D1234377

Catharine Maria Sedgwick

Unmounted carte-de-visite photograph (albumen print) with darkroom retouching (Rare Books and Manuscripts, Special Collections Library, Pennsylvania State University Libraries), accompanied by a letter, which reads:

My dear Miss Mary Lee.
The signature to your note has captivated me into a very prompt reply (which in truth its modesty deserves).
For the prettiest English name
That ever was, or can be,
For sonnet, ode, or Madrigal
Is the name of *Mary Lee*.
And so—my dear Miss Mary Lee (how merrily it goes!)
I remain with many thanks for your kind expressions, yrs truly

C M Sedgwick.
Lenox 13 Nov '52

Catharine Maria Sedgwick

C R I T I C A L   P E R S P E C T I V E S

Edited by

Lucinda L. Damon-Bach and Victoria Clements

With a Foreword by Mary Kelley

N O R T H E A S T E R N   U N I V E R S I T Y   P R E S S • *Boston*

Northeastern University Press

Judith Fetterley's "'My Sister! My Sister!': The Rhetoric of Catharine Sedgwick's
Hope Leslie" originally appeared in *American Literature* 70:3 (September 1998): 491–516.
Copyright 1998 by Duke University Press. All rights reserved. Reprinted with permission.

Library of Congress Cataloging-in-Publication Data

Catharine Maria Sedgwick : critical perspectives / edited by Lucinda L.
Damon-Bach and Victoria Clements ; with a foreword by Mary Kelley.
        p. cm.
Includes bibliographical references and index.
    ISBN 1–55553–548–8 (alk. paper)
    1. Sedgwick, Catharine Maria, 1789–1867—Criticism and interpretation.
2. Women and literature—New England—History—19th century.   3. New
England—In literature.   I. Damon-Bach, Lucinda L.   II. Clements, Victoria,
[date]
PS2798.Z5 C38 2003
813′.2—dc21   2002006725

Designed by Gary Gore

Composed in Adobe Garamond by Coghill Composition Company in Richmond, Virginia.
Printed and bound by Thomson-Shore, Inc., in Dexter, Michigan. The paper is Glatfelter
Supple Opaque Recycled, an acid-free sheet.

MANUFACTURED IN THE UNITED STATES OF AMERICA
07 06 05 04 03   5 4 3 2 1

To our families, both given and chosen,
with gratitude for the many ways you have sustained us

Contents

Illustrations

Foreword

MARY KELLEY

When I made an initial visit to the Massachusetts Historical Society in the summer of 1973, I knew that the papers of Catharine Maria Sedgwick's parents, siblings, and descendants had been deposited at the nation's oldest historical society. In search of letters, diaries, and journals that Sedgwick herself might have left, I anticipated spending three to four days doing research in her papers. Little did I expect to find the exceptionally rich and diverse collections housed at the Society—169 boxes of the Sedgwick Family Papers and 21 boxes filled with Sedgwick's manuscripts. The days became three to four weeks in the first of my many visits. I was then one of the very few scholars who were trying to navigate the collections, which had neither an inventory nor a more general guide. The scholarship on Sedgwick the author presented a different challenge. The woman who had been one of antebellum America's most prominent writers, Sedgwick had been virtually erased. Mentioned in a handful of surveys of American literature, Sedgwick's novels were presented as footnotes to James Fenimore Cooper. Forgotten by cultural historians and literary critics, the fiction that had commanded a national readership had with one exception been out of print for more than a century.

In the intervening years, all of this has changed. With generous funding from the National Endowment for the Humanities, the papers of all the Sedgwicks have been catalogued. The most thorough and detailed of inventories, the four volumes date and annotate each of the manuscripts. The Sedgwick materials are now some of the most frequently consulted collections at the Society. Reissuing Catharine Maria Sedgwick's novels has become a many-volumed enterprise. *Hope Leslie*, the first to be reissued in 1987 and the volume I edited, appeared in the American Women Writers Series published by Rutgers University Press. It is no coincidence that contributors to the present volume edited several of the novels that have been reissued. With an introduction by Carolyn Karcher, *Hope Leslie* has appeared a second time under the Penguin imprint. Victoria Clements edited *A New-England Tale*, which Oxford University Press issued in 1995; and Susan Harris will serve as editor for the Penguin reissue due in 2003. Most recently, Maria Karafilis prepared an edition of *The Linwoods* for the University Press of New England, which appeared in 2002. Sedgwick's short fiction has been reprinted in a host of anthologies, including the pathbreaking *Provisions: A Reader from Nineteenth-Century Women,* which Judith Fetterley published in 1985. And a digitized Sedgwick now appears at a Web site created by the Catharine Maria Sedgwick Society, where readers of the screen can find a growing collection of Sedgwick's stories, including "Slavery in New England" and "Our Burial Place."

Catharine Maria Sedgwick: Critical Perspectives represents the coming of age in what we can now call "Sedgwick studies." I invoke this phrase rather than the more conventional label "scholarship" for several reasons. Designed to serve a variety of purposes, *Catharine Maria Sedgwick: Critical Perspectives* is a multidimensional volume. For the first time, we have a complete bibliography of Sedgwick's literary production. We have a chronology that locates Sedgwick's professional career in the context of a personal life shaped by profoundly intimate relationships with her six brothers and sisters. This chronicle illuminates the degree to which the fabric of family was woven from these relationships, and we see that Sedgwick, who was welcomed into the families of all her siblings, alternated between the homes of Charles in Lenox, Massachusetts, and Robert in New York City. Acting as literary escorts, Sedgwick's brothers Theodore, Henry, Robert, and Charles also played a signal role in their sister's career. Strongly and consistently supportive, they encouraged the initially reluctant author, applauded the novels and stories, and negotiated with publishers. In dedicating *Clarence,* the fourth of her six novels, "To my Brothers—my best friends," Sedgwick marked their importance, professionally and personally.

The volume's editors, Lucinda Damon-Bach and Victoria Clements, introduce us to one of antebellum America's most prolific writers of fiction. The woman who entered the literary marketplace with the publication of *A New-England Tale* in 1822 published five more novels in the next three decades. Cultural historians and literary critics who are already familiar with the longer fiction may well be surprised to find that the novels constitute only a fraction of Sedgwick's many appearances in print. Antebellum Americans read the scores of stories Sedgwick contributed to periodicals and annuals. They traveled with Sedgwick in the two volumes of *Letters from Abroad to Kindred at Home,* the correspondence that was written during the fifteen months she spent in Europe. They took to the highly popular domestic trilogy, *The Poor Rich Man and the Rich Poor Man, Live and Let Live,* and *Home,* the last of which remained in print until 1900. And they instructed their children using Sedgwick's eight volumes designed for "young people," beginning with *The Travellers,* which appeared in 1825, and concluding with *Memoir of Joseph Curtis, A Model Man,* published in 1858.

Damon-Bach and Clements's introduction sets the stage for the volume's

"Critical Perspectives," each of which is interleaved with excerpts from nineteenth-century reviews of Sedgwick's work. This series of essays not only builds upon earlier scholarship but reassesses and revises that scholarship. Melissa Homestead's essay is emblematic in this regard. In the five decades Sedgwick spent in the literary marketplace, she achieved a striking visibility on the basis of anonymous publication. The fact that the name of one of antebellum America's most prominent authors appeared on the title page of only one of her books is more than an irony. The question scholars, including myself, have asked is whether Sedgwick's cloaking of her authorial identity should be interpreted as deferring to gender conventions, or as negotiating those conventions and crafting a liminal identity, or, as Homestead argues, as deliberately staging a literary persona. The answer depends on the sources in which the interpretation is grounded. The deeply felt ambivalence about transgressing cultural norms that is scattered through Sedgwick's letters, diaries, and journals suggests that the woman, who, out of step with her culture's past, wrote in public, tacked back and forth between observing gender conventions that limited a woman's influence to the members of her household and using those conventions as a point of departure in fashioning a more autonomous identity. The public record, the title pages and the reviews of Sedgwick's fiction, lead to an alternative interpretation in which Sedgwick's ambivalence is elided and the female body of the unnamed author is clearly discernible. Not simply any female body, as Homestead shows, the author is a carefully crafted representation of a "lady." And, again, not simply any "lady." I would suggest that Sedgwick is an author who, in committing herself and her fiction to the reform and regeneration of society, bases her authority on the role articulated by advocates of Republican Motherhood. Whichever the emphasis or the sources deployed, these interpretations are relatively congruent, at least in terms of highlighting Sedgwick's dazzling negotiation of gender conventions.

The essays that chart narrative structure and character development open outward, providing readers with striking insights into previously neglected characters. Victoria Clements's illuminating analysis decodes the riddle of Crazy Bet. The character with whom Sedgwick begins and ends *A New-England Tale*, Crazy Bet appears almost as an appendage whose presence does little if anything to advance the narrative. Why, then, did Sedgwick write her into the novel's pages? Is she the embodiment of a woman's unfettered imagination, as some critics have suggested? Clements locates Crazy Bet's narrative presence in the experiences of an author who had rejected Congregationalism for the more controversial Unitarianism the same year in which she embarked on her literary career. Historical experience and discursive representation were woven together in the character of Crazy Bet, a woman who destabilizes churchly orthodoxy. She speaks as well for the author's concern with the secular institution of marriage, which Sedgwick also rejected. Sedgwick was assuredly not as "crazy" as Bet; however, like the character she invented, Sedgwick would not be contained, insisting instead on the freedom to choose for herself. The issues before her—decisions regarding religious affiliation and marital identity—had enormous implications for women in a century in which they were expected to subordinate individual needs and desires to men. From Crazy Bet onward, Sedgwick sent subversive characters on an errand that informs the rest of her fiction—the interrogation of gender conventions that limited women's claims, both to a literary vocation and to a larger authority in the public world.

As Lucinda Damon-Bach demonstrates, Sedgwick's *Redwood* dismantles gender conventions that call for female deference and dependence and installs in their stead heroines who are able to "act" and "transact," including making the decision to marry or to remain single. Tellingly, as Damon-Bach reminds us, two of the six female characters in *Redwood* elect the latter choice. *Hope Leslie,* in addition to addressing the issue of a woman's marital status, elaborates the implications of Sedgwick's claim to public authority. In a reading of Sedgwick's third novel that takes us beyond the polarities of unalloyed celebration or critique, Judith Fetterley shows how the author translated Republican Motherhood into a more powerful Republican Sisterhood that called for women to play a visible role in public life. In positing "woman" as her category, Sedgwick appeared to offer readers a universal sisterhood that included women of all classes and races. However, the characters that Sedgwick identified as members of the sisterhood and the moral authority she ascribed to them looked very much like the representation Sedgwick had crafted for herself. Like the author of *Hope Leslie,* they claimed the mantle of a "lady." The role Sedgwick expected this more exclusive sisterhood to play is manifest in Brigitte Bailey's essay, "Tourism and Visual Subjection." Bailey's texts are *Letters from Abroad* and "An Incident in Rome"; the site is Italy, which, like the tea tables and salons at which women in post-Revolutionary America presided, is gendered feminine. In the female-centered institutions of tea table and salon, elite women had superintended the behavior of men, polishing their manners, enlarging their sympathies, and aiding in the cultivation of their moral sense. Their nineteenth-century counterparts touring Italy perform the same role, cultivating members of America's male elite and transforming the seductive power of the country's beauty into a lesson in the importance of affiliation with and sympathy for others.

Patricia Kalayjian sounds a complementary note in highlighting the "Disinterest as Moral Corrective" that animates the pages of Sedgwick's fourth novel, *Clarence.* Concerned that antebellum Americans were engaged in a relentless pursuit of profit, social status, and material possessions, Sedgwick called for the alternative embodied in the character of Gertrude Clarence, a quintessential member of Sedgwick's sisterhood. In contrast to the emulative consumption in which *Clarence*'s other females engage, Gertrude is the model republican citizen who acts on behalf of the larger good of the community.

Anyone reading the newly published edition of *The Linwoods* will want to reckon with Robert Daly's rereading of Sedgwick's fifth novel. The Sedgwick that Daly presents is as postmodern as his critical analysis, which shows that rather than presenting readers with familiar models of feminine behavior, Sedgwick populates the novel with women who elect to remain single, who refuse to be taken in by rakes, and who display the physical strength of males. The lesson with which Sedgwick leaves readers is embodied in the characters who flourish in *The Linwoods*. Instead of conforming to a unitary model based on prevailing expectations, they develop a repertoire of virtues selected from different races, classes, and genders.

Sedgwick's final novel directly addresses the most persistent theme in her fiction: the statuses and the compromises entailed in being either *Married or Single?* Deborah Gussman's groundbreaking essay locates the novel and its author in the context of the nineteenth-century women's rights movement and the rhetoric its advocates engaged. Moving beyond the earlier interpretations of cultural historians and literary critics, Gussman shows that Sedgwick did not align herself either with a classical republicanism that presumed female deference and dependence or with a liberal feminism that called for equal rights. The position adopted by Sedgwick, which had already been articulated by post-Revolutionary essayists Judith Sargent Murray and Hannah Mather Crocker, claimed the masculine rights and responsibilities of classical republicanism for women. Sedgwick did not stop there, however. Neither Murray nor Crocker had extended this revisionary republicanism to unmarried women. Sedgwick has characters who remain single enact this republicanism, and thereby eliminates marital status as a qualification for membership in the sisterhood.

The politics embraced by Sedgwick and her sisterhood are the subject of several essays. In her essay on "a Slave story I began and abandoned," as Sedgwick labeled a manuscript that is now deposited at the Massachusetts Historical Society, Karen Woods Weierman maps the trajectory taken by Sedgwick as she grappled with antebellum America's most divisive moral and political issue. From Sedgwick's perspective, the "dark and fearful subject," as she described the institution of slavery and the controversy it generated in a letter to Lydia Maria Child, needed to be approached with more caution than had been exhibited by radically inclined abolitionists. Weierman demonstrates the intensity with which Sedgwick struggled personally and professionally with the tenets and practices of William Lloyd Garrison's abolitionism. And well she might have—opposition to slavery was one of her father's legacies to all his descendants. United States Senator and Speaker of the House of Representatives, Theodore Sedgwick represented Elizabeth Freeman in her successful suit for freedom in the courts of Massachusetts. Later generations entered the public debate to oppose slavery at critical junctures. Sedgwick's brother, Henry Dwight Sedgwick, published a pamphlet that argued for *The Practicability of the Abolition of Slavery*. The lawyer Theodore Sedgwick III, Sedgwick's contemporary and one of her nephews, argued for the defense in the *Amistad* slave mutiny case. The lawyer and politician Charles Baldwin Sedgwick, the son of one of Sedgwick's cousins, defended the individuals who defied the Fugitive Slave Law and freed a fugitive slave from a jail in Syracuse, New York. This legacy and, still more important, Sedgwick's devotion to Elizabeth Freeman, or "Mumbet," as she came to be known after she became the family's servant, inform the pages of the story Sedgwick abandoned. In the unfinished manuscript, Meta, the character drawn from Elizabeth Freeman, stands as a brief for African American equality: Racially prejudiced scientific arguments are dismantled, and a variety of strategies for gradual emancipation are presented. But Sedgwick still hesitated—both in completing the narrative and in committing herself to Garrisonian immediatism. Weierman's splendidly assembled evidence shows us why: No matter how strong her opposition to slavery, Sedgwick was still more deeply committed to securing the survival of the Republic, which she believed was threatened by the controversy surrounding abolitionism. Ironically, the advocates of the more moderate position Sedgwick adopted were no more successful in sustaining national unity than was the author in finishing the "pages of a Slave story."

Sedgwick also engaged class relations, a second pressing issue that generated no little controversy in antebellum America. Sondra Smith Gates's essay looks at *Home, The Poor Rich Man and the Rich Poor Man*, and *Live and Let Live*, the trilogy that documents the presence of poor people in the midst of the ascendant middle classes. How, she asks, does Sedgwick reconcile poverty with the nation's claims to freedom and equality? From Timothy Dwight to Lydia Maria Signourney, writers engaged in the cultural work of nationalism, which grounded the nation's identity in its common people. The repository of disinterested virtue, the people so construed, not only confirmed America's exceptional status but also constituted its model of republican citizenship. Sedgwick distinguished herself from other writers in staging characters who are explicitly marked as poor, as Gates observes. Vehicles for schooling readers in the lessons of meritocracy, they achieve mobility through the practice of republican values rather than through the acquisition of capital. Protagonists William Barclay, Harry Aiken, and Lucy Lee live in and through this promise of opportunity. They are the virtuous poor of a mythic America; their poverty is only temporary. However, as Gates's illuminating analysis shows, race and class intersect to eliminate all but Anglo-Americans from the nation's promise of mobility and its corollary full-fledged citizenship. Susan Harris charts a similar series of intersections, showing how Sedgwick limited candidacy for citizenship in America's republic. Support for the emancipation of slaves did not translate into support for their right to all the privileges of citizenship. Class and race limited the potential of those in the lower orders, all of whom would continue to require leadership from the middle and elite classes. In arguing less for equality than for meritocracy, Sedgwick revalued instead of dismantling the class and race hierarchies of antebellum America.

In her fiction, as in her life, Sedgwick registered the social and political debates through which Americans grappled with the freedoms and the anxieties, the rights and the contradictions they had inherited from the Revolution. The contributors to this collection of essays limn Sedgwick in all her complexity. They chart the evolution of her perspective on the signal issues that resonate through the decades from the establishment of the Republic to the coming of the Civil War. It is a measure of this collection's achievement that Sedgwick can now serve as a lens through which we glimpse an America negotiating the valences of many-voiced and always changing identities.

Acknowledgments

While the idea for this project had been conceived prior to our meeting, it began to take shape in 1996 when Susan Harris introduced us to one another at the landmark 19th-Century American Women Writers Conference held at Trinity College, and our collaboration began. We codirected the first Catharine Maria Sedgwick Symposium held in Stockbridge, Massachusetts—Sedgwick's birthplace—in June, 1997, with Judith Fetterley delivering the keynote address, an early version of the essay included in this volume. The Sedgwick Society was formed shortly thereafter, and a second symposium followed in June, 2000. To Susan, Judith, and all the symposia presenters we owe our thanks for their shared enthusiasm and rigorous scholarship, and we owe them as well to Mary Kelley, whose biographical research on Sedgwick and personal encouragement have been vital to our work.

Several members of the Sedgwick family have provided generous assistance with our quest for information about and greater understanding of their renowned ancestor, and we are deeply appreciative of their willingness to share Catharine with the rest of the world. In particular, we thank the Sedgwick Family Society and Trust, Arthur and Ginger Schwartz, Ellery Sedgwick, and Stephen Delafield for their contributions.

The Office of the Vice President for Academic Affairs at Salem State College provided a Faculty and Librarians Research Grant during the initial stages of research for this project; an additional grant through the graduate school this past fall provided us with the invaluable help of graduate assistant Allison Roepsch, who worked diligently, along with Martha-Jane Moreland, Becky LeMon, and Doreen Hill in Salem State Library's interlibrary loan office, tracking down copies of nineteenth-century reviews of Sedgwick's work as well as the works themselves.

Financial support from the College of Southern Maryland allowed us to reproduce the images of Sedgwick included herein. For their assistance in our acquiring these images we especially thank Paul Rocheleau, photographer, and Sedgwick Society member William Bell. We are also indebted to Sandra Stelts, associate curator for rare books and manuscripts at the Paterno Library at Penn State.

We offer our thanks as well to the volume's contributors for their collegial spirit and for their extraordinary efforts in shaping the book into a cohesive whole. Elizabeth Swayze, Emily McKeigue, and Jennifer Wilkin at Northeastern University Press have guided both volume and editors along the perilous route to publication.

Finally, true collaboration is a remarkable thing, and we are ever grateful for the gift of each other. The trust we have developed in one another's skills, talents, and ideas has helped us grow, both as scholars and as human beings. We have inspired, supported, and learned from one another in a creative process that has been an honor to share.

We also have individual thanks to offer.

Lucinda: My colleagues at Salem State College—in particular those in the Faculty Writing Workshop sponsored by the Office of the Vice President for Academic Affairs in the summer of 2001 and led by Nancy L. Schultz, as well as those in the ad hoc faculty writing group led by Elizabeth Kenney—have offered continued encouragement and help. I am fortunate to be working with such dedicated and generous scholars, including Nancy, Elizabeth, Peter Walker, Gayle Fischer, Avi Chomsky, and Julie Whitlow. To my family, both near and far, I am infinitely grateful. The nourishment they have provided me—physical, emotional, and spiritual—and their patience with me have paved the way for my work on this book.

Victoria: My family and friends have been steadfast cheerleaders along the sometimes seemingly endless road that has led to this volume; their faith in me and acceptance of my frequent unavailability have bolstered my efforts from the outset. Were it not for my partner Dean Hebert, my contributions to this volume could not have been made. His strength, humor, patience, constancy, and willingness to take on far more than his share of our mutual responsibilities have made this work as much his accomplishment as mine.

Introduction

LUCINDA L. DAMON-BACH AND VICTORIA CLEMENTS

Catharine Maria Sedgwick: Critical Perspectives examines the work of one of the most popular and highly respected American writers and thinkers of the nineteenth century. Sedgwick's considerable literary output—which includes novels, short stories, children's books, domestic novellas, travel writing, biography, nonfiction sketches, and religious tracts—addresses the central social and political issues of both her day and ours: nation building, the role of women, relations between races and classes. She is, as one nineteenth-century reviewer put it, "our Sedgwick," deeply concerned by the cultural divisions that erupted in the decades leading up to the Civil War and that have been the source of national discord ever since.[1] Bringing together new critical essays and nineteenth-century reviews, the present volume situates Sedgwick historically, shows her evolution as a writer, and analyzes, from a range of theoretical approaches, twelve of the twenty books she published, as well as one unpublished manuscript. Included as well are the first widely available and substantially updated bibliography of Sedgwick's work, a detailed chronology of her life, and rarely seen images from both public and private collections. Providing as it does the first extended critical overview of her understudied oeuvre, the collection reveals the breadth and complexity of Catharine Sedgwick's contributions to American literature, thereby challenging prevailing twentieth-century paradigms of U.S. literary history and suggesting new directions for twenty-first-century scholarship.

Sedgwick was uniquely positioned to address both political and domestic issues in the developing United States, and her published work exhibits her lifelong engagement with real-world challenges to the success of nation, family, and individual. Choosing to remain unmarried in a century in which only one out of ten women did,[2] she was a shrewd observer of the impediments to domestic stability that resulted from patriarchal culture and was an early advocate of what she considered women's natural rights: the right to a practical and intellectual education, the right to choose whom—and whether—to marry, and the right to work outside the home. Raised in a family of politicians and lawyers, she was supremely aware of the differing sociopolitical ideologies that struggled for authority in the early nineteenth century, and she shaped from these the political stance that characterized her life and work: a firm commitment to universal moral and civic responsibility, practical activism, and freedom of religion. Although she in fact participated in hands-on social work, the primary vehicle of Sedgwick's activism was writing—about the lessons of history, the legal and economic status of women, corruption in religion and government, labor conditions for domestic help, the rehabilitation of convicted criminals, and many other subjects that garnered the nation's attention in her lifetime. Living for part of each year in western Massachusetts and otherwise in New York City, Sedgwick understood the problems and pleasures of both country and city life. Indeed, she traveled widely and maintained many international friendships, which informed her thoughtful and principled nationalism. Although she socialized with the rich and politically powerful, she maintained all the while a consciousness derived from her direct contact with the poor and defenseless. A busy, successful professional writer, she was nevertheless intimately involved with her large immediate and extended family. From this broad, multifaceted perspective, Catharine Sedgwick speaks to us today with striking authority of the intersections of nation, home, and literature, shedding light on a period in U.S. history in which the foundations for American culture were being laid.

Born in Stockbridge, Massachusetts, in 1789, George Washington's election year, Sedgwick was the sixth of seven surviving children of prominent Federalist politician Theodore Sedgwick and Pamela Dwight, who was descended from the powerful colonial Connecticut family that would eventually include three presidents of Yale University. Catharine and her siblings were from early childhood privy to the inner workings of national politics through the window of their father's career—when he was elected to the first of six terms in the United States Congress in 1791, Catharine was two years old. Speaker of the House under Washington and a justice of the Massachusetts Supreme Court in the years following his last congressional term, Theodore Sedgwick was usually away from home for more than half of each year, and almost always for the long, cold Stockbridge winter. Pamela's correspondence and Catharine's autobiography suggest how keenly Pamela felt this absence. By 1791 she had given birth to ten children in nine years, three of whom had died in infancy, and her final descent into crippling depression began that year.[3] By the time she died—when Catharine was just seventeen—Pamela's diminished mental state had resulted in several lengthy but apparently unsuccessful hospitalizations. With both parents thus unavailable, the household was held together primarily by Elizabeth Freeman, the freed slave known to the family as Mumbet and to whom Catharine referred in more than one instance as "mother." In the face of these domestic worries and throughout the remainder of their lives, the Sedgwick siblings relied heavily on one another for practical and emotional support. Their voluminous correspondence testifies to a network of deeply felt, mutually satisfying relationships, extending eventually to include one another's spouses, children, and grandchildren.

Sedgwick's single status allowed her to move among her siblings' families throughout her lifetime, living with one or the other for months at a time in Albany, New York; Stockbridge or Lenox, Massachusetts; or New York City; and, in her later years, with her niece in Boston. As a full member of several different households and the favored aunt of more than thirty nieces and nephews, Sedgwick was firmly enmeshed in a rich domestic life. She was as well, however, an avid traveler. The chronology of her life included in this volume suggests the extent of her frequent trips—north to New Hampshire, Vermont, and Quebec; as far west as Minnesota and from there down the Mississippi River to Missouri; and south to Pennsylvania, Washington, D.C., and Virginia. In 1839 and 1840, she spent fifteen months in Europe, visiting England, Belgium, Germany, Switzerland, France, and Italy. Her acute observations of this wide variety of cultural milieux informed her work, manifesting not only in her choice of subjects and ideological agendas, but also in her choices of genre, narrative structure, and style.

Sedgwick was undoubtedly a leading figure in American letters in her own time, her works published widely on both sides of the Atlantic and translated into French, German, Italian, Swedish, Dutch, and Danish. Though not the first successful female writer in the new nation—both Susanna Rowson's *Charlotte, a Tale of Truth* (1791) and Hannah Foster's *The Coquette* (1797) had enjoyed considerable success before the turn of the century—Sedgwick established new ground for the American woman's novel, rejecting the temptation of seduction for her self-reliant heroines and presenting them with an entirely different set of social, moral, and intellectual hurdles. In 1834, based on the reputation she had gained in her first decade of writing, Sedgwick was selected for inclusion in the first volume of the *National Portrait Gallery of Distinguished Americans*, a Who's Who of generals, politicians, ministers, and other cultural leaders who had played a significant role in shaping the nation. Among the thirty-five dignitaries in volume 1 are George Washington, Henry Clay, Andrew Jackson, Daniel Webster; Martha Washington and Sedgwick are the only women, and only four writers appear—Joel Barlow, Washington Irving, Sedgwick, and James Fenimore Cooper. Of these, Sedgwick earns the second-longest entry, shorter than Irving's by two pages, but twice as long as Barlow's or Cooper's. Although her inclusion in the book is not surprising—she had already been recognized, along with Irving, Cooper, and William Cullen Bryant, as one of the founders of a truly American literature—what is perhaps surprising is that in 1834 she had published less than 25 percent of her eventual output, and her most widely read books had yet to appear.

As Mary Kelley suggests in her foreword, few today are familiar with the extent of Sedgwick's oeuvre, with its sheer quantity or the variety of genres Sedgwick explored during her forty-year career. The updated bibliography shows her extraordinary range and output, including not only six novels, but also domestic novellas, advice manuals, and more than one hundred short pieces. Although a portion of these were nonfiction essays or sketches, the majority were fiction, and editors of gift books and annuals reportedly clamored for her contributions. Even today's readers who have managed to find all of Sedgwick's novels may be surprised to discover that she created eight books and a quarter of her short works specifically for children. Also included in this large and catholic body of work are a travelogue, two biographies, several introductions to other writers' works, and a nearly one-hundred-page translation from the Italian of *My Prisons, Memoirs of Silvio Pellico of Saluzzo* (1836).[4] As both Melissa Homestead's and John Austin's essays make clear, Sedgwick worked and understood herself as a professional writer, and her popularity suggests that her readers and fellow writers did as well.

James Fenimore Cooper inaugurated Sedgwick's critical reception in the United States with his lengthy review of *A New-England Tale* in 1822. He was especially pleased with the novel's realism, praising its presentation of "the multitude of local peculiarities, which form our distinctive features" and comparing it favorably to Irving's "burlesque . . . [which does] little towards forming a history of the diversities of passion, sentiment, and behavior . . . of our little communities." William Cullen Bryant offered similar praise for Sedgwick's realistic characterizations three years later in his review of *Redwood* in the *North American Review*, calling her dialogue—to him, the most difficult part of a novel—"exceedingly natural, spirited, and appropriate." Writing just over twenty years later for *Godey's Lady's Book*, Edgar Allan Poe averred that *Redwood* established Sedgwick "as the first female prose writer of her country," but was himself "best pleased" with *The Linwoods* (1835), which he praised for its "ease, purity, pathos, and verisimilitude."[5] As these and dozens of similarly laudatory reviews suggest, Sedgwick's central position in American literature and culture was securely established early in her career. The review excerpts provided throughout this volume, from both American and English periodicals, provide a sense of the great affection and respect that were generally accorded her work.

Her widespread popularity may have stemmed in part from the variety of genres she consistently worked in throughout her career. In the first ten years, for example, she wrote four of her six major novels, a religious tract (for the New York Unitarian Book Society), a children's novel, and twenty-one short stories (ten for children). Sedgwick's commitment to diversity of subject and style is demonstrated even within her shorter works, which present a wide range of characters—a Catholic Iroquois, a sailor, a Quaker martyr, young lovers, old maids, and loyal dogs—and her children's works naturally feature children. In the second decade of her career (1832–41), when she was in her forties, Sedgwick's short fiction output nearly doubled. She averaged a remarkable four to five new stories per year, nearly half of which were aimed at young readers—of the two collections of children's stories published during this period, one was composed of entirely new works. In this exceptionally productive decade, Sedgwick published not only a lengthy advice manual for adolescent girls, but also six more full-length works for adults: her fifth major novel, her two-volume European travelogue, her first collection of short stories, and three domestic novellas.

These last, *Home* (1835), *The Rich Poor Man and the Poor Rich Man* (1836), and *Live and Let Live* (1837), proved to be Sedgwick's most widely read works. *Home* appears to have gone through as many as twenty editions, remaining in print until 1900. The novellas are also the most difficult to characterize, referred to variously as "tracts" or "didactic tales," perhaps because the first was written for a series inaugurated by Unitarian minister Henry Ware Jr., and also because their moral design seems clear. They are perhaps most accurately termed domestic novellas, for they focus on the home and are not, as the term "didactic" might suggest, monologically instructive, but polyvocal, entertaining, and sociopolitically provocative, much like Sedgwick's other realist works. Writing in London's *Westminster Review* in 1838, prominent British journalist Harriet Martineau declared *Home* and *The Rich Poor Man* to be "the first complete specimens of a higher kind of literature than the United States have hitherto possessed." Sedgwick, she declares, "relies on fact and on her own American heart and eyes; . . . she gives us perhaps the first true insight into American life." Although these novellas received their share of the jibes with which such moralistic fiction was routinely met—Herman Melville, for example, satirized *The Rich Poor Man* twenty years after it first appeared—they were far more often granted acclaim: Ralph Waldo Emerson was sufficiently impressed with *Live and Let Live* to note in his journal that reading it made him "glow."[6]

In the third decade of her career, Sedgwick became increasingly involved in public service, volunteering with the Women's Prison Association, with which she was associated for nearly twenty years, and teaching, both in her sister-in-law's school for girls in Lenox and in various Sunday schools. By then in her fifties, she published thirty-nine more short works between 1842 and 1851—compiling in 1844 her second collection of short fiction for adults—as well as three new books for young readers, all of which emphasize moral responsibility to others. With her reputation as a major American author firmly in place, she also revised three of her earlier novels for new, uniform editions. Apparently tireless, Sedgwick continued to write throughout her sixties, producing her last major novel, nine more short stories, and a biography of Joseph Curtis, founder of the New York House of Refuge for juvenile delinquents. Her last known short story was published in 1862, when she was seventy-two.

For most of her professional life, Sedgwick wrote in the company of other writers, including members of her own family, and editors. Early in her career, two of her sisters-in-law, reportedly her closest friends—Susan Livingston Ridley Sedgwick, one of Catharine's schoolmates, who had married Theodore, and Elizabeth Dwight Sedgwick, wife of Charles—were both writing and publishing, often with Catharine's advice. Theodore, too, was a published author.[7] According to Edward Halsey Foster, these siblings, "together with Shakespearean actress Fanny Kemble . . . formed the 'inner circle'" of Berkshire literary society for nearly a quarter of a century. While Sedgwick may have begun her career "behind the veil" of anonymous publication, that anonymity, as Melissa Homestead argues, was short-lived: readers knew who Sedgwick was and flocked to visit her. As Foster notes, her "fame and the fame of her novels, several of which were set in the Berkshires, first brought the Stockbridge-Lenox area to the attention of the public." Sedgwick was "the social leader of [what was known as] the American Lake District" from roughly 1835 to 1860.[8] In fact, her national and international renown, dating from her inclusion in the *National Portrait Gallery of Distinguished Americans* up to the Civil War, parallels the twenty-five-year prominence of the Berkshires in American literary life, suggesting her significance to it. Nearly every American author of note, as well as politicians and activists—women's rights champion Lucy Stone among them—called on Sedgwick during this period; renowned international figures, such as Irish novelist Anna Jameson, Swedish writer Frederika Bremer, British travel writer Basil Hall, and members of Queen Victoria's court, all considered a visit with Sedgwick a highlight of their itinerary.[9]

They came, as Charlene Avallone makes evident, to talk: Sedgwick, a noted conversationalist, participated in "interrelated conversation communities in Europe, as well as in the Berkshires, New York, Boston, Washington, and Saratoga," and saw these conversations not merely as social gatherings, but as "opportunities for professional exchange and for literary, intellectual, and political influence." In her essay for this volume, Avallone persuasively identifies conventions of nineteenth-century women's conversation that not only illuminate Sedgwick's rhetorical practices but also suggest a lens through which the work of other contemporary women writers must be considered.

The conversations that characterized Sedgwick's professional social environment typified the vigorous discursive atmosphere of the young Republic. Debates that had led to the formation of the new nation in the eighteenth century were only multiplied in the nineteenth, as widely varying ideologies struggled with and against one another to shape the United States. Susan Harris's and Brigitte Bailey's essays situate Sedgwick's novels and travel writing within that nation-building discourse, showing that Sedgwick establishes through both genres a central role for white Protestant women in American culture and thereby resists developing paradigms for the location of authority. Both essays also suggest, however, the limits of this resistance, noting the white, class-based hegemony the texts uphold. Sondra Smith Gates and Charlene Avallone also identify in their essays the various methods by which Sedgwick's discourse restricts authority according to then typical race and class distinctions. But, like Harris and Bailey, they also demonstrate that Sedgwick's texts are never easily dismissed as simply conserving a patriarchal culture, but are in their dialogism always questioning existing structures and their effects. Sedgwick, long before Whitman, "contains multitudes."[10]

Notably, a signal rhetorical strategy in Sedgwick's considerations of nation building is a pervasive polyvocality, as several essays show. Carolyn Karcher identifies the democratic nature of Sedgwick's novels in their multivocal structure; when Sedgwick includes characters' letters, for example, those characters are, as Karcher puts it, allowed "to speak for themselves." Robert Daly's exploration of *The Linwoods*, Sedgwick's Revolutionary War novel, identifies a chorus of voices that seek to define the nation. Only by listening carefully to all of these and drawing from many can both characters and readers make the wisest choices for self and nation. A demand for careful reading is shown as well through Lucinda Damon-Bach's study of *Redwood*'s "reinterpretation strategies," which considers the voices that populate the novel's paratext and joins Susan Harris in showing Sedgwick's commitment to process rather than finite product. Sedgwick emerges from these readings as rhetorically feminist, enacting what Hélène Cixous calls a "nonclosure that is . . . confidence and comprehension; . . . an opportunity for . . . wonderful expansion."[11]

As Deborah Gussman points out in her essay on *Married or Single?*, though, the term "feminist" as we understand it today is one that Sedgwick would never have applied to herself or her work. Gussman shows, however, that the novel's regendering of the discourses of republicanism and Christian virtue interrogates traditional roles for both men and women, and that this, alongside the novel's participation in a literary debate over the injustices of patriarchal marriage, suggests the transformative nature of Sedgwick's vision for women. Lucinda Damon-Bach's discussion of *Redwood* joins Gussman's in its investigation of the novel's critique of contemporary marriage practices and the limited alternatives available to women in patriarchal culture.

Sedgwick's stance on women's rights and roles may appear limited to modern readers, but she was nevertheless profoundly committed to the cultural and personal benefits of female agency. In her introduction to British author Barbara Leigh Smith Bodichon's tract "Women and Work" (1859), for example, Sedgwick proposes that women of all classes should be allowed and prepared to work, asserting, "Qualification for work should be the stamp of citizenship—the badge of nationality. Our women of every class have a right to this qualification. They are not to be resolved into non-entities, and to have no . . . effective existence in the republic." Warning that fortunes in America can fluctuate quickly and dramatically, Sedgwick urges women to be ready to provide for themselves and their families if necessary, and agrees with Bodichon that satisfaction can be derived from "'leaving the world a little better than we find it,'" presumably through financial agency. Rich women are not exempt from this imperative to useful employment, "bidden" by their wealth to "charitable work."[12]

Sedgwick had been concerned with this issue nearly thirty years earlier in *Clarence* (1830), in which she criticized women who are of no "use to society." Patricia Kalayjian's study of "disinterestedness" in *Clarence* uncovers the responsibilities the novel assigns to women in its sociopolitical solutions to what Sedgwick clearly saw as the increasingly negative effects of the Jacksonian economy. Wealthy Gertrude Clarence certainly improves the urban world she "finds." So, too, did women such as Sedgwick and her fellow writer Caroline Kirkland, who visited hospitals and volunteered their services for the Women's Prison Association of New York. As Jenifer Banks's examination of Sedgwick's correspondence shows, direct contact with the female convicts heightened Sedgwick's awareness of gender inequality, which manifested in her presentation of increasingly complex female characters, particularly those who, like *A New-England Tale*'s Crazy Bet, "deviate" from the traditional path. Victoria Clements's essay identifies Bet as an early example of Sedgwick's literary sophistication, a site for the post-Kantian author's negotiations with the real. Perhaps Sedgwick's most flamboyant figure, Crazy Bet is also the first of her many female characters who interrogate patriarchal cultural models in the uncharted territory of nineteenth-century female authority.

Judith Fetterley's powerful reading of *Hope Leslie* (her keynote address at the first Sedgwick Symposium in 1997, published the following year in *American Literature*) suggests that in Sedgwick's rhetorically complex third novel the problem of gender difference is left wholly unresolved, caught up in a fundamental failure of Western culture to ford the gulf of alterity. Exploring the Native American–white relationships that lie at the center of this novel, Fetterley shows that Sedgwick, ever the realist, appears unable to imagine a cultural or rhetorical model that can easily contain both white and racial Other, both man and woman. We are left instead, Fetterley points out, with Sedgwick's memorable Magawisca, "disfigured and disarmed," representing the challenges ahead for those cultural pioneers who would "risk engagement with the actual mess of America." Karen Woods Weierman's study of a similarly disarmed—i.e., unfinished—text, the antislavery novel contained in the Sedgwick Papers at the Massachusetts Historical Society, suggests that an equivalent hopelessness led to Sedgwick's final abandonment of this manuscript. Weierman's careful analysis of Sedgwick's contemporary private papers uncovers the personal and literary struggle that Sedgwick undertook in her effort to address the nation's greatest crisis.

The essays and accompanying documents contained in *Catharine Maria Sedgwick: Critical Perspectives* provide a fascinating, varied, sometimes disturbing, and invariably provocative look at the work of a woman who began writing when both the nation and its literature were beginning to take shape and who took an active role in their struggles for identity. In the course of her lifetime, Sedgwick witnessed the War of 1812, westward expansion to the Pacific, wars between the United States and Native American tribes and the tribes' subsequent removal to western reservations, the United States' war with Mexico, the first women's rights convention, the California gold rush, the invention of the telegraph, the Civil War, the completion of the transcontinental railroad, three economic depressions, and seventeen different presidents (for none of whom, of course, she cast a vote). As a writer, she took seriously her responsibility to join with others in creating a national culture that would support its citizens in their pursuit of physically, emotionally, and spiritually fulfilling lives.

In the nineteenth century, Sedgwick enjoyed a popularity equivalent to, if not greater than, that of Cooper, Irving, Melville, or Poe. That she was virtually obliterated from the literary landscape by the modernist critical tradition of the early twentieth century should be profoundly disturbing to scholars of both American literature and history. But is it? As an index of scholarly concern, let us consider, along with the statistics that Dana Nelson provides in her inspiring conclusion to the volume, the number of high-school American literature textbooks that contain Irving's "Legend of Sleepy Hollow," Poe's "Cask of Amontillado," or an excerpt from *Moby Dick,* as compared to the number that contain even Sedgwick's name. Sedgwick's work has yet to be recovered for secondary schools, which means that a nation of students is currently absorbing an incomplete, inaccurate picture of American literary history, one still dominated by the male writers that were canonized in the first half of the twentieth century. And Sedgwick, of course, is only one example of the dozens of major American writers who remain unrepresented in our nation's libraries, public schools, and postsecondary institutions. Though the recovery efforts of the last twenty-five years have made significant headway toward appropriately locating Sedgwick and other formerly "vanished" writers in a responsible American literary history, much work, clearly, remains. Carolyn Karcher's essay suggests the magnitude of the ongoing project of integrating Sedgwick—and, by extension, other noncanonized writers—into the current curricular model of American literature: it demands that we reshape scholarship, reshape textbooks, reshape syllabi, reshape lesson plans, and, perhaps most uncomfortably but most excitingly, reshape the critical and historical paradigms through which we have come to understand our world. It means reading, teaching, writing, and publishing in what seems to many scholars and instructors an overcrowded, uncertain territory with few reliable guideposts. The essays that follow, along with the texts they address and the vast body of Sedgwick's work that remains to be explored, point us in a wise and hopeful direction.

NOTES

1. Mrs. E[mma] C. Embury, "Essay on American Literature," *The Ladies Companion* (1835): 84.

2. Mary Kelley, introduction to *The Power of Her Sympathy: The Autobiography and Journal of Catharine Maria Sedgwick* (Boston: Massachusetts Historical Society and Northeastern Univ. Press, 1993), 22.

3. Child Sedgwick, b., d. 27 March 1777; Catherine Sedgwick, b. 11 July 1782, d. 4 March 1783; Henry Dwight Sedgwick, b. 18 April 1784, d. 1 March 1785.

4. This translation had not been located when the present volume went to press, but appears in the *Bibliography of American Literature* entry for Sedgwick, item 17370; see short works bibliography. Sedgwick is also known to have translated works by Swiss writer Jean Charles L. S. de Sismondi; see *Life and Letters of Catharine M. Sedgwick*, ed. Mary E. Dewey (New York: Harper, 1871), 231. In "Miss Sedgwick's Novels," *Ladies Magazine* (May 1829): 234–38, Lydia Maria Child also notes that Sedgwick had translated several of Sismondi's works. These also had not been located at press time.

5. James Fenimore Cooper, review of *A New-England Tale*, *Literary and Scientific Repository and Critical Review* (May 1822): 336; [William Cullen Bryant], review of *Red-*

wood, North American Review (April 1825): 271; Edgar A[llan] Poe, "The Literati of New York City—No. V," *Godey's Lady's Book* (September 1846): 126.

6. Harriet Martineau, "Miss Sedgwick's Works," *The Westminster Review* (October 1838): 64, 59–60; Laurie Robertson-Lorant identifies Melville's "nod" to Sedgwick in *Melville: A Biography* (Amherst: Univ. of Massachusetts Press, 1996), 246–47, 222; Paul Lewis also develops the connection in his essay "'Lectures or a Little Charity': Poor Visits in Antebellum Literature and Culture," *New England Quarterly* 73 (June 2000): 246–73, demonstrating that Melville's "Poor Man's Pudding and Rich Man's Crumbs" (*Harper's New Monthly Magazine*, June 1854) makes "direct satirical thrusts . . . at all comforting pieties about the poor," including Sedgwick's; *Journals of Ralph Waldo Emerson*, ed. Merton M. Sealts, vol. 5 (Cambridge: Belknap Press of Harvard, 1965), 503.

7. Theodore Sedgwick published *Hints to My Young Countrymen* in 1826; in 1828 Elizabeth Dwight Sedgwick published her first of several books, *The Beatitudes;* and in 1829, Susan L. R. Sedgwick published her first book, *The Morals of Pleasure.* See Edward Halsey Foster, *Catharine Maria Sedgwick*, Twayne's United States Authors Series 233 (New York: Twayne, 1974), 35, on friendship; see Dewey, *Life and Letters,* 191, for Sedgwick advising Elizabeth on how to revise *The Beatitudes* for publication.

8. Foster, *Catharine Maria Sedgwick*, 35, 20.

9. Writers and editors who lived in or visited the region included Nathaniel Hawthorne, Herman Melville, Fanny Fern, Nathaniel P. Willis, William Ellery Channing, Ralph Waldo Emerson, Henry Wadsworth Longfellow, Lydia Sigourney, James Russell Lowell, Oliver Wendell Holmes, Henry James, Evert Duyckinck, and publisher James Fields; some, like William Cullen Bryant and Caroline Kirkland, became long-term friends. See Foster, *Catharine Maria Sedgwick*, 19–20, 35–37.

10. Walt Whitman, "Song of Myself," in *Heath Anthology of American Literature*, 4th ed., ed. Paul Lauter, vol. 5 (Boston: Houghton Mifflin, 2002), 2913.

11. Hélène Cixous, "Sorties: Out and Out: Attacks/Ways Out/Forays," *The Feminist Reader: Essays in Gender and the Politics of Literary Criticism*, ed. Catherine Belsey and Jane Moore (New York: Blackwell, 1989), 106.

12. Catharine Maria Sedgwick, introduction to *Women and Work*, by Barbara Leigh Smith Bodichon (New York: C. S. Francis, 1859), 3, 9–10.

Chronology of Sedgwick's Life and Work

1781 In *Brom and Bett v. Ashley,* Elizabeth Freeman ("Mumbet") wins freedom from slavery in a Massachusetts court with Theodore Sedgwick as her attorney; she begins to work for Sedgwick family shortly thereafter.

1785 Sedgwick family settles in Stockbridge, Mass. (from Sheffield, Mass.), in house built for them. Father, Theodore, elected to Continental Congress.

1787 Father elected to second term in Continental Congress, joins Massachusetts convention to ratify U.S. Constitution.

1788 Father elected to U.S. House of Representatives, serves four consecutive terms (1789–90, '91–92, '93–94, '95–96).

1789 Catharine Maria Sedgwick (CMS) born December 28, third daughter and second-to-last (surviving) child of Theodore and Pamela Sedgwick. Siblings: sisters Elizabeth (known as Eliza, b. 1775) and Frances (b. 1778), brothers Theodore (b. 1780), Henry Dwight (b. 1785), Robert (b. 1787), and Charles (b. 1791). For next twelve years, father in Philadelphia between three and eight months per year, mostly during winter, home in Stockbridge summers.

1791 Mother begins to suffer from attacks of severe depression, which continue until her death.

1793 Mother recuperating Nov.–Jan. (away from home).

1794 Mother and sister Eliza visit Theodore in Philadelphia. Family together in Stockbridge during summer.

1795 Mother held in isolation in Sheffield under medical supervision, Dec.–Jan.

1796 Father elected to U.S. Senate at midterm.

1797 Marriage of sister Eliza to Thaddeus Pomeroy (Oct.).

1798 Attends school and spends the summer in Bennington, Vt., with father's eldest living sister, Mary Ann, wife of Rev. Job Swift. Father reelected to U.S. House of Representatives.

1799 Father elected Speaker of the House.

1800 Father does not seek reelection.

1801 Marriage of sister Frances to Ebenezer Watson (Apr.). Father home for most of year.

1802 Reading constantly, especially novels. Living with Watsons in New York City; studies dancing with M. Lalliet and begins to study French. Father appointed Supreme Court Justice for Massachusetts (which includes Maine); leaves in May and is frequently absent from home for next ten years.

1803 Attends Mrs. Bell's school in Albany, develops skills in embroidery. Reads Rollin's multivolume *Ancient History*, as well as collections for children by Anna Barbauld and Arnaud Berquin.

1804 Attends Mrs. Payne's school in Boston; studies French.

1805–6 Spends the winter in New York with sister Frances; sister Eliza and family move back to Stockbridge (from Albany), in part to be near mother, who is ill.

1807 Death of mother (Sept.).

1808 Marriage of father to Penelope Russell (7 Nov.); they reside in Stock-bridge. Marriage of brother Theodore to Susan Ridley, one of Catharine's friends (28 Nov.). Until her father's death, CMS divides her time between Albany (with brother Theodore's family), New York (with sister Frances's family), and Stockbridge. Elizabeth Freeman leaves household.

1809–21 CMS a member of Dr. Mason's Congregationalist church in New York.

1812 Breaks engagement with first known suitor, William Jarvis, who marries Harriet Marsh in Pittsfield, Mass. (20 July).

1813 Death of father, who converts to Unitarianism on his deathbed, attended by Rev. Channing and CMS. CMS moves back to Stockbridge.

1817 Marriage of brother Henry to Jane Minot (June).

1819 Prior to March breaks her "arrangement" with "Mr. B.," Harmanus Bleecker, brother Theodore's law partner. Marriage of brother Charles to Elizabeth Dwight (Sept.).

1820 Meets William Cullen Bryant, encourages his writing.

1821 Travels from Albany to Niagara Falls and back through Montreal and Vermont with brother Robert, "Mrs. B.," brother Theodore and wife Susan (Ridley), their son Theodore III (b. 1811), probably also their daughter Maria (b. 1813), 22 June to end July. Starts her first journal in the summer. Becomes a member of the Unitarian Society in New York City, along with brothers Robert and Henry. Develops friendship with Mr. and Mrs. Frank (Susan) Channing (William Ellery Channing's brother).

1821–22 Brother Charles moves his family to Lenox; brother Theodore and his family move into Stockbridge house. CMS begins to spend her summers in Stockbridge/Lenox and winters with siblings in New York.

1822 Marriage of brother Robert to Elizabeth Ellery (Aug.). Publishes *A New-England Tale*. Publishes "Mary Hollis" (tract) for the New York Unitarian Book Society. Visits Hancock Shaker Village; spends two days there.

1823 Reads *The Pioneers*. Receives a letter from Maria Edgeworth.

1824 Publishes *Redwood* (dedicated to Bryant). Visiting in Washington, D.C., attends publication party for Margaret Bayard Smith; James Fenimore Cooper also attends.

1825 Publishes *The Travellers*, first book for children. In dispute over repayment of loan made in 1818, brother Robert takes J. F. Cooper to court in three lawsuits, 1825–26. In June CMS meets Gen. Lafayette at Mrs. Quincy's; hears Webster's Bunker Hill oration. Publishes "The Catholic Iroquois," in *The Atlantic Souvenir*, first of more than one hundred short stories and sketches over next thirty-seven years.

1826 Spends five weeks in Boston among Unitarian followers of William Ellery Channing, including her good friends Susan Higginson Channing (Mrs. Frank) and writer Eliza Lee Cabot (later Follen), as well as educators Elizabeth and Mary Peabody.

1827 Publishes *Hope Leslie*. Sister Eliza (Pomeroy) suffers stroke in June, dies in October. December, CMS receives "most gratifying letter" from Sismondi; their correspondence spans twenty years. Brother Henry's mental illness and eye problem developing. British travel writer Basil Hall visits Stockbridge. Beginning of recognized importance of Berkshire culture and "pilgrimages" by noted Europeans to visit CMS.

1828 Moves to Lenox, Mass., to live with brother Charles; visits New York, Boston, Salem (attends Bicentennial of Salem, dines with Justice Story).

Winter, helps in sister-in-law Elizabeth Dwight Sedgwick's Young Ladies' School at Lenox, which taught pupils from elite families, many of whom became accomplished in their own right (1828–64). Attends court murder trials. Takes one of many summer holidays at Saratoga Springs.

1829 Death of Elizabeth Freeman, who is buried next to space reserved for CMS in Sedgwick family "pie" in Stockbridge Cemetery. January, brother Henry's mental condition has deteriorated; April, he moves into asylum. CMS spends three weeks in Pennsylvania. Sister-in-law Susan Ridley Sedgwick's first book published (*Morals of Pleasure*).

1830 Publishes *Clarence*. Beginning of acquaintance with writer Harriet Martineau. Travels to Philadelphia.

1831 Trip to Washington, D.C., in January; sees family friend Vice President Martin Van Buren; introduced to President Jackson. Visits Supreme Court (Justice Story speaks with her party there); Chief Justice John Marshall visits her, plans to read her new work. Visiting the legislature, CMS appalled by vehemence of Southerners' debate as nullification crisis emerges. Harper Brothers, publisher, invites CMS to contribute to the *Library of Select Novels* ("Le Bossu" appears, along with works by Bryant, Paulding, Verplanck, Leggett, and Sands, in *Tales of Glauber Spa* in 1832.) February, brother Henry delivers antislavery lecture in Stockbridge; dies in December.

1832 Beginning of friendship with actress Fanny Kemble. In April opposes Home for Discharged Convicts in Stockbridge. CMS in Lenox; wing has been built onto Charles's house for her. Lydia Maria Child dedicates *The Coronal* to CMS.

1833 Takes trip to Virginia with brother Robert and wife Elizabeth (Ellery); tours Randolph plantation, "Wilton," on James River (150 slaves). Pays "visit of lasting importance" to Fanny Kemble in New York; introduces Kemble to Elizabeth (Dwight, Mrs. Charles) Sedgwick and Elizabeth's daughter Kate—both become Kemble's most intimate lifelong friends in the United States.

1834 Responds to Lydia Maria Child's gift of her *Appeal in Favor of that Class of Americans Called Africans* (May); fears presenting herself as an "advocate of the principles of the abolitionists," saying some are "foolish and doubtful zealots." CMS included in *National Portrait Gallery of Distinguished Americans;* first Charles Ingham portrait featured in this volume.

1835   Publishes *The Linwoods* and *Home*. Height of Berkshires' popularity with writers, 1835–60. CMS gathers Lydia Sigourney, Fanny Kemble, Harriet Martineau, and others in Stockbridge. Washington Irving, Daniel Webster, President Van Buren visit Theodore Sedgwick Jr.

1836   Publishes *The Poor Rich Man and the Rich Poor Man, Memoir of Lucretia Maria Davidson*, and *Tales and Sketches* (dedicated to Harriet Martineau); translates ninety-five pages of *My Prisons, Memoirs of Silvio Pellico of Saluzzo*, from Italian. Sits for second portrait with Charles Ingham (July). William Jarvis, former suitor, shoots himself through the heart (Oct.).

1837   Publishes *Live and Let Live;* finishes writing *A Love Token for Children*. Visited by Joseph Curtis in New York (founder of New York City Homes for Juvenile Delinquents; see also *Memoir*, 1858). In March, meets Sarah and Angelina Grimké at Mrs. Follen's in New York; attends abolition party. Anna Jameson stays with CMS in Berkshires during negotiation of separation from her husband, inaugurating intense friendship and lifelong correspondence. Death of brother Theodore (Nov.). Visited by Italian exiles. Fanny Fern and brother Nathaniel Willis spend summers in Stockbridge (through 1846).

1838   Brother Robert suffers stroke; CMS becomes primary caretaker.

1839   Publishes *Means and Ends, or Self-Training*.

1839–40   Travels for fifteen months in Europe with brother Robert and his family; visits England, Belgium, Germany, Switzerland, France, Italy. Publishes *Stories for Young Persons*.

1840–60   CMS maintains rooms in both Charles's home in Lenox and family home in Stockbridge.

1841   Death of brother Robert (Sept.). Publishes *Letters from Abroad to Kindred at Home*. Visited by Lord Morpeth (later Earl of Carlyle) and Augusta Murray, both of Queen Victoria's court.

1842   Death of sister Frances (Watson) (June). William Ellery Channing delivers his definitive antislavery address on eighth anniversary of emancipation in the West Indies (1 Aug.) in Lenox while vacationing with the Sedgwicks in Stockbridge.

1844   Publishes *Tales and Sketches*, Series Two (a.k.a. *Wilton Harvey and Other Tales*). Travels to Philadelphia, visits Kemble. Writes Jameson, following publication of Margaret Fuller's *Woman in the Nineteenth Century*, about women's rights. Corresponds with Cassius Clay on his antislavery scheme.

In August, participates in Berkshire Jubilee, festival organized by Bryant and held in Pittsfield, Mass.

1845   Becomes active in Female Department of the New York Prison Association. In June, formally opens the Home for Discharged Female Convicts.

1847   Caroline Kirkland visits CMS in Lenox.

1848   Publishes *The Boy of Mount Rhigi* and *Facts and Fancies for School-Day Reading*. Becomes first directress of the New York Women's Prison Association; also active in the Isaac T. Hopper Home (teaches Bible classes and gives Sunday afternoon readings). Associates with Abbie Hoffman Gibbons, Caroline Kirkland, and other prison reform workers. In the late 1840s and early 1850s socializes in elite Anne Lynch's New York City salons.

1849   Lucy Stone visits.

1850   In August, Nathaniel Hawthorne meets Herman Melville; day's activities include a climb up Monument Mountain. Sedgwick reportedly part of festivities, along with Oliver Wendell Holmes, Cornelius Mathews, publisher James T. Fields, lawyer David Dudley Field, and publishers and critics Evert and George Duyckinck. Holmes replies to Hawthorne's request to judge writing contest in Albany, recommending CMS "as the most natural person to look to" for third member of committee. CMS sees Caroline Kirkland frequently. Visited by James Russell Lowell, Rev. Orville Dewey, James, Longfellow.

1851   Begins writing autobiography for great-niece Alice Minot, granddaughter of brother Charles (10 Oct.). Dinner at Charles and Elizabeth's in Lenox with the Melvilles, Hawthorne, and Mrs. G. P. R. James.

1854   Travels 3,740 miles with brother Charles and excursion party on trip that includes St. Paul, Minn.; Chicago, Ill.; and passage on Mississippi River to St. Louis and Hannibal, Mo.; returning to New York via Niagara Falls.

1856   Death of brother Charles, last remaining sibling (Aug.).

1857   Publishes *Married or Single?*, her last novel.

1858   Publishes *Memoir of Joseph Curtis*, her last book.

1862   Publishes "A Sketch from Life," last known short story.

1863   Epileptic seizure, unconscious for twenty-four hours. Writes letter of resignation as Directress of the Women's Prison Association.

1864 Visited by Whittier. Death of Elizabeth Dwight (Mrs. Charles) Sedgwick (Nov.).

1865 Visits Stockbridge for the last time. Most of last years spent living with niece Kate Minot (Charles's daughter) in West Roxbury, Mass. (near Boston).

1867 Susan Ridley Sedgwick dies (Jan.). CMS dies of paralysis, 31 July, age 77.

1871 *Life and Letters of Catharine Maria Sedgwick* published (edited by Mary E. Dewey).

This chronology benefited from the research of Charlene Avallone.

Sources consulted in the development of this chronology include:
Edward Halsey Foster, *Catharine Maria Sedgwick*. New York: Twayne, 1974.
Jane Giles, "Catharine Maria Sedgwick: An American Literary Biography."
    Ph.D. diss., City Univ. of New York, 1995.
Tim Kinslea, "Awakening the Heart: Courtship, Engagement, and Marriage
    Among the Sedgwicks of Berkshire County in the Generation after the
    Revolution." Ph.D. diss., Boston College, 1999.
The Life and Letters of Catharine Maria Sedgwick. Ed. Mary E. Dewey. New
    York: Harper's, 1871.
*The Power of Her Sympathy: The Autobiography and Journal of Catharine Maria
    Sedgwick*. Ed. Mary Kelley. Boston: Massachusetts Historical Society,
    1993.
Audrey J. Roberts, "The Letters of Caroline M. Kirkland." Ph.D. diss., Univ.
    of Wisconsin, Madison, 1976.
Henry Dwight Sedgwick, "Reminiscences of Literary Berkshire." *Century Maga-
    zine* 50, V 4 (August 1895): 552–68.

Catharine Maria Sedgwick

I

⁊ Excerpts from Early Overviews of Sedgwick's Career

[Signed] F. [Lydia Maria Francis Child]. "Miss Sedgwick's Novels." *Ladies Magazine* (May 1829): 234–38.

There is hardly one among the crowd of pretenders at the present day, who has not received more newspaper praise than the author of these excellent and highly interesting volumes. Even the reviewers, though they have spoken of her with the deepest respect and admiration, have hardly satisfied our enthusiasm upon the subject. Her claims have, however, sunk deeply into the hearts of her countrymen; and her fame is destined to be far more durable than that of any other female writer among us. In America, she deserves the rank accorded to Miss Edgeworth in England; and an hundred years hence, when other and gifted competitors have crowded into the field, our country will still be as proud of her name. She has been a close observer of all the shadings of human characters, —in kind and playful humour she has penetrated into all the hiding places of the heart; and she has brought them before us in pictures as simply beautiful as nature herself. Her style is unambitious—it has none of the pomp of metaphor, or the trickery of arrangement—it is always pure, graceful, and fascinating. Language with her, is the breath of the soul; and that breath is "articulate melody." (Pp. 234–35)

"Catharine M. Sedgwick." In *The National Portrait Gallery of Distinguished Americans.* Ed. James Herring, James B. Longacre, and American Academy of the Fine Arts. Vol. 1. New York: Monson Bancroft, 1834, 1–8. Note: No through-numbering of pages; each "portrait" numbered separately. Reprinted as "Caroline [*sic*] Maria Sedgwick." *American Ladies' Magazine* (Dec. 1835): 656–65.

We cannot omit a passing remark upon Miss Sedgwick's style. We have often thought, that in the hands of a master, the subject of style would afford an admirable opportunity for establishing a new school of philosophy. It is very certain, that style affords a truer index of the mind, than the theory of physiognomy. . . .

Whatever our readers may think of the depth of this philosophy, we are sure they will agree with us, that there is a peculiar grace, fitness, and beauty in Miss Sedgwick's style: it is entirely devoid of mannerism, and we like it a thousand times better on that account. The drapery of her thoughts [is] negligee, gay, rich, grave, or solemn, as becomes them. There is one particular in which we especially admire her costume: there is no variety of it which ever exhibits a single blue thread, in a certain quarter where that color is too apt to attract attention. She always leads us to regard her rather as an accomplished lady, than as a brilliant author. Her style is never marked by pedantry, and is equally free from stiffness and negligence—it is more distinguished by delicacy and grace than strength. The purity of her English may afford a model to some of our learned scholars; and with that of Miss Edgeworth, it furnishes for their consideration the very interesting problem how far a knowledge of the learned languages is essential to an English writer in the use of his vernacular tongue.

Our [page] limits will not permit us to speak of Miss Sedgwick's powers of invention, and imagination, nor of her great truth and skill in the delineation of character. We cannot, however, wholly omit to notice that power, which speaks from heart to heart. In matters of taste, we may adopt the opinions of others, but we must feel for ourselves. . . . [S]he never attempts to convulse our hearts with hopeless and unprofitable agonies; and if there be anything painful in the emotions which she calls forth, it is more than compensated by the healing influence which they possess—the kindly sympathies they elicit, or the sense of justice which they satisfy; and this, we think, is the limit beyond which fictitious misery should never pass. (Pp. 7–8)

Chapter 1

Catharine Maria Sedgwick in Literary History

CAROLYN L. KARCHER

The recovery of Catharine Maria Sedgwick's oeuvre that this ambitious collection of essays promotes simultaneously forces a radical reconceptualization of American literary history. As scholars acquaint themselves with *A New-England Tale* (1822), *Redwood* (1824), *Clarence* (1830), *The Linwoods* (1835), *Tales and Sketches* (1: 1835, 2: 1844), and *Married or Single?* (1857), Sedgwick emerges as much more than a major contributor to the dominant genres of the 1820s—the frontier romance and the historical novel—a status she has secured since the republication of *Hope Leslie*. Thanks to the survey of her corpus the editors of the present volume have compiled, we can now recognize Sedgwick as the founder of a homegrown novel of manners tradition that American literature has long been erroneously supposed to lack; a pioneer in the development of realism, which has customarily been dated after the Civil War and credited to male writers; a prolific and trendsetting author of short fiction; and even, as Patricia Kalayjian's essay on *Clarence* demonstrates, an early architect of the urban novel that Howells, Crane, Dreiser, and Wharton would later perfect.

Restoring Sedgwick to her rightful place in American literary history thus requires challenging paradigms that have obscured both the genres she helped shape and the direct and indirect influence she exerted on her contemporaries and successors. Three paradigms have maintained an especially tenacious hold on scholars: those of the romance, the sentimental novel, and the scribbling woman. They can be summarized as follows. First, American writers have persistently shied away from the realistic depiction of society, preferring to work in the mode of what Nathaniel Hawthorne called the romance—a mode best suited to probing the individual psyche. Second, nineteenth-century American fiction can be divided into serious novels produced by men and sentimental novels produced by women, the former addressing significant human issues and occasionally articulating social or political insights, the latter limited to retailing the trivia of the domestic sphere. Third, men's fiction alone displays self-conscious artistry and formal innovation, while women's fiction endlessly duplicates formulaic plots; hence, new literary trends (such as the shift from romanticism to realism) can only be discerned by studying male writers.[1]

Of these paradigms, none has more completely marginalized Sedgwick and the school of women writers she started than that of the romance, as the critic Richard Chase has defined it. Chase identifies the romance as the "most original and characteristic form" of the American novel, locating its Americanness in its departures from the British and European novel. Unlike the novel, he contends, the romance disregards the "requirements of verisimilitude, development, and continuity" and "ignore[s] the spectacle of man in society." Whereas the "novel renders reality closely and in comprehensive detail," the romance, according to Chase, "veer[s] toward mythic, allegorical, and symbolistic" representations. Similarly, whereas the novel emphasizes "character" over "action and plot" and sets characters in "explicable relation to nature, to each other, to their social class, to their own past," the romance subordinates character to action, treats characters as "two-dimensional types . . . not . . . complexly related to each other or to society or to the past," and abstracts them so entirely from their milieu that it does "not matter much what class people come from."[2]

Sedgwick's works contradict Chase's premises point by point. The very title of her first novel—*A New-England Tale; or, Sketches of New-England Character and Manners*—announces at the outset that delineating the character and manners of a particular society is Sedgwick's primary concern, and the opening sentence of her preface specifies that she intends thereby "to add something to the scanty stock of native American literature."[3] For Sedgwick, in other words, the project of Americanizing the novel and adapting it to the creation of a "native" literature distinct from its British and European models does not involve transforming the novel into the romance; instead, it involves limning daily life in her own country with close attention to the values, mores, and social gradations that differentiate her compatriots from other peoples.

Thus, in *A New-England Tale*, Sedgwick situates her heroine Jane Elton in a village whose class structure consists of well-to-do merchants and landowners, clergymen, teachers, small farmers, domestic servants, and outcasts, but she also shows that in contrast to the old world's class structure, this one is unstable and mutable, making it an unreliable foundation on which to build Jane's future. Jane's father, "formerly a flourishing trader" (*NET*, 9), dies bankrupt by the third page of the novel, and her dissipated cousin David Wilson wastes his fortune and turns highwayman in the end. Jane herself occupies three different class positions over the course of the novel, sinking from her parents' elite status to servitude in her Aunt Wilson's household, climbing back into middle-class respectability as a self-supporting schoolteacher, and finally regaining her original rank by marrying the wealthy philanthropist Robert Lloyd, who has bought her father's home.

Although Sedgwick carefully maps her characters' class relations, she centers her "sketches" of a New England village on the role religion plays in molding their "manners"—a role she observes from her perspective as a recent convert from Calvinism to Unitarianism. Through her portrayals of Jane's Calvinist relatives and their minister, Sedgwick presents a blistering exposé of the evils Calvinist theology begets: an obsession with "sound doctrine" at the expense of "benevolent practice"; a mean-spiritedness masked by ostentatious contributions to tract societies, foreign missions, and programs for evangelizing "the Cherokees, or Osages"; and a ban on "appropriate pleasures" that drives church members into "sins of a much deeper die" (*NET*, 13, 23, 47). Through her contrasting portrayals of the Quaker Robert Lloyd and the Methodist servant Mary Hull, Sedgwick illustrates the spirit of true religion—a spirit that transcends sectarian barriers and manifests itself in ethical behavior and faith in a loving God. Lloyd and his family live "after the plain way of their sect; not indulging in costly dress or furniture, but regulating all their expenses by a just and careful economy" and devoting their savings to charity (*NET*, 27). Their lower-class counterpart Mary Hull, who possesses such "virtues of her station" as "practical good sense, industrious, efficient habits," and tact in her interactions with social superiors, teaches Jane to submit humbly to her servitude and to rely on God for consolation (*NET*, 12, 20).

Sedgwick's realistic rendition of New England character and manners Americanizes the British novel in a double sense. Not only does it illuminate the class mobility, religious fluidity, and democratizing tendency that set American society apart from old-world analogues, but it turns conventions that had previously served to reinforce class hierarchies into vehicles for inculcating republican virtues and nonsectarian Christian principles. Sedgwick's achievement stands out even more clearly in the light of British literary history, for she began writing only a decade after Jane Austen, when the novel of manners was still young.

Because of her commitment to accurate representation of her society, the novel of manners, as Sedgwick developed it, can also be seen as lying at the origins of American literary realism. *A New-England Tale* inaugurates the mode of women's regional fiction that Judith Fetterley, Joanne Dobson, and Joan Hedrick, among others, have cited as a far earlier source of realism than the works of William Dean Howells and the European writers from whom he drew inspiration.[4]

Just as Sedgwick's oeuvre refutes the claim that the romance ranks as the "most original and characteristic form" of the American novel, so the social and political criticism she weaves into all her works, beginning with *A New-England Tale*, dispels the belief that women confined themselves to writing about trivial domestic matters, leaving the province of serious fiction to men. Although feminist critics like Nina Baym, Jane Tompkins, and Joanne Dobson have eloquently defended the sentimental novel against its detractors, demonstrating that it performed the serious "cultural work" of fostering an ethos of "human connection" as a corrective to American society's selfish individualism, they have not challenged the gendered division of American fiction that the paradigm of the sentimental novel furthers.[5] By concentrating on the sentimental novel, moreover, feminist critics have inadvertently perpetuated the notion that nineteenth-century women wrote primarily in that genre. I have already suggested that Sedgwick can better be appreciated as a novelist of manners and a pioneering realist. Here I would like to propose that we also consider her an early political novelist.

Critics now universally acknowledge the political dimensions of *Hope Leslie* as a novel that rewrites the history of the Pequot War and engages ongoing debates over Indian Removal. In her essay for this volume, Susan Harris argues that *A New England-Tale*, *Redwood*, *Clarence*, and *The Linwoods* can likewise be considered political novels in that they grapple with the questions, "What are the limits to legitimate authority? When is it appropriate to defy king, magistrate, father?" *Redwood*, however, still awaits recognition as the first novel to tackle the issue of slavery.

Published four years after the Missouri Crisis of 1819–20 raised the specter of an internecine war between North and South, *Redwood* explores scenarios for peacefully ending the "curse of slavery" that Harriet Beecher Stowe would later entertain in *Uncle Tom's Cabin* and *Dred*.[6] In an episode foreshadowing the martyrdom of Uncle Tom, the slave Africk, beaten to death for shielding a slave woman from a whipping, exhorts a sympathetic young slaveholder with his last breath: "Do not pray for me, nor for mine. . . . But pray for your father's land, and your father's children. . . . I hear the cry of revenge; I hear the wailings of your wives and your little ones; and I see your fair lands drenched with their blood. Pray to God to save you in that day, for it will surely come" (*R*, 1:56). This slaveholder subsequently emancipates his slaves after preparing them for freedom, and his son then sells the plantation and uses its proceeds to train himself for a profession from which he can earn his own living. In another episode that anticipates the increasing resistance of Northern citizens to turning in fugitive slaves, a slave taken north by her owner escapes to Massachusetts, where "the white inhabitants would be very backward to enforce her master's rights" (*R*, 2:271). The main solution *Redwood* offers to the problem of ending slavery without causing civil war, however—the regeneration of the South by a patiently forbearing North and the ultimate reconciliation of the two regions—is implied by the novel's symbolic ending. As the "infidel" planter Henry Redwood, a precursor of Stowe's Augustine St. Clare, sees the contrasting effects of a Southern and a Northern upbringing on his daughters Caroline and Ellen—the former a spoiled belle reared in South Carolina, the latter a self-reliant and principled young woman reared among New England farmers after her deserted mother's death—he repents of his errant ways. Meanwhile, Ellen's generous renunciation of her rightful share of the Redwood fortune wins over the hostile Caroline, and when Caroline dies prematurely, Ellen not only receives her full inheritance, but gives her sister's child the benefit of the New England education responsible for her own virtues. A prime example of how "Sedgwick uses family and social relationships as models for political relationships" (to quote Susan Harris again), *Redwood* thus intervenes in the controversy over slavery much the way *Hope Leslie* does in the controversy over the Indian question.

One reason critics have failed to give *Redwood* its due as an antecedent of the antislavery novel is that Sedgwick, unlike her friend Lydia Maria Child and her successor Stowe, never joined the abolitionist movement, despite her strong sympathy for the slaves and her family's championship of their cause. In her fascinating essay on Sedgwick's abandoned antislavery manuscript, which she finds to be "one of the earliest examples of antislavery fiction," Karen Woods Weierman hypothesizes that Sedgwick refused to align herself with the abolitionists because she feared their uncompromising stand would destroy the Union (see chapter 7 in this volume). This explanation accords with Sedgwick's emphasis on reconciliation in *Redwood*. Yet notwithstanding Sedgwick's inability to move beyond the political position she staked out in 1824—a position radical for its day, though conservative by the time Child published *An Appeal in Favor of That Class of Americans Called Africans* in 1833—*Redwood* provided Child and Stowe with an empowering model for their own political fiction.

Sedgwick's novels deserve critical reassessment not just for their compelling dramatization of key national problems, but for their artistry, as Judith Fetterley underscores.[7] Indeed, the praise Sedgwick received from her contemporaries clearly indicates that unlike the twentieth-century architects of the American literary canon, nineteenth-century readers of both sexes fully appreciated her artistry and ranked her with her leading male peers. Edgar Allan Poe eulogized Sedgwick as "one of our most celebrated and most meritorious writers." Hawthorne paid tribute to Sedgwick's realism by commending her as "our most truthful novelist." Rufus Griswold's landmark anthology, *The Prose Writers of America*, pronounced her "delineations of New England manners . . . decidedly the best that have appeared." William Cullen Bryant, Lydia Maria Child, and John S. Hart, editor of *The Female Prose Writers of America*, all acclaimed Sedgwick's "skill in the drawing of characters," her "close observation" of human psychology, and her success at capturing "minutely individual" traits. Readers also singled out favorite characters for special mention. The British novelist Maria Edgeworth, for example, particularly admired the six-foot-tall spinster, Aunt Deborah Lenox, who peppers *Redwood* with her sententious wisdom. "[She] is to America what Scott's characters are to Scotland," opined Edgeworth, "—valuable as original pictures, with enough of individual peculiarity . . . to give the feeling of reality & life as portraits, with sufficient also of general characteristicks [*sic*], to give them the philosophical merit of portraying a class." Bryant, who shared Edgeworth's estimation of Aunt Deborah, considered the Shaker Susan Allen almost as memorable. The Swiss historian Jean Charles Leonard Sismondi hailed *Hope Leslie*'s Magawisca as "the noblest conception imagination ever formed"—a judgment with which Child concurred. The *North American Review* likewise found Magawisca a creation of "genius," but delighted equally in the "lovely" Esther Downing and the high-spirited Hope Leslie, "sparkling with gaiety and wit." Along with her realistic depictions of character and manners, reviewers repeatedly extolled Sedgwick's "limpid" style.[8]

Although overlooked by her contemporaries, Sedgwick's sophisticated narrative strategies constitute perhaps the most impressive evidence of her self-conscious artistry and gift for innovation. One of these strategies, with which she begins experimenting in *Redwood*, is to share authorship with her characters by letting them narrate parts of the story through interpolated letters. Combining the intimacy of the epistolary novel with the broader horizon an omniscient narrator affords, this technique enables Sedgwick to present multiple perspectives on events and to give voice even to marginal or evil characters. She exploits it to its fullest potential in her novels' denouements. In *Redwood*, for example, Sedgwick delegates to Aunt Deborah the responsibility for tying up loose ends and bringing the narrative to a close. "We fancied we had finished our humble labours," she alleges playfully, "when by a lucky chance a letter, written by Deborah Lenox . . . fell into our hands. . . . [W]e immediately transmitted it to our printer," intact except for the spelling, which he purportedly insisted on correcting (*R*, 2:281). Sedgwick goes even further in *Hope Leslie*, where she allows Esther Downing to alter the outcome of the plot in a letter breaking her engagement with Everell Fletcher and encouraging his "immediate union" with Hope.[9]

The multivocal narrative strategy Sedgwick devises in *Redwood* and *Hope Leslie* serves to effect formally the democratization of American society that these novels seek to advance through their plots. In her last novel, *Married or Single?*, which shifts the focus from North-South conflict and Indian Removal to the controversy over women's rights, as Deborah Gussman shows in her essay for this volume, Sedgwick adapts the technique of interpolated letters to new purposes. By opening the novel with extracts from "old family letters" that her heroines are preparing to burn, she suggests the continuities in women's lives from one generation to the next. As these letters "spell backward one's own future," they foreshadow the flawed marriages that will ensue from the heroines' courtships.[10] Accordingly, they reinforce the novel's realistic portrayal of marriage. *Married or Single?* also features another innovation—a plot that does not end with marriage, but instead unveils the trials and tribulations of married life. In exploring this theme, and thereby challenging a long-standing fictional convention, Sedgwick anticipates such novels as Dinah Mulock Craik's *A Brave Lady* (1869–70), Elizabeth Stuart Phelps's *The Story of Avis* (1877), and William Dean Howells's *A Modern Instance* (1882).

Resurrecting Sedgwick's corpus, in sum, changes our understanding of American literary history by displacing the romance as "the most original and characteristic form" of the American novel;[11] by restoring to visibility the native novel-of-manners tradition Sedgwick initiated in *A New-England Tale*, and with it the beginnings of literary realism; by establishing women as thoughtful social critics and innovative artists rather than mere "scribblers" who churned out nothing but formulaic tearjerkers; and by highlighting women's contributions to the development of American literature.

So far, I have been outlining the reconfigurations that follow from placing Sedgwick at the source rather than in the margins of nineteenth-century American literature. I would now like to situate Sedgwick in relation to both the male writers who chose divergent literary paths and the women writers who emulated her example.

As his review of *A New-England Tale* indicates, James Fenimore Cooper immediately recognized Sedgwick's aptitude for "perfectly and agreeably" "illustrat[ing] American society and manners"—an endeavor at which he himself had failed when he had imitated Jane Austen in his first novel, *Precaution* (1820).[12] He also seems to have recognized in Sedgwick a writer who might threaten the preeminence he had just won with *The Spy* (1821), a historical novel of the American Revolution in the mode of Sir Walter Scott. When Sedgwick had the temerity to invade Cooper's domain by challenging his Scott-inspired frontier romance, *The Last of the Mohicans* (1826), set during the French and Indian War, with her version of the genre, *Hope Leslie* (1827), set in the aftermath of the Pequot War, Cooper countered with a novel of King Philip's War, *The Wept of Wish-ton-Wish* (1829), similarly based in Puritan New England and featuring an Indian-white marriage. The two authors' revisions of each other's plots reflect more than literary rivalry (though such rivalry furnishes a significant index of Sedgwick's status as a woman writer with whom male competitors had to reckon). At stake in their jousting is whether patriarchal or protofeminist ideol-

ogy will shape the frontier romance and the vision of American history it en-
codes; whether war between whites and Indians must be judged inevitable, or
models of peaceful coexistence—economic and cultural exchange, friendship,
interracial marriage, voluntary emigration—can provide alternatives; and
whether the right to determine the nation's destiny must remain in white male
hands or be shared with white women.

If Cooper perceived Sedgwick as an interloper in the territory he had
claimed, Hawthorne seems to have perceived her as a predecessor in the field he
hoped to cultivate—New England history. A vignette from *A New-England Tale*
that reappears in *The Scarlet Letter* (1850) shows how carefully Hawthorne read
Sedgwick. On a "solitary walk" through the woods, Sedgwick's heroine Jane
Elton finds a "wild rose-bush" growing beside a grave, and "plucking one of the
flowers," she soliloquizes: "[F]ragrant and transient, thou art a fit emblem of
the blasted flower below!" (*NET*, 116). Coyly remarking that this wild rosebush,
"by a strange chance, has been kept alive in history," Hawthorne figuratively
replants it beside the portal of Hester Prynne's prison door and "pluck[s] one
of its flowers" for the reader, to whom its "fragrance and fragile beauty" offer a
"token that the deep heart of Nature [can] pity and be kind" to the "condemned
criminal."[13]

Whatever hints Hawthorne took from Sedgwick, he opted for a very different approach to dramatizing New England history. Indeed, nothing better illustrates Richard Chase's distinctions between the romance and the novel than a
comparison of *The Scarlet Letter* with *Hope Leslie*. Hawthorne dispenses with
the detailed social canvas in which Sedgwick places Hope. The Puritan community in *The Scarlet Letter* functions as an ominous symbolic backdrop, not as an
integral element of the characters' daily lives. Whereas in *Hope Leslie* we eaves-
drop on theological debates in Puritan households and social centers, attend the
serving and setting of meals, watch the plying of needles and the wielding of
brooms and mops, join in evening prayers, and participate in the rites of the
Puritan Sabbath, in *The Scarlet Letter* we see Puritan life only in such emblematic scenes as the arraignment of Hester on the scaffold and the procession in
which Dimmesdale marches to deliver his election sermon.

By rejecting Sedgwick's novelistic realism for what Chase calls the "formal
abstractness" of the romance, Hawthorne simultaneously rejects the picture she
presents of women.[14] In contrast to Sedgwick, who enmeshes Hope in a dense
female network that includes her Puritan friend Esther Downing, her Indian
friends Nelema and Magawisca, her surrogate mothers Mrs. Winthrop and Bertha Grafton, the fallen woman Rosa, and the meddling servant Jennet, Hawthorne isolates Hester from other women, characterizing them as her "most
pitiless" judges. He also brings his rebellious heroine to accept society's punish-

ment, unlike Sedgwick, who allows Hope to triumph over the Puritan magistracy.

Precisely the aspects of Sedgwick's legacy that most disturbed her male rivals most inspired her female peers. Child confessed a desire "to *think*, and *write*, and *be*, like" the author of *Hope Leslie*, to whom she dedicated her first collection of stories, *The Coronal* (1831). *A New-England Tale*, which Child read aloud to her class at the school she was running, helped embolden her to publish her own first novel, *Hobomok, A Tale of Early Times* (1824). Child apparently regarded Sedgwick as a role model rather than a literary model, however. Not only did she eschew the realistic delineation of manners that was Sedgwick's forte, but she created women characters quite unlike the virtuous Jane Elton and Ellen Redwood. Instead, the heroines of *Hobomok* and *The Rebels; or, Boston Before the Revolution* (1825) actually anticipate Child's favorite Sedgwick characters, Magawisca and Hope Leslie, in challenging patriarchal authority. Moreover, Mary Conant of *Hobomok*—who elopes with an Indian, bears him a son, and then divorces him to marry her first love—enjoys a sexual freedom that Sedgwick would never allow her heroines. Child would ultimately go beyond Sedgwick in advocating intermarriage as a solution to America's race problem, championing the abolitionist cause, defending sexual desire as natural, and endorsing women's rights as indispensable to combating the abuses of a society in which "men made all the laws, and elected all the magistrates." She would also adopt genres more suited to forwarding these ideals than the novel of manners, such as antislavery fiction, science fiction, and journalism.[15]

The writer on whom Sedgwick exerted the strongest literary influence was Stowe. Stowe's borrowings from *Redwood* in *Uncle Tom's Cabin* represent only one aspect of that influence. "A New England Sketch," which inaugurated Stowe's career as a fiction writer in 1834 with a memorable characterization of a "regional type," the New England farmer,[16] acknowledges a debt to Sedgwick in its very title. Stowe's greatest New England novel, *The Minister's Wooing*, emulates Sedgwick both thematically and formally: by lovingly depicting the manners of her native region, by articulating a trenchant critique of Calvinism, by creating a piquant New England character type and according her a prominent role in the denouement, and by interspersing letters from the characters throughout the narrative as a means of allowing multiple voices to speak. Stowe even ends *The Minister's Wooing* with a letter from the gossipy seamstress Miss Prissy, just as Sedgwick ends *Redwood* with a letter from Deborah Lenox.

Sedgwick's legacy and its implications for American literary history will become increasingly clear as scholars bring her works back into print and pursue the leads this collection of essays suggests. Future literary historians will trace the chain of influences farther, exploring the links between Sedgwick and other early realists, such as Susan Warner and Caroline Kirkland, and examining possible connections with successors such as Elizabeth Stuart Phelps and Sarah Orne Jewett. They will also extend the study of Sedgwick's dialogue with her male peers to encompass Cooper's novels of manners, Hawthorne's *The House of the Seven Gables*, Melville's *Pierre*, and George Lippard's urban novels. Above all, they will reconceptualize American literary history no longer as a single thread spun from contemplation of a white male canon, but as a rich multistranded tapestry interweaving a variety of traditions.

NOTES

1. For influential formulations of these paradigms, see Richard Chase, *The American Novel and Its Tradition* (Garden City, N.Y.: Doubleday, Anchor Books, 1957); Fred Lewis Pattee, *The Feminine Fifties* (New York: D. Appleton-Century, 1940); Leslie A. Fiedler, *Love and Death in the American Novel*, rev. ed. (New York: Stein & Day, 1966); and Ann Douglas, *The Feminization of American Culture* (New York: Knopf, 1977).

2. Chase, *American Novel*, viii–ix, 12–13. For more recent exponents of these theories, see Joel Porte, *The Romance in America: Studies in Cooper, Poe, Hawthorne, Melville, and James* (Middletown, Conn.: Wesleyan Univ. Press, 1969); Edgar A. Dryden, *The Form of American Romance* (Baltimore: Johns Hopkins Univ. Press, 1988); and Terence Martin, "The Romance," in *Columbia History of the American Novel*, ed. Emory Elliott (New York: Columbia Univ. Press, 1991), 72–88.

3. Catharine Maria Sedgwick, *A New-England Tale; or, Sketches of New-England Character and Manners*, ed. Victoria Clements (1822; reprint, New York: Oxford Univ. Press, 1995), 7. Subsequent page references appear parenthetically in the text with the abbreviation *NET*.

4. Judith Fetterley, ed., *Provisions: A Reader from Nineteenth-Century American Women* (Bloomington: Indiana Univ. Press, 1985), 10–11; Joanne Dobson, "The American Renaissance Reenvisioned," in *The (Other) American Traditions: Nineteenth-Century Women Writers*, ed. Joyce W. Warren (New Brunswick, N.J.: Rutgers Univ. Press, 1993), 164–82; and Joan D. Hedrick, *Harriet Beecher Stowe: A Life* (New York: Oxford Univ. Press, 1994), chap. 8. For recent accounts of the origins of realism that adhere to the traditional view, see Eric J. Sundquist, "Realism and Regionalism," in *Columbia Literary History of the United States*, ed. Emory Elliott (New York: Columbia Univ. Press, 1988), 501–24; and Robert Shulman, "Realism," in *Columbia History of the American Novel*, 160–88.

5. Nina Baym, *Woman's Fiction: A Guide to Novels by and about Women in America, 1820–1870* (Ithaca: Cornell Univ. Press, 1978); Jane Tompkins, *Sensational Designs: The Cultural Work of American Fiction, 1790–1860* (New York: Oxford Univ. Press, 1985); and Dobson, "American Renaissance Reenvisioned," 170–71.

6. [Catharine Maria Sedgwick], *Redwood: A Tale*, 2 vols. (1824; reprint, New York:

Garrett Press, 1969), 1:183. Subsequent page references appear parenthetically in the text with the abbreviation *R*.

7. Judith Fetterley, " 'My Sister! My Sister!': The Rhetoric of Catharine Sedgwick's *Hope Leslie*," *American Literature* 70 (September 1998): 491–516, esp. 492; and "Nineteenth-Century American Women Writers and the Politics of Recovery," *American Literary History* 6 (fall 1994): 600–611, esp. 605.

8. *The Works of Edgar Allan Poe*, vol. 8, *The Literati—Minor Contemporaries, Etc.*, ed. Edmund Clarence Stedman and George Edward Woodberry (1895; reprint, Freeport, N.Y.: Books for Libraries Press, 1971), 142; *The Centenary Edition of the Works of Nathaniel Hawthorne*, vol. 7, *A Wonder Book and Tanglewood Tales*, ed. William Charvat et al. (Columbus: Ohio State Univ. Press, 1962), 169, quoted in Edward Halsey Foster, *Catharine Maria Sedgwick* (New York: Twayne, 1974), 137; Rufus Wilmot Griswold, *The Prose Writers of America. With a Survey of the History, Condition, and Prospects of American Literature* (Philadelphia: Carey and Hart, 1847), 358; [William Cullen Bryant], Review of *Redwood*, *North American Review* 20 (April 1825): 271; F. [Lydia Maria Francis Child], "Miss Sedgwick's Novels," *Ladies Magazine* 2 (May 1829): 234–35; John S. Hart, *The Female Prose Writers of America. With Portraits, Biographical Notices, and Specimens of their Writings* (Philadelphia: E. H. Butler, 1855), 19; Maria Edgeworth, quoted in Rebecca Lazarus to Catharine Maria Sedgwick, 16 July 1826, Catharine Maria Sedgwick Papers II (hereafter abbreviated as CMS), Massachusetts Historical Society (MHS), quoted by permission of MHS; Review of *Hope Leslie*, *North American Review* 26 (April 1828): 418, 420. Sismondi is quoted in Child's review, 237–38, above. His original letter, in French, is enclosed in CMS to Henry D. Sedgwick, 19 Dec. 1827, CMS III.

9. [Catharine Maria Sedgwick], *Hope Leslie; or Early Times in the Massachusetts*, ed. Carolyn L. Karcher (1827; reprint, New York: Penguin Books, 1998), 368.

10. [Catharine Maria Sedgwick], *Married or Single?* 2 vols. (New York: Harper and Brothers, 1857), 1:9.

11. Chase, *American Novel*, viii.

12. James Fenimore Cooper, Review of *A New-England Tale*, *Literary and Scientific Repository and Critical Review* 4 (May 1822): 336.

13. Nathaniel Hawthorne, *The Scarlet Letter* (1850; reprint, New York: Penguin Books), 45–46.

14. Chase, *American Novel*, ix.

15. Lydia Maria Francis [Child] to Catharine Maria Sedgwick, 28 August [1827] and 21 August 1826, CMS III, MHS, quoted by permission of MHS; Lydia Maria Child, "Rosenglory," *Fact and Fiction: A Collection of Stories* (New York: C. S. Francis, 1846), 255. For a full-length study, see Carolyn L. Karcher, *The First Woman in the Republic: A Cultural Biography of Lydia Maria Child* (Durham, N.C.: Duke Univ. Press, 1994).

16. Hedrick, *Harriet Beecher Stowe*, 87.

2

✍ Excerpts from Biographical Sketches

"Sketches of Distinguished Females." *The New-York Mirror, and Ladies Literary Gazette* (21 April 1827): 310–11.

Author of two very popular novels, the "New-England Tale," and "Redwood," is the daughter of Judge Sedgwick, and was born at Stockbridge, Massachusetts, in the year 1790 [*sic*]. She is deservedly ranked among the most elegant prose writers of the day; and is understood to be now engaged in the preparation of a series of Tales, founded on scenes in New-England. (P. 310)

"Catharine M. Sedgwick." In *The National Portrait Gallery of Distinguished Americans*. Ed. James Herring, James B. Longacre, and American Academy of the Fine Arts. Vol. 1. New York: Monson Bancroft, 1834, 1–8.

Our readers must be aware that the license which is allowed us in the sketch of a lady, precludes us from borrowing from memory or asking from friends any of those details without which that strong individuality which is, or might be engraven on our own minds, could not be transferred to others. Were it no trespass we should, to the best of our ability, present those charms of conversation and those traits of moral excellence which render Miss Sedgwick's society and character the objects of admiration, and of the most partial attachment to all who enjoy her acquaintance and friendship.

But, doubting our license on these points, we must leave those who have never enjoyed this happiness, to form what conjectures they may, in these respects, from her writings, and from the engraving which precedes these pages; a copy from a very fine picture by Ingham, taken, as we are informed, some few years since.

We may be permitted, nevertheless, to speak as we think, of her writings. The first published of her works was the *New England Tale*. There is a circumstance relating to this work, which, if we have been correctly informed, shows that the public are indebted, not so much to love of literature or distinction, as to accident, for her writings as a novelist. It is quite proverbial that many important events which affect the fortunes of our race, are often independent of any human design, but we are not aware that the annals of literature are often signalized by such occurrences. Be this as it may, the New England Tale, (the fact is vouched by the preface of that charming work,) was originally intended for publication as a religious tract; but it gradually grew beyond the necessary limits of such a design. It was thus extended without any intention of publication, and finished solely to amuse the writer. Such was her distrust of her abilities, and so great her reluctance to appear before the public in a work of this magnitude, that her consent to its publication was finally extorted rather than given. (Pp. 2–3)

Mrs. E[mma] C. Embury. "Essay on American Literature." *The Ladies Companion* (1835): 83–85.

How it irks the ear of a patriot when the names, however honored, of the gifted in another land are applied to our own writers. Who has not felt indignant at hearing Miss Sedgwick styled the Edgeworth of our country? Whether her hand pourtrays [*sic*] the sweet Hope Leslie, the stately Grace Campbell, the noble Magawisca, or the excellent Aunt Deborah, she is alike feminine, natural and American. Why then should we bestow on her the mantle which has fallen from the shoulders of another? She is no copyist of another's skill: she has now a name for herself—she is one of our national glories—our Sedgwick. (P. 84)

Chapter 2

Behind the Veil? Catharine Sedgwick and Anonymous Publication

MELISSA J. HOMESTEAD

Catharine Sedgwick's name appeared on the title page of only one of her books published during her lifetime, her 1835 *Tales and Sketches*, a volume collecting pieces that had originally appeared in the annually published "gift books" in the preceding nine years. Sedgwick is the earliest writer included in Mary Kelley's influential book on women's authorship, *Private Woman, Public Stage: Literary Domesticity in Nineteenth-Century America*, and Kelley claims that women writers published anonymously or pseudonymously because of the great anxiety that appearing in public through the medium of print caused them: "The literary domestics could write and, as it were, attempt to hide the deed. Psychologically as well as physically they could make the gesture of writing behind closed doors. They could write hesitantly for the world and try to stay at home. The invisible figure . . . could become the secret writer."[1] By simultaneously going public and denying it, Kelley claims, such "secret writers" "demonstrated that their social condition was powerful enough to cripple their efforts, if not prevent them."[2] In her remarks on Sedgwick's anonymity in particular, Kelley quotes a number of Sedgwick's letters to family and friends in which she makes such statements as "I have a *perfect horror* of appearing in print" and "I did hope my name could never be printed except on my tomb."[3]

Private Woman presents the most fully developed analysis of American women's anonymous publication in the nineteenth century and the one bearing most directly on Sedgwick, but Kelley is not alone in reading women's anonymous and pseudonymous publication as symptoms of gendered anxiety. The idea that women in past centuries withheld their names because they experienced their own authorship as shameful or scandalous has achieved the character of received wisdom. Ask a typical lower-level undergraduate what she knows about women's authorship in the United States during the years of Sedgwick's greatest productivity (the 1820s through the 1840s), and she will tell you: "It wasn't considered respectable for women to write back then, so they didn't give their names, or they took male pseudonyms."[4] I argue instead that Sedgwick's anonymity was a market strategy for constructing an authorial persona rather than an absence of an author or a denial of authorship, and her anonymity serves as a useful example through which we can reconsider the function of women's anonymous publication in the 1820s, '30s, and '40s.

Michel Foucault argues in "What is an Author?" that the name of the author serves to classify certain texts, grouping them together, defining them, and differentiating them from and contrasting them to others under the sign of the name of the author,[5] but reviewers of Sedgwick's books managed to perform this task of classification in the absence of the author's name. As Robert Griffin astutely notes in his analysis of anonymous publication practices in eighteenth- and nineteenth-century Britain, Foucault's "author function . . . can be shown to operate quite smoothly in the absence of the author's name,"[6] and the example of Catharine Sedgwick bears out this observation. My analysis of Sedgwick's authorship shifts the focus away from Sedgwick's privately expressed doubts about authorship and publicity (the basis of Mary Kelley's portrait of her) to the public record of her authorship available to her early-nineteenth-century readers. This record consists of three elements: her fictional texts (especially the self-effacing heroines of these texts, who function to construct a public persona for the author who created them), the "paratext" (as defined by theorist Gerard Genette, the "threshold" between the "inside" and the "outside" of a text: the materials such as title pages, dedications, and prefaces that "[enable] a text to become a book and to be offered as such to its readers"), and contemporary reviews of her fiction.[7] Sedgwick's withholding of her name from her books' title pages did not orphan her texts, leaving them without an author. Instead, those title pages and the reviews of those books construct the female body of an unnamed author behind the books.

Although her anonymity may not have functioned as received wisdom suggests, Sedgwick nevertheless clearly performed her anonymity as a "lady," and for her contemporary readers, gender provided an important key for decoding anonymous texts. A few examples of anonymous publication by Sedgwick's male and female peers (James Fenimore Cooper, Nathaniel Hawthorne, and Lydia Maria Child) demonstrate that anonymity itself was not gendered exclusively female but was instead a variable practice that produced variable effects. Although some of Sedgwick's readers may have decoded a private history of pain and conflict in her anonymous publication, most would have perceived a very particular kind of authority and security in her public persona constructed in part through that anonymity. If we interpret Sedgwick's anonymous publication strategies as her contemporaries did, Sedgwick emerges as a secure and authoritative figure rather than as a conflicted and defeated one, as a woman at the center of American cultural production rather than as a crippled figure at its margins.

At the center of Sedgwick's first novel, *A New-England Tale*, published anonymously in 1822, is the presentation of the local school prize for the best student composition. The name of the winner does not appear on the program for the academy exhibition. Instead, the winner's identity is kept secret until a curtain is withdrawn to show the winner seated on a "throne." Elvira, cousin to heroine Jane Elton, appears first on the throne, tricked out in a befuddled array of borrowed finery, but when a member of the audience reveals that her "original" composition is a plagiarism from an old newspaper, the curtain opens again to reveal Jane "seated on the throne, looking like the 'meek usurper,' reluctant to receive the honour that was forced upon her."[8]

Although the drawing aside of the curtain reveals Jane's identity as a prize-winning author, anonymous publication would seem to have kept the curtain drawn in front of Sedgwick. Sedgwick's name did not appear on the "program" for her literary debut, but that book and its paratext nevertheless staged the presence of its unnamed author. *A New-England Tale* carried no name on its title page, but the dedication—"To Maria Edgeworth, as a slight expression of the writer's sense of her eminent services in the great cause of human virtue and improvement"—signals the author's alliance with a clearly defined (and lady-like) authorial persona (5). Sedgwick and her publisher could have been slightly more direct by designating the author as "a Lady" or "an American Lady" on the title page, as was the case with other novels, but her dedication to Edgeworth is more subtle while still being effective. As Genette observes, although a dedication ostensibly addresses the dedicatee, the author "speak[s] over that addressee's shoulder" to the reader, using the dedication to proclaim "a relationship, whether intellectual or personal, actual or symbolic, and this proclamation is always at the service of the work, as a reason for elevating the work's standing or as a theme for commentary."[9] Reviewers obligingly followed Sedgwick's paratextual direction in the novel's dedication, taking up the relationship of her works to those of Edgeworth as a "theme for commentary" in their reviews, and this theme served to "elevate" the text and its author to Edgeworth's established level. A brief notice of *A New-England Tale* in the *North American Review*, for instance, reads, "If rumor has rightly attributed this excellent production to a female pen, we may with far greater confidence boast of a *religious* Edgeworth in our land, than of a wonder-working Scott."[10] Reviewers repeatedly return to this analogy to Edgeworth to define both Sedgwick and her works, sometimes finding her artistry inferior to Edgeworth's but generally praising her religious and moral tone as superior and as characteristically American (Sedgwick's paratextual direction also shaped this literary nationalistic line of commentary—she begins her preface by stating, "The writer of this tale has made an humble effort to add something to the scanty stock of native American literature" [7]). In an unsigned review of *A New-England Tale* in the *Literary and Scientific Repository*, James Fenimore Cooper praises the author for being a true "historian" of American life, but claims (probably disingenuously) not to know the gender of the author, "whomsoever *he* or *she* may be."[11] This is the only review, however, that indicates any ambiguity about the author's gender. For the rest of her career of anonymous book publication, Sedgwick's reviewers, taking a cue from this early dedication to Edgeworth (and, in some instances, relying on inside knowledge), expressed no doubt that they were reviewing the works of a "lady."

Her second novel, *Redwood*, also appeared without a name on the title page, but reviewers obligingly began the process of constructing an author function to classify a growing body of texts. Helping this process along, in her preface to the novel Sedgwick adopts a similar pose to that in her *New-England Tale* preface, avowing her "reluctance to appear before the public" but claiming that the extensive "love and habit of reading" in America had persuaded her to attempt to fulfill the need for amusement and instruction. "We will, at least, venture to claim the negative merit often ascribed to simples," she self-deprecatingly writes, "that if they can do no good, they will do no harm."[12] Reviewers clearly felt that readers would want to know the gender of this self-deprecating author, and they present both their conclusions concerning the author's gender and the bases for their common conclusion. A reviewer of *Redwood* in the *Port Folio*, who praises the novel as "the first *American* novel, strictly speaking," cites inside knowledge and a reading of the novel itself as evidence of the author's gender: "If we had not other evidence of the fact, we should have suspected the authoress to be a lady, from the partiality that is shown" to female characters in the novel.[13] In an unsigned review in the *North American Review*, William Cullen Bryant, who was an intimate friend of the Sedgwick family (and the person to whom the novel is dedicated), delicately identifies the author of *Redwood* as "the same lady to whom the public is already indebted for another beautiful little work of a similar character."[14] A review in the *United States Literary Gazette* is more direct, stating, "Common fame attributes these works—Redwood, and the New-England Tale—to a lady."[15]

The title pages of subsequent books continue this intertextual construction of their author: *The Travellers*, *The Deformed Boy*, and *Hope Leslie* are all "By the Author of Redwood"; *Clarence* is "By the Author of Hope Leslie"; *Home* is "By the Author of Redwood, Hope Leslie, &c."; *The Linwoods* is "By the Author of Hope Leslie, Redwood, &c."; and so on. Many of her tales published in the annuals in the late 1820s and early 1830s often follow the same format (e.g.,

"Romance in Real Life" in *The Legendary* for 1828 is "By the Author of Red-wood," and "The Berkeley Jail" in *The Atlantic Souvenir* for 1832 is "By the Author of Hope Leslie"). Although *A New-England Tale* never appeared in any of these title-page genealogies, the novel nevertheless had a secure status in reviews and biographical sketches as part of Sedgwick's oeuvre.

In the early years of Sedgwick's career, reviews and title pages built the elaborate web of intertextuality supporting and suspending her as an author without mentioning her name, but eventually, Sedgwick's name circulated in association with her anonymous publications.[16] Some of her tales published in annuals during the 1830s are identified as "By Miss Sedgwick," but in 1827, before her name ever appeared on a title page or in a byline in an annual, the *New-York Mirror and Ladies Literary Gazette* (edited by the poet George Pope Morris) featured her in a series of "Sketches of Distinguished Females." The *Mirror* identified "Catharine Sedgwick" as the "Author of two very popular novels, the 'New-England Tale,' and 'Redwood'" in this sketch (a sketch placed, fittingly enough, next to a sketch of Maria Edgeworth). Two months later in a review of *Hope Leslie*, the *Mirror* identified the novel's author as "Miss Sedgwick." In the wake of this revelation, a review in the *Port Folio* more coyly refers to her as "Miss S." and as "our *Fair Unknown*." This allusion to Sir Walter Scott, who was known as "The Great Unknown" when he published *Waverley* anonymously and a subsequent series of novels as "the Author of Waverley," seems to indicate a genuine mystery. However, Scott's identity was always an ill-kept secret (recall the mention of him as a novelist in that 1822 review of *A New-England Tale*), and he publicly acknowledged his authorship in 1826, so the allusion acknowledges the transparency of the identity of "Miss S." rather than a genuine continuing mystery.[17] By 1835, with the publication of her *Tales and Sketches*, which identified the author on the title page as "Miss Sedgwick, Author of the Linwoods, Hope Leslie, &c.," reviewers were no longer even pretending to accord Sedgwick anonymity, although her books continued to appear without her name on their title pages.

Throughout Sedgwick's career, there is a remarkable consistency in the public construction of Sedgwick as an "anonymous" author, spurred, I would suggest, by a consistent public performance of humility, genteel appropriateness, and (female) republican virtue. In one of the early reviews to identify Sedgwick by name (an 1828 review of *Hope Leslie* in the *Western Monthly Review*), the reviewer also notes approvingly that Sedgwick "appears to move onward, with a becoming modesty; and if her track is not distinguished by the splendor, which belongs to some among her predecessors, and cotemporaries [*sic*], it will at least lead no one astray."[18] That very lack of splendor, the lack of obvious attempts at self-aggrandizement, gave Sedgwick moral authority and the right to true fame. Even this praise for Sedgwick's seeming lack of authorial power evidences her carefully subtle deployment of that power. In claiming that Sedgwick's works have "led no one astray," the reviewer echoes Sedgwick's own statement in her preface to *Redwood* that her works at least will "do no harm." Thoroughly conditioned by Sedgwick's early prefaces and authorial modesty, this reviewer does not take umbrage at Sedgwick's much more combative tone in her preface to *Hope Leslie* (in which she defends the accuracy of her portrayal of her Indian characters) or to the character of her Puritan heroine, who spends much of the novel leading others astray.

Her novels proper as well as their paratexts produced this consistent public authorial persona. Through her heroines, she staged for herself the same sort of public character that she staged for Jane Elton. At the dawn of the age of self-promotion and publicity, Sedgwick appeared in public without appearing to seek publicity. In Sedgwick's second novel, *Redwood* (1824), Grace Campbell, a headstrong young society woman, tells Ellen Bruce, the modest, countrified heroine, that "the days are past when one might 'do good by stealth, and blush to find it fame'—this is the age of display—of publication" (II: 152). Nevertheless, both Sedgwick and her heroines manage to "do good by stealth" and thus achieve fame without appearing to seek it. In her third novel, *Clarence* (1830), Sedgwick again successfully negotiated her public authority through a virtuous, self-effacing heroine (Gertrude Clarence) who, significantly, performs a series of heroic and selfless good deeds on behalf of others while withholding her name. The male protagonist, Gerald Roscoe, witnesses Gertrude's first act of heroism at the dramatic moonlit location of Trenton Falls, where she tries to lead her feverish and mentally deranged art teacher, Louis Seton, down a treacherous rocky path so that he will not throw himself into the falls because of his unrequited love for her. Both Gerald (who is at the falls trying to prevent the forced marriage of Emilie Layton to the villainous Pedrillo) and Gertrude hide their identities because both are trying to prevent harm and embarrassment to others. Gerald's cloak, which he wraps around Gertrude, betrays his identity when she finds his name stitched inside, but Gertrude successfully maintains her anonymity through several more such episodes, including her attendance at Louis Seton's deathbed and her daring attempt to foil Pedrillo's abduction of Emilie at a masquerade ball. She indeed proves herself to be, as the narrator describes her, "a fit heroine for the nineteenth century; practical, efficient, direct and decided—a rational woman—that beau-ideal of all devotees to the ruling spirit of the age—utility" (I: 239–40), with the essential caveat that she is not, as Sedgwick was not, direct about her own identity. She acts directly so that others may be saved from evil and allowed to live and die godly lives, but she effaces her own agency in these dramatic rescues. Just as with Sedgwick's, Gertrude's anonymity does not ultimately obscure her value, but instead, when her identity is inevitably revealed, her "audience" (Gerald Roscoe) only admires her more for her purity and disinterestedness.

To put a slightly different spin on Sedgwick's performance of anonymity, we might turn to the words of Miles Coverdale, narrator of Hawthorne's novel *The Blithedale Romance*, who says of a woman writer's use of a pseudonym, "Zenobia . . . is merely her public name; a sort of mask in which she comes before the world, retaining all the privileges of privacy—a contrivance, in short, like the white drapery of the Veiled Lady, only a little more transparent."[19] Indeed, Sedgwick's brother Harry used exactly the same image of a veiled lady in a letter to a family friend describing the impending publication of *A New-England Tale:* "[W]e all concur in thinking that a lady should be veiled in her first appearance before the public."[20] But although her brother stressed the need for absolute secrecy concerning her identity, his use of the figure of the veiled lady belies that intention. In specifying that the lady should be veiled for her first publication, he implicitly acknowledges the inevitability of the lady's being revealed upon subsequent publication. And the veil itself both reveals and conceals—it conceals her identity, but it reveals that the person wearing it is not just a woman or a female, but a "lady."

Throughout Sedgwick's career, reviewers and others who wrote about her praised her for just the sort of genteel appropriateness in publication that the veiled lady suggests. Perhaps the best example is a biographical sketch of Sedgwick published in *The National Portrait Gallery of Distinguished Americans* (1834), which demonstrates how her contemporary critics responded extremely positively to Sedgwick's public authorial persona staged through the means of anonymous publication. In this sketch (a portion of which is reproduced above), the writer notes the difficulty inherent in describing a "lady" such as "Miss Sedgwick," because it is not permissible to ask others to convey details of her person and her private life.[21] The article thus gives very few such details, but the writer nevertheless describes approvingly one "private" story, the story of the genesis and publication of *A New-England Tale*, including Sedgwick's modest initial plan to write a tract and her reluctance to publish something as ambitious as a novel.[22] The story described correlates closely to the private manuscript record that is the basis of Mary Kelley's portrait of Sedgwick in *Private Woman*, but by circulating this story publicly, the sketch transforms her reluctance to publish into a qualification for literary vocation. Although we might wish for a literary foremother who forthrightly proclaimed her own ability rather than one who apologized for appearing in public at all, such apologies ultimately underwrote rather than undermined her public authority.

Indeed, although the writer of the *Portrait Gallery* sketch does not comment specifically on Jane Elton as a character or on the academy exhibition scene in the novel, he or she implicitly collapses the two authorial performances, writing about Sedgwick's "accidental" writing and publishing of her first novel as if she were its heroine. Sedgwick thus effectively staged her own entrance into an appropriately modest public role through Jane, and her contemporaries read Sedgwick's performance in exactly the same way that Sedgwick invites us to read Jane's. Echoing the praise of many reviewers, the *Portrait Gallery* essay also praises the beauty, purity, and appropriateness of her style. Drawing on the same image that Sedgwick used in *A New-England Tale*, language as dress, the reviewer praises Sedgwick for dressing appropriately (like plain Jane rather than ostentatious Elvira). Rather than displaying blue threads of pedantry to draw attention to herself (the same blue threads of which Alice Courland expresses a horror in "Cacoethes Scribendi"), she uses language to draw attention to the substance of her works. Clearly this biographical sketch (and passages from many reviews I have not quoted here) reflects gendered expectations for Sedgwick as an author, but the expectation is not that ladies should not appear in public through the medium of print. Instead, the expectation is that they should appear dressed "appropriately"—while making certain formulaic demurrers about their reluctance to so appear. The standards of appropriateness for ladylike publication placed limits on Sedgwick's literary production, but all authors, if they hope to be published and to communicate with their audience, must work within certain limits for their work to be intelligible. By working within certain limits, an author may also gain the authority to subvert others (see my remarks above regarding how critics responded to Hope Leslie as a character).

By the late 1830s and through the 1840s, Sedgwick shifted much of her energy from writing books to writing tales and sketches for the booming magazine market for American-authored works; her name almost always appears on these short works (most often as "Miss C. M. Sedgwick," but also as "Miss Sedgwick" and "Miss Catharine M. Sedgwick").[23] Despite the vestigial absence of her name from the title pages of her books in the 1840s, paratextual elements in the volumes, such as text printed on the cloth covers and in publisher's catalogs and advertisements bound into them, routinely undermined that absence by giving her name.[24] Some of the most popular monthlies of the 1840s, such as *Godey's Lady's Book*, *Graham's Magazine*, *Columbian Lady's and Gentleman's Magazine*, and Sartain's *Union Magazine*, sought her out as a regular contributor, with *Graham's* and *Godey's* adding her name to the promotional list of "principal contributors" featured on their covers.[25] In 1838, the poet Emma C. Embury, one of Sedgwick's peers who published in the annuals in the 1830s and who became a prolific magazinist in the late 1830s and the 1840s, featured "Miss Sedgwick" prominently in an "Essay on American Literature" published in the

Ladies' Companion. At the height of Sedgwick's literary reputation, Embury returned to the analogy to Edgeworth that grounded Sedgwick's entry into the literary market in 1822 in order to repudiate it:

> Who has not felt indignant at hearing Miss Sedgwick styled the Edgeworth of our country? Whether her hand pourtrays [*sic*] the sweet Hope Leslie, the stately Grace Campbell, the noble Magawisca, or the excellent Aunt Deborah, she is alike feminine, natural and American. Why then should we bestow on her the mantle which has fallen from the shoulders of another author? She is no copyist of another's skill; she has a name for herself—she is one of our national glories—our Sedgwick.[26]

In 1838, Sedgwick had emerged from behind the veil and was a "name" to be claimed for American literature, but despite Embury's complaint, the Edgeworth label had not been unjustly imposed on Sedgwick but taken up at her suggestion.

A brief detour through the anonymous publication practices of some of Sedgwick's contemporaries highlights just how carefully and consistently Sedgwick (and her publishers) staged her anonymity and her subsequent emergence as a sought-after "name" contributor to magazines. Sedgwick's transparent and consistent anonymity created an unanxious public authority for her, but anonymous and pseudonymous publication are complex practices that produce varying effects. The prevalence of anonymity and its gender dynamics are necessarily difficult to quantify—the authors of many anonymously published novels remain unidentified, and quantifying anonymous publication in periodicals is a practical impossibility—but one scholar who bases her calculations on books included in Lyle Wright's *Bibliography of American Fiction* finds that from the 1820s to the 1840s, men were more likely than women to "veil" their authorship through anonymity or pseudonymity.[27] While Sedgwick's anonymity in the 1820s informed her readers about the character of the unnamed republican lady author, male fiction-writers also took up anonymity as an informative tool, and other writers, male and female, used anonymity in a way that misinformed and obfuscated.

The most closely related example to Sedgwick is her contemporary and competitor, James Fenimore Cooper. Like Sedgwick, he published his first novel, *Precaution*, anonymously in the early 1820s, and then published a string of other novels that omitted his name from their title pages. As in the case of Sedgwick, his anonymity did not remain true anonymity for long. Planning for the publication of his first book, Cooper found anonymity to be a pleasurable game and hoped it would pique public interest in his novel (he thought it might be good for sales if readers thought Washington Irving might be the author).[28]

American readers and critics virtually ignored *Precaution*, but it was so derivative of its British models (the works of Amelia Opie and Jane Austen) in both style and subject matter that it passed for the work of a British author in the British reviews, where it received considerably more attention than it did in the United States.[29] Nevertheless, Cooper did not attempt to disavow the novel: The title page of his first successful "American" novel, *The Spy*, identifies the author as "the Author of *Precaution*." By 1824, reviewers routinely mentioned Cooper's name in their reviews despite its continuing absence from his title pages. The greater speed, relative to Sedgwick, with which his name publicly circulated most likely has less to do with public deference to a lady's modesty than to Cooper's extraordinary level of productivity—in four years, he published four novels, whereas Sedgwick took eight years to publish the same number. In 1823, however, after his authorship of *Precaution*, *The Spy*, and *The Pioneers* was established and his fourth novel, *The Pilot*, was being widely noticed as "in press," Cooper published *Tales for Fifteen* under the pseudonym "Jane Morgan" (once again, his model was Amelia Opie, but his scenes and characters were American). Cooper effectively created a separate (and never repeated) authorial identity, and reviewers never caught on to the game.[30] More sustained attention to Sedgwick's career may uncover similar charades, but the likelihood seems low.[31] With the exception of Cooper's brief masquerade, then, both Cooper and Sedgwick built consistent public reputations in the 1820s through anonymous book publication.

Nathaniel Hawthorne's anonymous publication practices during the 1820s and 1830s provide a particularly telling contrast to Sedgwick's and highlight Sedgwick's consistency and transparency in opposition to Hawthorne's fragmentation and opacity. Like Sedgwick and Cooper (but a few years later, reflecting his relative youth), Hawthorne began his public authorial career by publishing a novel anonymously. *Fanshawe* (published in 1828) received positive reviews, but it languished in obscurity. Seemingly embarrassed by its poor literary quality, its autobiographical character, and its failure to find an audience, Hawthorne asked his friends to destroy their copies and refused to acknowledge his authorship of the novel for the rest of his life.[32]

Rather than building a reputation as "the author of *Fanshawe*," Hawthorne allowed his tales to be published in annuals and magazines during the 1830s in a way that prevented readers (except for his editors and close associates) from classifying them together under the sign of a single author, named or unnamed. His publications in *The Token* (and later the merged *Token & Atlantic Souvenir*) under the editorship of Samuel Goodrich provide a particularly stark contrast to Sedgwick, whose works appeared in the same venues during the same years. When Hawthorne first sent Goodrich the manuscript for a group of tales, hoping that Goodrich could help him publish them together as a book, Goodrich countered with an offer to publish a few of them in *The Token*. Hawthorne suggested that they appear as "by the Author of the *Provincial Tales*," an interrelated collection of tales that he had not yet (and never) succeeded in publishing together as a book. He reasoned that "an unpublished book is not more obscure than many that creep into the world, and your readers will suppose that the *Provincial Tales* are among the latter."[33] Rather than follow Hawthorne's suggestion, which would have at least classified the *Tales* as the work of a single author, Goodrich instead created over the course of several years the fiction of multiple anonymous authors to disguise his heavy reliance on one author for his annuals.[34]

Consistently identified as "Miss Sedgwick" in Goodrich's annuals, Sedgwick used the annuals to continue to build and consolidate her reputation and market identity, but Nathaniel Hawthorne, his works published with no attributions, under pseudonyms, and under many different "by the author of" tags, had no public identity. Whereas "Miss Sedgwick" was a market presence in the early 1830s, as far as ordinary readers were concerned, no single author function classifying the works produced by the man we know as Nathaniel Hawthorne existed, a situation only partially remedied by the publication in 1837 of many of his gift-book contributions as *Twice-Told Tales* with his name on the title page.[35] In contrast, the public record of Sedgwick's authorship demonstrated a consistent will and desire to appear in print and to claim her literary productions as her own.

Lydia Maria Child's first novel provides yet another example of the variability of anonymity as an authorial practice and the interpretive conventions through which readers deciphered (correctly or not) the gender of an anonymous author. Child published her first novel, *Hobomok*, in 1824. The first novels of Sedgwick, Cooper, and Hawthorne bear no authorial designation at all—the space under the title on each title page is simply blank. The title page of *Hobomok*, in contrast, designates its author as "an American" (not "an American Lady" or "an American Gentleman"). All of Catharine Sedgwick's prefaces are what Gerard Genette calls "authorial prefaces," in which the author writes as the author addressing the reader. Child's preface to *Hobomok*, however, is part of an elaborate fictional game, the rules of which were not decipherable to many of her readers in 1824 in the absence of an author's name on the title page. In Genette's taxonomy, the preface to *Hobomok* is both allographic (purporting to be written by "Frederic" rather than by the "author," whose production of the book "Frederic" describes) and "fictive" (both "Frederic" and the unnamed male author, designated "*******," are fictional characters created by Child).

Even literary critics, whom one might designate "professional readers," were confused by the status of the preface, believing (quite reasonably) that the author of a tale thus prefaced was a man.[36] One review that groups Sedgwick's *Redwood* and *Hobomok* together as novels treating American subject matter illustrates clearly the grounds for such confusion. The reviewer correctly identifies the unnamed author of *Redwood* as "she" and an "authoress," but identifies the author of *Hobomok* as male. "[T]he author," writes the reviewer, "as he informed us in his preface, was induced to write it, by reading the eloquent article by Mr. Palfrey, in the North American Review."[37] Not only does the reviewer mistake the fictive status of the preface, even within that fictional world, but the "author" of the novel is not the "author" of the novel's preface. Instead, "Frederic" reports a conversation in which "*******" claims the *North American Review* article as his inspiration.[38]

While Sedgwick began and ended her career consistently publicly identified as "lady author," Child's beginning was more tentative and her ultimate trajectory far different. *Hobomok* did not remain orphaned or misattributed to an unnamed American gentleman because Child's identity as a "lady author" eventually became known and because she included the novel in her "by the author of" genealogies in annuals and on title pages. Unlike Sedgwick, who continued to keep her name off the title pages of her books, Child's name (usually as "Mrs. Child") appears on many of her title pages in the 1830s and afterward, including the title page of her controversial antislavery treatise, *An Appeal in Favor of that Class of Americans Called Africans* (1833). In the eyes of many of her contemporaries, her abolitionism unsexed her, undermining her status as a "lady author" and the authority that came with that status.[39] Perhaps if Sedgwick had completed and published her intended antislavery novel during the early 1830s, she would have suffered a similar fate.[40] Instead, she avoided direct intervention in political controversy and became "a name for herself . . . one of our national glories—our Sedgwick."

In the one book on whose title page Sedgwick's name appeared, *Tales and Sketches*, Sedgwick includes a story about women's authorship, "Cacoethes Scribendi." The story features dual female protagonists, one who seeks the publicity of print and one who refuses it. The widowed Mrs. Courland is inspired to take up authorship by reading an annual. She picks up a new volume and finds "the publisher had written the names of the authors of the anonymous pieces against their productions," and among those names, "she found some of the familiar friends of her childhood and youth."[41] Her daughter Alice, however, resists the entreaties of her mother and her aunts to take up the pen because, as the narrator tells us, "she would as soon have stood in a pillory as appeared in print" (55). When her mother and aunts publish her school composition in a magazine without her knowledge or consent, Alice, prefiguring Jo March in the second book of *Little Women*, throws the volume "into the blazing fire" and chooses marriage over authorship (59).

Although Sedgwick was still nominally anonymous when she first published this story in 1829 (it was "by the author of Hope Leslie"), we should resist the temptation to equate Sedgwick with either Alice or Mrs. Courland. When the story first appeared, "the author of Hope Leslie" was a thrice-published American novelist, dividing her time between the Berkshires and New York City, whose presence lent luster to the *Atlantic Souvenir* rather than the other way around. In private (and perhaps ironically), she may have claimed that she had "a *perfect horror* of appearing in print," but what eventually grew to a long record of publication (some of it anonymous, some of it not) testifies that print was not a pillory she sought to avoid. Alice Courland throws her essay into the fire because it was published against her will, but Sedgwick clearly wanted to publish and to have her works publicly recognized as hers. The fact that she kept her name off the title pages of most of her books speaks only a partial truth about her relationship to print. That absence—maintained even as Sedgwick changed publishers, crossed genres, and survived many shifts in market practices over decades of active publication—suggests a certain ladylike reticence, but it also suggests a consistent and carefully staged authorial presence.

NOTES

Thanks to Victoria Clements, Barbara Ryan, and Karen Woods Weierman for comments on earlier drafts of this essay. Research for this essay was funded in part by a Mellon Post-Dissertation Fellowship at the American Antiquarian Society.

1. Mary Kelley, *Private Woman, Public Stage: Literary Domesticity in Nineteenth-Century America* (New York: Oxford Univ. Press, 1984), 125.

2. *Ibid.*, 128.

3. *Ibid.*, 129–30. In her work on Sedgwick since *Private Woman*, Kelley has shifted her focus to emphasize Sedgwick's agency as an author and how Sedgwick achieves that agency by "negotiating . . . highly charged gender conventions and designing a readily identifiable persona from those conventions" (*The Power of Her Sympathy: The Autobiography and Journal of Catharine Maria Sedgwick*, ed. Mary Kelley [Boston: Massachusetts Historical Society and Northeastern Univ. Press, 1993], 36). Rather than seeing Sedgwick as unable to imagine herself as a producer of culture, Kelley more recently has argued that Sedgwick reconceptualized what it meant to be a producer of culture—my claims concerning Sedgwick's authorship thus share a strong affinity with Kelley's more recent work. Kelley's account in *Private Woman* remains enormously influential, however, shaping critical readings both of Sedgwick's works and of female authorship in nineteenth-century America, even though Kelley has subsequently modified that interpretation. See, for example, Andrew J. Scheiber, "Master and Majesty: Subject, Object, and the Power of Authorship in Catharine Sedgwick's 'Cacoethes Scribendi,'" *American Transcendental Quarterly* 10 (1996): 41–58, and T. Gregory Garvey, "Risking Reprisal: Catharine Sedg-

wick's *Hope Leslie* and the Legitimation of Public Action by Women," *American Transcendental Quarterly* 8 (1994): 287–98, two readings of Sedgwick's texts that rely heavily on Kelley's psychological portrait of Sedgwick in *Private Woman*.

4. Virginia Woolf's *A Room of One's Own* is probably the first twentieth-century articulation of what has become the received wisdom concerning the nineteenth century: "Currer Bell, George Eliot, George Sand, all the victims of inner strife as their writings prove, sought ineffectively to veil themselves by using the name of a man. Thus they did homage to the convention . . . that publicity in women is detestable. Anonymity runs in their blood. The desire to be veiled still possesses them" (New York: Harcourt Brace Jovanovich, 1981), 50. For a persuasive refutation for this claim as applied to Charlotte Brontë and George Eliot, see Catherine A. Judd, "Male Pseudonyms and Female Authority in Victorian England," in *Literature in the Marketplace: Nineteenth-Century British Publishing and Reading Practices*, ed. John O. Jordan and Robert L. Patten (Cambridge: Cambridge Univ. Press, 1995), 250–68.

5. Michel Foucault, "What is an Author?" in *The Foucault Reader*, ed. Paul Rabinow (New York: Pantheon, 1984), 107.

6. Robert J. Griffin, "Anonymity and Authorship," *New Literary History* 30 (autumn 1999): 879. Griffin's specific example is a series of Victorian novels published with "by the author of" claims on their title pages, the same practice that links Sedgwick's novels together (see below).

7. Gerard Genette, *Paratexts: Thresholds of Interpretation*, trans. Jane E. Lewin (Cambridge: Cambridge Univ. Press, 1997), 1–2.

8. Catharine Maria Sedgwick, *A New-England Tale; or, Sketches of New-England Character and Manners*, ed. Victoria Clements (New York: Oxford Univ. Press, 1995), 54. Subsequent page references are cited in the text.

9. *Paratexts*, 124, 135.

10. Review of *The Spy*, *North American Review* (July 1822): 279 (the notice of Sedgwick's book appears in a footnote to a review of this Cooper novel). [James Fenimore Cooper], Review of *A New-England Tale*, *Literary & Scientific Repository* (May 1822): 336–70. Review of *Redwood* and *Hobomok*, *Atlantic Magazine* (July 1824): 234–36. Review of *The Travellers*, *New York Review* (June 1825): 34–38. Review of *Hope Leslie*, *Western Monthly Review* (September 1828): 289–95.

11. [Cooper], Review of *A New-England Tale*, 337.

12. Catharine Maria Sedgwick, *Redwood*, 2 vols. (New York: E. Bliss and E. White, 1824), 1: ix. Subsequent page references are cited in the text.

13. Review of *Redwood*, *Port Folio* (July 1824): 67.

14. Review of *Redwood*, *North American Review* (April 1825): 245.

15. Review of *Redwood*, *United States Literary Gazette* (15 July 1824): 101.

16. Kelley acknowledges this fact of the literary market in her analysis of anonymity in *Private Woman*, but in keeping with her thesis, Kelley sees this process as unintentional and painful and "dramatiz[ing] in public the private subjugation of [women writers'] lives" (128). Again, I am arguing that the drama visible to readers was not one of Sedgwick's subjugation but of her ascension.

17. "Sketches of Distinguished Females," *New-York Mirror* (21 April 1827): 310–11. Review of *Hope Leslie, New-York Mirror* (23 June 1827): 383. Review of *Hope Leslie, Port Folio* (July–Dec. 1827): 29, 41. The first gift-book publication to bear the name "Miss Sedgwick" is "Mary Dyer" in *The Token* for 1831. After this publication (which was, as was the custom, actually released in the fall of 1830), all of her tales and sketches published in *The Token* and the subsequent merged *Token & Atlantic Souvenir*, both published under the editorship of Samuel G. Goodrich, appeared with a "Miss Sedgwick" byline. For interesting recent discussions of Scott's anonymous publication practices, see Genette, *Paratexts*, especially 43–46, 248–49, 284–88; Fiona Robertson, *Legitimate Histories: Scott, Gothic, and the Authorities of Fiction* (Oxford: Clarendon Press, 1994), 123–41; and Jane Millgate, *Walter Scott: The Making of the Novelist* (Toronto: Univ. of Toronto Press, 1984), 59–65, 107–9. Instances in which European translators erroneously attributed *Redwood* to James Fenimore Cooper might seem to point to Sedgwick's obscurity (these European attributions are apparently the source of Judith Fetterley's claim that "Since [*Redwood*] was published anonymously . . . and since it was both American and good, many took *Redwood* to be the work of James Fenimore Cooper." See Judith Fetterley, ed., *Provisions: A Reader from Nineteenth-Century American Women* [Bloomington: Indiana Univ. Press, 1985], 43). However, these instances instead testify to the fact that some Europeans encountered the novel apart from the broader para- and extratextual context in which American readers encountered the novel (no American reviews attribute *Redwood* to Cooper).

18. Review of *Hope Leslie, Western Monthly Review* (Sept. 1828): 286.

19. Nathaniel Hawthorne, *The Blithedale Romance*, ed. Seymour Gross and Rosalie Murphy, *Norton Critical Editions*, 2nd ed. (New York: W.W. Norton, 1978), 8.

20. *Private Woman*, 129.

21. *National Portrait Gallery*, 2. Sarah Josepha Hale reprinted the essay without attribution in her *American Ladies' Magazine* ([Dec. 1835]: 656–65) under the title "Caroline [*sic*] Maria Sedgwick."

22. *National Portrait Gallery*, 3. Actually, despite the reference to the preface of the novel as authority for these statements, the writer apparently possesses and conveys information concerning the genealogy of the book that was not previously publicly available. In the Preface, Sedgwick writes that the "original design" for the book was "if possible, even more limited and less ambitious than what has been accomplished," which was "to produce a very short and simple moral tale of the most humble description," but she makes no reference to "religious tracts" or an unwillingness to be published.

23. On the general shift to named publication in the magazines in the 1840s, see Susan Barrera Fay, "A Modest Celebrity: Literary Reputation and the Marketplace in Antebellum America" (unpublished dissertation, George Washington Univ., 1992), chap. 6. I discuss Fay's statistical analysis of anonymous and pseudonymous book publication below, and although I do not agree with all of her findings, her broader analysis of "veiled" authorship during the period has been crucial to my own analysis of Sedgwick's practices.

24. I have found the following examples (which may not be duplicated in all extant

copies, especially if they have been rebound): in *Letters from Abroad to Kindred at Home* (1841), a brief catalog of new works bound into the front of the volume identifies *Letters* as "by Miss C. M. Sedgwick," and a full Harper's catalog bound into the back includes an entry for "Miss Sedgwick's Works"; catalogs for two Harper's School Library Series that reprinted Sedgwick's works identify them as "by Miss Sedgwick," and these catalogs are bound into series editions of Sedgwick's works; and some editions of her works issued by Harper's independent of the library series include her name on their spines (e.g., an 1845 edition of her *Tales & Sketches*, Second Series, identifies her as "Miss Sedgwick," and the spine text for *A Love Token for Children* identifies the author as "Miss C. M. Sedgwick"). Late in her career, when Sedgwick returned to the novel with the publication of *Married or Single?* (New York: Harper & Brothers, 1857), Harper's kept her name off the title page, using the "by the author of" formula, but put "by Miss C. M. Sedgwick" on the spine. Also note that though several European translators misidentified *Redwood* as by Cooper (see bibliography), an 1822 English edition of *A New-England Tale* (London: John Miller) includes "Miss Sedgwick" on the spine, if not on the title page.

25. See the bibliography included in this volume for Sedgwick's magazine contributions.

26. Emma C. Embury, "Essay on American Literature," *Ladies' Companion* 9 (1838): 84.

27. "Although men continued to outwrite women by large margins in each of these three decades, publication patterns indicate that men, rather than women, were more likely to resort to literary veils and were slower to part with these disguises" (Fay, "Modest Celebrity," 70—the statistical tables appear on pp. 327–30).

28. James D. Wallace, *Early Cooper and His Audience* (New York: Columbia Univ. Press, 1986), 79.

29. See George Dekker and John P. McWilliams, eds., *Fenimore Cooper: The Critical Heritage,* in *The Critical Heritage Series* (London: Routledge & Kegan Paul, 1973), and additional reviews collected on microfilm by the American Antiquarian Society, which houses Cooper's papers.

30. See James Franklin Beard's preface to a facsimile edition, *Tales for Fifteen (1823) by James Fenimore Cooper. A Facsimile Reproduction* (Gainesville, Fla.: Scholars' Facsimiles & Reprints, 1959).

31. The appearance of "Le Bossu" in the *Tales of Glauber Spa* collection, which consists entirely of anonymous contributions from American authors, might appear to be such a charade, but the authorship of individual pieces in the volume seems to have been an open secret. The *Portrait Gallery* identifies Sedgwick as the author of "Le Bossu" without even mentioning the supposed anonymity of its authorship.

32. Fredson Bowers, Introduction to *The Blithedale Romance and Fanshawe*, vol. 3, *Centenary Edition of the Works of Nathaniel Hawthorne* (Columbus: Ohio State Univ. Press, 1964), 301–16; James R. Mellow, *Nathaniel Hawthorne in His Times* (Boston: Houghton Mifflin, 1980), 41–50; Arlin Turner, *Nathaniel Hawthorne, a Biography* (New York: Oxford Univ. Press, 1980), 50; and Edwin Haviland Miller, *Salem is my Dwelling Place: A Life of Nathaniel Hawthorne* (Iowa City: Univ. of Iowa Press, 1991), 77–78.

33. Thomas Woodson, L. Neal Smith, and Norman Holmes Pearson, eds., *Nathaniel Hawthorne, The Letters, 1813–1843*, vol. 15, *Centenary Edition* (Columbus: Ohio State Univ. Press, 1985), 205.

34. For the complex (and contested) history of Hawthorne's pre–*Twice-Told Tales* publications, see Mellow, *Nathaniel Hawthorne*, 46–48, 69–76; Turner, *Nathaniel Hawthorne*, 49–54, 69–79; J. Donald Crowley, "Historical Commentary," in *Twice-Told Tales*, vol. 9, *Centenary Edition* (Columbus: Ohio State Univ. Press, 1974), 485–533. For complete bibliographical information, including bylines, see C. E. Frazer Clark, *Nathaniel Hawthorne: A Descriptive Bibliography* (Pittsburgh: Univ. of Pittsburgh Press, 1978), 376–83, 411–18.

35. Ironically, two Massachusetts newspapers reprinted his "A Shaker Bridal" (first published in *The Token* for 1838 as "by the Author of The Twice-Told Tales") and attributed it to "Miss Sedgwick" (Clark, *Nathaniel Hawthorne*, 382–83).

36. For Child's literary celebrity in Boston, see Carolyn Karcher, *The First Woman in the Republic: A Cultural Biography of Lydia Maria Child* (Durham: Duke Univ. Press, 1994), 16–17; Deborah Pickman Clifford, *Crusader for Freedom: A Life of Lydia Maria Child* (Boston: Beacon, 1992), 47–50.

37. Review of *Redwood* and *Hobomok*, *Atlantic Magazine* (July 1824): 234.

38. The first review of *Hobomok* in the *North American Review* similarly misgenders Child and confuses the fictional status of certain elements ([July 1824]: 262–63). The second review of *Hobomok* in the *Review* ([Jared Sparks], "Recent American Novels" [July 1825]: 78–104) avoids misgendering Child by avoiding all pronominal references to the author of *Hobomok;* but Child indirectly solicited this second review through George Ticknor, so Sparks had inside knowledge (Clifford, 44–45). The nine other novels included in this omnibus review, authored about equally by men and women, were all published anonymously or pseudonymously.

39. On the effects of her abolitionism on Child's authorial career, see Karcher, *First Woman*, chap. 8.

40. Karen Woods Weierman's essay in this volume persuasively dates the composition of this manuscript fragment to the early 1830s.

41. In Fetterley, *Provisions*, 53. Subsequent page references are cited in the text.

Portrait of Catharine Maria Sedgwick by Charles Cromwell Ingham, painted between 1816 and 1834. Oil on canvas. Courtesy of Sedgwick Family Society and Trust.

3

🖎 Excerpts from Reviews of *A New-England Tale; or, Sketches of New-England Character and Manners*

[William Howard Gardiner.] Review of *The Spy*, by James Fenimore Cooper. *North American Review* (July 1822): 250–83.

When those remarks were prepared for the press, we had not read the New England Tale, a beautiful little picture of native scenery and manners, composed with exquisite delicacy of taste, and great strength of talent. Had we seen this, we should not have needed a stronger confirmation of our opinion respecting the abundance of original character we can supply to the domestic tale.—If rumor has rightly attributed this excellent production to a female pen, we may with far greater confidence boast of a *religious* Edgeworth in our land, than of a wonder-working Scott. (Footnote, p. 279)

[Signed] F. [Lydia Maria Francis Child]. "Miss Sedgwick's Novels." *Ladies Magazine* (May 1829): 234–38.

The "New England Tale," on which her reputation was first founded, is unquestionably, our most successful portraiture of New England. (P. 235)

[James Fenimore Cooper.] Review of *A New-England Tale*. *Literary and Scientific Repository* (May 1822): 336–69.

Our political institutions, the state of learning among us; and the influence of religion upon the national character, have been often discussed and displayed; but our domestic manners, the social and the moral influences, which operate in retirement, and in common intercourse, and the multitude of local peculiarities, which form our distinctive features upon the many peopled earth, have very seldom been happily exhibited in our literature. It is true, that Mr. Washington Irving, in his Knickerbocker, Rip Van Winkle, and the Legend of Sleepy Hollow, has given, in inimitable burlesque, very natural, just, and picturesque views of one class of people in the land; but they are all ludicrous subjects, and do little towards forming a history of the diversities of passion, sentiment, and behaviour, as they are manifest, in any of our little communities, detached, as it were, from the great world. (P. 336)

We love an interesting fiction, because, however paradoxical the assertion may appear, it addresses our love of truth—not the mere love of facts expressed by true names and dates, but the love of that higher truth, the truth of nature and of principles, which is a primitive law of the human mind, and only to be effaced by the most deplorable perversion. (P. 338)

[Crazy Bet] is one of that extraordinary class of females which Shakespeare, Otway, and the author of Waverly, have employed with such effect; and which, perhaps, was originally taken from the Grecian Pythoness, or the Roman Sybil; or which, to be more natural, and less erudite, is probably to be found exemplified in some individuals of all times and places. . . . Crazy Bet is one of those unfortunate beings, in whom a naturally fine genius, excess of sensibility, a neglected education, and a severe disappointment of the heart, have produced such predominance of the sensitive, and such infirmity of the intellectual and active faculties, as to destroy the equilibrium of powers; and by dethroning reason to leave the whole soul a prey to itself; yet sparing partial memory and unappropriated affections; and these affections, delivered up to undisciplined enthusiasm, entering into every wild conception of God, of nature, and of human beings, and inspiring ideas the most sublime, and the expressions of the most original and affecting.

. . . The style of the maniac's broken discourse displays a fine power of imagination, and an equal command of expression in the recorder of the character, if the language imputed to her be not taken from the original; and, in relation to the poor creature, it reminds us of those flowers which are said to spring up from the soil recently deluged by the fiery showers of volcano, that derive their glowing colours and their sweet odours from the elements which have changed beauty to ashes and joy to mourning. (Pp. 346–47)

"Catharine M. Sedgwick." In *The National Portrait Gallery of Distinguished Americans*. Ed. James Herring, James B. Longacre, and American Academy of the Fine Arts. Vol. 1. New York: Monson Bancroft, 1834, 1–8.

The plan of the *New England Tale* did not admit of the variety, the extent, or power of delineation, which her subsequent writings have exhibited; but it contains passages of deep tenderness—descriptions of nature, for example, in the scenery of "the Mountain Caves"—and notes of eloquence in the wild songs or rhapsodies of Crazy Bet, which the author has seldom, if ever, surpassed. (P. 3)

Chapter 3

"A Powerful and Thrilling Voice": The Significance of Crazy Bet

VICTORIA CLEMENTS

S edgwick published *A New-England Tale; or, Sketches of New-England Character and Manners* in 1822, just as American literature was beginning to define for itself an identity separate from that of Europe. Although lauded in Sedgwick's lifetime, the novel has received little attention since. Those twentieth-century critics who have addressed *A New-England Tale*, however, have followed their nineteenth-century forebears in invariably noting the impact on the narrative of Crazy Bet, the self-proclaimed "wild woman" who "indulge[s] her vagrant inclinations, in wandering from house to house, and town to town . . . arrayed" in a "fanciful medley." Bet, reportedly driven mad by grief over the drowning death of her lover on the day before they were to have married, frequents darkened graveyards and every "awakening" and "camp meeting" in her vicinity, consumed by a religious fervor and "original sensibility" that reject churchly hypocrisy in favor of a naturalist experience of the divine.[1]

Bet occupies a privileged position in the novel in several ways. Significantly, the book begins with her—she is the only character named in the preface—and the narrative ends with her—the novel's final scene is devoted to her death. The centrally located and certainly most dramatic scene in the book, Jane's mysterious midnight journey to the home of John Mountain, is dominated by Bet's otherworldly appearance and her moonlit, author-izing testimony: "Her head . . . was fantastically dressed with vines and flowers; her eyes were in a fine 'frenzy, rolling from earth to heaven, and heaven to earth;' she looked like the wild genius of the savage scene, and she seemed to breathe its spirit, when, after a moment's silence she sang, with a powerful and thrilling voice, which waked the sleeping echoes of the mountain . . ." (*NET*, 87–88).

Given this narrative prominence, we might expect Bet to play a material role in advancing the plot, but in fact she is completely unnecessary to the central characters' movement through time and space. The trek to John's house on which Bet leads Jane could easily have been led by someone else; in fact, we might legitimately expect Jane's guide to be John, who presumably travels the treacherous route himself in order to tell Jane that Bet will be her guide. Nor is Bet essential to the development of any central character, although she herself is as painstakingly drawn as any character is. We know nearly as much about Bet as we do about Lloyd, the novel's hero—indeed, in Sedgwick's 1852 revised edition of the novel, we know more, for Lloyd's family history is there deleted.

Bet's indistinct purpose does nothing to diminish her effect in the novel, though, as critical response has amply shown. In his review of *A New-England Tale* in the May 1822 issue of the *Literary and Scientific Repository and Critical Review*, James Fenimore Cooper devotes two long paragraphs to the characterization of Bet, noting an "extraordinary interest to all that she says," and provides a four-page excerpt that includes Bet's big scene—her nocturnal testimony above "the caves of the mountain."[2] Edward Halsey Foster in 1974 calls Bet "the most fully, or at least the most interestingly, developed person in the book."[3] Jane Giles agrees that Bet is the novel's "most interesting character," asserting further that Bet "runs through the novel like a bright discordant thread" and "has the best lines."[4] Lucinda Damon-Bach suggests Crazy Bet is "a figure of woman's unleashed imagination" who guides both heroine Jane Elton and the reader through the "'wild trackless region'" of woman's moral and literary development.[5] Cathy Davidson calls the wandering madwoman "an emblem of unfettered emotion and unrestricted movement."[6] As the responses of these and other critics demonstrate, Crazy Bet demands our attention. How are we to account for the extraordinary narrative presence of this seemingly minor character?

Sedgwick's correspondence reveals that early in 1821, at the age of thirty-one, she withdrew from the Congregationalist church in New York of which she had long been a member and that some months later she joined the Unitarian Society. That same year, her domestic situation began to change. Her recently married younger brother Charles, who with his wife Elizabeth and new baby had been occupying the family home in Stockbridge, found that his business dealings in Lenox warranted his relocating there. As this grew apparent, Sedgwick wrote in June to her brother Robert, "I have never felt so oppressed by the changes in our family. The house is so still and solitary. . . . [T]hose beloved ones whose hearts responded to mine as 'face answereth to face in the water' are all gone, or far away."[7] That Robert himself, whom Sedgwick called "as much a part of me as the lifeblood that flows through my heart,"[8] was engaged by the end of the year to Elizabeth Ellery no doubt contributed to her sense of her own social dis-engagement, to her awareness of her marginalized status as a single woman in a culture organized by couples.

Out of this year in which Sedgwick quit the religious institution that had once been her spiritual home, provoking some censure from friends and family, and in which her sociopolitical vulnerability as a single woman must have seemed especially apparent, she produced her first novel. In a letter to Susan Channing written shortly after the book's appearance, Sedgwick declared she began the tale because she "wanted some pursuit, and felt spiritless and sad."[9] That Crazy Bet arose from this spiritual, sociopolitical, and emotional context perhaps accounts in some way for her being Sedgwick's most radical vision of a woman alone in the nineteenth century—homeless by choice, uncontrollable, going where and when she pleases, profoundly spiritual, equally outspoken, powerfully articulate. In her undeniable decentralization of central characters in *A New-England Tale*, Crazy Bet sheds light on Sedgwick's personal and ideological concerns, regarded by many as a provocative reflection of national ones.[10] Bet's greatest significance, though, both for Sedgwick's oeuvre and for the developing American literature in which that oeuvre would so substantially figure, lies in her embodiment of a fundamental dilemma for all American writers in the nineteenth century and beyond: the capacity of language to convey the object world, or what Eric Sundquist calls the "containment" of "'the real.'"[11]

Until relatively recently, realism in American literature was generally regarded as a post–Civil War phenomenon. The inaccuracy of this periodization has been identified by numerous critics, including Joanne Dobson, who points out that "literary realism existed alongside romanticism and was well in place in the sketches and tales of women as early as the 1830s."[12] *A New-England Tale*, in its prominent deployment of verisimilar settings, regional characteristics, and the representation of ordinary Americans and their voices, suggests Sedgwick's participation in the early development of American literary realism. Given the general ontological instability of the era that was ushered in by Kant's challenge to the authority of the object in his 1781 *Critique of Pure Reason*, this effort on the part of writers to assert a fixed reality is hardly surprising. Morse Peckham suggests the "original source" of the flood of sentimental literature that characterized the late-eighteenth and nineteenth centuries lay in "the necessity to discharge the tension consequent upon the [Enlightenment] affirmation that the world is radiant with order and value . . . and the inconsistent perception that it is not. . . . [T]he more the basic instability became apparent, the more necessity there was to fall back upon an . . . affirmation of order, value, and identity as qualities structured into the real world."[13] Katharine Kearns similarly observes of realism that "[t]alking about the real is a way to stay in the world, to keep alive the loved objects whose loss one fears." But of course, as Kearns goes on to point out, "Realism's faith in materiality is problematized by a post-Kantian suspicion that [material] markers are compromised, delusory artifacts of one's own blind insight."[14] In a post-Kantian universe, the project of realism is inevitably doomed to failure: " '[T]he real,' " as Sundquist puts it, "resists containment."[15]

The literary manifestation of this painful tension between subject and object, arguably identifiable in U.S. literature from the early nineteenth century onward, has been remarked in the nineteenth-century male canon by prominent twentieth-century critics such as Sundquist, F. O. Matthiessen, Richard Chase, and Northrop Frye.[16] That this philosophic and aesthetic struggle has heretofore gone largely unobserved in nineteenth-century women's texts comes as no surprise, given the critical myopia of the first half of the twentieth century, when "melodramas of beset manhood" were canonized while popular nineteenth-century genres were dismissed as unworthy of critical attention.[17] When we look beyond this critical bias, we see that *A New-England Tale*, heralding in 1822 a genre that would dominate the literary market for the next fifty years, seeks to retain "the loved object" as much in its realism as in its sentimental Christian ideology. In so doing, the novel reveals, long before the tortured efforts of Hawthorne,[18] James, or Crane, the paradoxical nature of the realist project: In its effort to retain the object through fiction, or, as Howells put it, "to present life just as it is,"[19] realism necessarily engages the potential authority of the subject in ordering the world. In *A New-England Tale*, this paradox is played out in the novel's most actively disruptive agent: the conspicuously unrestrained signifier of Crazy Bet.

The preface to *A New-England Tale* identifies Crazy Bet as the primary locus of the novel's realism: the paratextual, putatively nonfiction voice promises that "no personal allusions, however remote, were intended to be made to any individual, unless it be an exception to this remark, that the writer has attempted a sketch of a real character under the fictitious appellation of 'Crazy Bet' "(*NET*, 7).[20] But the idea that Bet is based on someone "real," on an object that exists in a world external to the novel, is destabilized at the same time that it is advanced. A "real character"? The oxymoronic juxtaposition of the word "real" with "character," a term associated with fiction, problematizes the claim: The character is based on a character. Even if we rely for interpretation on a secondary definition, in which the term "character" denotes an individual who is "odd, extraordinary, or eccentric" (as it has, according to the *Oxford English Dictionary*, since at least 1773), we find a fiction, someone who was textualized when she was termed "eccentric." Certainly, this appears to have been true in the case of Sedgwick's reported source for Bet.

Foster identifies as the model for Bet a woman named Susan Dunham, who, he says, "for fifty years made a destinationless pilgrimage of mourning throughout the towns of Berkshire County."[21] Foster's source is the *Berkshire Hills*, a "Historical Illustrated Sketch Monthly" published in 1900. The inaugural issue contains an article entitled "Sketch of Crazy Sue: A Remarkable Berkshire Character of the Past," in which we learn, "Catherine [*sic*] Sedgwick in her New England Tales, Crazy Sue being a frequent visitor at the Judge Sedgwick mansion, alluded to her as 'Crazy Bess' [*sic*], and represented her as having died upon the grave of her youthful lover, but this assertion was never verified and was undoubtedly a liberty allowed to the fiction of this celebrated Berkshire lady novelist and authoress." A long string of anecdotes follows, ending with the editor's request for stories about Bet from the article's readers. These are provided two months later in a second article, "More Anecdotes of Crazy Sue: Her Most Interesting Wild Pranks and Witty Rejoinders as Contributed by Our Readers."[22] As the chorus of voices relate their "Sue stories," the inaccessibility of the object Sue becomes readily apparent. And although these articles appeared nearly eighty years after the publication of *A New-England Tale*, they nevertheless provide telling evidence of the Berkshire textualization of Susan Dunham, a process that was no doubt well under way in 1822, when Dunham would have been approximately fifty-five.

In addition, it seems likely that Crazy Sue was not the sole antecedent for Bet, as some nineteenth-century critics pointed out.[23] The similarity of Crazy Bet to Madge Wildfire, a character in Sir Walter Scott's *The Heart of Midlothian*, published in 1818, seems more than accidental. Like Bet, Madge has reportedly lost her wits as the result of a lost love. Like Bet, "she aften sleeps out, or rambles about amang thae hills the haill simmer night."[24] She, too, "trick[s] herself out with shreds and remnants of beggarly finery" (*H*, 332), is harassed by children, and provides amusement to adults. Madge looks after Jeanie Deans, the young heroine, guiding her through the Scottish hills much as Bet guides Jane in the Berkshires. Madge is "well-acquainted" with Bunyan's *Pilgrim's Progress* (*H*, 330); as does Bet, she interprets events through a fractured lens of Protestant doctrine. She is especially known for singing "her own wild snatches of song and obsolete airs," which provide "oblique . . . or collateral" commentary on "her present situation" and by which her listeners are "particularly moved" (*H*, 431–33). Her familiarity with the rough countryside results at one point in her leading a party on a moonlit climb that cannot help but call to mind the journey of Bet and Jane through the "Caves of the Mountain." Madge leads her followers through "mony crags and stanes," and "the ascent of the moon, supposed to be so portentous over those whose brain is infirm, made her spirits rise in a degree tenfold more loquacious than she had hitherto exhibited" (*H*, 180–82). That Sedgwick admired Scott's novels is clear from her autobiography and journal and in the frequent references to him throughout her oeuvre[25]—it seems likely that Crazy Bet is in some measure an homage to "the author of Waverly."

Behind Crazy Bet, then, the one element in the novel for which we are overtly promised a "real" referent—promised object—we find instead fictions, representations, or, in other words, subject. And the text can offer only a representation of these representations, or, more subject. Seen in the light cast by Madge Wildfire and the legend of Susan Dunham, Crazy Bet's "realness" recedes, illustrating Barthes's claim that "the 'realistic' artist never places 'reality' at the origin of [her] discourse, but only and always, as far back as can be traced, an already written real."[26] Her object status thus effaced, Bet is revealed as a product of the author-izing subject, and as such she is a powerful feminist revision of Scott's Madge: Madge's seduction, subsequent abandonment, and pariahdom are replaced by the drowning death of Bet's lover and Bet's being "welcome wherever she went" (*NET*, 16). Madge's solitary death in a public hospital, the result of her beating at the hands of a violent mob, is replaced by the gentle attentions of Mary Hull and her husband, who care for Bet tenderly but do not prevent her dying where she chooses, "her head resting on the grassy mound that covered the remains of her lover" (*NET*, 165).

Crazy Bet's status as a creation of the author-izing subject is further emphasized in the one striking violation of verisimilitude that disturbs this otherwise realist text: Bet makes the feathers stuffing a mattress disappear—potentially, inasmuch as no accounting of the feathers is ever made—into thin air. Vague intimations of Bet's supernatural abilities are offered through the episode. Jane hears a noise in a bedroom of her aunt's house and when she investigates discovers "a scene of the greatest confusion. The bedclothes had been hastily stripped from the bed and strewed on the floor, and Bet stood at the open window with the [feather] bed in her right hand. She had, by sudden exertion of her strength, made an enormous rent in the well-wove home-made tick, and was now quite leisurely shaking out the few feathers that still adhered to it." Jane asks the black "servant" why she did not prevent Bet's action, and Sukey replies, "'Stop her, missy? the land's sake! I could just as easily stop a flash of lightning! missy must think me a 'rac'lous creature, respecting me to hold back such a harricane.'" When Jane asks, "'But, Bet, . . . where are the feathers?'" Bet replies, "'Where? child . . . where are last year's mourners? where is yesterday's sunshine, or the morning's fog?'" (*NET*, 81). At Mrs. Wilson's entrance, Bet beats a hasty exit, and the narrator claims, "Bet . . . sprang through the window quick as thought, and so rapid, and as it were, spiritual, was her flight, that a minute had scarcely passed, when the shrill tones of her voice were heard rising in the distance" (*NET*, 82). Bet can evidently move farther in a minute than would be possible for one less "spiritual," and the location of the feathers is as numinous as that of "the morning's fog."

This passage, which appears immediately prior to the novel's literal center-piece, the midnight journey upon which Bet delivers her sermon on the mount, presents a surprising interruption in the verisimilar fabric of this text, fore-grounding the author-izing subject's dominion over the fictional realm. In this episode, we glimpse a world in which objects inexplicably disappear, a world that is unmistakably created. The narrative hints and omissions permit an inter-pretation of Bet's vanishing act as the performance of magic—she transforms matter. In this it is tempting to see Bet as a figure for the author, who does the same: In producing fiction, she creates a world—she generates something from nothing.

Indeed, Bet's authority in the narrative is derived from her exercise of what Robert Scholes calls "textual power: the power to select (and therefore to sup-press), the power to shape and present certain aspects of human experience."[27] When Bet speaks, or selects and re-presents the various texts she quotes in her unique, "crazy" arrangement of them, she makes a compelling assertion of the female author-izing self. When we first meet her, for example, Bet deconstructs Mrs. Wilson's uncharitable suggestion that supporting Jane for more than "'a little while'" would amount to "'taking [her] children's meat [and] throw[ing] it to the dogs,'" commenting, "'It [would be] more like taking the prey from the wolf,'" and singing a verse from a hymn that recommends against selfishness (*NET*, 16–17). Jane has heard the story of "poor Lucy," at whose grave the two women pause before their hike, "'a thousand times,'" but only Bet's version of herstory leaves Jane "deeply interested," moved to tears, and prompts her to exclaim, "'Poor Lucy! I never felt so much for her'" (*NET*, 85). When the two women emerge on their moonlit journey "into an open space, completely surrounded and enclosed by lofty trees," Jane kneels in worship with Bet—she has "caught a spark of her companion's enthusiasm" (*NET*, 85–86). The female authorial act serves in the novel to raise the question of the authority of the individual subject, a question that reverberated throughout Western philosophy and culture in 1822.

As the text's most conspicuous product and representation of the author-izing subject, Crazy Bet also serves to interrogate dominant institutions that rely for their authority on the fixity of the object—most notably the Church and the social and economic status of women. A woman's fortune in the early republic, regardless of her class, was determined by her marital status. As the cultural object *ne plus ultra* for women, marriage generates the plots of both seduction and courtship novels. In *A New-England Tale*, though, the narrative supremacy of the marriage plot is significantly sidetracked by the figure of Crazy Bet. From the outset, Jane's quest for both happiness and protection is shadowed by a deluge of disastrous marriages. As well as the unhealthy marriages of Jane's parents and the Wilsons, we are provided the tragic tale of Lucy, who drowned herself after her Federalist lover was used as a human shield by rebels in the "Shays war" and killed by his own forces. Added to these are the fatal pairing of David Wilson and Mary Oakley, the tragic end of Martha Wilson in her early twenties through alcoholism and domestic abuse, and the little-more-hopeful image of Martha's sister Elvira, riding into the sunset with a confidence man who has just narrowly escaped tar and feathers. Even the idyllic union of the Lloyds, which Susan Harris rightfully identifies as the book's model for a happy marriage, is cut short by young Rebecca's death from tuberculosis. Against the backdrop of these marital outcomes, Bet's freedom to roam the Berkshire hills alone cannot but suggest some appeal, her madness notwithstanding. While she can certainly be read, as Harris points out, as a warning against emotional excess, no attic confines Crazy Bet.[28] Her pitiable mental state gives her license to speak freely and creatively—Bet is unencumbered by the cultural structures that govern every other woman in the text. As an indigent vagrant, she lives outside the social and economic mainstream—she is literally in a class by herself. Her flagrant challenge to the culturally sanctioned options available to her evokes Alfred Adler's suggestion that various forms of neurotic behavior in women are at their base a protest against the condition of patriarchy.[29] The charismatic figure of Crazy Bet provides *A New-England Tale* with an anti-marriage "plot" that competes successfully for narrative focus with the heroine's marriage plot and thereby decentralizes the cultural object marriage.

One of the text's apparent purposes, to critique the rigid New England Calvinism within which Sedgwick had been raised, is also carried out by Bet, in her kind protection of Jane and her unflinching, often humorous exposure of Calvinist hypocrisy. And although Bet's religious discourse appears rooted in the Protestant sources she brings together in her intertextual religious tapestry, she lives outside their social contexts and aligns herself materially with no single group. She is presented essentially as a mystic, who hears at the moment of Mary Oakley's death "a voice saying, 'Her sins are forgiven'—she is one 'come out of great tribulation'" (*NET*, 93), and who sees and hears "'the spirits of heaven'" before her own death (*NET*, 165). As Cathy Davidson has suggested, Bet's midnight testifying can be seen as a "pantheistic celebration of nature in which [she and Jane] . . . enact Transcendentalism in a personalized, intimate, passionate, and sentimental register."[30] The outspoken "wild woman" who sleeps under the stars prefigures the "majority of one" glorified by Emerson and Thoreau some fifteen and twenty years later, thereby bringing into relief the constraints of religious orthodoxy.

Bet's literary importance is emphasized in the devotion of the novel's final scene to her death, a move that simultaneously deconstructs the object-centered plots of courtship and seduction novels and testifies to the power of the authorizing subject. The final scene of the courtship novel is regularly given to the heroine's marriage; the closing of the seduction novel highlights the heroine's death.[31] *A New-England Tale* resists these models, filling the space traditionally occupied by the heroine's narrative ancestors with Bet, a character who arrantly resists literary and cultural stability. Moreover, the unsettling conflation of the real and the fictional with which the book begins—the paradoxical assertion in the preface of Bet's "realness"—is answered on the narrative's final page. Bet's death attests finally to the sovereignty of the author: Even the most "real," the most overtly object-identified figure in the book can be destabilized, executed, erased, by the novelizing subject.

The book itself, however, does not close with Bet's death. Its last pages are devoted to a lengthy endnote, prompted by the story of Lucy's perished lover, that describes the "Shays war," a largely class-based armed uprising against the Massachusetts state legislature over the issue of taxation that took place during six months in 1786 and 1787. The tone of the note favors the legislature; Foster points out that Sedgwick's father was active in the suppression of the insurrection and suggests that this may account for the note's appearance, as Sedgwick "always noted her father's deeds with care." He cannot help but note, though, that the rebellion's "relevance to [*A New-England Tale*] is something of a moot point."[32] Certainly, the details of the rebellion are in no way essential to the plot of the novel or to the development of its central characters—even Lucy's suicide does not require that her lover die under these particular circumstances. The style of the note is distinctly that of nonfiction—specific dates, the names of Massachusetts towns in which conflicts occurred, and the names of military officials who took part are included. The implied author's final comments indicate that Minot's 1788 *History of the Insurrections in Massachusetts in 1786 and of the Rebellion Consequent Thereon* was the note's source.

Such assiduous attention to the supposedly objective referent of a relatively insignificant narrative moment raises questions as to the note's purpose. Why this deliberate imposition of a history lesson in the midst of a work of fiction? Arguably read when the reference to it appears, just as Bet is telling the story of Lucy—and telling it, as Jane attests, with great skill—the note serves to pull the reader out of the narrative, back to reality, as it were. In presenting the reader this lifeline to the supposed object world, the note warns against the bewitching power of the author-izing subject. In its hyperbolic assertion of a reality outside the text, though, the endnote recapitulates the discomfort over the uncertain status of the object evidenced in the preface. The two distinctly object-identified texts bracket *A New-England Tale*, as if to contain the power of the subject located in Crazy Bet. But the rhetorical peculiarities of the paratext undermine the effect. Bet, it appears, will not be contained.

In her embodiment of this central issue of representation for American authors—the writer's negotiation with the "real"—Bet suggests significant loci of that negotiation for nineteenth-century women writers: paratext, the marriage plot, characterization of women. Countless women's fictions that appear after the publication of *A New-England Tale*—including her own—continue the work that Sedgwick here begins, addressing through various narrative and rhetorical means the challenges to the human subject presented by both an object-driven culture and an objectless world. In this, they take an active role in the literary exploration of a philosophical debate that preoccupies Western thinking following Kant's Copernican Shift.

No single character in Sedgwick's own subsequent work, though, is as sociopolitically subversive and as literarily provocative as Crazy Bet. While each ensuing novel and many tales include female characters who live in one way or another at odds with their social milieux, none presents as sensational a combination of wholesale cultural interrogation and writerly display. In light of events in Sedgwick's life, it seems reasonable to suggest that the thoughtful, sophisticated young authoress, who had for some time been painstakingly contemplating the nature of the spirit, was in her first literary effort perhaps especially aware of the philosophical problems any writer of realist fiction would necessarily face in representing the world. It seems equally reasonable to imagine that the exceptional presence of Crazy Bet in this first novel figures both Sedgwick's enthusiasm for and her apprehension about the challenges to prevailing cultural roles for women that were implied by her own choices—to remain unmarried and to raise her voice in fiction in the public sphere. While Bet is undoubtedly powerful, she is also vulnerable to the "continual amusement [of] the curious" and the "unfailing mirth of the young and vulgar" (*NET*, 16).

In 1821, more than ever before, Sedgwick must have been considering the options available to a single, childless woman in a culture that positively identified women almost exclusively with marriage and family. At thirty-one, she was a woman alone. Her mother had died when Sedgwick was nearly eighteen; in the following year, Elizabeth Freeman, who cared for Sedgwick from birth (and whom Sedgwick called "mother" in the epitaph she wrote in 1829), had left the family's service. By the time Sedgwick was twenty-three, her father had died, and in the years that followed, her brothers Harry and Charles had both married. Robert's engagement in December 1821, which came as no surprise, left Sedgwick finally "first to none."[33] Where she would live was uncertain, and her financial status must have been of some practical concern. (While the Sedgwick family lived "comfortably," they were not, as Mary Kelley notes, "among the very wealthy."[34]) Having made, for whatever reasons, the socially divergent choice to remain unmarried, Sedgwick was faced with potential economic strain and the cultural stigma she identifies in 1857 in *Married or Single?*—"the name of 'old maid,'" the "smile . . . of . . . the vulgar." In 1821 she began to craft for herself "a mission of wider and more various range" than that generally available to an unmarried woman in the domestic realm.[35] Eventually, that mission would not only assure her financial stability but also give her a say in the national social, political, and literary debates of her time. Perhaps accordingly, the challenge to patriarchal authority located in Crazy Bet is, as Lucinda Damon-Bach has observed, in Sedgwick's later work divided, various elements situated on less "crazy," if still unconventional, characters—Aunt Debby in *Redwood,* Magawisca in *Hope Leslie,* Bessie Lee in *The Linwoods.*[36] As Sedgwick's work becomes increasingly available in the twenty-first century, our understanding of the course of her gender politics will no doubt become clearer. In the meantime, Crazy Bet sounds a keynote, her flamboyant resistance to categorization and her impassioned voice resonating across time, eloquent testimony to the power of the female author-izing subject.

NOTES

I am indebted to Charlene Avallone and Lucinda Damon-Bach for their thoughtful contributions to the development of this essay.

1. Catharine Sedgwick, *A New-England Tale* (1822; reprint, New York: Oxford Univ. Press, 1995), 16. Page references hereafter provided parenthetically with the abbreviation *NET.*

2. James Fenimore Cooper, review of *A New-England Tale, Literary and Scientific Repository and Critical Review* (May 1822): 347.

3. Edward Halsey Foster, *Catharine Maria Sedgwick,* in *Twayne's United States Authors Series* 233 (New York: Twayne, 1974), 52–53.

4. Jane Giles, "Catharine Maria Sedgwick: An American Literary Biography" (Ph.D. diss., City University of New York, 1984), 52–53.

5. Lucinda Linfield Damon-Bach, "'The Joy of Untamed Spirits and Undiminished Strength'": Catherine Sedgwick's and Susan Warner's Revisionary Romances" (Ph.D. diss., State University of New York, 1995), 55, 61–62.

6. Cathy N. Davidson, preface to *A New-England Tale* (New York: Oxford Univ. Press, 1995), viii.

7. *Life and Letters of Catharine Maria Sedgwick,* ed. Mary Dewey (New York: Harper, 1871), 121.

8. Catharine Maria Sedgwick quoted in Mary Kelley, introduction to *The Power of Her Sympathy: The Autobiography and Journal of Catharine Maria Sedgwick* (Boston: Massachusetts Historical Society and Northeastern Univ. Press, 1993), 25.

9. *Life and Letters*, 153.

10. See, for example, essays in this volume by Weierman, Daly, Gates, Kalayjian, Gussman, and Harris.

11. Eric Sundquist, "Introduction: The Country of the Blue," in *American Realism: New Essays* (Baltimore: Johns Hopkins Univ. Press, 1982), 6.

12. Joanne Dobson, "The American Renaissance Reenvisioned," in *The (Other) American Traditions: Nineteenth-Century Women Writers* (New Brunswick, N.J.: Rutgers Univ. Press, 1993), 172. See also Judith Fetterley's introduction to *Provisions: A Reader from Nineteenth-Century American Women* (Bloomington: Indiana Univ. Press, 1985), 10–11, and Carolyn Karcher's essay in this volume.

13. Morse Peckham, "Toward a Theory of Romanticism: II. Reconsiderations," in *The Triumph of Romanticism: Collected Essays* (Columbia: Univ. of South Carolina Press, 1970), 31.

14. Katherine Kearns, *Nineteenth-Century Realism: Through the Looking-Glass* (New York: Cambridge Univ. Press, 1996), ix, 6.

15. Sundquist, "Introduction," 6.

16. See F. O. Matthiessen, *American Renaissance: Art and Expression in the Age of Emerson and Whitman* (London: Oxford Univ. Press, 1941), 42; Northrop Frye, *The Secular Scripture: A Study of the Structure of Romance* (Cambridge, Mass.: Harvard Univ. Press, 1976), 35–61; Richard Chase, *The American Novel and Its Tradition* (Baltimore: Johns Hopkins Univ. Press, 1957), 12–14.

17. Nina Baym, "Melodramas of Beset Manhood," in *Feminism and American Literary History* (New Brunswick, N.J.: Rutgers Univ. Press, 1992), 3–18.

18. Hawthorne is not traditionally recognized as a realist, but R. C. De Prospo has persuasively identified the repressive sense of ubiquitous human subjectivity that nullifies the myth of object autonomy in *The Marble Faun* (1860), Hawthorne's last important book. The novel is weighed down by a surfeit of humanity: the thousands of voices singing on the night of the murder of the model, the pestilential air, the bones that turn up everywhere (especially in the priests' graveyard, so full of bones that the brothers must be exhumed after five years in order to make room for new occupants), the age and quantity of Roman artwork (human subjectivity as ancient, persistent), and the claustrophobically crowded carnival scene at the novel's close. Kenyon, Hilda, and Miriam are busily engaged in the exercise of their individual subjectivities; as artists they are obsessed with the subject-object relation. Their attempts to capture the object are naturally thwarted by the subjectivity that is employed in the production of art. Lecture (Chestertown, Md.: Washington College, 1991).

19. William Dean Howells, "Novel-Writing and Novel-Reading: An Impersonal Explanation," in *W. D. Howells: Selected Literary Criticism*, vol. 3, *1898–1920* (Bloomington: Indiana Univ. Press, 1978).

20. The assertion of Bet's realness anticipates the anxiety over the loss of the object

evinced by the narrator of Rebecca Harding Davis's 1861 "Life in the Iron Mills," whose urgent insistence that she make her story "a real thing to you" betrays her fear that she cannot. (In *Life in the Iron Mills and Other Stories*, ed. Tillie Olsen [New York: Feminist Press, 1985], 13–14.)

21. Foster, *Catharine Maria Sedgwick*, 52.

22. *Berkshire Hills* 1 (October, November, 1900): n.p.

23. See, for example, "Catharine M. Sedgwick," in *The National Portrait Gallery of Distinguished Americans*, vol. 1 (New York: Monson Bancroft, 1834), 1–8; and H. M. [Harriet Martineau], "Miss Sedgwick's Works," *The Westminster Review* (October 1838): 42–65.

24. Walter Scott, *The Heart of Midlothian* (1818; reprint, New York: Holt, Rinehart and Winston, 1962), 181. Page references hereafter provided parenthetically with the abbreviation *H.*

25. Sedgwick, *Power*, 38, 77–78, 79, 82, 98, 130.

26. Roland Barthes, *S/Z: An Essay*, trans. Richard Miller (New York: Farrar, Straus and Giroux, 1974), 167.

27. Robert Scholes, *Textual Power: Literary Theory and the Teaching of English* (New Haven: Yale Univ. Press, 1985), 20.

28. Susan Harris, *19th-Century American Women's Novels: Interpretive Strategies* (New York: Cambridge Univ. Press, 1990), 54–58. I refer here, of course, to Gilbert and Gubar's monolithic *The Madwoman in the Attic: The Woman Writer and the Nineteenth-Century Literary Imagination* (New Haven: Yale Univ. Press, 1979).

29. Alfred Adler, *Understanding Human Nature*, trans. Walter Beran Wolfe (London: George Allen & Unwin, 1928), 133–36.

30. Davidson, preface to *A New-England Tale*, ix.

31. See, for example, the novels of Jane Austen in the courtship genre; see Susanna Rowson's *Charlotte Temple* or Hannah Foster's *The Coquette* in the seduction genre.

32. Foster, *Catharine Maria Sedgwick*, 27–28.

33. Sedgwick, *Power*, 122.

34. Mary Kelley, *Private Woman, Public Stage: Literary Domesticity in Nineteenth-Century America* (New York: Oxford Univ. Press, 1984), 13.

35. [Catharine Maria Sedgwick], preface to *Married or Single?* vol. 1 (New York: Harper, 1857), vii–viii.

36. Lucinda Damon-Bach, "Heroines and Monsters in Catharine Maria Sedgwick's *Redwood*" (paper presented at Northeast Modern Language Association Convention, Hartford, Conn., March 2001).

4

*Excerpts from Reviews of *Redwood: A Tale*

The Atlantic Magazine (July 1824): 234–39.

The promise held forth by the "New England Tale," has been more than abundantly realised in "Redwood"; and, without any extravagant, or indeed extraordinary incidents, or any overstrained exhibitions of passion, we are insensibly carried through two highly entertaining volumes, acknowledging the fidelity of every scene to nature. (Pp. 235–36)

The contrast between the sisters [Caroline and Ellen] is finely preserved; and the character of Ellen, who . . . had enjoyed the double advantage of learning what was practically useful, and cultivating highly her intellectual powers, is drawn by the author in a manner which evinces the pleasure she took in its description. . . .

There is a character . . . that cannot be passed over, being the most original in the work. It is that of Deborah, a Yankee maiden of a certain age. . . . Her decided, though not coarse vulgarity, is more than redeemed by the shrewdness of her judgment, and goodness of her heart. . . .

As a mere novel, the correctness of style, the interest of the fiction, and the excellence of the descriptions, would entitle this work to high praise. But the vein of pure moral feeling which runs through it, and the instructive lesson it is designed to teach, demand for the authoress no common place among writers of this class. It has been said that America has never produced a female writer of eminence. If the writer of "Redwood" is not the only exception, she is certainly the brightest; and we trust, that a long career is before her, of still increasing utility and fame. (Pp. 238–39)

Port Folio 18 (July–Dec. 1824): 66–69.

"Who is there to fill [Washington Irving's] place in the description of American manners[?]" . . . In reply to the desponding question of Mr. Christopher North, we hold up the "Spy," and "Pioneers" of Mr. Cooper, and . . . we may exulting claim the honour for the work whose title honours the head of our page:—a performance which we pronounce to be *American*, exclusively, in scenery, manners, and sentiments. . . .

. . . The *dramatis personae* are sufficiently numerous and varied. . . . Without being dull or tedious, they are generally such people as we have all seen at one time or another—neither too wise nor too weak, too virtuous nor too wicked for our common nature. Even its fair heroine is not an angel. If we should demur in the least, it might perhaps be to Miss Deborah. She is rather too active and efficient a personage. . . . Nothing, however, supernatural, is attributed to the all-sufficient maid, . . . and we do sometimes see, that an uneducated woman, whether married or single, may be gifted with a head to devise, and a heart to perform. . . .

If we had not other evidence of the fact, we should have suspected the authoress to be a lady, from the partiality that is shown to that sex. Her females are more virtuous, more active, and more engaging, than her males. (Pp. 66–67)

Let it be recollected that the field is entirely new; for this is the first *American* novel, strictly speaking, which has appeared. (P. 69)

[William Cullen Bryant.] *North American Review* (April 1825): 245–72.

We have called . . . [*Redwood*] a comparatively hazardous experiment, and this, because it seems to us far more difficult to deal successfully with the materials which the author has chosen [current domestic incidents], than with those which she has neglected [historical events]. (P. 246)

[Debby's] mixture of intelligence and simplicity, of good nature and decision, of masculine habits with those of her sex, of strong feelings and attachments, with a strong understanding, and great warmth of imagination . . . altogether form a striking and novel combination. She has much to do in the course of the plot, and we are always glad to observe her agency. If any should be found who are of opinion, that she sometimes talks a little too long, none, we imagine, will think that she talks too often. (Pp. 266–67)

Next to the character of Debby, that of Susan [the Shaker eldress] is sketched with the greatest spirit and originality. Either of these would of itself suffice to give a reputation to the work. (P. 271)

[Lydia Maria Child.] "Miss Sedgwick's Novels." *Ladies Magazine* (? 1829): 234–38.

We considered Redwood far better than the "New England Tale." If there be an artist who hopes to surpass "Aunt Debby Lennox," he may as well lay down his pencil and die. . . .

Of Grace Campbell we have but a sketch—but it is eminently successful and spirited. This highly intellectual and elegant woman is drawn with as much truth to nature, as our humble friend Aunt Debby. . . . [Sedgwick] is at home in the higher circles, and refinement is a graceful habit; yet it is evident she loves to watch the comparatively unfettered developments of nature in middle life. Her own sentiments are, doubtless, uttered by Grace Campbell. . . . (Pp. 236–37)

Chapter 4

To "Act" and "Transact": *Redwood*'s Revisionary Heroines

LUCINDA L. DAMON-BACH

> It is only by attention that as our eyes pass over a book, we transfer its knowledge into our own minds. No book will improve you which does not make you think; which does not make your own mind work.
>
> Catharine Maria Sedgwick, *Means and Ends, or Self-Training*[1]

Hailed as "the first *American* novel, strictly speaking," Catharine Sedgwick's second novel, *Redwood: A Tale*, was widely praised in America and abroad.[2] Early reviewers lauded the novel's "fidelity . . . to nature," its lack of "any extravagant, or indeed extraordinary incidents, or any overstrained exhibitions of passion," and its believable characters, "generally such people as we have all seen . . . neither too wise nor too weak, too virtuous nor too wicked for our common nature. Even its fair heroine is not an angel."[3] In a lengthy *North American Review* essay published a year after the novel's successful debut, William Cullen Bryant declared that *Redwood* proved that "American Society" was indeed a "valid field for fiction." Bryant wrote, "We look upon the specimen before us as a conclusive argument, that the writers of works of fiction, of which the scene is laid in familiar and domestic life, have a rich and varied field before them in the United States." To Bryant, Sedgwick's domestic novel was on the frontier of American fiction. Her decision to write about "the very days in which we live, . . . presenting us not merely with the picture of what she has imagined, but with the copy of what she has observed," was a brave one, according to Bryant, "a more hazardous experiment of her powers" than the efforts of others who continued to cater to nineteenth-century readers' love for "narratives of the romantic kind."[4]

Redwood's female characters struck critics as Sedgwick's most stunning work. In 1825, Bryant claimed that the New England spinster Deborah Lenox and the Shaker eldress Susan Allen were "sketched with the greatest spirit and originality. Either of these would of itself suffice to give a reputation to the work."[5] Maria Edgeworth and Lydia Maria Child concurred that *Redwood* was "far better" than its predecessor, *A New-England Tale*, basing their opinions on *Redwood*'s heroines, in particular farm woman Debby Lenox, but Child also singled out the heiress Grace Campbell: "This highly intellectual and elegant woman is drawn with as much truth to nature, as our humble friend Aunt Debby."[6] Bryant also admired scenes featuring Caroline Redwood and Ellen Bruce, while another reviewer concluded that Sedgwick's "females are more virtuous, more active, and more engaging, than her males."[7] Indeed, *Redwood: A Tale* is full of women, and not, as its title might imply, a single story about a man named Redwood, but instead a complex work comprised of several intertwined tales that address—and challenge—early-nineteenth-century ideas about gender, class, slavery, religion, American and British relations, and relations between Northern and Southern states. Although the novel opens by focusing on the title character, Southern "infidel" Henry Redwood, it is primarily about the two women—also "Redwoods"—whose lives his irreligious behavior adversely affects. As the reviewers' comments suggest, however, several additional female characters are also central to the story. Throughout the novel Sedgwick uses these characters to explore both the limits and possibilities of life for women in antebellum America, exploring in particular the ways that women's lives could be lived more freely and fully within the conventions of the time.

Following the many interpolated tales of women's lives in *Redwood* is challenging. As Nina Baym has noted, in comparison to *A New-England Tale*, *Redwood*'s "many more characters and several subplots" yield a tangled narrative that Mary Kelley understandably calls "murky."[8] Kelley also notes that despite its potentially confusing plot, the tale is nevertheless "predictably clear" in its focus on Henry Redwood's self-acknowledged, multiple moral failings.[9] But Redwood's redemption and religious conversion are almost a footnote to the novel, tacked on in one of the book's final chapters. And while Redwood's attitude toward slavery—which evolves in spite of his slave-holding status—could prompt a reading of the novel as a political allegory, as Jenifer Elmore has persuasively argued, neither Elmore's nor Kelley's reading accounts for two main threads of the narrative: the Shaker episode that takes up a fourth of the book (seven out of twenty-seven chapters, from which Redwood is entirely absent), and Grace Campbell's story, presented in the final quarter of the book (ch. 17, 21–27).[10]

Most reviewers who noted the Shaker presence were fascinated by it, since Sedgwick's representation was one of the first (if not the first) portrayals of the sect.[11] The British reviewer Harriet Martineau was one of the few who criticized it sharply: "[T]he exhibition of a faulty religion, here offered in the form of a Shaker community, is as distasteful as that kind of exposure always is."[12] She missed Sedgwick's point, however, as did Bryant when he dismissed Ellen's encounters with Grace Campbell and the Armsteads, a family she meets while traveling, as the "least interesting part of the book. . . . There is a great deal of conversation here . . . and of consequence the interest suffers."[13] But as Charlene Avallone argues, Sedgwick's attention to conversation is no small matter.[14] Significantly, these two episodes, comprising half the novel, focus on alternatives for women's lives. My reading accounts for the narrative attention paid to these two plot elements and both continues Nina Baym's examination of the roles of women of the novel.[15]

Throughout, the novel challenges romantic notions with moments of realism—and Sedgwick is not offering a "copy of what she has observed" without purpose. She declares in her first preface that America is "a country which is, beyond parallel, free, happy, and abundant," but she asserts further that it is "no Arcadia," and that she will not represent it as such.[16] Implied here is a question: What might be wrong in antebellum America? But while she points to various problems, Sedgwick does not tell her reader what to think or dictate solutions—these must be figured out by each reader, who will determine them only by giving the book appropriate "attention."[17] As does all of Sedgwick's later work, *Redwood* schools its audience in the reading process—ultimately the process of interpretation and reinterpretation—encouraging readers to become participants in the creation of cultural meaning. As characters in the novel explore various options for their lives, growing ever more capable through the process of reinterpreting themselves, the novel's readers engage in this process with them, thereby developing skills that will enable them to interpret and reinterpret both their culture and their own lives—especially in terms of roles and possibilities for women.

In a chapter called "Reading" in *Means and Ends, or Self-Training* (1839), Sedgwick rehearses for her "young countrywomen" the importance of the reading process she had established fifteen years earlier in *Redwood.* "Next to 'what to read,'" Sedgwick writes, "comes the great question 'how to read,' and I am not sure the last is not the weightier of the two." Rather than blindly accepting the words or views of others, she urges, her young female audience must read with "*attention* . . . without it you can succeed in nothing, and certainly without it, books might as well be blanks to you" (emphasis in original). "When you read," she continues,

> do not *take for granted*, believing, with ignorant credulity, whatever you see stated in a book. Remember an author is but one witness, and often

a very fallible one. Pause in your reading, reflect, compare what the writer tells you with what you have learned from other sources on the subject, and above all, use your own judgment independently, not presumptuously (*Means*, 247–49, emphasis in original).

Leading its reader from questioning to comparing alternatives to interpreting, *Redwood* both models and teaches this critical reading process. Sedgwick frames the narrative of *Redwood* with Henry Redwood's own reeducation as a reader, showing his progression toward a fuller appreciation of women's capabilities in particular. At the beginning of the novel, an injury lands Redwood at a remote Vermont farmer's house, which happens also to be housing Ellen, the daughter he does not know he has. His convalescence provides Redwood with the opportunity to reevaluate his own life and the ways he views others. In the course of the novel, Redwood heals—both in body, through the ministrations of Debby, and in soul, in part through the act of reading the Bible that Ellen gives him. By the end of the novel Redwood demonstrates that he now reads beneath the surface of both people and books, and, most importantly, that he has begun to act on what he knows.

The Role of the Paratext

The reading process that *Redwood* demands and models is set up in the novel's structure. From the start, the reader is offered a dialectic that depicts and promotes the process of interpretation and reinterpretation as it reinforces the novel's realism and calls attention to its female characters. In essence, the novel begins before it begins, with a preface (or two, depending on the edition), an epigraph to the whole novel, and an epigraph to chapter 1, all before the narrative starts. This initial paratext, along with subsequent epigraphs, editorial interjections, and even footnotes, frames the novel, demanding readers' active engagement in the interpretive process even as they read. The novel's complex narrative is given additional layers through this external commentary, suggesting that Sedgwick is, to borrow a phrase from Judith Fetterley, "policing her literary territory," steering attention toward (or away from) the novel's central message.[18] Sedgwick's paratextual commentary, at times in untranslated French, forces her reader to interpret, presaging the pluralism that Robert Daly identifies in *The Linwoods*.[19]

The initial epigraph to the book introduces the importance of faith and of inquiry simultaneously: "Whilst the infidel mocks at the superstitions of the vulgar . . . it does not occur to him to observe that the most preposterous device by which the weakest devotee ever believed he was securing the happiness of a future life is more rational than unconcern about it. Upon this subject nothing is so absurd as indifference;—no folly so contemptible as thoughtlessness or levity" (iii).[20] Both echoing and forecasting Sedgwick's own liberal views of religion, expressed in particular in *A New-England Tale* and *Hope Leslie*, the epigraph steers the reader's attention toward the character of Redwood, who we learn in chapter 3 is an unfaithful man (in both marriage and religion). The next words, however—those of the preface—turn our attention to "the sketch . . . of the society of Shakers," the religious sect founded in 1774 by Mother Ann Lee, which "was drawn from personal observation" (x). In the second preface to the 1850 edition of *Redwood*, Sedgwick clarifies further that she has told the history of a particular Shaker woman "of rare gifts . . . substantially as she told it to me" (xv).

Only fools would laugh thoughtlessly at others' religious practices without at least asking questions; even the strangest of faiths may be better than none— these references are followed by the mention of a relatively new and, to most, strange Shaker religion. Clearly, the juxtaposition of epigraph and preface primes the reader to read attentively, to question actively, and to consider more than one perspective. But it is the epigraph to the first chapter that most obviously presents the dialectical reading process in which successful readers will necessarily engage, by raising two of the novel's main concerns: what this book is (really) about and how to read it. The anonymous epigraph introduces two conflicting cultural tropes for nineteenth-century American female identity, as it floats above the initial scene, suggesting two gossiping voyeurs commenting on what they see:

"A fine heroine, truly?"

"A Patagonian monster without a show of breeding" (17). Despite the second speaker's definitive response, the reader is left with only a question: To whom are these speakers referring?

The novel's opening scene reveals Henry Redwood, a wealthy Virginian, and his beautiful eighteen-year-old daughter Caroline on a ferry approaching the shore of Lake Champlain in Vermont. Recognizing that his abandonment of his daughter following his second wife's death has led to her being spoiled by her grandmother, Redwood has brought the debutante Caroline on this trip north in an attempt to "repair his fault" (72). At this moment, he learns that he has so far been unsuccessful: While he comments on the incredible beauty of the landscape before them, she has eyes only for the fine horses and fancy carriage waiting for them on the shore, which then prompt her to complain at length about how "excessively mortifying" it was for her to make her entrée into Montreal in "little vile caleches": "Grandmama says that people of fortune should never lay aside the insignia of their rank." Redwood is appalled and responds sarcastically: "Your grandmother's jumble of fortune and rank have a strong savor of republican ignorance. I would advise you, Miss Redwood, not to adopt her wise axioms as rules for the conduct of your life" (19).

This scene, following the epigraph, encourages the reader to consider whether Caroline, despite her wealth, "breeding," and privileged upbringing, is indeed the "fine heroine" she may initially appear to be, or whether she is not perhaps a "Patagonian monster," a foreign misfit, not just from another part of the United States, but from another country entirely. Thus the epigraph, floating anonymously in its privileged location above the narrative, models the reading process and raises questions that other characters, as well as Sedgwick's readers, must negotiate from that point on. Who is a "fine heroine"? What makes a woman "monstrous"? Is "breeding" the primary criterion for a heroine? The first chapter's epigraph orients the reader as to what to read for or expect in *Redwood*, and, by providing no single perspective, schools the reader in the role of questioning and thinking independently in order to clarify an interpretation.

This pattern of reading and reassessing is demonstrated by the characters themselves. As noted, Henry Redwood initially has a particularly low estimation of both women and religion, which he reveals in one of the novel's interpolated letters. Writing about his clandestine first marriage to his "infidel friend," he states: "I am married to a young creature without fortune, without connexions; innocent, and beautiful, and *religious*; an odd union, is it not? I have not intimated my free opinions to her, for why should I disturb her superstition? It is quite becoming to a woman, and harmonizes well with the weakness of her sex, and is perhaps necessary to it" (56, original emphasis). By the end of the novel, however, through his witnessing of Debby's and Ellen's ability to "act" and "transact" for themselves and on the behalf of others, Redwood has come to appreciate fully the integrity and many strengths of at least two women who are without fortune, connections, or significant beauty, and has come to realize the necessity of religion for himself (107). He is now able to see beyond the superficial, external aspects of women—the accidents of birth or "breeding"—to deeper levels of character, having disbanded his notions of what women are or should be and broadened it to include what he has now witnessed as their at times superior intellectual, spiritual, and even physical strength. These two changes are shown most obviously when Redwood graciously welcomes Debby to a fashionable dinner party, despite her Malvolio-like dress—a yellow and purple "lutestring changeable"—and when, following his conversion at the novel's close, he calls the Bible he received from Ellen "an inestimable treasure" (334, 450).

Monster? or Heroine?

A prime mover in Redwood's—and by extension the reader's—reeducation in women's capabilities is the spinster Aunt Deborah Lenox. "Original," "peculiar," "interesting," and "real," according to early critics, Aunt Debby was indeed a new kind of gender-crossing heroine, whose "stature and . . . weatherbeaten skin" suggest that "her feminine dress was a vain attempt at disguise, had not her voice, which possessed the shrillness . . . of a woman's, testified to Miss Debby's right to make pretensions which at the first glance seemed monstrous" (31). Like Crazy Bet before her in *A New-England Tale*, Debby surprised the reviewers, and, like Bet's, her appearances interrupt the narrative and steer readers' interpretations of characters and events. Described in the novel as "Amazonian" due to her six-foot-one-inch height (32), Debby "has much to do in the course of the plot," Bryant notes, "and we are always glad to observe her agency."[21] Debby's "hints" help the characters within the novel, as well as the reader, to comprehend the meaning of key scenes. It is tempting to conjecture that again, like Bet's, Debby's presence in the novel provides an uncensored voice for Sedgwick. Regardless, through Debby's striking originality and candid assessments of others, the text demands that readers reconsider what lies within the range of appropriate behavior for women and what it means for a woman to be "heroic."

Aunt Debby—farmer, veterinarian, nurse, hostler, and matchmaker—acknowledges the romantic but privileges the pragmatic. When the injured Redwood inquires about the qualifications of the country doctor Debby has just sent for, she acknowledges that his questions are "rational; and I like him all the better for it; none but your parfect [*sic*] fools believe in any thing and every body" (29). Later, when young Charles Westall—son of Henry's childhood friend and a potential suitor for Caroline Redwood—arrives for an extended visit, Debby hints to him "that all in Caroline [is] not as fair and lovely as it seem[s]" (167). Like Redwood, Westall is, at first, an inaccurate "reader" of women who needs to be reeducated, and Debby becomes his instructor. In one particular exchange, Debby initiates a transference of his affections from Caroline to Ellen. In Caroline's presence, Westall "forgot Miss Deborah's hint—forgot every thing but the power and the presence of his beautiful companion" (167). So when Deborah later overhears him comment to himself, "Thank Heaven! . . . I have awoke before it is too late," she decides to clinch this change of heart by challenging him, paradoxically, to defend Caroline's beauty (189–90).

To each of Westall's confident remarks—he is "sure no knight ever had a fairer cause for his chivalry"—Deborah responds, acting as Ellen's "knight" with equal confidence. In response to his description of Caroline's "incomparable hair, black and glossy as a raven's plumage, turning into rich curls whenever it escapes from the classic braids that confine it," Deborah parries,

> Now tell me, Mr. Westall, on your conscience, if you can think that black hair plaited, and twisted, and fussified, to be compared with Ellen's beautiful brown hair? . . . [I]t reaches almost to the tops of her shoes; and then, when she doubles it into them rich folds, and fastens it with her comb, and parts it from the front in a kind of a wave—did you ever see any thing that had a cleaner, prettier look? And so bright and polished as if the sun was shining into it. (193–94)

Westall "yield[s] the point of the hair" and, ultimately, confesses himself "vanquished" in terms of the face, but still holds "that Miss Redwood has the finest figure; so tall and graceful—she moves like Juno." Debby again convincingly argues against him: "That I won't deny. She is just like one of them heathen idols: every motion—sitting or rising, walking or standing—seems to say, look at me! worship me!—but Ellen—she is behind a cloud just now; but if you had seen her as I have her, every step as light and springy as a fawn's . . . " (194–95).

The comedy of this exchange highlights how difficult it can be for men and women to see beyond conventions. Like Westall, the reader is forced to reassess the many qualities of all three women—Ellen, Caroline, and Debby. Although in a letter to her grandmother Caroline initially calls Debby "a hideous monster—a giantess: I suspect a descendant of the New-England witches" (106), Caroline is later revealed to be both a thief and a liar, the true "Patagonian monster" of the novel.[22] Debby, it turns out, is not only a good judge of appearance, but of character.

How both women and men read each other is, of course, crucial to the marriage plots in *Redwood*. A scene that appears mid-novel, in which the gathered family members listen to and discuss a portion of Maria Edgeworth's *The Absentee* (1812), showcases the interpretive process (and shows that both Westall and Redwood have progressed as independent thinkers). Ellen Bruce, Redwood, Caroline, and Westall compare the situation of the novel to their own lives.

> Ellen resumed the book, and read with feeling and expression the ever-memorable scene of Colambre's declaration to Grace Nugent, till she came to the passage where Colambre says there is an "invincible obstacle" to their union. Her voice faltered, but she would have had enough self-command to proceed, had not Mr. Redwood inquired, "what obstacle could be invincible where a creature so artless, so frank, so charming, was in question?"

"A sufficient obstacle, papa," interposed Caroline; "Lord Colambre believed that Miss Nugent's mother was not 'sans reproche.'"

"That may be a sufficient obstruction in a work of fiction," replied Mr. Redwood, "but in real life, with a man of sense and feeling, a man deeply in love too, I fancy it would not be a very serious objection. What say you, Charles, you are a young man of the class I have named?"

Mr. Redwood looked to Westall for a reply; he perceived his question had disconcerted him—he looked at Ellen, her face was crimson—the application that had been made of the fictitious incident instantly flashed across his mind. (214–15)

Like Edgeworth's heroine, Ellen does not know her parentage. At this point in the novel, aware of Charles's growing affection for her, she believes that her possible lack of "breeding" may well be an obstacle to marriage. In *The Absentee,* it is Lord Colambre who raises the problem of Grace's heritage, and he clearly will refuse her if the worst proves true. But Sedgwick's Charles Westall responds differently, rejecting this social code and making an important distinction between "conventional ethics" and "natural justice": "the fault of one person cannot be transferred to another . . . it cannot be right to make an innocent child suffer for the guilt of its parent" (215). Through Westall's example of challenging and revising a fictional situation, the reader is invited similarly to question appearances in Sedgwick's novel.

By mid-novel, the reader knows that the most significant difference between the half-sisters Ellen and Caroline lies not in their appearance or their "breeding," but in their ability to, as Debby puts it, "act" and "transact." Unlike spoiled, lazy, selfish Caroline, whom Debby calls "that *Caroliny gal,* with all her flaunting ruffles and folderols," Ellen has been "brought up to business; but as to that useless piece [Caroline], she could neither act nor transact" (107, emphasis in original). This crucial difference is demonstrated in an earlier scene, when Ellen, rather than Westall, physically rescues Caroline during a boating mishap. Caroline impulsively jumps into a canoe, which she does not know how to paddle, in order to pick some flowers for her hair that are growing out of a cliff at the water's edge. When the boat subsequently careens into the rock face and begins to tip, Caroline grabs a vine and is left hanging as the canoe floats out from under her. Sedgwick's description of Ellen's reaction emphasizes her ability to think quickly and act independently: "She ran around the curve of the shore, ascended the rock where the ascent was gradual, and letting herself down as gently as possible into the canoe, she rowed immediately to the relief of the distressed damsel, whose arms already trembled with the weight which they sustained" (159–60).

Sedgwick emphasizes Westall's ineffectiveness at this moment and later underscores the gender reversal involved. Approaching this scene from a distance, Westall "had been a witness of Miss Redwood's danger, and had hastened on in the hope of being so fortunate as to assist at her rescue; but fate had been unkind to him, for the pleasure of playing the hero on this occasion was not only wrested from him, but he was forced to witness and admire the celerity with which the rescue had been effected without his aid" (161). Afterward, Caroline not only neglects to acknowledge Ellen's help, she complains that Ellen's act "deprived me of the romance of being rescued by you, Mr. Westall, which you know would have been a charming opening to our acquaintance—quite an incident for a novel" (177). *Redwood,* the attentive reader learns, is not the type of novel to which Caroline refers, but one that actively denies Caroline and Westall the romantic roles of "damsel" and "hero" through Ellen's practical (and athletic) agency. From the outset of the novel, the reader learns that this is not a typical romance but a book that instead requires a rethinking of women's roles.

Sedgwick interrupts her narrative to explore women's inner resourcefulness and ability to help one another when she again breaks the mold of the romance and assigns Debby and Ellen the conventionally male task of "rescuing" Emily Allen from the Shakers. Their three-part rescue mission begins at the Shaker community in Hancock, Massachusetts, continues on a densely wooded back road somewhere near the border of New York, and concludes at a Lebanon Springs resort. The two women cross a societal boundary first by leaving home and second by driving their "old-fashioned chaise" themselves (230). But their most obvious transgression is their errand into the wilderness, when they literally leave the "beaten highway" and end up in the woods. This story again involves the reader in reevaluating women's traditional roles.

In the first of seven chapters that present Ellen and Debby's "crusade to the Shakers," attention shifts from them to the pair of Shaker women who temporarily assume center stage: young Emily Allen, identified by the narrator as "the simple amiable little fanatic" (214), and her aunt, Susan Allen, whom Deborah identifies as "half crazy woman and half saint" (79). The mission to rescue Emily, a lengthy diversion from the supposedly central plot of Ellen Bruce, forces the reader into the interpretive act, to ask, "Why is this incident included in this novel?" Here Sedgwick presents options for women without dictating which is best, in fact preserving, instead, the range of possibilities by showing that what is good for one woman may not be good for another. Although both Emily and Susan are seen as partially insane by the other characters in the novel because they have opted to trade their conventional homes and roles for the celibate practices of the Shaker religion, ultimately their individual experiences are completely opposite to one another and equally rational. The same Shaker practices paradoxically offer Susan more freedom and authority than she might have experienced had she stayed in her "natural" family, but limit Emily so much that she becomes critically ill. Emily's loss of physical health due to the constraints of Shaker life, juxtaposed with Susan's rise to power under the same circumstances, underscores the importance of choice in the matter. Significantly, the theme that links this interpolated tale to the rest of *Redwood*'s narrative is the issue of a woman's right to choose not only whom to marry (revising the perspective of *The Absentee*), but whether to marry at all.

As the narrative turns to Susan, one of the "elder sisters," or female leaders, in the community, and Emily, her recently (and somewhat reluctantly) converted niece, the text reveals a surprisingly destructive relationship. Because Susan "saved [Emily] from the efforts of self-dependence" (82), Emily's spirit and physical strength have languished: "[H]er love for the elder sister . . . had produced such habitual dependence on her, that she had become a mere machine governed by a power which she could neither understand nor resist" (279). Susan's presence at times overwhelms Emily, and others as well. As Debby notes, Susan "has that in her that she can make people a mind to do what they would hate to do for any body else. I don't know what it is, she is not a stern woman, but it is a kind of nat'ral authority, as if she was a born-queen" (88). Membership in the society empowers Susan, who rises to the highest rank, equal to or higher than that of the male elders, but Emily needs to be back out in "the world," at the side of her lover, in order to be fully functioning again.

Although Susan's and Emily's stories are featured at the novel's center—the place where, Susan Harris has alerted us, nineteenth-century women writers often offered their readers alternatives to conventions—the attentive reader can see that these two are clearly not women to emulate, but are instead cautionary examples.[23] Emily's silent passivity and "habitual dependence" lead her to follow a religion in which she does not wholly believe and to become the dupe of a selfish, irreligious man. Because she stops thinking for herself, she nearly becomes the sexual victim of the corrupt elder Reuben Harrington, whose role in "healing" the dejected Emily is to abuse her mentally and then kidnap her, planning to marry her and live on the money he has embezzled from the Shakers. On the other hand, Susan's decision to join the Shakers provides her with significant authority. Although she initially accedes to Reuben's "treatment" of Emily, she later becomes suspicious and challenges his authority by pulling rank on him: "Remember I am your elder; I fear you not, Reuben; I suspect you" (50).

Yet the truly attentive reader will realize that Susan's story is not a clear-cut cautionary tale. While it appears that Susan's rejection of her former lover in favor of a celibate life with the Shakers leads to his premature death, the novel's paratext reveals Sedgwick's admiration of the eldress on whom her character is based. Calling this woman "a saint" in her second preface to *Redwood,* Sedgwick reveals both her respect for her and her goal of preserving this woman's "true" story within *Redwood:* "The sister . . . whose history, under the name of Sister Susan, I have told substantially as she related it to me, has long since passed to the reward of a self-sacrifice, a holy self-denial that places her among the Christian saints, no matter by what earthly sectarian designation named" (xv). Susan's autobiography—a putatively nonfictional interjection—makes the fictional narrative more real, becomes the centerpiece of Sedgwick's portrait of the Shakers, and requires careful rereading.

After arriving at the Shaker Society and discovering that Emily has inexplicably disappeared the night before with Reuben, Ellen and Debby temporarily give up their search and head on toward Lebanon. Assuming that their mission to rescue Emily—or as Debby initially proposed it, their "crusade to the Shakers"—has failed, they (and the reader) are surprised when they not only discover where Emily is being held captive but also are able to free her (261).

In his review of *Redwood,* Bryant was not "satisfied with the circumstances of Emily's escape from the thraldom in which she is held among this strange community. The adventures connected with the Indian and his cabin are too extraordinary and romantic, to harmonise well with the general strain of the narrative."[24] His two-sentence dismissal, however, draws attention to this uncharacteristic moment in the novel—the purpose of which depends precisely on the fact that it does not "harmonise well" with the rest of the book—and raises questions about its meaning in the reader's mind.

Interestingly, Deborah and Ellen prefigure Bryant's criticism with their own comments on the unfolding scene, which, though it marks the climax of their "crusade"—the moment at which Emily is finally rescued—is surprisingly anti-climactic, even accidental. As they walk up a remote shortcut over the mountain that separates the Shaker Society at Hancock, Massachusetts, from Lebanon, New York, Debby and Ellen are surprised by a whining and fawning dog that convinces Ellen (once rescued herself from a house fire by a dog) to follow it into the woods. Deborah emphasizes that "for two rational women, we are in an odd place and following a strange leader," to which Ellen responds, "And that is as it should be . . . two errant damsels as we are, in quest of adventures—danger there is not, cannot be here, and we will not go much farther" (321). Ellen's language is telling: Although she presumably recasts the moment in romantic terms in an effort to make light of their situation, she nevertheless actively revises romantic conventions. In calling herself and Debby "two errant damsels . . . in quest of adventures," she conflates the role of the rescuing "knight errant," traditionally male, with that of the typically passive "damsel." Once again, the narrative voice reminds us, the "incidents for [this] novel" will be different; like Ellen's earlier rescue of Caroline, this moment will rewrite the scene we might expect.

An alternative meaning for the word "errant"—not "wandering in quest of adventure," but "erring or doing something wrong"—reinforces the scene's revision of its medieval prototype. Ellen's use of "errant" points toward their going not only out of narrative "bounds" for women, but also, in their unescorted nocturnal wandering against conventional social expectations for women's appropriate or acceptable behavior.[25] Both the Shaker subplot and Emily's rescue emphasize at *Redwood*'s center that women are capable of remarkable vision and action outside the realm of contemporary literary and cultural boundaries. Like Debby, Susan has chosen to be single; both characters demonstrate the viability of that option for women. Early on in the novel, when Westall wonders why Debby has "chosen a single life," the narrator describes Debby's reaction fully:

> Deborah's smile showed she was not insensible to the compliment implied in the word *chosen;* for like other maidens, she preferred it should be understood that she did not walk in the solitary path of celibacy by compulsion. "Oh, it was a whim of my own," she replied, "and there is no danger of such whims being catching—sooner or later every body slides off into the beaten road of matrimony." (192)

The self-reliant Aunt Debby anticipates Emerson's "Self-Reliant" man, who leaves the domestic scene on a "whim": "I shun father and mother and wife and brother when my genius calls me. I would write on the lintels of the doorpost, *Whim*."[26]

The material, psychological, and social functions of marriage for women are central to the novel. Ellen has already rejected her first proposal of marriage from a man she doesn't love, saying "my path is a solitary one," and Susan's story provides an additional, based-on-real-life example of a woman who, of her "own good will," elects not to slide "off into the beaten road of matrimony."[27] Nevertheless, in detailing the emotional and physical ramifications of Susan's decision to join the Shakers and swear celibacy, including the suggestion that her decision led to the death of her former lover, the text problematizes the choice of celibate singlehood. Even though the voice of the preface calls Susan a "saint" twenty-six years after the first publication of the novel (preface to the second edition, x), Sedgwick's "mostly true" sketch of Susan reveals her ambivalence about Susan's decision to walk "a solitary path." What does seem unambiguous, however, in Debby's, Susan's, and Emily's stories, is Sedgwick's belief in a woman's right to choose whether or not to marry, and if choosing marriage, her right to choose her partner.

Sedgwick reinforces the importance she attaches to the issue of marriage and choice of partner in the novel's final subplot—Grace Campbell's courtship, which provides yet another possible choice and resulting outcome for women. Her name recalls Edgeworth's heroine in *The Absentee*, but her situation reverses that of the eighteenth-century novel, since she (as a wealthy woman, not Edgeworth's wealthy man) must decide whether to choose the man she loves and lose her inheritance, or agree to the conditions of her uncle's will, marry the man he has designated, and keep her money. Grace's importance to the novel is signaled by the epigraph to the chapter that introduces her: "Proud of her parts, but gracious in her pride— / She bore a gay good nature in her face, / And in her air was dignity and grace."²⁸ The epigraph not only suggests that Grace will be, in part, a revision of Caroline, as they share—to differing extents—the flaw of pride, but also suggests one answer to the question of the epigraph to chapter 1, "A fine heroine, truly?"

Though Grace is introduced in the narrative through an accident (when Ellen pulls Grace's nephew out of the way of a runaway horse and carriage), her presence in the novel seems anything but accidental. Grace's marital decision is significant because it comes down to a choice (she thinks) between money and love. Like Caroline, she is a beauty, an heiress, and courted by a British man. One significant distinction between the two women, however, is in the kind of man each elects to marry. Grace's suitor, Fenton, is, unbeknownst to her, the cousin she is "required" to marry if she wants to retain her inheritance. Because he knows this, Fenton has decided to hide his identity (anticipating Gertrude Clarence's similar move in *Clarence*, six years later) to provide Grace with the opportunity to meet him without the pressure of the will. (If it becomes apparent that there is no attraction, he will withdraw.) Under these circumstances Grace indeed falls in love and subsequently chooses the man, not the money, even though she realizes she is defying her beloved uncle's will. Sedgwick's approval of Grace's values seems evident in that she is then "rewarded" by being able to retain her inheritance, since Fenton is revealed to be the man she was supposed to marry.

Caroline faces a similar parental injunction: She, too, will lose her inheritance if she marries against her father's wishes. But Sedgwick's point here is more subtle: Caroline is not truly in love with Fitzgerald—she seems to choose him because he is handsome, he flatters her, and she thinks she "ought" to be married. In this novel, however, Caroline's default to romance conventions and her inability to act or transact productively lead to her premature death.

Thirty-three years before Sedgwick raises the question again in her final novel, *Married or Single?*, She argues in *Redwood* that freedom regarding the choice to marry defines freedom for women and is not simply an aspect of their freedom. Sedgwick's dedication to realism prevents her from writing a novel in which all of the women fulfill the ideal; instead, she provides a range of choices and outcomes that encourages the reader toward careful inquiry into what is best for each individual. Ultimately, she includes two women who decide not to marry (Debby and Susan), one who makes a good marriage choice (Grace), one who chooses poorly (Caroline), one who remains passive and is chosen (Emily—though she wants to marry, she doesn't act), and one who chooses not to marry and then changes her mind (Ellen). Although, early on in the novel, Ellen refuses George Lenox's offer of marriage, saying "my path is a solitary one," [149], by the end of the novel, she and Westall have indeed fallen in love—with full parental approval—and are engaged to be married. By the close of *Redwood*, Grace Campbell has revised her predecessor Grace Nugent's role in Edgeworth's earlier novel and thereby provided a more assertive model for women in the nineteenth century. Both Grace's and Ellen's marriages confirm the importance of marriage based on love, not determined by familial or societal expectations, while Debby's and Susan's lives demonstrate two versions of single life; significantly, all four exemplify women who can both "act" and "transact." The carefully schooled reader can answer the question raised in the epigraph by paying attention to the novel's realism, which provides female characters that are, for the most part, neither "heroines" nor "monsters," but are instead, in at least some cases, a blend of the two—both noble and flawed.

This realism, foreshadowed in the prefatory attention to the spinster Shaker, Sister Susan, is foregrounded one last time at the end of the novel. Aunt Debby, another woman who has chosen to stay single, has perhaps most profoundly challenged the reader's notion of a heroine, and she is awarded the last word. Structurally anticipating the end of *Hope Leslie,* which also closes by focusing on a woman who has elected not to marry (Esther Downing), *Redwood* closes with a letter from Debby, written two years after "the date of these memoirs," that the narrator declares "fell into our hands." In an elaborately detailed editorial address, Sedgwick describes the process of transmitting the letter to the printer, who sent it back, requesting "that the spelling might be rectified." Finally, though, Debby's "pot-hooks and trammels" are presented, and we learn, among other things, that the man Ellen chose not to marry has recovered and married a southern woman, who despite this "disadvantage" is, according to Debby, "as likely and prudent and notable a woman as if she had the good fortune to be brought up in New-England." She goes on to remark that this instance "leads a reflecting person to consider that it is best to lay aside their prejudices, and to believe there are good people every where" (455). In this final performance of "reading" a woman, Debby serves to remind the novel's reader of the process that has brought her to this point—of interpretation and reinterpretation—and thus emphasizes the importance of that process not only in shaping the cultural possibilities for women but also for regional understanding. For a "reflecting person," Deborah's story, as one early reviewer noted, reminds the reader "that an uneducated woman, whether married or single, may be gifted with a head to devise, and a heart to perform."[29] If, like this reviewer, we have read *Redwood* with "attention," we will have noticed that Sedgwick has challenged early-nineteenth-century interpretive conventions in three important ways: by choosing a realistic framework, by presenting characters whose actions challenge expectations, and by actively engaging her readers in the reading process, involving them in the challenging of conventions that can lead them to achieve fuller lives for themselves.

NOTES

This essay has benefited greatly from the generous and thoughtful rereadings of John Canaday, Victoria Clements, Gayle Fischer, Nancy Schultz, and Elizabeth Kenney.

1. [Catharine M. Sedgwick], *Means and Ends, or Self-Training* (1839), 249.

2. *Port Folio* (July–Dec. 1824), 69. Within six years of its publication in the United States and England, *Redwood* was translated into French (1824), German (1825), Swedish (1826), and Italian (1830). That the novel was well-known and liked—and that association with *Redwood* might help sell later books—is also apparent in publishers' use of the novel's title as her anonymous byline ("By the Author of Redwood"), not only on the three works that immediately followed, *The Travellers* (1825), *The Deformed Boy* (1826), and *Hope Leslie* (1827), but even on books published over the next twenty years, despite the later renown of *Hope Leslie*, *Clarence* (1830), and *The Linwoods* (1835). Though *Redwood* is included in many of her anonymous bylines within a string of other novels, four subsequent works—*A Short Essay to Do Good* (1828), *Home* (1835), *Means and Ends, or Self-Training* (1839), and *The Boy of Mt. Rhigi* (1848)—all appeared attributed specifically (and solely) to "the Author of *Redwood*."

3. *Atlantic Magazine* (July 1824): 235–36; *Port Folio*, 66, 69.

4. William Cullen Bryant, *North American Review* (April 1825): 248; 246–47.

5. Bryant, *North American Review*, 271.

6. See Carolyn Karcher's essay, "Catharine Maria Sedgwick in Literary History," in this volume, for text of Maria Edgeworth letter, which is also reprinted in *Life and Letters of Catharine Maria Sedgwick*, ed. Mary E. Dewey (New York: Harper and Brothers, 1871), 169. Lydia Maria Child, "Miss Sedgwick's Novels," *Ladies Magazine* (May 1829): 236–37.

7. Bryant, *North American Review*, 260, 264–65, 271; *Port Folio*, 67.

8. Nina Baym, *Woman's Fiction: A Guide to Novels by and about Women in America, 1820–1870* (Ithaca, N.Y.: Cornell Univ. Press, 1978), 56. Mary Kelley, *Private Woman, Public Stage: Literary Domesticity in Nineteenth-Century America* (New York: Oxford Univ. Press, 1984), 310.

9. Kelley, *Private Woman, Public Stage*, 311.

10. Jenifer Elmore, "Parti-Colored Fiction: Political Allegories and National Anxieties in Sedgwick's *Redwood* and 'A Reminiscence of Federalism'" (paper presented at the Catharine Maria Sedgwick Symposium, Stockbridge, Mass., June 2000).

11. *Atlantic Magazine*, 238; Bryant, *North American Review*, 265.

12. Harriet Martineau, *Westminster Review* (October 1838): 49.

13. Bryant, *North American Review*, 266.

14. See Charlene Avallone's essay, "Catharine Sedgwick and the 'Art' of Conversation," in this volume.

15. Baym, *Woman's Fiction*, 58.

16. [Catharine Maria Sedgwick], *Redwood* (1824), Author's Revised Edition (New York: George Putnam, 1850), xi. Page references hereafter provided parenthetically.

17. Sedgwick, *Means and Ends*, 247.

18. Judith Fetterley, *Provisions: A Reader from Nineteenth-Century American Women* (Bloomington: Indiana Univ. Press, 1985), 45.

19. See Robert Daly's essay, "Mischief, Insanity, Memetics, and Agency in *The Linwoods*," in this volume. In his review of several novels, including Lydia Maria Child's *Hobomok* (1824), Jared Sparks declares that these novelists "are uniformly deficient in taste and skill in the selection of mottos for their chapters. These scraps form an important part of a novel, and require more attention and knowledge, than the authors of most of them seem to be aware. The mottos of those, which we have now noticed, are far too frequently either hackneyed, pointless, or without sufficient bearing on the subject of the chapter" (103). "Recent American Novels," *North American Review* 21 (July 1825): 78–104.

20. The epigraph is identified as from "Paley," likely Reverend William Paley's *Principles of Moral and Political Philosophy* (1785).

21. Bryant, *North American Review*, 266.

22. Caroline steals the contents of the box that Ellen Bruce's mother gave to Ellen with instructions not to open it until she is twenty-one or engaged to be married. It contains a letter and a miniature that reveal Henry Redwood to be Ellen's father.

23. Susan Harris, *19th-Century American Women's Novels: Interpretive Strategies* (New York: Cambridge Univ. Press, 1990), 34.

24. Bryant, *North American Review*, 266.

25. In addition to his objection that the incident was "too extraordinary and romantic," perhaps it was this aspect of the scene that felt "wrong" to Bryant: A journey into the wilderness of this kind was "male" territory; what was Sedwick doing invading it with capable women?

26. Ralph Waldo Emerson, "Self Reliance" (1841), in *Ralph Waldo Emerson: Selected*

Essays, Lectures, and Poems, ed. Robert D. Richardson Jr. (New York: Bantam, 1990), 152. Emphasis in original.

27. See *Redwood,* 92, 149, 139–42, 146–48.

28. Crabbe, epigraph to chapter 17, *Redwood,* 291.

29. *Port Folio,* 66.

5

🖎 Excerpts from Reviews of *Hope Leslie; or, Early Times in the Massachusetts*

"The Novels of Miss Sedgwick." *American Monthly Magazine* (January 1836): 15–25.

It is not Miss Sedgwick's great gift to contrive the incidents of a story. It is, however, true, that she does not give us the old hackneyed routine. But in avoiding this, her drama wants a regular beginning, middle, and end; it is often improbable, and sometimes inconsistent; and we never read one of her stories without smiling at a certain spirit of adventure, which always comes out somewhere in the conduct of her young girls. . . . (P. 15)

Western Monthly Review (September 1827): 289–95.

Magawisca is the first genuine Indian angel, that we have met with; and we must give our authoress credit, for having manufactured the savage material into a new shape. This angel, as she stands, is a very pretty fancy; but no more like a squaw, than the croaking of a sand-hill crane is like the sweet, clear and full note of the redbird. Dealers in fiction have privileges; but they ought to have for foundation, some slight resemblance to nature. (P. 295)

North American Review (April 1828): 403–20.

We hold it to be a fortunate thing for any country, that a portion of its literature should fall into the hands of the female sex; because their influence, in any walk of letters, is almost sure to be powerful and good. This influence appears to us to be so peculiar in its nature, and so important in its action, that we venture to demand the attention of our readers to some remarks upon it, however unworthy of the subject our exposition may be.

To speak first of the influence of female literature on females themselves, we presume that the mere fact of the existence of such a literature produces a very sensible effect on the mental character of those, whom, if it were only for gallantry's sake, we must call the best part of our race. A woman feels a laudable pride in the knowledge that a sister has distinguished herself in an intellectual career; has won a prize in the competition of the mind; has vindicated for her sex that equality with the other, which has been both doubted and denied. Her success is an argument which can be wielded at pleasure, and doubtless with pleasure, against all who would underrate feminine capacity. And it is something more and better than an argument. It is a stimulus; acting on the generous ambition of the whole sex; prompting all to an exertion of their highest faculties; inducing a general disposition to read, to study, to think; making something desirable beside personal attraction, and something enviable, which shall last longer, and be more attainable, than beauty. The objects of pursuit will be exalted and refined. The consciousness of power will produce self-respect, and self-respect will lead to improvement. (Pp. 403–4)

Hope Leslie, the white heroine of the work, is a finely drawn character, full of enthusiasm, affection, truth, and yet sparkling with gaiety and wit. Her friend and rival—yes, both friend and rival—Esther Downing, is lovely too, in her way, which, as was to be expected in those times, was rather a precise one and her loveliness is as distinct from Hope's as possible. Magawisca too is another friend and rival, as we before hinted. Here are three ladies, who seem to love and admire each other as much as they do Everell Fletcher; who, by the way, excellent as he is, hardly deserves such an accumulation of honor. Is this, or is it not, a greater improbability than the character of the Indian heroine? We are afraid to leave the decision of the question to our authoress, who, if the truth must be told, appears to entertain a decided partiality for her own sex. Nor can we blame her for it. We are in no humor, indeed, to find fault with her at all, or for anything. We only hope, that as we have been tardy in noticing the last production of her pen; another will very soon be ready for our inspection. We pray her to go on, in the path in which she must excel, and has excelled, and which she ought consequently to make her peculiar one. We pray her to go on, in the name of her friends, for the public's sake, and for the honor of our youthful literature. (P. 420)

Godey's Lady's Book (November 1842): 249.

Those who remember the lively sensation produced by the first appearance of this delightful historical novel, will not be surprised at its republication. Miss Sedgwick was particularly fortunate in the selection of the period and the scene of the novel, and she has brought to the task of illustrating the early colonial annals of Massachusetts, her native state, a vivid power of conception and a happy talent of delineation and characterization. It is gratifying to see the unrivalled talents of such a writer devoted to so patriotic an object as that of increasing the interest of the American people in the history of their own country. The best pens among our female writers, we are happy to notice, are chiefly devoted to national subjects. While the lady writers are thus patriotic, we need not despair of ultimately building up a sound and elegant national literature. (P. 249)

Chapter 5

"My Sister! My Sister!": The Rhetoric of Catharine Sedgwick's *Hope Leslie*

JUDITH FETTERLEY

Hope Leslie is arguably one of the most under-analyzed texts of nineteenth-century American literature. While sales figures from the Rutgers University Press American Women Writer series indicate its extensive use in classrooms across the country, and perhaps its interest for the general reader as well, scholarly and professional readings of the text have not developed proportionately.[1] This lag gains further resonance if we recognize that in little over a decade Sedgwick wrote five major novels—a fictional output equaled only by Cooper. Responding, like Cooper, to the call for a distinctively American literature, she rivaled him in her own day as the writer who could answer Sydney Smith's sneering question, "[W]ho in the four quarters of the globe reads an American book?" by putting America on the literary map. Moreover, like her contemporary, Lydia Huntley Sigourney, she created a space for the woman writer to participate in creating an American literature and hence in constructing the new Republic. While Nina Baym claims that if Sigourney "had not existed, it would have been necessary to invent her," Catharine Sedgwick could never have been made up, for she exceeds the imagination that did, in fact, as Baym goes on to point out, invent Sigourney as the "epitome of the specifically *female* author in her range of allowed achievements and required inadequacies."[2] In a certain sense, Catharine Sedgwick is too good to make up, and if she could not have been invented in her own day, neither has she been successfully reinvented in our own.

An essay seeking to explain this phenomenon would, I believe, work against efforts to "reinvent" Catharine Sedgwick, for it would inevitably address the conversations surrounding the construction and reconstruction of nineteenth-century American literary history more than Sedgwick's own texts. In an earlier essay on American women writers and the politics of recovery, I argued that "those of us interested in nineteenth-century American women writers may need to find ways to revitalize modes of criticism no longer fashionable because these modes may represent stages in the process of literary evaluation that we cannot do without," and I referred specifically to the techniques of close reading associated with the New Criticism of the 1950s and 1960s.[3] While those techniques were designed to establish and justify the canonization of a limited set of texts, I believe it is possible to disengage the methodology of New Criticism from its ideology and to use that methodology to serve very different political ends. Indeed, in recovering and reading women's texts from the last century, I think it is not only possible but desirable to use the master's tools to dismantle the master's house. For if a primary effect of New Critical methodology was to accord value to the objects of its attention—to find them worthy of intensive, sustained analysis, to assign them, in a word, the status of the analyzable—then to apply this methodology to texts that the ideology of New Criticism rejected as unworthy has a potentially radical effect. I would argue further that it is essential to undertake this activity at this moment in the construction of American literary history in order to prevent the possibility that a text such as *Hope Leslie* will be "re-vanished" on the grounds that there was really nothing to say about it anyway. It is in the effort to prevent such a disappearance that I offer the following unabashedly close reading.

I offer this essay as well as a way of reading texts by nineteenth-century American women that balances the polarity between the hagiography characteristic of the first phase of recovery, a hagiography directly proportional to the misogyny informing previous treatment of these writers and texts, and the critique associated with the second phase, a critique that implicates these writers and their texts in a variety of nineteenth-century racist, classist, and imperialist projects.[4] Like other late-twentieth-century readers of these texts, themselves recovering from the intensity associated with the alternating phases of celebration and critique, I want to move beyond the binary opposition of these impulses by proposing that what is admirable about *Hope Leslie* cannot be separated from what is problematic, and that, moreover, it is this very entanglement that makes the text worth recovering in the first place. In proposing this approach, I am also writing against what has been a primary model for the work of recovery, namely, the assumption that these works can be best understood in terms of a dominant text and a subtext—a conventional surface text that covers and contains a radical subtext (or vice versa, depending on the reader's politics). While such a model may indeed be useful for reading certain works, it tends to produce a false sense of coherence and to rationalize too readily what are clearly incompatible stories. My own approach, based on rhetorical analysis and informed by Joan Scott's work on French feminists, relies more on the concept of paradox than on coherence. Given Scott's analysis of the importance of coherence to the legitimation of ideological/political systems such as the French and American republics, and given her understanding of the role played by the production of "sexual difference" in achieving such coherence in the face of women's actual exclusion from the categories of individual and citizen, we may well conclude that those texts that have "only paradoxes to offer" are the ones we should most work to recover.[5]

Pre-text

Sedgwick opens *Hope Leslie* in England with the words of William Fletcher the elder, who represents all that is "old"—loyalty, obedience, sovereignty, authority, law: "Take good heed that the boy be taught unquestioning and unqualified loyalty to his sovereign—the Alpha and Omega of political duty. . . . One inquiry should suffice for a loyal subject. 'What is established?' and that being well ascertained, the line of duty is so plain, that he who runs may read. . . . Liberty, what is it! Daughter of disloyalty and mother of all misrule—who, from the hour that she tempted our first parents to forfeit paradise, hath ever worked mischief to our race."[6]

Fletcher's admonitions construct a "pre-text" that enables Sedgwick to propose her own theory for the origins of America. In contrast to the efforts of some of her contemporaries who gendered the nation's origins in intensely masculine terms—heroic forefathers battling a howling wilderness and warring against savage enemies—and equated republican America with manliness, Sedgwick offers a different vision of the relation of gender to the new nation. A good rhetorician, Fletcher places his most powerful argument last, convinced that by gendering "Liberty" feminine he will have created a natural and hence insuperable barrier to his nephew's identification with the concept. In the context of Sedgwick's text, however, Fletcher's strategy serves to associate the gendering of America, whether as feminine or masculine, with a specific set of political interests understood as emphatically un-American. Thus, for Sedgwick, America begins with the history of men like the younger William Fletcher who refuse to accept the gendering of "liberty" and are therefore immune to the gender terrorism of being labeled "women." Though her initial emphasis is on those men willing to pass as "women," Sedgwick's real agenda is the construction of a rhetoric that will enable women in America to become "men."

The pre-text of *Hope Leslie* provides Sedgwick with a pretext for beginning her work as well. Through the story of Alice Fletcher, forcibly prevented from joining her lover in passage to America, returned to her father's home against her will and ordered to marry a man of her father's choosing, Sedgwick represents the fate of biological women in a country where they have no chance of becoming "men." Though William Fletcher the younger is no seducer, Alice's attempted elopement to America evokes the history of Charlotte Temple. In *Hope Leslie*, Sedgwick defines *Charlotte Temple,* one of the most popular stories in America, even in 1827, as essentially un-American, a story of the old country, for whether dragged off by a seducer or dragged home by a father, women in stories like *Charlotte Temple* are subject to patriarchal control. Committed to the structures of heterosexual romantic love, both Charlotte and Alice seek America for the wrong reasons. In preventing Alice from reaching America, Sedgwick in effect reverses and undoes the story of Charlotte Temple, clearing the ground for a new and different story based on a different understanding of America. Moreover, Sedgwick embeds *Charlotte Temple* in the text of *Hope Leslie* through the story of Rosa and Sir Philip, and, as Christopher Castiglia has observed, when she concludes her own novel with an explosion that blows up both seduced and seducer, we recognize her desire to annihilate romantic love with its plot of "seduced and abandoned" as a basis for the story of America.[7]

Romantic love stands between women and the possibility of becoming "men" in part because it reifies the separation of public and private by gender, thus supporting a model of the civic in which events in the private sphere cannot or need not have any effect on the public sphere. In challenging this model, Sedgwick not only goes beyond the postulates of Enlightenment liberal feminism that did not, for the most part, challenge the division between public and private but only argued for women's larger inclusion in the public sphere; she also rewrites her own family history. As Mary Kelley has noted in her introduction to *The Power of Her Sympathy*, Sedgwick's father, whom she admired, even adored, assumed that service to one's country required putting aside the claims of the domestic and the private, even when doing so led to the depression, illness, and death of his wife.[8] According to Kelley, in the autobiographical memoir Sedgwick began when she was in her sixties, she articulates, however indirectly, the cost to women like her mother of her father's definition of citizenship, one that led him to serve twelve years in Congress and to be absent from home for long periods of time despite the evident distress this caused his wife. Much earlier, however, in *Hope Leslie*, Sedgwick had argued that there can be no meaningful understanding of public good separate from a recognition of its "private" cost, that in fact the true America cannot be built by men and women like her father and mother. Rather, the construction of America falls to the decidedly antiromantic Hope Leslie and to her "brother" Everell, whose understanding of citizenship makes no distinction between the public and private. When Everell rejects Governor Winthrop's argument for refusing to release Magawisca—namely, that "private feelings must yield to the public good"—he does so because he recognizes that in such formulations one person's private needs are in fact recast as public good (234).[9]

Republican Sisterhood

When the younger William Fletcher arrives in Boston, he almost immediately finds it necessary to move further west to achieve the condition of liberty for which he left the mother country. When the new so quickly becomes the old, when here becomes there, "America" emerges as a future possibility, perhaps an ever-receding one, but certainly one not yet realized in colonial Boston or the early republic of the United States. In this context the ahistoricity of Hope Leslie, a republican heroine two hundred years before her time who still occupies a space of future possibility in relation to "the girls of today," becomes legible as well. And if "America" is essentially a future possibility, then fiction provides an appropriate space for its construction through an imaginative act that might move the present toward that desired future. In *Women of the Republic*, Linda Kerber argues persuasively that in the years between 1790 and 1820 American women "were left to invent their own political character" and that they did so primarily by devoting their political imagination and energy to the construction of Republican motherhood.[10] Writing some few years after the end of the period Kerber analyzes, Sedgwick proposes in *Hope Leslie* a different and more radical model for the inclusion of women in the American Republic, a model I call "Republican sisterhood." While Republican motherhood brought women into the public and political sphere by focusing on a woman's role as the mother of sons and hence a producer of the nation's future citizens, *Hope Leslie* emphasizes the figure left out of this picture, the daughter, and holds out the hope that a daughter need not be a mother. Indeed, if Republican motherhood left the daughter out of the picture, absorbing her into the figure of the mother by conceiving of her as merely a mother in the making, *Hope Leslie* reverses the image, imagining the disappearance of the mother through her absorption into the daughter. Equally significant, the removal of the mother allows the son to be reconfigured as brother and substitutes the relation of brother and sister for the iconography of mother and son. In *Hope Leslie*, then, the daughter imagined primarily as a sister occupies the center of the picture, and because she inhabits the same subject position as her brother—in contrast to the Republican mother, whose subject position differs significantly from that of her son—she offers a different basis and hence an alternative model for women's inclusion in the American republic.

Sedgwick begins the text proper of her novel with Hope Leslie writing a very long letter to her absent "brother," Everell Fletcher. Since letters in *Hope*

Leslie figure as the site where one's "true" identity is revealed (for example, when we read Sir Philip's letters we discover who he "really" is), introducing Hope Leslie through letters authenticates her character, giving the reader grounds for believing that she really is what she appears to be. Moreover, if letters provide evidence of one's "true" identity, they by necessity provide evidence of identity itself. By writing, Hope reveals not only who she *really* is but that she really *is;* she establishes her ability to construct a coherent and functioning "I" and hence her possession of the kind of literacy that matters for citizenship—the literacy of subjectivity that makes her capable of writing her own version of "history." Further, with this epistolary opening the narrative voice is displaced by a character's voice, signaling from the outset the degree to which character voice and narrative voice are one and the same. In this text, then, whose pre-text includes the removal not only of Hope's biological mother but also of her potential surrogate mother, Mrs. Fletcher, the attack on Republican motherhood implicit in the violence of Mrs. Fletcher's removal extends even to narrative strategy, for in *Hope Leslie* there will be no "mother" voice to cover and contain the daughter.

Though the logic of Republican sisterhood requires the prior existence of the brother as ground for the claims of the sister, Sedgwick's narrative imaginatively inverts this priority to create a subliminal argument more radical still than the one she makes explicitly. This opening scene presents Everell as removed: Hope writes to him on the anniversary of his "recovery" from his first removal because he is once again removed, this time to England. Thus Sedgwick positions Hope as the original American, Eve preceding Adam in the garden.[11] Though this American Eve clearly needs her Adam/Everell, this need is not the need of romantic love, of opposites attracting and completing each other; rather, it is the need to discover someone just like her, someone who will identify with and be identical to her, who will mirror and support her. Though Hope possesses the literacy of subjectivity without Everell, her ability to construct him as identical to her plays a considerable part in her ability to construct herself through writing. Reporting her testimony to the magistrates on the question of Nelema's escape, Hope writes, "What I would fain call courage, Mr. Pynchon thought necessary to rebuke as presumption:—'Thou art somewhat forward, maiden,' he said, 'in giving thy opinion; but thou must know, that we regard it but as the whistle of a bird; withdraw, and leave judgment to thy elders'" (109). Clearly speech can be equivalent to silence, depending on who listens; and just as clearly Hope's literacy—her ability to write her own history, in which defending Nelema is understood as courage, not presumption—depends upon Everell's sympathetic ear.

Sedgwick's argument for the inclusion of women as equal partners in the American republic, whether now or in the future, depends upon the rhetoric of identity between brother and sister, a key component of Enlightenment liberal feminism. Thus Sedgwick carefully positions Everell as Hope's brother—his father should have been hers, her mother should have been his, they are raised together, and Hope signs her letter "sister," addressing him as "brother." Moreover, Sedgwick's initial description of Everell could easily describe Hope as well: "His smooth brow and bright curling hair, bore the stamp of the morning of life; hope and confidence and gladness beamed in the falcon glance of his keen blue eye; and love and frolic played about his lips. . . . [H]is quick elastic step truly expressed the untamed spirit of childhood" (22). We hardly need the word "hope" here to recognize the identity of this boy to the girl who bounds from the litter carrying her to Bethel and dashes forward to be reunited with her sister.

When, in the second half of the text, Sedgwick reintroduces her characters to each other upon Everell's return from England, she is even more careful to employ the rhetoric of sameness. She describes Hope as "open, fearless, and gay," with a face that reflects her "sportive, joyous, and kindly" feelings. Physically, Hope has the "elastic step and ductile grace which belongs to all agile animals"; intellectually, she has "permitted her mind to expand beyond the contracted boundaries of sectarian faith" (122, 123). In Everell, we find "a youth in manhood's earliest prime, with a frank, intelligent, and benevolent countenance over which . . . joy and anxiety flitted with rapid vicissitude" (124). Later we hear of his "unsubdued gaiety," his "unconstrained freedom," and the charm of his "ease, simplicity, and frankness" (136). Thus Hope is open and Everell frank; Everell is intelligent and Hope has an expanded mind; Hope is filled with kindly feelings and Everell is benevolent—the list could be expanded but the point is clear.

Though Sedgwick creates an escape hatch that will allow her to conform at the eleventh hour to the conventions of the novel and specifically of the historical romance, the relationship between Hope and Everell is decidedly antiromantic. Moreover, Everell's "universal" desirability—all the girls adore him—leads one to suspect that he functions less as an object of love than as the sign of a desired state of being, a desired subjectivity. He is what girls want to be more than to have, the brother as mirror and ground for what the American sister can also become, the point of comparison that enables women in America to imagine themselves as "men."

What Then Is the American, This New Person?

Writing to Everell, Hope describes how she managed, despite the initial resistance of her "father" and aunt, to become one of a party of men venturing to climb a nearby mountain: "I urged, that our new country developes faculties that young ladies, in England, were unconscious of possessing" (98). In this carefully crafted comment, Sedgwick indicates the difference America makes: Young women in England possess the same faculties as young women in America, but England keeps women unconscious and therefore undeveloped. America allows a woman like Hope Leslie to recognize in herself the same faculties developed and promoted in her "brother"—namely, those quintessential American virtues of independence, self-reliance, and self-determination. America develops in women the ability to think critically and hence to challenge established authority. Hope insists not only on the physical freedom to climb mountains and visit graveyards alone at night; she insists on intellectual freedom as well, having learned from the arguments of those around her to doubt all dogma and to let her mind expand "like the bird that spreads his wings and soars above the limits" (123). Perhaps most crucially, America develops in women that "reverence of self" that Judith Sargent Murray claimed was essential for the success of the new Republic in her essay of 1784, "Desultory Thoughts upon the Utility of Encouraging a Degree of Self-Complacency, Especially in Female Bosoms." Proposing that she "would early impress under proper regulations, a reverence of self . . . , that dignity, which is ever attendant upon self-approbation, arising from the genuine source of innate rectitude," Murray further suggests that such reverence for self would cure the "depression of soul" that she, like Mary Wollstonecraft, saw as afflicting many women "all their life long."[12]

Though Sedgwick gives Murray's concept a far more radical cast, Hope Leslie is clearly characterized by a "reverence of self . . . arising from the genuine source of innate rectitude." As Aunt Grafton puts it, "It's what everybody knows, who knows Hope, that she never did a wrong thing" (177)—and her hopefulness can be directly linked to her self-approbation. Moreover, Hope's reverence for self leads her to a decided lack of reverence for established authority, simply because it is established. Though rebuked for her "levity" and irreverence in suggesting to Mr. Holioke that they name the mountain they have just climbed after him, she observes that "the good man has never since spoken of his name-sake, without calling it '*Mount Holioke*,'" an observation designed to indicate to Everell that she has taken the measure of such men (101).

Hope's lack of reverence for authority manifests itself more seriously, however, in her willingness to challenge decisions on matters pertaining to the state and the "public good." Despite the disapproval of authority, Hope speaks out in defense of Nelema and when she fails to be heard takes matters into her own hands, releasing the prisoner and effecting her escape. Similarly, Hope agrees to participate in Everell's plan to free Magawisca, thereby risking her freedom and even her life by putting herself in the way of Sir Philip Gardiner and his plot. Indeed, Hope's courage in choosing to challenge the authority of the state becomes more pronounced when we recognize the degree to which the state perceives itself to be in danger and is willing to mobilize against such danger, whether real or apparent. References to treason and sedition, to plots against the state, appear with considerable frequency in *Hope Leslie,* a story that takes place against the background of the English Civil War with its monitory icon of a beheaded king. Within the text we have the multiply treacherous Sir Philip, the imprisoned Thomas Morton, instances of treachery within and among Indian tribes and between Indians and whites, and the threat of a possible conspiracy among the Indians to annihilate the English settlers. Though Sedgwick minimizes the reality of the last threat by portraying the Indian tribes as weak, dispirited, and internally divided, Hope's decision to free Magawisca suggests that she is indeed willing to take treason as her text in order to realize the possibility of America.[13] Thus the model of citizenship Sedgwick proposes as necessary to actualize the rhetorical premise of the equality of brother and sister requires acts of civil disobedience that may be labeled treason. Founded in the original treason of defying gender terrorism, the true and gender-neutral America may require continued acts of treason for its ultimate realization.

Sedgwick refrains, however, from making this claim an overt part of her text, for Magawisca's release in fact provokes no reprisal. Though Governor Winthrop does occasional duty as a patriarchal heavy, "impatient to put jesses on this wild bird of yours, while she is on our perch" by marrying her to William Hubbard, future author of the infamous portrayal of the slaughter of the Pequods whom Sedgwick quotes in her text, he also figures as the reconstructed father, reborn during the passage to America because he is willing to embrace the identity of "mother" and "daughter" in the pursuit of America (155). Thus we are led to believe that Winthrop too secretly desires Magawisca's release and approves of, even identifies with, Hope's act. In *Hope Leslie*, then, Sedgwick accomplishes nothing less than the deployment of biological woman as the representative American. Witty, smart, compassionate, gutsy, Hope Leslie is a lover of self and a challenger of arbitrary authority who, while insisting on her physical and intellectual freedom, is willing to take extreme risks for what she believes. She is a remarkably "American" figure, yet one whom we will not see again in American fiction for a long time. And despite the treasonous implications of her text, Sedgwick manages to keep Hope out of jail, both literally and figuratively. Yet we might well be justified in asking at what cost Sedgwick has produced this amazingly hopeful story. I turn now to a complex answer to this question, one that will, not surprisingly, present a far more complicated and less hopeful story.

Slippage and Modulation

Hope Leslie is clearly meant to be hopeful, yet whether by design or slip its title acknowledges the existence of a different tonality and a text that might as accurately be named *Hope-lessly*. As Dana Nelson observes in her own analysis, "tension and ambivalence mark the [text]," and "*Hope Leslie* is finally equivocal."[14] While Nelson locates this ambivalence partly in Sedgwick's investment in "Anglo-America's historical inheritance" and partly in the uneven developments of critique ("cultural hegemony is pervasive, and enlightenment not always foolproof"),[15] reading Sedgwick as both radical and conservative, I wish to argue that contradictions are an inevitable element of Sedgwick's project and that one cannot separate *Hope Leslie* from *Hope-lessly*. Slippages occur in the hope-ful text that operate as a kind of modulation, enabling us to move from one tonal register to another and to recognize that they are both part of the same composition. Writing to Everell, Hope remarks, "As you already know, Everell, therefore it is no confession, I love to have my own way" (114). While this phrase can seem a gender-neutral assertion of independence, a version of that "universal" American quality celebrated, for example, in Thoreau's "different drummer," in this context it has overtones of the willful, the self-indulgent, and the personal that can make it seem gender-specific, not indeed the locution of a "brother." Later, when Hope insists on remaining alone overnight on the island where Digby, the former family servant now himself modulated into the independent supervisor of the Governor's garden, resides, he situates her desire to have her own way in the context of America: "Why this having our own way, is what every body likes; it's the privilege we came to this wilderness world for" (225). Yet he also subtly undercuts the legitimacy of Hope's insistence by suggesting the potential irresponsibility of her willfulness: "I always said, Miss Hope, it was a pure mercy you chose the right way, for you always had yours" (225). Moreover, as events unfold, it becomes clear that Hope does not always choose the right way and that her insistence on having her own way places others as well as herself in danger. "Having my own way" becomes similarly gendered still later when Hope has recourse to methods of manipulation that can easily be labeled "feminine." In order to persuade Barnaby to let her visit Magawisca even though she does not have the authorizing pass, she bursts into tears, knowing that Barnaby will be unable to refuse "this little kindness" to "one who had been an angel of mercy to his habitation" (308).

Sedgwick similarly problematizes Hope's "reverence of self." In one of the novel's strangest scenes, she acknowledges certain anxieties on the subject of Hope's self-love, anxieties perhaps aggravated by her refusal to create a narrative voice that would itself put "jesses" on her character through narrative distance. Hope escapes being raped by the drunken sailors she encounters on her flight from Oneco by impersonating a Catholic saint; and while she justifies her act by claiming that the woman who became a saint "might not have been a great deal better than myself" (271), the excessiveness of her claim reminds readers that, where women are concerned, it may be hard to distinguish between an appropriate reverence for self and an inappropriate willingness to let the self be reverenced, for in a historical context in which self-love is specifically proscribed for women and in which women are socially constructed as selfless, self-love may seem, and even be, narcissistic. Thus while Sedgwick does present the rhetoric of "sister equals brother" as fixed and absolute, providing the theoretical ground for a gender-neutral America, she also, like Scott's French feminists who argue both "for the identity of all individuals and the difference of women,"[16] allows gender to function as a powerful field of force, destabilizing the rhetoric of equality and suggesting significant distinctions between sisters and brothers. If we return to the scene in question for a moment, we can move still closer to an understanding of the rhetorical complexity of *Hope Leslie*, for the very mechanism Sedgwick uses to restabilize her rhetoric of equality points to and opens up the central rhetorical fissure of the text.

When Esther rebukes Hope for taking her rescue out of the hands of providence and into her own, and for supporting superstition even to save her own life, Everell turns "disappointed away," recognizing only the difference between Esther and Hope (272). Implicitly asserting his identification with Hope, his response returns her reverence of self to the gender-neutral context of American self-reliance. In this scene, however, Esther becomes the scapegoat, attracting all the negative energy that might otherwise be directed at Hope. Indeed, throughout the text Hope is compared explicitly and implicitly to various "sisters" and, with the exception of Magawisca, always to her advantage. Primary among these sisters are, of course, the "English" twins, Rosa and Esther. Both are women who accept male authority and see their own position as subordinate, who regard romance and religion as the main concerns of women, and who accept the separation of public and private, which entails their own confinement to the latter. Though superficially Rosa appears the opposite of the severe, chaste, and religious Esther, their equal susceptibility to romantic love, with its attendant addiction to masculine authority and consequent lack of self-reverence, links them and distinguishes them from Hope.

But what are we to make of a text in which the logic of the sister-sister relationship is so different from the logic of the sister-brother relationship? What are we to make of a text that seeks to establish equality between brother and sister while insisting on distinctions among sisters, thus presumably arguing that only some sisters get to be equal to brothers, only some women get to be sisters? What are we to make of a text that is so hard on "sisters," in which Rosa commits suicide, Jennet is blown up, and Esther is exiled? This question becomes particularly acute and particularly painful when we turn our attention to the real sisters in the text. But it is only when we turn our attention to these figures that we can begin to grasp the complexity of *Hope Leslie* and to comprehend the extent of Sedgwick's "hopelessness."

"My sister! my sister!"

Perhaps no scene in *Hope Leslie* is so troubling as the one in which Hope is temporarily reunited with her long-lost sister, Mary/Faith/White Bird. (This sister, we might note, has another name, the Indian words translated as White Bird, that even Sedgwick recognizes cannot be uttered within her text.) This scene becomes less strange, however, if we read it as the moment when "Hope Leslie" encounters "Hope-lessly," when Sedgwick confronts the contradictory impulses of her text and her own rhetorical dilemma. In this scene, we see a different Hope, one who is revolted by rather than respectful of difference, one who cannot imagine that her sister has made choices or even that she has any life at all. Hope seems desperate to recover her sister, yet her efforts place that sister in actual danger; she is obsessed with keeping her sister, yet she loses her by resorting to cheap tricks. While we may understand why Hope views her sister as lost, we are less able to see why she should care so much, since she has been separated from this sister for years and has lived quite hopefully without her. Nor can we readily understand why she finds her sister's Indianness sickening and disgusting, since up to this point Hope's interactions with Indians have fallen within the liberal humanist and unitarian position of respect, recognition of essential sameness, and, in the case of Nelema, one might argue, even covert identification. Here, as elsewhere, Sedgwick's narrative voice doubles Hope's perspective, for Hope too constructs Mary as simply not there, without language or memory: Her face "pale and spiritless was only redeemed from absolute vacancy by an expression of gentleness and modesty" (229). Though one might expect Sedgwick to recognize the implications of the word "vacant," echoing as it does the phrase *vacuum domicilium* used by the English to justify their appropriation of Native American lands (126), like Hope she seems suddenly to be confronted with a difference so profound that she can only represent the fact that she cannot represent it.[17] But the difference of this scene, its strangeness and excessiveness, as well as its obvious contradictions—Hope wants to keep her sister but goes about it in a way guaranteed to lose her—forces us to confront extraordinary embedded questions: Why does Hope wish to recover her sister, why is she unsuccessful, and why is the experience of loss and failure so traumatic, placing her in both literal and spiritual danger? Answers to these questions become clearer if we raise another query: Who is the sister whom Hope has really lost and seeks to recover?

When Hope first encounters Magawisca disguised as a stranger selling moccasins who shows her a "necklace of hair and gold entwined together," she exclaims, "'My sister! my sister!'" (183). As Sandra Zagarell has observed, Sedgwick carefully constructs the relation of Hope and Magawisca as that of "metaphoric sisters. Their first meeting takes place in the Boston cemetery in which their mothers are buried. . . . In Winthrop, Magawisca and Hope share a symbolic Puritan father, . . . and they are literal sisters-in-law."[18] Moreover, when Hope finally meets Magawisca she is in effect recovering her "brother's" lost "sister." In this context we might be justified in reading Mary's "vacantness" as a sign that she represents a space actually occupied by someone else; she is not there because she is in fact not the "true" sister. If we imagine this sister to be Magawisca, then indeed we can begin to understand Hope's hopelessness.

In her preface, Sedgwick identifies Magawisca as the figure who represents her own creativity; in imagining Magawisca she allowed herself to move from the "actual" to the "possible." Given that in this text America itself is conceived as the possible, we might reasonably assume that for Sedgwick the fate of America is inextricably linked to the fate of Magawisca. Rhetorically speaking, Magawisca's function in the text is clear; she makes the argument, articulated by Sedgwick in her preface, "that the elements of virtue and intellect are not withheld from any branch of the human family" and "that the difference of character among the various races of the earth, arises mainly from difference of condition" (6). In other words, she makes the argument that "red equals white," just as Hope makes the argument that "sister equals brother." Moreover, Magawisca realizes the more radical implications of Sedgwick's rhetoric, for having "obtained an ascendancy over her father's mind by her extraordinary gifts and superior knowledge," she has acquired substantial political power in the world of the fathers, effectively displacing her brother in her father's affection and, more significantly, in his council (326). In a word, she is the daughter understood as son.

Presumably, when Magawisca returns to Boston, Hope has the opportunity to recover this sister as well as her birth sister, but ultimately Magawisca is as lost to her as Mary. We must then ask the final and most painful question: Why can't Hope keep this sister; why, like Rachel seeking her lost children, must she continue to lament, "'Oh, my sister! my sister!'" (188)?

Interlude

At the end of *Hope Leslie* both Hope and Everell beg Magawisca to remain in Boston and become "American," and to the degree that Sedgwick's rhetorical model has constructed her as same and equal this plea seems eminently reasonable. During Magawisca's trial, Sir Philip has been noticeably unsuccessful in his effort to render her as "other," since she so clearly possesses those virtues understood as "universal" and particularly those understood as universal to women (note, for example, the reference to "the modesty of her sex" [282]). Yet from the outset Sedgwick has also constructed Magawisca under the mark of difference. Though introduced as one "beautiful even to an European eye," in contrast to Everell, who "bore the stamp of the morning of life; hope and confidence and gladness," Magawisca's expression is one of "thoughtfulness, and deep dejection . . . , the legible record of her birth and wrongs" (23, 22, 23). Indeed, it is Magawisca's difference as much as her sameness that makes her attractive to Everell. In describing the interaction of Everell and Magawisca to her absent husband, Mrs. Fletcher describes a relationship that we might now identify as ideally multicultural:

> The boy doth greatly affect the company of the Pequod girl, Magawisca. If, in his studies, he meets with any trait of heroism, (and with such, truly, her mind doth seem naturally to assimilate) he straightway calleth for her and rendereth it into English, in which she hath made such marvellous progress, that I am sometimes startled with the beautiful forms in which she clothes her simple thoughts. She, in her turn, doth take much delight in describing to him the customs of her people, and relating their traditionary tales, which are like pictures, captivating to a youthful imagination. (31–32)

Similar enough to inhabit the same world, Magawisca and Everell are yet different enough to provide opportunities for each other's growth. Indeed, one could argue that Everell's and Hope's "expanded" minds depend upon Magawisca's difference, for they could not present themselves as open, tolerant, and unprejudiced if there were no differences to overcome. Yet Sedgwick's rhetorical model has no way of recognizing difference as an argument for equality. If Magawisca were to agree at the end to remain in "America," she would not in fact be able to retain those differences of race, religion, and culture that actually constitute her value. For if one argues for citizenship by invoking the rhetoric of equality, how can one at the same time promote a respect for difference? In thus confronting the limitations of her rhetorical model, Sedgwick indicates that political situations are actually far more complex than the rhetorical models designed to address them. We might recognize the persistence of this problem today in the language of affirmative action, for the phrase "women and minorities," by making women white and minorities male, excludes minority women. Since in the rhetoric of liberalism white men are understood as grounding all claims for equality, those who cannot be equated with them by either race or gender have no basis for their claims. One could make the affirmative action phrase inclusive by specifying "white women and minorities" or "women and minority males," but only at the cost of rhetorical power and the risk of being meaningless.

In this context we might acknowledge Sedgwick's courage in seeking to accomplish the rhetorically difficult and culturally unimaginable move of equating the racialized woman with the white man. Though her primary energy is clearly devoted to the equation of white women with white men, the relationship of Magawisca and Everell actually precedes that of Hope and Everell and constitutes an unprecedented and unduplicated moment in American literary history. That such an extraordinary equation should ultimately prove unstable and the strategy for accomplishing it unworkable is hardly surprising. Indeed, I have already indicated the inherent incompatibility of the value of difference with the rhetoric of equality. If we consider as well the issue of rhetorical power, we will find a further source of difficulty, for the rhetorical power of the equation of sister and brother finds its ground in the nonnegotiable privilege of the brother. To argue for the equation of sister with brother so as to make gender the sole and hence potentially insignificant variable requires from the outset a certain occlusion of race and class privilege. In making this argument, Sedgwick inevitably commits herself to a construction of the sister and brother as equally privileged except in the area of gender. Like Everell, Hope is rich, white, literate, and the beloved child of a member of the ruling elite. If we return for a moment to our first encounter with her, we may discover that her understanding of the privilege attendant upon difference is as powerful as her recognition of the privilege to be gained from similarity.

We first see Hope exercising her American sense of independence, which is also her feminine insistence on having her own way, when, over the protests of the Indian men who are carrying her, she leaps from the litter, giving each a tap on his ear "for," as she puts it, "your sulkiness" (70). That Hope's motive for exercising the privilege of race is her overwhelming desire to be reunited with her sister who has in fact just then "gone native" only underscores the extraordinary complexity of this text. Placing the problematic of the sister-sister relationship at the heart of a text designed to propose optimistically and even breezily the nonproblematic equation of brother and sister requires Sedgwick to critique the very rhetoric that structures her text. For a rhetoric designed to bring privileged white women into citizenship may not do much for their differently raced (or classed) sisters. To put it slightly differently, as long as the rhetoric of equality begins from the ground of the "brother," there will be no place in America for "my sister! my sister!"

Hopelessly

We might, however, be advisedly suspicious of an argument that explains Hope's loss solely in terms of the limitations of a rhetorical model, for hopelessness seems an excessive response to rhetorical frustration. To understand the text of *Hope-lessly*, we must look more closely at the relationship of Magawisca and Everell and at the reasons for the instability of this particular equation. In so doing we may discover not only an additional rhetorical complexity; we may also uncover the more profound emotional and political causes of this complexity and instability, for such an investigation leads inevitably to a recognition of the difference between the sister-sister relationship and the brother-sister equation.

Though Sedgwick clearly constructs *Hope Leslie* as an alternate history of relations between whites and Native Americans with Magawisca as an alternative to the image of both the savage savage (she is noble) and the noble savage (she is "white"), nothing in her text suggests that Sedgwick can imagine a future for Magawisca within America. Indeed, as we have noted, while Everell is introduced in terms of future possibility ("the morning of life"), Magawisca is consistently described by images that suggest the "evening" of life—something fading, disappearing. In her final exchange with Everell and Hope, Magawisca herself points to the impossibility, and perhaps even the speciousness of their hopes: "It cannot be—it cannot be. . . . [T]he Indian and the white man can no more mingle, and become one, than day and night" (330). While we surely would not fault Sedgwick for failing to imagine what no one of her time seemed capable of imagining—that is, how there could be a nation within a nation, persons who could be at once Indians and Americans—we might well fault her for participating in the "cult of the Vanishing American," that "elegiac mode" so common to the literature of the period that by asserting the inevitability of Indian removal naturalizes as it deplores it. Sedgwick's text could be said to accomplish what Lora Romero has called "the historical sleight-of-hand crucial to the topos of the doomed aboriginal: it represents the disappearance of the native as not just natural but as having already happened."[19] Though Sedgwick acknowledges at various points within *Hope Leslie* the actual motive behind the removal of native Americans (the desire for their land), and though she herself may well have protested the Indian Removal Act of 1830, she does not choose to use her text as an opportunity to challenge American complacency and complicity in removal or to propose that the failure to solve the conundrum of difference lies more in a lack of commitment than in the limitations of rhetorical models or a failure of imagination. Given the extent of Sedgwick's investment in Magawisca, we might well ask why she is willing to let her go. Or, to put it somewhat differently, we might ask whether or not Magawisca's removal serves interests still more powerful than those that would be served by her inclusion.

In the scene that begins a sequence of events that by their strangeness, their difference bring all the problems of the text to the surface, Digby makes an observation that seems to come out of nowhere: "Time was," says Digby, speaking to Everell, "when I viewed you as good as mated with Magawisca"; and Everell himself acknowledges, "I might have loved her" (214). Digby continues, however, by observing that it was just as well that Magawisca had "disappeared" before Hope's arrival at Bethel, "for I believe it would have broken [her] heart, to have been put in that kind of eclipse by Miss Leslie's coming between you and her," and he concludes by saying, "Now all is as it should be" (214). Digby's sense of resolution is, of course, premature, as it precipitates Hope's announcement of Everell and Esther's "engagement." In her haste to give Everell away to someone else, we might read an acknowledgment of Hope's discomfort with Digby's model of "natural" succession; indeed, we might read her response as evidence of her sense of the "unnaturalness" of her displacement of Magawisca and of the violence required to bring about the "should be" of her possession of Everell. While, as I have argued, the text of *Hope Leslie* is decidedly antiromantic, it may be more than just the conventions of the novel that brings about the intrusion of romance at this point in the text. Indeed, it may be that romance here serves to identify the heart of the problem in the relationship of sister to sister. For if Hope and Magawisca are constructed as rivals for the possession of Everell, then the relationship of sister to sister becomes antagonistic to that of sister to brother. And if this is so, we might expect to see as much effort directed to disrupting as to constructing the equation between sister and sister. In this context, we can better understand the relentless construction of difference between Hope and her sisters—Rosa, Esther, and Jennet—for this cumulative construction of difference supports the key distinction between Magawisca and Hope, which is muddled by the presentation of Magawisca as the red who equals white yet is clearly essential to removing Magawisca from competition with Hope.

To return, then, to the question of why Hope is unsuccessful in recovering her sister, we might say that the answer lies in the fact that as much as she wishes to recover her she equally wishes to remove her. And if we reconsider what Hope sees when she looks at her sister, we may understand more fully why she might desire her removal. In Mary's "vacantness" Hope confronts the terror of nonidentity—that absence of and from self she hopes to escape through identification with her brother—to which her identification with her sister inevitably leads. And in Mary's "degradation" Hope confronts the reality of her position as a woman, whether white or red, in the American republic of then and now. In this context, Sedgwick's assumption of the insignificance of gender, so essential to the hopeful part of *Hope Leslie*, turns into a fantasy designed to obscure the actual fact of women's radical inequality. References to the degraded condition of women break through the text in figures like Mrs. Fletcher, Madam Winthrop, Rosa, Esther, and even Magawisca, for in this context Magawisca's "redness" can be read less as a sign of race and more as a sign of gender. The rhetoric of sibling equality, then, works differently for sister and sister than for brother and sister; indeed, the one destabilizes the other as it threatens to reinforce the actual inequality of sister and brother by underscoring the significance of gender. For sisterhood, however powerful it may become, begins with the recognition of mutual misery, perhaps the reason that Hope flees the weeping Rosa. If equation with the brother represents for the sister a securing of identity and an accession to power, and if equation with the sister represents a potential threat to these possibilities, then we can appreciate the value of the construction of difference between sisters, for such difference provides the sole protection against the disintegration of identity embodied in sister Mary, "gone native."

Yet we must finally return to the implications of Sedgwick's decision to racialize the figure I have been calling the "real" sister. If we assume that her primary goal was to equate Hope and Everell and secondarily to equate Magawisca and Everell, and that these two equations would result in a third, that of Hope and Magawisca, we must ask what went wrong. The answer to this question lies not simply in the limitations of a rhetorical model that cannot at once argue for equality through sameness and promote a recognition of the value of cultural difference as an alternative basis for equality. Nor does it lie simply in the fact that the claim for the insignificance of gender is compromised by the equation of sister with sister. Rather, it also lies in the fact that Sedgwick had ultimately to confront her fear that her case for the equality of white women would be undermined if she made the same case for racially other women, that her argument for gender would be hopelessly compromised by the issue of race. Unable to imagine how she could both be and have her brother if she must also serve as the ground for her sister's equation with the brother, indeed if she must share him with her sister, Hope chooses to lose her sister.[20] In *Hope Leslie*, then, racial passing comes to seem as impossible and incomprehensible as gender passing seems obvious and simple, and the opportunity to become "men" is reserved for white women. And since the text imaginatively presents racial passing as more possible than gender passing—sister Mary becomes Indian, Magawisca could be white, but Rosa is unconvincingly male—we might argue that the construction of racial difference implicit in Hope's losing her sister is in fact essential to the argument for gender equality. If such be the case, then the rhetoric of *Hope Leslie* is hopelessly at odds with itself.[21]

Removal?

Hope Leslie provides powerful evidence of the anxiety that accompanies an argument for the equality of white middle-class "American" women. When Sir Philip Gardiner visits Magawisca in jail and is accidentally locked up in a cell with Thomas Morton, he experiences a terror out of proportion to either his situation or his character. We might therefore be justified in reading this terror symptomatically—somebody is afraid of being caught, imprisoned, and driven mad as the consequence of challenging the state. In *Declarations of Independence*, Bardes and Gossett acknowledge "the repeated concern with prisons and imprisonment found in Sedgwick's novels," and suggest that this pattern derives from Sedgwick's recognition that those who challenge authority, particularly women, may well end up in prison.[22] Indeed, within the text of *Hope Leslie* we find a representation of the woman whose claim to equality met with banishment and death, not indulgence and acceptance. This figure serves to remind us of the radical nature of *Hope Leslie*'s rhetoric of gender equality and of the potential danger in making such a claim. I refer, of course, to the figure of Anne Hutchinson, who makes her appearance almost immediately in the America of *Hope Leslie*. When Mr. Fletcher haltingly tries to tell his wife that the two children of his beloved Alice have arrived in Boston, she is "perplexed by his embarrassment," and immediately inquires, "[H]as poor deluded Mrs. Hutchinson again presumed to disturb the peace of God's people?" (19) That Hope Leslie's arrival in America should be marked by a reference to Anne Hutchinson seems hardly accidental. Although, according to Amy Lang, the view of Anne Hutchinson as "prompted to dissent by her resentment of the lowly status assigned women in New England" is "doubtful on a number of counts," what is clear, as Lang further observes, is that she came to be seen as the embodiment of the radical possibilities for women of the American experiment, the transformation attendant upon that North Atlantic passage.[23] In this light, her fate came to be understood as representing the danger attendant upon the argument for gender equality because it exposed the lengths to which male authority would go to protect its own interest.

This reading of Anne Hutchinson was, of course, particularly true for the early nineteenth century, and to find Hutchinson so immediately on the threshold of our text suggests that she provides a powerful interpretive frame for what follows, just as she does later for Hawthorne. Her significance is further underscored by the prominence in *Hope Leslie* of Governor Winthrop, historically the architect of her persecution, and by the fact that the trial of Magawisca corresponds with the date of Anne Hutchinson's death. Since the supporters of Hutchinson refused to take part in the expedition against the Pequods, we might be justified in reading the trial of Magawisca as a coded representation of the trial of Anne Hutchinson. But what, then, would we make of this "fact"?

For one thing, as previously suggested, the presence of Anne Hutchinson signals the radical nature of Sedgwick's argument for gender equality and identifies the dangers of taking up such an argument. For another, the displacement of the figure of Anne Hutchinson from Hope Leslie to Magawisca suggests that Sedgwick determined to handle this danger by removal, creating a text that potentially argues for the equality of race but ultimately abandons that potential to participate in the ideology of removal, the "inevitable" and "natural" disappearance of the Indian. That such a move serves the purpose of making the argument for gender equality look less radical by comparison seems clear. However, that the price Sedgwick pays for this strategy may be so extreme as to call into question the value of her entire rhetorical enterprise seems equally clear, for the identities of Catharine Sedgwick, Hope Leslie, Magawisca, and Anne Hutchinson are hopelessly entangled in this text, and to exclude Magawisca from the rhetoric of equality leaves a text as disfigured and disarmed as Magawisca herself. Yet the power of *Hope Leslie* lies in this very entanglement, and Sedgwick's most radical act may be to propose that a text so disfigured and disarmed is the only meaningful, whole text possible for an author willing to risk engagement with the actual mess of America in the effort to realize its potential. Textually speaking, Sedgwick refuses a model of separation and removal, insisting instead on a single text whose contradictions, compromises, and complicities she thrusts upon us, exposed and raw.

NOTES

1. Paperback sales for *Hope Leslie* from the date of publication by Rutgers Univ. Press (June 1987) to December 1997 are listed at 17,182. In the same series, comparable texts and figures include Fanny Fern's *Ruth Hall* (June 1986) at 17,775; Maria Cummins's *The Lamplighter* (October 1988) at 2,906; and Caroline Kirkland's *A New Home, Who'll Follow?* (April 1990) at 3,547.

2. Nina Baym, "Reinventing Lydia Sigourney," *American Literature* 62 (September 1990): 385.

3. Judith Fetterley, "Nineteenth-Century American Women Writers and the Politics of Recovery," *American Literary History* 6 (fall 1994): 605.

4. For an analysis of these two phases of recovery, see June Howard, "Unraveling Regions, Unsettling Periods: Sarah Orne Jewett and American Literary History," *American Literature* 68 (June 1996): 365–84. For examples of what I am calling the hagiographic phase as applied to *Hope Leslie*, see Christopher Castiglia, "In Praise of Extravagant Women: *Hope Leslie* and the Captivity Romance," *Legacy* 6 (fall 1989): 3–16;

and Sandra Zagarell, "Expanding 'America': Lydia Sigourney's *Sketch of Connecticut,* Catharine Sedgwick's *Hope Leslie,*" *Tulsa Studies in Women's Literature* 6 (fall 1987): 225–45. For readings of nineteenth-century American women and their texts as "complicit," see Richard Brodhead, *Cultures of Letters* (Chicago: Univ. of Chicago Press, 1993); Lori Merish, "'The Hand of Refined Taste' in the Frontier Landscape: Caroline Kirkland's *A New Home, Who'll Follow?* and the Feminization of American Consumerism," *American Quarterly* 45 (December 1993): 485–523; and more recently, Rosemarie Garland Thomson, "Benevolent Maternalism and Physically Disabled Figures: Dilemmas of Female Embodiment in Stowe, Davis, and Phelps," *American Literature* 68 (September 1996): 555–86.

5. See Joan Wallach Scott, *Only Paradoxes to Offer: French Feminists and the Rights of Man* (Cambridge, Mass.: Harvard Univ. Press, 1996), 1–18.

6. Catharine Maria Sedgwick, *Hope Leslie; or, Early Times in the Massachusetts* (1827; reprint, New Brunswick, N.J.: Rutgers Univ. Press, 1987), 7–8. All future references are to this edition and will be cited parenthetically in the text.

7. Castiglia, "Extra-vagant Women," 9–10.

8. *The Power of Her Sympathy: The Autobiography and Journal of Catharine Maria Sedgwick,* ed. Mary Kelley (Boston: Massachusetts Historical Society, 1993), 12–15.

9. Sedgwick identifies the public nature of "private" space at various points within her text. For example, the Indian guests of Governor Winthrop refuse their placement at a side table during a family dinner, aware that this apparently private act has major implications for public policy.

10. Linda K. Kerber, *Women of the Republic* (Chapel Hill: Univ. of North Carolina Press, 1980), 269. See especially Kerber's introduction, 7–12.

11. In arguing for the existence in the 1820s of "an admittedly short-lived female alternative" to the male construction of the genre of frontier fiction, Leland Person proposes as one of its components "an alternative, female, frontier fantasy—a pact between Indians and women, an Eden from which Adam rather than Eve has been excluded" ("The American Eve: Miscegenation and A Feminist Frontier Fiction," *American Quarterly* 37 [winter 1985]: 670). While I share Person's recognition of Sedgwick's manipulation of the Edenic myth, I do not see her as seeking to exclude Adam/Everell since he is so essential to the larger rhetorical strategy of her text. Indeed, it is his necessary inclusion that finally disrupts "the pact between Indians and women."

12. *Selected Writings of Judith Sargent Murray,* ed. Sharon M. Harris (New York: Oxford Univ. Press, 1995), 48.

13. The phrase "treason as her text" is intended to evoke the title and content of Lillian Robinson's "Treason Our Text: Feminist Challenges to the Literary Canon," *Tulsa Studies in Women's Literature* 2 (spring 1983): 83–98.

14. Dana D. Nelson, "Sympathy as Strategy in Sedgwick's *Hope Leslie,*" in *The Culture of Sentiment,* ed. Shirley Samuels (New York: Oxford Univ. Press, 1992), 200, 202.

15. *Ibid.,* 202, 199.

16. Scott, "Only Paradoxes," 11.

17. While one might argue, as would Nina Baym, that Hope's reaction stems from

her belief that Christianity is the only true faith and that she cannot bear to think of her sister as other than Christian, in the graveyard scene in which Hope and Magawisca meet to arrange for Hope to see her sister, Sedgwick actually distances herself from Hope's position. While Hope is relieved to discover that her sister is at least a Catholic, "for," as the narrator observes, "she thought that any Christian faith was better than none," Sedgwick does not indicate that this is her position and indeed she gives Magawisca the last word in the exchange (189). See Nina Baym, *American Women Writers and the Work of History, 1790–1860* (New Brunswick, N.J.: Rutgers Univ. Press, 1995), 156–62, and chap. 2.

18. Zagarell, "Expanding 'America,'" 237–38.

19. Lora Romero, "Vanishing Americans: Gender, Empire, and New Historicism," *American Literature* 63 (September 1991): 385.

20. Though I am focusing here on the rhetorical interests at stake, one might argue that Sedgwick's text is haunted by the economic interests at stake as well. In a footnote to the text of Sedgwick's *Autobiography*, Mary Kelley points out that the socioeconomic standing of Sedgwick's maternal grandparents was achieved by the profit they made from their management of the Stockbridge Indian School. If this is the case, then Sedgwick's own socioeconomic standing, essential to her career as author, indirectly derived from the act of Indian Removal. See Kelley, *Autobiography*, 46.

21. In "Catharine Sedgwick's 'Recital' of the Pequot War" (*American Literature* 66 [December 1994]: 641–62), Philip Gould arrives at a similar analysis of Sedgwick's rhetorical dilemma, though from a rather different if not necessarily oppositional understanding of her purpose. Arguing that Sedgwick's primary agenda in *Hope Leslie* is to redefine Republican Manhood as savagery and to replace this definition of virtue with one that reflected feminine values, he suggests that this gender agenda is subverted by her equal desire to humanize and defend the Pequots through an appeal to the very rhetoric of manhood she is seeking to displace. Therefore she presents them as people who "admirably chose to live free or die" and valorizes them "within the culturally sanctioned terms of masculine republican heroism." Thus he concludes that Sedgwick's text "demonstrates the difficulty of carrying on simultaneous revisions of gender and race." For Gould's discussion of this issue, see 651–52.

22. Barbara Bardes and Suzanne Gossett, *Declarations of Independence* (New Brunswick, N.J.: Rutgers Univ. Press, 1990), 35.

23. Amy Schrager Lang, *Prophetic Woman: Anne Hutchinson and the Problem of Dissent in the Literature of New England* (Berkeley and Los Angeles: Univ. of California Press, 1987), 41, 42.

6

𝒯 Excerpts from Reviews of *Clarence; or, A Tale of Our Own Times*

North American Review (January 1831): 73–95.

We know of nothing for which she is more remarkable, than her nice and discriminating habits of observation, and that fine tact, which with the directness of instinct, seizes upon what is important for the description of men and things, and rejects what is superfluous. She has an "eye practised like a blind man's touch," and she can distinguish instantly those minute shades which are so imperceptibly blended in nature as to seem but one color to common observers. . . . The same remark will apply to her descriptions of artificial life and manners;—such as . . . the picture in the second volume of Clarence, of the tone, dress, and conversation of the fashionable society of New York. . . . We are disposed to think more highly of this habit of discriminating observation, as a means of intellectual development, than most persons. He who goes about among men with his eyes open, will learn something better than the lore that is hidden in books. This is a thing in which women writers excel men; it is a merit almost peculiar to female writers. (Pp. 74–75)

Clarence is a tale of our own times, descriptive of the manners of the present day and of this country. . . . The spirit of sympathy makes us feel a keener interest in the adventures of characters who wear the same dress, dwell in the same land, speak the same language and are interested in the same subjects as ourselves—while on the other hand, the matter-of-fact air and garb of sober reality which the world now-a-days wears, precludes the possibility of romantic delusion; and the creative power is both limited in its materials and checked by severe laws in the employment of them. (P. 80)

In the second volume we are introduced into the gay world of New-York, and among the gilded swarm that enact the solemn farce of fashion; we breathe the scented air of drawing-rooms, our eyes are dazzled with the glare of candelabras, and our ears are familiar with the language of *persiflage*, and the shining counters that pass current in the *beau monde* for the sterling coin of sense. Our author seizes and embodies with magic skill the fleeting colors and changing forms of fashionable society, and the tone and manner of those who regard life as one long drawing-room, of the heartless and fascinating woman of the world, full of sentiment and devoid of virtue, of the curled fop, whose soul seems lost in the folds of his cravat, of honest and respectable vulgarity and of worthless refinement. (Pp. 83–84)

The most valuable and characteristic scenes are those in which the lash of playful satire is applied to the lesser foibles of life, and the unostentatious *home-bred* virtues are set forth and eulogised; for these are the traits which women have the most frequent opportunities of observing, and are the most skilful in catching and delineating. . . . (Pp. 89–90)

The Literary World (6 October 1849): 297–98. [Refers to the 1849 reissue of *Clarence*].

Ever since her first entrance into the world of letters her literary productions have been mainly, in every sense of the word, American. Not only have the scenes and incidents of her works of fiction been drawn from the history of this country or its domestic manners, but her more directly useful and perhaps most praiseworthy efforts have been in illustration of its social habits and tendencies. Besides this, there are perhaps none of our writers whose works in their spirit and style more completely reflect the prominent characteristics of the American mind. They are marked less by the refinements of highly cultivated taste and imagination than by a rigorous straightforwardness of purpose and a practical energy, of which the principal ingredient is that rare quality in authorship, good common sense.

. . . We think . . . that [*Clarence*] has a surer foundation—the foundation of good sense, active and enlightened sympathies, a genial warmth of sentiment, and an earnest energy of thought, ingredients which, while they would give the assurance of success to literary efforts of almost any description which taste or inclination might prompt, receive a higher impulse and a more satisfactory recompense when applied to advance the real and immediate interests of society, and to promote the culture of a *genuine* nationality. (P. 297)

Chapter 6

Disinterest as Moral Corrective
in *Clarence*'s Cultural Critique

PATRICIA LARSON KALAYJIAN

Catharine Maria Sedgwick's fourth novel, *Clarence; or, A Tale of Our Own Times*[1] (1830), opens by observing a physical and metaphorical urban landscape that announces the fiction's thematic content. The narrative voice describes—as from a second-story window—a wide-angle view of contemporary Lower Manhattan on a crisp February morning, when "*Broadway*, the thronged thoroughfare through which the full tide of human existence pours, the pride of the metropolis of our western world, presented its gayest and most brilliant aspect" (I, 7). In this vista are St. Paul's and Trinity Churches, but the narrator most highlights the "ostentatious brilliancy" of a city decorated with ice crystals, making New York appear "the very temple of art and fashion" (I, 8). What follows is a Whitmanesque catalog of the gradually arriving morning throng. The earliest to arrive are the poor charwomen and shopboys, who then give way to merchants and clerks; all are preparing to serve the array of stylish, gossiping customers who come to see and be seen on Broadway. Then the focus narrows on a "lonely being . . . who felt the desolateness of that deepest of all solitudes—the solitude of the crowd" (I, 10). We follow him as he passes Trinity Church and turns onto Wall Street, where the "butterfly world of Broadway" is replaced by an even more intense area of commercialization and exchange. Here pennies are clutched more tightly, and vendors are driven to more desperate measures to realize a profit for the day. In these opening pages, Sedgwick announces that *Clarence* is a critique of contemporary urban America that appraises a new society principally interested in material goods and profit making, a society that daily ignores its religious and social responsibilities by preferring gewgaws to good works, upward social mobility to spiritual improvement, and competition to compassion. As a corrective to such destructive tendencies, Sedgwick, via *Clarence*'s heroine Gertrude, offers the individual and society the option of disinterested action, the accomplishment of social good without regard to personal benefit.

Despite its timely and insightful evaluation, *Clarence* received little attention when it first appeared, and that trend has continued; when mentioned at all, it is as one of Sedgwick's lesser works.[2] Ironically, perhaps the current lack of attention may be attributable to a contemporary tendency to label or, as I would argue, mislabel *Clarence* as "domestic fiction." Domestic fiction is defined in the *Oxford Companion to Women's Writing in the United States* as "didactic and exemplary fiction centered in the 'women's sphere' and focusing on the concerns of women's lives." Indeed, Sedgwick is named therein as author of "the first full articulation of the form" in *A New-England Tale* (1822), and *Clarence* is included as a part of her domestic oeuvre.[3] Scholarship has largely rehabilitated domestic fiction from influential detractors like Fred Lewis Pattee in *The Feminine Fifties* (1936) and identified much of it as both subversive and empowering to its readers.[4] Whether we value or dismiss the category of domestic fiction, however, it seems to include every novel—occasionally excepting historical fiction—written by a woman between 1820 and 1880. As Susan K. Harris observes in *19th-Century American Women's Novels: Interpretive Strategies*, the problem with terms such as "domestic" and "sentimental" as genre descriptives "is that the terms themselves encourage us to continue approaching women's novels . . . within a particular hermeneutic that focuses on the social/sexual context and that, consequently, restricts our access to the novels' verbal, structural, and thematic adventures."[5] It is perhaps futile to argue that *Clarence* does not fit in such a capacious category, but I want to suggest that not only *Clarence* but also its critics are ill served when the novel is presupposed as part of such a vast designation.

Indeed, in categorizing *Clarence* as domestic fiction, our assumptions disable us, for we discover only that which we know we will find. We fail to entertain the notion that the text might be experimental and groundbreaking, a nascent novel of manners,[6] one of the first novels of the modern American city, and, within each of these subgenres, a powerful and insightful critique of contemporary society. Who would expect to find, in 1830, a "domestic" novel that takes as its subjects the effects of urbanization on American society, of industrialization and the rising middle class on the role of women, of surplus income on consumers, and of consumerism on the nation's soul? When we presuppose a gendered text, we may miss the central economic and political issues the novel engages: money, capitalism, consumerism, and the effects of all three on the contemporary urban landscape, both physical and moral. Nor are we likely to see that Sedgwick easily predates those major American figures—Emerson, Thoreau, Hawthorne, Melville—who achieved modern literary fame for having engaged similar subjects. Although Sedgwick's subjectivity may be distinctly female, it is anachronistic for us to read *Clarence* as women's fiction when Sedgwick herself would not have narrowed her field of readers in a like manner. Michael Davitt Bell emphatically points out that the "differentiation of men's and women's fictional tradition, never absolute in any case, took place later" than the 1820s and 1830s; he dates this gendered division to the 1850s.[7]

When we read *Clarence* outside the prescriptive category of domestic fiction, we see that Sedgwick uses her familiarity with New York City (two of her brothers lived there, and she generally spent every winter and spring in their homes) to describe the newly realized urbanization of the city. New York by 1820 "had become a center of capitalist development, a staging ground of the great transformations of the industrial wage system."[8] Henry James would complain decades later of the thin fabric of American society, but Sedgwick ably weaves together a remarkable tapestry of New York City's various classes and ethnic groups against a background of shops and homes, gambling halls and masquerades, auction houses and courtrooms. As her readers would expect her to do, the author as moralist moves beyond objective representation to offer a subjective critique of the just-emerging urban culture of excess income and the consumption of unnecessary goods and services. Sedgwick's fiction always has an improving message, and *Clarence* is no exception to this rule. Here, the lessons to be learned have to do with money and how to use it for the public good rather than for personal aggrandizement.

Sedgwick succinctly outlined her literary intentions in the preface to the earlier *A New-England Tale:* to "add something to the scanty stock of native American literature" and to provide some "sketches of the character and manners of our own country" via a "simple moral tale." Along with the feminine desire to remain a private woman that Mary Kelley describes in *Private Woman, Public Stage* (1984), Sedgwick's choice to publish anonymously suggests a wish to be read without her gender factoring into the writer-reader equation. As she does in her other novels (in which she tackles such diverse issues as religion, regionalism, relations with Native Americans, slavery, the emerging class system, and the Revolutionary War), in *Clarence* Sedgwick engages every theme as a citizen, a patriot, a social critic, a moralist. Despite her possible discomfort with her role as author and with her consequent fame, Sedgwick felt obliged to write, as she made clear in a 17 December 1835 journal entry: "When I feel that my writings have made anyone happier or better I feel an emotion of gratitude to Him who has made me the medium of any blessing to my fellow creatures. And I do feel that I am but the instrument."[9] God had given her talents, and, equally importantly, her family had given her a sense of public responsibility. Her society denied her the option of public service in her family's preferred role of lawyer or statesman, and she herself rejected Republican Motherhood, the conventional patriotic option open to women.[10] Writing, though it troubled the boundaries of women's accepted roles, offered Sedgwick an alternative for public service.[11]

Sedgwick's focus on the potentially destructive qualities of capitalism, consumerism, and commodification in *Clarence* suggests her dis-ease with the current moral state in the new republic. She was not alone in believing that the American character needed improvement. In *The Radicalism of the American Revolution*, Gordon S. Wood points out that American values had changed rapidly from those espoused by colonial monarchism to those of classical republicanism and then to an entirely unexpected social construct determined by liberal democracy. "America had . . . emerged as the most egalitarian, most materialistic, most individualistic . . . society in Western history," according to Wood. "People in the early nineteenth century sensed that everything had changed."

> In the early republic, then, America suddenly emerged a prosperous, scrambling, enterprising society not because the Constitution was created or because a few leaders formed a national bank, but because ordinary people, hundreds of thousands of them, began working harder to make money and "get ahead." Americans seemed to be a people totally absorbed in the individual pursuit of money.[12]

Sedgwick recognized these cultural changes, and, from those opening pages of *Clarence* described above, the reader encounters the bustling marketplace that is modern America. When the narrator describes a man turning his back on Trinity Church and walking up Wall Street (already long-identified with the stock market), it is clearly a symbolic as well as literal act. Sedgwick's *Clarence* is not only a depiction of the urban landscape where this process of "getting ahead" seems most intense, but also a challenge to capitalism and the selfish pursuit of profit, social status, and material possessions.

Clarence is the story of three families: the Clarences, the Roscoes, and the Laytons. The first quarter of the novel focuses on the Clarence family (in typical Sedgwick fashion, these chapters predate the main events). The novel begins with the saga of a modestly comfortable working-class family, who, through the young son Frank, meet and eventually take into their home an ailing man of no apparent means who proves to be Frank's grandfather. The long-lost parent makes it clear that his vast wealth has never brought him happiness; indeed, it has broken up his marriage and separated him from both his sons—one legitimate (Frank's father, Charles) and the other illegitimate and biracial. When the old man dies, he endows the family with substantial property. The Clarence family fortunes rise, but important lessons about true value are painfully learned; the inheritance indirectly brings about the death of the angelic Frank. The Roscoe family experiences not a gain in fortune but a loss. When Mr. Roscoe dies, he leaves his wife and son Gerald with considerable debt, which they choose to discharge by reducing their lifestyle. Gerald goes to work as a lawyer. In contrast, the Laytons (who enter the plot with the main time frame, several years later) are an aristocratic family who live on an economic margin continually threatened by both Mrs. Layton's grand lifestyle and Mr. Layton's gambling. When Mr. Layton cheats at cards, he is discovered by a wealthy stranger named Pedrillo; Pedrillo holds Layton hostage to this slanderous information and claims the family's eldest daughter, Emilie, as the price of his silence.

Sedgwick weaves the three families' fortunes together, introducing into the tale a variety of other characters, including a lovesick artist, Louis Seton; a brother and sister, the former in love with Emilie; and several suitors for Gertrude Clarence, the novel's heroine, who is now considered a desirable "fortune." Gertrude perceives this economic reality, and she endeavors throughout the novel to keep herself from becoming a mere commodity on the marriage market. She has her eye on Gerald Roscoe, but she hides her identity in order to assure herself that he loves her and not her money, that he is, in the parlance of the times, "disinterested" in his affection. In a parallel plot, Gertrude intercedes on Emilie's behalf in order to prevent her being sold to Pedrillo to pay off her father's dishonorable debt. Sedgwick's special emphasis on the negative effects of money on the young nation's children—its future citizens—is surely no accident but rather intentional and cautionary. From the outset of *Clarence*, money, far from securing happiness and stability, drives families apart and often buys children either orphanages or early graves.

Money has become the only measure of success in fashionable society. Mrs. Roscoe is urged to declare bankruptcy when her husband dies so that she can repay his debts with pennies on the dollar. When she refuses and can no longer keep up appearances, she is snubbed by friends who value only the status money buys. In contrast, to maintain an elaborate façade of money and standing and later to protect his reputation, Mr. Layton and his wife both place their status above everything else, even their parental duties, using their daughter as a marker against the father's financial and social debts. Layton continues his self-destructive lifestyle, and his wife remains the aging but magnetic belle of New York's *haut monde*. He blames her for her spending and her failure to be a moral corrective; she finds him merely a bore. Both are willing to force their daughter into marriage with a man Emilie despises and fears. Whatever the commodity—whether goods, privilege, status, or a marriage partner—Sedgwick seems to be saying, it is for sale in New York City in the early nineteenth century.

Urban prosperity has other deleterious effects on society, according to Sedgwick, than superficiality and commodification. Nor are these social crises confined to the upper class. The working class and the emerging middle class are also susceptible to the allure of money and the easy flexibility of social status. Scanning the social landscape of the city, the narrator finds that the role of middle-class women is eroding into a round of meaningless social gatherings and a compulsion to buy unnecessary goods. One scene late in the novel places Gertrude Clarence with Gerald Roscoe at an estate auction. There Gertrude encounters several women from the poor neighborhood in which she grew up. These women's fortunes have also improved; their husbands have had success in business and have moved up a social ladder built of dollar bills, business contracts, and emulative consumption. The women—the families' principal consumers—now maintain large households with "immense parlor[s] overloaded with costly, ill-assorted, and cumbrous furniture, where the very walls . . . seemed to say, 'we can afford to pay for it'" (II, 56). Many of these assorted goods are acquired at auction; the thrifty natures of these newly enriched matrons make bargains irresistible, even when they have no use for what they purchase. Gertrude observes of one old friend, Mrs. Stanley, that nothing "in life seems to interest her so much as an auction bargain" (II, 72).

Of this same Mrs. Stanley, Sedgwick writes that she had been "a bustling notable woman" but "had been thrown out of her natural orbit" by good fortune and now was "'of no farther use to society.'"

> She would have made a most meritorious shop-keeper, or a surpassing milliner. There are few persons fit to be trusted with the selection of a mode of life, or who suspect how much they owe to Providence, for assigning to them an inevitable occupation. In our country, the idlers of fortune are to be compassionated. We have as yet no provisions for such . . . ; they are not numerous enough to form a class, and each individual is left to his own resources. A rich, motherless, uneducated, unintellectual woman, is one of the most pitiable of these sufferers. If she has no taste for the management of public charities, and no nerves to keep her at home; if she is healthy and active, she takes to morning visiting, shopping, frequenting auctions, and to that most vapid of all modes of human congregating—tea-parties. (II, 64–65)

Sedgwick actually describes and decries what we recognize as conspicuous consumption and leisure, phenomena named and defined seventy years later by the controversial social scientist Thorstein Veblen in *The Theory of the Leisure Class* (1899) as the necessary but unpaid occupations of middle-class women.[13] As performers of meaningless acts, such as those Sedgwick enumerates, and purchasers of unnecessary goods, women serve to affirm the "pecuniary strength" and middle-class rank of their laboring husbands. Sedgwick also understands that, for such upwardly mobile women, these time-consuming and tedious pursuits replace the pleasure of useful, productive employment, or what Veblen calls "the instinct of workmanship."[14] Whereas Veblen observes and explains capitalist culture with at least a show of objectivity, Sedgwick's authorial voice does not hesitate to offer a moral judgment on the new capitalism. These modern social realities, the novel warns, conspire to destroy the old community-value system of Puritan moderation and godliness and encourage both profligacy and superficiality as the dominant qualities of the new individualistic urban American landscape.

Against her descriptions of this new society, engaged as it is in mindless consuming and pointless activity, Sedgwick privileges an alternative use for a citizen's money or time or talents: to do something good without a reward—to be disinterested. According to Wood, disinterestedness is "the term the eighteenth century most often used as a synonym for civic virtue," and a disinterested person is "someone who is capable of rising above private advantage and being unselfish and unbiased." However, in the original context of the term, a social hierarchy exists, and the disinterested person must always be a gentleman and therefore "free from dependence" on such externals as the vicissitudes of the marketplace. Women and working people—all of whom are by definition dependent on others—can never achieve disinterest in this era's social construct.[15] Later, as the political formulation of the new United States evolves toward democracy (from its origins as an English colony and therefore a republican monarchy), the designation of gentleman takes on new meaning. "Gentleman" had traditionally meant a man who was born to the rank and who did not need to work. In the new democratic environment of early-nineteenth-century America, however, "[l]eisure became idleness, work became respectable, and nearly every adult white male became a gentleman."[16] Disinterest in its older application becomes obsolete since all men—even gentlemen—work and are therefore "interested" or vested (by their pursuit of profit) in public decision-making. For all practical intents, America's democracy makes work universal and, hence, no one above the temptation of self-interest. The inverse also applies: Disinterest is universally accessible, too, and not exclusively the province of the rich. Disinterest is unbound from its earlier class restrictions and, for Sedgwick, becomes a Christian virtue perhaps akin to altruism. As the authorial voice in *Clarence* explains, a "perfectly disinterested action is a demonstration to the spirit of its alliance and communion with the divine nature—an entrance into the joy of its Lord" (II, 190). If all men and women face the temptation to behave only in their own self-interest, each can choose to act in a disinterested or benevolent fashion as well.

Clarence records a kind of social battleground between these contrary impulses, the lower impulse of self-aggrandizement and the higher one that emphasizes the good of the community. In her novel, Sedgwick criticizes a particular politician, who, without the constraints either of a tradition of civic virtue or of personal morality, seeks added power, influence, and status. He is disapproved of as " 'a calculating sensualist, governed by one object and motive, his own interest' " (I, 58), a man who "flattered women for their love, men for their favor, and the people for their suffrages. From the first he received all grace, from the second, consideration, and from the last, office and political distinction" (I, 129).[17] The novel clearly laments such interested actions—whether in the public or private sphere—as destructive to the national good. Sedgwick does not, however, agree that self-interest must be the inevitable and universal response to contemporary life. A cynical old man warns a child early in the novel " 'that there are no disinterested services in this world!' " (I, 23), but his faith in humanity is restored when he does in fact find " 'what I believed did not exist—a disinterested man' " (I, 66). Again, in the private sphere, Mr. Clarence remarks that a suitor to his wealthy daughter " 'is not all I could have wished for you . . . but he is pure, and disinterested, and talented' " (I, 160). Gertrude cannot love this man, but "she felt a glow of satisfaction that she had excited one pure, disinterested sentiment" (I, 235). Out of the home and family and in the public tumult of a court trial during which testimony has been bought and sold, Sedgwick describes a young man who testifies honestly as having the "disinterested enthusiasm of a young friend" (I, 84). Nor is disinterest in the public world confined to men. A gentlewoman who is teaching poor children is acclaimed for being " 'as much engaged in [her teaching] as if it was [in] her own interest' " (II, 80). Nor are the poor excluded from the possibility of true generosity, for, says one character, the " 'most energetic, self-denying, and disinterested persons I have ever known, have been made so by the force of necessity' " (I, 49). The term "disinterest" here potentiates a range of positive responses, from the passive—not exhibiting selfish motives—to the active performance of benevolent acts. In the new American democracy, not only the poor are venal and not only the rich are generous; women as well as men have opportunities to contribute in a disinterested fashion to the larger well-being of the community.

Gertrude Clarence is a model of this disinterest as she scrupulously avoids even the appearance of self-interest when she gives Mr. Layton sixty thousand dollars to redeem Emilie from a marriage to Pedrillo. The text makes it clear that Gertrude has no hope or even desire of being repaid this enormous sum of money. Her only reward is "the consciousness of benevolent and successful efforts for others; of efforts to which one is not impelled by any authorized claim, which the world does not demand, nor reward, nor can ever know—which can have no motive, nor result in self" (II, 190). Of course, not every young woman could hope to make such a magnanimous and costly gesture, so

Sedgwick shows Gertrude performing innumerable small acts of kindness and generosity in the course of the novel. (Hers are the virtues of Sedgwick's heroines in general, each of whom seems a magnet for those in need and each of whom acts without regard for personal gain or safety.) Gertrude exists in marked contrast not only to the venality of both the above-mentioned politician and the aristocratic Mrs. Layton but also to the material excesses of the middle-class women at the auction. Gertrude avoids the shallowness of others, according to the text, because Mr. Clarence raised her in the New England countryside, since the "formation of Gertrude's character was the first object of his life, and he wished, while it was flexible, to secure for it the happiest external influences" (I, 147). Kept from the superficial values of New York City's fashionable society until her adulthood, Gertrude appreciates the arts, reads widely and with insight, runs her father's household with calm ingenuity and minimum effort, enjoys travel, and attends lectures with the expressed intention of learning something—not simply to see and be seen as is the more common case among the "flippant idlers of fashionable life" (I, 148). Because she needs nothing, she buys nothing; money not spent on things is available to afford her "the luxury of giving" (I, 47).

If Gertrude sounds just a bit too good to be true for skeptical modern tastes, Sedgwick's narrator describes her as a "fit heroine for the 19th century; practical, efficient, direct, and decided—a rational woman—that beau-ideal of all devotees to the ruling spirit of the age—utility. But it must be confessed she had certain infirmities of olden and romantic times clinging to her" (I, 239–40), including a romantic imagination and a love of nature. Not a beauty, Gertrude is what is crassly referred to as a "fortune," a depersonalizing recognition of the vast wealth to which she is the sole heir. Witnessing pretty Emilie commodified as a bride to be sold for her looks, Gertrude fears she herself might become merely an expensive prize to be won by the most enterprising suitor. Within the economy of the novel, the only way Gertrude can be assured of a suitor's "disinterestedness" is to withhold her identity during courtship.

Gerald Roscoe's disinterest is ascertained only through a complex game whereby Gertrude keeps her identity secret only from him—a plot device that strains the reader's suspension of disbelief well into the last chapters of the six-hundred-page novel. One contemporary critic quipped that Gerald exhibits a "want of shrewdness very discreditable, if not to a hero, then certainly to a man. . . . [He] does not find out till the last moment the name of his fair enslaver; and he a lawyer, strange to say. The story, if it ever spread much, must have been fatal to his rise at the bar."[18] Although this plotting does create a series of awkward junctures that undermine the text's probability, it serves its moral economy. Before they meet, Gertrude knows of Gerald first because he was a childhood friend of her dead brother and second because he is in the employ of her father. But Gertrude has spent her youth in the country, and so they have remained strangers. What Gerald has heard of Gertrude is that she is a "comely little body—amiable and rather clever" (I, 135); this damning faint praise, along with a nature he assumes ruined by her fortune, makes him uninterested in her—disinterested, in fact.

Gertrude is indeed a fit heroine for the nineteenth century, in that she is an object of desire to most in direct proportion to her market value. Though her other suitors may like her, she has reason to believe they like her money more. Gerald's ignorance of her allows Gertrude to create her identity in his presence solely by what she does and says, free of preconceptions tainted by her good "fortune." Sedgwick alters the system of value rhetorically, denying the desirer Gertrude's true market value and thereby revising the cultural and literary marriage plot. By esteeming Gertrude's generosity more highly than her fortune, her intelligence more than her social status, and her sense of moral purpose above all else, the novel offers an implicit critique of the consumerist cultural ideology that Sedgwick clearly found so troubling. Neither selfless (had she been, she might have married the man who loved her but whom she did not love in return) nor selfish, Gertrude may not have the sassy appeal of Hope Leslie, but Sedgwick is writing a realistic novel of her own times—not a historical romance.

Mrs. Layton is actually the more intriguing character—smart, witty, wily, and sufficiently weak to seem human and comprehensible. But she is a symptom of her culture's malaise, not a cure. Indeed, she is an excellent example of the miseducated woman that Mary Wollstonecraft deplores in *A Vindication of the Rights of Woman* (1792), a woman trained only to be desirable and flirtatious, who then has no means to satisfy herself after marriage except by continuing to work her charms. Wollstonecraft argues that male writers like Jean-Jacques Rousseau, who "have warmly indicated that the whole tendency of female education ought to be directed to one point—to render them pleasing," are, in fact, creating unforeseen problems for women and for men alike. When a woman is educated only to please, Wollstonecraft asks, will she after years of marriage "have sufficient native energy to look into herself for comfort, and cultivate her dormant faculties? or is it more rational to expect that she will try to please other men? . . ."[19]

Women like those Wollstonecraft describes and like Mrs. Layton value themselves only as commodities, as objects of desire needing potential consumers to validate their worth. In her need to remain desirable, Mrs. Layton has become so selfish that she cannot resist buying a bauble with the money she has scraped together to pay her desperate maid's back wages, and she is willing to see her daughter married against her will because it is profitable. Mrs. Layton will not even listen to Emilie's pleas; without a touch of irony the wretched daughter regrets that her "mama . . . suffers so much when any thing crosses her" (I, 173). Within this culture of unrestrained materialism and egocentric individualism, which again threatens the well-being of the nation's children, Gertrude is indeed formed for utility, for usefulness. She and the disinterestedness she exemplifies are the social glue necessary to bind together a society Sedgwick must have felt was relentlessly fragmenting.

As a keen observer of contemporary life, Sedgwick focuses *Clarence* on two related themes: On one hand, she critiques the new national obsession with making and spending money, and, on the other, she explores evolving concepts of disinterestedness—an important civic notion she refines and applies socially across boundaries of class and gender. Whereas disinterest was historically the province of the wealthy, who alone could be above the pettiness of self-interest, democracy made disinterest possible to both rich and poor. Gertrude has great wealth that enables her to help a desperate girl escape an unwanted marriage, but in the earliest pages of the novel a little boy also performs acts of unselfish benevolence to a man in need of physical and emotional relief. In these and multiple instances throughout *Clarence*, disinterestedness becomes a pure benevolence affiliated with Christian tenets. Sedgwick identifies disinterest as a necessary corrective to the new American obsession with acquisition, and it is the urban phenomena of capitalism, consumerism, and self-involvement that she ably associates with a range of citizens from Mr. and Mrs. Layton to Mrs. Stanley and others of the rising middle class. If she could not stem the tide of American materialism with one novel, Sedgwick did, through *Clarence*, give American readers a view of the negative potential inherent in capitalist individualism and a vision of a community both more democratic and more generous than one governed by mere self-interest and competition.

NOTES

1. Catharine Maria Sedgwick, *Clarence; or, A Tale of Our Own Times,* 2 vols. (Philadelphia: Carey and Lea, 1830). All page numbers are provided parenthetically with the volume number.

2. *Clarence* was reviewed at some length in the *North American Review* (32 [1831]: 73–95), but went unnoticed by other contemporary critics. When the novel was reissued in 1849, *Sartain's Union Magazine* (8 [1851]: 142) and *The Literary World* (5 [1849]: 297–98) gave it brief attention. Because it is concerned with life in New York City, we might expect it to find some consideration in studies about the American urban experience

and, indeed, *Clarence* rates a rare and admiring mention in George Arthur Dunlap's *The City in the American Novel* (New York: Russell and Russell, 1934). More recent examinations of literature and the American city, however, ignore both Sedgwick and *Clarence*. For example, Robert A. Gates's *The New York Vision* (Lanham, Md.: Univ. Press of America, 1987), and Sidney H. Bremer's *Urban Intersections* (Urbana: Univ. Press of Illinois, 1992), each considers James Fenimore Cooper's *Home as Found* but makes no mention of *Clarence*. A search of the Modern Language Association index yields no articles listed on *Clarence* in modern scholarly journals.

3. Cathy N. Davidson and Linda Wagner-Martin, eds., *The Oxford Companion to Women's Writing in the United States* (New York: Oxford Univ. Press, 1995), 253.

4. For seminal discussions of the nature, history, and definition of the domestic novel, see Nina Baym, *Woman's Fiction: A Guide to Novels by and about Women in America, 1820–1870* (Ithaca, N.Y.: Cornell Univ. Press, 1978); Nina Baym, *Novels, Readers, and Reviewers: Responses to Fiction in Antebellum America* (Ithaca, N.Y.: Cornell Univ. Press, 1984), 201–7; Jane Tompkins, *Sensational Designs: The Cultural Work of American Fiction, 1790–1860* (New York: Oxford Univ. Press, 1985); and Mary Kelley, *Private Woman, Public Stage: Literary Domesticity in Nineteenth-Century America* (New York: Oxford Univ. Press, 1985). The concept is continued, theorized, and questioned in such works as Ann Romines, *The Home Plot: Women, Writing and Domestic Ritual* (Amherst: Univ. of Massachusetts Press, 1992); Helen Fiddyment Levy, *Fiction of the Home Place: Jewett, Cather, Glasgow, Porter, Welty, and Naylor* (Jackson: Univ. Press of Mississippi, 1992); and in several essays in Joyce W. Warren, ed., *The (Other) American Traditions: Nineteenth-Century Women Writers* (New Brunswick, N.J.: Rutgers Univ. Press, 1993).

5. Susan K. Harris, *19th-Century American Women's Novels: Interpretive Strategies* (Cambridge: Cambridge Univ. Press, 1990).

6. Hugh H. Holman and William Harmon's *A Handbook to Literature*, 5th ed. (New York: Macmillan, 1986), defines the novel of manners as a novel "in which the dominant forces are the social customs, manners, conventions, and habits of a definite social class at a particular time and place. In the true novel of manners the mores of a specific group, defined and described in detail and with great accuracy, become powerful controls over characters. The novel of manners is often, although by no means always, satiric; it is always realistic in manner, however." Nineteenth-century writers closely associated with this subgenre include English author Jane Austen (Sedgwick's near-contemporary), but America's most famous exemplars—Henry James and Edith Wharton—did not begin their careers until the late 1870s and late 1890s, respectively.

7. Michael Davitt Bell, in *The Cambridge History of American Literature*, vol. 2, *Prose Writers, 1820–1865*, ed. Sacvan Bercovitch (Cambridge: Cambridge Univ. Press, 1995), 43.

8. Christine Stansell, *City of Women: Sex and Class in New York, 1789–1860* (Urbana: Univ. of Illinois Press, 1987), 4.

9. *The Power of Her Sympathy: The Autobiography and Journal of Catharine Maria Sedgwick*, ed. Mary Kelley (Boston: Massachusetts Historical Society, 1993), 151.

10. Republican Motherhood is described by Nancy Woloch in *Women and the*

American Experience, vol. 1, *To 1920,* 2nd ed. (New York: McGraw-Hill, 1994), as a justification for female education in the new American Republic. The educated mother could, in addition to other benefits to her husband and family, "also fill a civic role. . . . Well-trained mothers . . . would be responsible not only for instructing daughters, whose upbringing had customarily been in their hands, but for shaping the values of their sons, who were likely to have a direct impact on the nation's success." Women were thus included "in the new nation, at least on the periphery of political life" (90).

11. This sense of literary mission intersects in an interesting way with Sedgwick's notions of class. Whatever her democratic protestations, this Federalist's daughter was always a recovering aristocrat—the result of which was a certain *noblesse oblige* we see most obviously in her later didactic tales. On 24 August 1837, after she had turned away from the writing of novels for a time and concentrated on writing didactic fictions, Sedgwick wrote to William Ellery Channing:

> I thank Heaven that I am not now working for the poor and perishable rewards of literary ambition. Unattainable they might be to me, but, whether so or not, they are not my object; and I think the time has gone by, or, perhaps, has not come to our country, when they are legitimate objects. With the great physical world to be subdued here to the wants of the human family, there is an immense moral field opening, demanding laborers of every class, and of every kind and degree of talent. Neither pride nor humility should withhold us from the work to which we are clearly "sent." (*Life and Letters,* 271)

Mary Kelley discusses Sedgwick's "lingering elitism" in *The Power of Her Sympathy,* 31. As a member of the educated and privileged gentry, her duty—as I believe she understood it—was not only a patriotic one to the nation but also a more personal one to its less privileged and less educated inhabitants. She applied her male relatives' progressive philosophies, the same Enlightenment beliefs in human improvement, to her descriptions of American life as well as to her prescriptions for the betterment of the national character.

12. Gordon S. Wood, *The Radicalism of the American Revolution* (New York: Vintage, 1991), 230, 306, 325.

13. Veblen has been the object of both praise and scorn during the twentieth century. The current scholarly response seems more inclined to the latter, prompted in no small measure by additional information regarding Veblen that has recently become available (at the Univ. Press of Chicago, Columbia Univ. Press, and Carleton College) to those who would assess both the man and his theories. In *Thorstein Veblen: Victorian Firebrand* (Armonk, N.Y.: M. E. Sharpe, 1999), Elizabeth and Henry Jorgensen call Veblen a

> dangerous man [who] challenged the *eternal verities* of America at the turn of the century. . . . Although his ideas were shocking to the Victorian-era conscience, they are no less shocking to many today, because they undermine the consumerist values inherent in the great American rat race. . . . For a century America has been in

denial about Veblen's ideas. They conflicted with the "American dream" of "winning" through perching atop a mountain of expensive possessions and becoming the envy of the neighbors. . . . Veblen's piercing insights were incompatible with the old-fashioned dream. It was easier to dismiss Veblen as a wacky eccentric, a womanizer, and a lecher. (3)

Rick Tilman, in *The Intellectual Legacy of Thorstein Veblen* (Westport, Conn.: Greenwood Press, 1996), calls Veblen "the great critic of American capitalism." Tilman admits that though "much has been written about America's most influential heterodox economist, there is no consensus among Veblen scholars, left, right or center . . . regarding the central meaning of his work. Nor does any general agreement exist regarding his influence on public policy or American intellectual history" (xi). Perhaps one pertinent point in drawing a comparison between the two authors' critiques of capitalism is that each encountered a public reluctant to admit the negative social implications of their observations.

14. Thorstein Veblen, *The Theory of the Leisure Class* (New York: Penguin, 1994).

15. Wood, *The Radicalism of the American Revolution*, 104–5.

16. *Ibid.,* 347.

17. Catharine Sedgwick's attitude toward self-interested politicians is apparently inherited from her father. Wood notes that at "a crucial moment during the debate over the assumption of state debts, Federalist congressman Theodore Sedgwick complained that Thomas Fitzsimmons and George Clymer were absorbed in their private affairs in Philadelphia, while Jeremiah Wadsworth of Connecticut 'has thought it more for his interests to speculate than to attend his duty in Congress, and is gone home'" (264–65).

18. *North American Review*, 83, 84.

19. Mary Wollstonecraft, *A Vindication of the Rights of Women* (London: Penguin, 1992), 110–11.

7

✎ Excerpt from Sedgwick's Unfinished Antislavery
   Manuscript

Labeled "Some pages of a Slave story I began and abandoned." Catharine Maria
Sedgwick Papers I, Massachusetts Historical Society. Sedgwick's deletions are
struck through; angle brackets indicate her insertions.

[In the scene provided here, the planter Mr. Cuthbert notices the severe
injury on his slave Meta's arm. The character of Meta is based on the former
slave Elizabeth Freeman ("Mumbet"), housekeeper and surrogate mother to the
Sedgwicks. This excerpt features Meta's resistance to her mistress, as well as the
conflict between Augusta Cuthbert and her stepmother.]

In passing Meta he exclaimed "God bless me! What ails your arm Meta?"

"Mistress can tell" she replied emphatically without moving a muscle of her
face. Every eye was directed first to Meta's arm which was disfigured with a long
blistered gash, and then to Mrs. Cuthbert's face ~~which was~~ still more disfigured
by the contortions & reddening of shame & anger.

"Why don't you put something on it Meta?" said Mr. Cuthbert. "The only
way to cool a burn is to cover it up."

"I feel cooler with it open sir." . . .

. . . As the secret of Meta's wounded arm has some bearing on our story the
reader must be put in possession of it though the company was not so favored.
~~It seemed that~~ Mrs. Cuthbert had on that day been particularly anxious for the
success of a favorite dish which she had ordered for dinner & she went herself
to the kitchen to see that it was in progress. ~~She found the cook had forgotten
it. The cook was a sister of Meta skilled in her art but a sickly creature~~

Meta & her daughter Mystilla—or Mysty as she was called were both in the kitchen assisting Izzy the cook in the unequal labors of the day. <The cook was skilled in her art but being sickly & timid, she had always received from Meta who was her sister the succor & tenderness that the strong & generous naturally accord to the weak.> and Augusta too was in the kitchen. Aware that Izzy was sick she was aiding the half-fainting drudge by instructing Mysty 'out of a book' in the complicated process of ~~making~~ compounding the ragout.

There was something in Augusta's manners to the servants & theirs to her that presented her in an annoying contrast to her mother in law. The lady herself perceived it through the thick veil of self-love. She happened to be particularly out of humor on this disastrous morning & she turned fiercely on Miss Cuthbert saying "I thought you were in the garden Miss Augusta. I am not obliged to you for meddling in my kitchen."

Miss Cuthbert did not indicate even by a glance of the eye that she ~~heard the~~ was conscious of the coarse attack. She preceded in an unaltered tone "a little mace, Mysty." Her coolness had no tendency to depress Mrs. Cuthbert's mercury. ~~She turned to the~~ cook, ~~who~~ sick weak & timid had felt from the moment of her mistress appearance a similar terror & bewilderment to that of the hen when the hawk is hovering over the poultry-yard. She was arranging and disarranging some coals under a stew.

"Is the lemon-pudding baked?" asked the mistress.

"Oh. I forgot it Mistress!"

"You did, did you? A pretty business truly! Where is your custard?"

"It got ~~turned over~~ burnt Mistress."

We have seen a calmer temper than Mrs. Cuthbert's ruffled by such adversities.

"~~turned over~~ burnt!" she cried "You deserve a burning richly. What are you putting more coals under that stew for? That will be burnt up next?"

The poor cowardly bird to whom we have already liked our poor drudge will if too hard pressed make battle. She dropped the shovel & spoke the words that rose to her lips. "You may cook it yourself. I reckon you are as used to the business as I am."

There was nothing this new-made lady could not bear better than any intimation that her former was lower than her present position. In general she affected entire ignorance of household details, but now & then she involuntarily betrayed her knowledge of the modus operandi in the humblest departments of house-affairs. The cook's last hit was too palpable. The mistress seized the dropped shovel & aimed a blow at the cook, but Meta who had watched the rising storm interposed her arm in time to receive it, "Strike on" she cried without shrinking a hair's breadth, "but touch Izzy at the peril of your life."

The power of external & accidental condition quails before the intrinsic superiority of the soul. Mrs. Cuthbert's arm dropped as if it were paralyzed. She let fall the shovel & retreated from the kitchen in a passionate fit of crying.

Chapter 7

"A Slave Story I Began and Abandoned": Sedgwick's Antislavery Manuscript

KAREN WOODS WEIERMAN

In her biography of the English actress Fanny Kemble, historian Catherine Clinton describes Kemble's close relationship with "abolitionist Catharine Sedgwick." This is not a title, however, that Sedgwick herself would have embraced: The literary and epistolary record reveals her opposition both to slavery and the "excesses" of the abolitionist movement. For such a prolific and influential author, her published treatment of slavery seems sparse indeed. Slavery plays a minor role in several of her novels, and she published a few essays on the slavery question. Yet the slavery question was a central concern within her family and social circle—many Sedgwick family members and friends played an active role in the movement, and Sedgwick's own letters and journals demonstrate her intellectual and emotional engagement with this issue of national importance. In this context, an unfinished, undated manuscript found among her papers at the Massachusetts Historical Society, labeled only "some pages of a slave story I began and abandoned," sheds some light on the "abolitionist problem" in Sedgwick literary history.[1]

Although scholars have not dated the manuscript with absolute certainty, Sedgwick likely wrote it in the early 1830s. At this time she struggled personally and professionally with the question of immediate abolition raised by radical William Lloyd Garrison and his converts. There is also a gap in her productivity in the early 1830s. After her 1830 novel *Clarence*, she published only a few sketches each year until 1835, when she published both *The Linwoods* and *Home*.

If Sedgwick did indeed draft her manuscript in the 1830s, it is also significant as one of the earliest examples of antislavery fiction. Sedgwick's 1824 novel *Redwood* and Sarah Josepha Hale's *Northwood* (1827) did incorporate the slavery issue into their plots, but as Carolyn Karcher notes, it was Sedgwick's sometime friend Lydia Maria Child who fully realized "the potency of fiction as a medium for overcoming readers' prejudices and converting them to abolitionism." Child "pioneered the genre of antislavery fiction" in the children's magazine *Juvenile Miscellany* (1830–34) and in the antislavery gift book *The Oasis* (1834). Sedgwick's manuscript may also predate two of the earliest known antislavery novels, Gustave de Beaumont's *Marie; or, Slavery in the United States* (1835) and Richard Hildreth's *The Slave; or, Memoirs of Archy Moore* (1836). Of course, the genre reached its peak in Harriet Beecher Stowe's watershed *Uncle Tom's Cabin* (1852).[2]

The reading of Sedgwick's manuscript requires the exploration of her cautiousness on the slavery question and her problematic relationship with the abolitionist movement. Her "slave story" is not merely an isolated curiosity; it is an important text in her oeuvre, as elements of the manuscript appear in prior and subsequent work. Ultimately, her failure to complete the manuscript foreshadows the failure of the moderate course of gradual abolitionism and national unity.

The Sedgwick Circle and Abolitionism

The Sedgwick family had worked to end slavery since the time of the American Revolution. Theodore Sedgwick, Catharine Sedgwick's influential father, played a role in the abolition of slavery in Massachusetts. In August 1781, he represented the slave Elizabeth Freeman in her suit for freedom against Colonel John Ashley. Decades later, following the excitement over *Uncle Tom's Cabin*, Sedgwick recounted this story in her 1853 article "Slavery in New England": "[I]t was the first practical construction in Massachusetts of the declaration which had been to the black race a constitutional abstraction, and on this decision was based the freedom of the few slaves remaining in Massachusetts." Upon receiving her freedom, Freeman, or "Mumbet," became a housekeeper for the Sedgwick family and a surrogate mother to Sedgwick.[3]

Despite this early activism, during the nation's fragile beginnings Theodore Sedgwick sometimes allowed political exigencies to compromise his commitment to the abolition of slavery. Along with his fellow statesmen, he sacrificed the slaves to what he saw as the greater good of the new union. In Congress he chaired the committee that sent the original Fugitive Slave Law of 1793 to the House. Some foreshadowing of this willingness to compromise with slaveholders can be found in his commentary on a 1787 fugitive slave case. Even though he wrote to a friend that the captured slave "has appealed to the laws and he certainly ought to be restored to his freedom," he also promised that "should it be determined that Sebring owns them I pledge my honor to do every thing in my power that he shall not be impeded in the exercise of his rights." Yet as Chief Justice of the Massachusetts Supreme Court, Judge Sedgwick dissented from the majority in *Greenwood v. Curtis* (1806), arguing that "an action could not be maintained in this commonwealth on a promissory note given in Africa for a balance due on a contract for the purchase of slaves."[4]

Later generations of Sedgwicks continued the family tradition of challenging slavery in high-profile court cases. In 1839, Theodore Sedgwick III, Sedgwick's nephew, joined the defense team in the *Amistad* slave mutiny case. The prominent lawyer and politician Charles Baldwin Sedgwick (the son of Sedgwick's first cousin) defended the "Jerry Rescuers," who had freed fugitive slave Jerry McHenry from a Syracuse jail on 1 October 1851. The Sedgwick family followed the trials with great pride and interest. Elizabeth Dwight Sedgwick wrote to her daughter Kate Sedgwick Minot that her cousin Charles of Syracuse "has just been at Albany to take care of the Syracuse fugitive law trials . . . he expects every indictment will be quashed."[5]

This antislavery advocacy was not just an abstract legal matter. For Sedgwick and her brothers, Elizabeth Freeman's role in their household influenced the development of antislavery sympathies. Henry Dwight Sedgwick, Sedgwick's beloved brother "Harry," gave a lyceum lecture in 1831, later published as a pamphlet, titled *The Practicability of the Abolition of Slavery*, in which he questions the idea that Africans should be enslaved because of their innate inferiority. As evidence, Henry Sedgwick tells Elizabeth Freeman's story in great detail, describing how she received a terrible blow on her arm while shielding her sister from their mistress, how she refused to return to her master after this violence, how she sought legal counsel from Henry's father, and how she was one of the first slaves to have the Massachusetts Bill of Rights—"all men are born free and equal"—applied to her. His personal relationship with Freeman made it impossible for him to believe in African inferiority: "Having known this woman as familiarly as I knew either of my parents, I *cannot* believe in the moral or physical inferiority of the race to which she belonged."[6]

Sedgwick's friends Rev. Charles Follen and Eliza Lee Follen praised Henry's lecture—"as you may suppose we were most deeply interested in it"—and by 1834 declared themselves abolitionists, despite the unpopularity of the cause. They urged Sedgwick to share her opinions: "We have often spoke of you dearest Catherine [*sic*] in connection with this subject & longed to talk with you about it & know what you thought. . . . Have you read Mrs. Child's *Appeal*? . . . What dear are your views & feelings upon the subject?" In her reply, Sedgwick wrote that her brother Harry would have agreed with them on the slavery question, but that her own position is more cautious: "I am not yet sufficiently acquainted with the subject to have made up my mind as to the expediency of immediate emancipation." Soon after Rev. Follen was appointed interim pastor of Sedgwick's Unitarian church, First Congregational in New York, he caused controversy with his antislavery Thanksgiving Day sermon in

1836. Sedgwick urged him to stop pushing the slavery issue so aggressively from the pulpit lest he not be offered a permanent position. As she wrote to Eliza, "[Y]our husband might do more good to the cause by not at present introducing the subject into the pulpit . . . than he can do if he loses this opportunity of commanding an avenue to mens minds & hearts in such a place as New York." Realizing that this cautious advice would disappoint her friends, she reminded them that "my heart & my exertions in my own way, are in the cause in which you have embarked all." In large part because of his radical antislavery beliefs, Follen was not offered a permanent position, and he resigned his interim position in January 1838.[7]

Eliza Follen and Sedgwick disagreed over abolitionism throughout their lifelong friendship. Eliza Follen's 1848 essay, "Harshness of Abolitionists," published in the abolitionist gift annual *Liberty Bell*, seems almost written for Sedgwick, who like other nervous antislavery supporters shrank from the "harsh," "uncompromising," and "severe" abolitionists. Follen argues that the horror of slavery requires strong words and that slavery itself sets the tone of the debate. Perhaps motivated by the events of the 1850s and worn down by her friends' appeals, Sedgwick attended the 1856 Antislavery Fair in Boston, "as a tribute to Eliza."[8] Nevertheless, Follen's invitation to the National Anti-Slavery Society anniversary in January 1860 reveals Sedgwick's problematic relationship to radical abolitionism. As Follen wrote to her old friend: "I know you do not agree with us in some things, but I am sure that our purposes you approve of & sympathize with. Come & hear us & let us meet as far as we can. The awful tragedy at Harpers Ferry has . . . sent a thrill of emotion through the civilized world. . . . I want to see you & hear your opinion. . . . Our hearts can never be divided."[9] But Sedgwick declined to attend, and, sadly, the invitation was the last letter she received before Follen's death. As she explained to Susan Channing, their hearts were indeed divided on the subject of John Brown:

> She wrote to me an earnest invitation to go with her to her annual festival. I declined it, assigning to her the true reason, that I shrunk from being with her on an occasion to her of the most elevating excitement which I did not partake. . . . The last time she ever put pen to paper—the pen that has done so much blessed work—was with the intention of kindly convincing me I was wrong. . . . You will not misunderstand me, my dear Susan, nor imagine that I do not feel heartily in the great question of humanity that agitates our people. It seemed to me that so much had been intemperately said, so much rashly urged, on the death of that noble martyr, John Brown, by the abolitionists, that it was not right to appear among them as one of them.[10]

Whereas the Follens were inspired by the abolitionist writings of Garrison and Lydia Maria Child, another family friend, the English actress Fanny Kemble, gave the Sedgwicks a firsthand account of slavery. In 1836, Kemble's new American husband Pierce Butler inherited the second-largest slaveholding estate in Georgia, and differences over slavery contributed to their eventual divorce in 1849. During a trip to the Georgia plantations in 1838–39, Kemble kept a journal in the form of letters to Elizabeth Dwight Sedgwick. During the summer of 1840, Kemble stayed with Sedgwick's brother Charles and his wife Elizabeth in Lenox, Massachusetts; they read her journal and urged publication for the abolitionist cause. This firsthand account of slavery by a close friend must have increased their commitment to abolitionism, and the epistolary record reveals that Charles and Elizabeth regularly attended abolitionist events and followed current events quite closely. The journal also circulated privately in abolitionist circles, and it is possible that Sedgwick read it as well. Kemble delayed publication until 1863, when she hoped that it would prevent England from aiding the Confederacy. When *Journal of a Residence on a Georgian Plantation, 1838–39* finally appeared, Sedgwick offered high praise: "We have all been reading Mrs. Kemble's book—the most impressive & important exposition of slavery we have ever had. . . . It seems providential that it should have been kept back for this momentous era." Through her friendship with Kemble, Sedgwick saw that slavery destroyed the family life of the slaves and the slaveholders alike, albeit in very different ways. Most telling, she described Kemble's divorce as a liberation from slavery: "I am sure she enjoys her release from galling shackles."[11]

As Sedgwick considered the slavery question, the experiences of family and friends, her belief in the rule of law, and her relationship with Freeman all shaped her thoughts. But as Jenifer Elmore has persuasively argued, Sedgwick believed in preserving the Union at all costs, and she feared that the radical abolitionists would destroy the nation.[12] These influences inspired and limited Sedgwick's creativity as she explored the national dilemma in fictional form.

The Manuscript: "Some pages of a Slave story I began and abandoned"

The manuscript itself is a fifty-page handwritten text, and according to Sedgwick's numbering system, it has ten pages missing from the middle. The fragment suggests a novel, because the story ends abruptly with many plot threads unresolved, but it also might be a lengthy short story or novella. In any case, the story lacks Sedgwick's typical narrative control, and its diverse genres—antislavery melodrama, political tract, scientific treatise—confuse rather than illuminate her message. Flaws and all, it is a fascinating look at Sedgwick's struggle with the most serious moral and political crisis of her time.

The story opens at a dinner party on the Cuthbert plantation in South Carolina. The characters include Jasper Cuthbert, "a South Carolinian who had an extensive plantation and large slave property"; Mrs. Cuthbert, his second wife, a Northerner who "imposed herself on superficial observers as a person of breeding"; and Augusta Cuthbert, the "beautiful and beloved" daughter of Jasper Cuthbert by his first marriage. Augusta's suitor, Duncan Fitzhugh, is a young gentleman from a neighboring plantation who is preparing his slaves for freedom. Meta, the Cuthberts' slave, is a skilled nurse whose character is clearly based on Elizabeth Freeman: "[H]er sound judgment, her incorruptible fidelity, her resistance of tyranny had given her that ascendance on the plantation that superior minds[,] stimulated by the energy of virtue[,] obtain in every sphere." Finally, the Cuthbert plantation is run by Mr. Agar, the overseer, who "had no more doubt of the inferiority of the African race than of his own existence" (1–3, 21, 23).

The plot has three main themes: resistance to slavery, race science, and gradual emancipation. The first theme centers around Meta's resistance to the abuses of slavery. As described above, the Meta character is clearly based on Elizabeth Freeman and her experiences as a slave. According to accounts by Sedgwick in "Slavery in New England" and by Henry Sedgwick in his lyceum address, Freeman shielded her sister from a blow with a hot oven shovel from their mistress Hannah Ashley. In the manuscript, Mrs. Cuthbert berates Meta's sister Izzy for her failures in the kitchen. When Izzy saucily alludes to Mrs. Cuthbert's lower-class origins in reply—"You may cook it yourself. I reckon you are as used to the business as I am"—Mrs. Cuthbert "seized the dropped shovel & aimed a blow at the cook." But like the real-life Freeman, "Meta who had watched the rising storm interposed her arm in time to receive it, 'Strike on' she cried without shrinking a hair's breadth, 'but touch Izzy at the peril of your life'" (13). Like Freeman, Meta leaves her serious wound open for all to see, and when people inquire about her injury, she replies simply and with unmistakable moral authority, "'Mistress can tell'" (11).[13]

Following this incident, the manuscript features a long digression on the question of black inferiority and race science, the second major theme.[14] During the course of the dinner conversation, Duncan contends that the slaves and the masters are "of one blood," alluding to the Biblical verse, popular among abolitionists, "For God hath made of one blood all nations of men for to dwell on all the face of the earth" (Acts 17:26). His host responds angrily: "'"Of one blood,"' echoed Mr. Cuthbert, 'devilish nonsense that. I dont know who believes it but Methodists & boys'" (9). The narrator then addresses the question of racial inequality directly. Turning to history to explore the belief in African inferiority, the narrator asks, "Are not all degraded and oppressed people rated by their oppressors below themselves. Did the Spartans admit the equality of the Helots? Do the Moors of the Barbary States allow that of their *white* slaves? Was not the Jew in his own opinion exalted far above the Gentile? The Roman above the barbarian & the turk over the Infidel?" (14). The narrator warns readers not to be blinded by difference: "That the black is different from the white cannot be controverted. But difference must not be mistaken for inferiority" (16).

The narrator goes on to debunk the "quackery" of phrenology, the "falsely so called" science which claims physiological evidence of African inferiority (20–21). She notes that "the strongest & it appears to us the conclusive argument in favor of the natural equality of the races" is that "[t]he colored children in the infant & primary schools make quite as rapid advances in all their studies as the white children" (21).

After seven pages of equality arguments, the narrator pulls back from political and scientific matters: "But we have perhaps extended these remarks too far—our readers may remind us that it is our *craft* to write for their amusement & to allow them to extract instruction for themselves if perchance so valuable an essence can be obtained from the light material of a tale" (21). Questions of phrenology and African inferiority remain on center stage, nevertheless, as the story continues. In order to prove his point about race science, the overseer Mr. Agar brings the skull of a slave to the table. In a highly wrought scene, Meta realizes that he holds the skull of her father, and in her outrage, she recites the litany of wrongs her family has suffered under slavery. Like Africk in *Redwood*, Meta warns Agar that the day of reckoning will come: "You make us like the brutes & then try to believe that God has made us so—but the day of vengeance is coming when you shall reap sorrow and death on the ground that has been wet with our blood & tears. In that day to some of you . . . we shall be—not monkies—but lions and wolves" (29). There is an amazingly similar scene in Beaumont's novel *Marie* (1835) when George, a free man of color, denounces the racial thinking that rationalizes slavery:

> Inferior race! So you say! You have measured the Negro brain and said "There is no room in that narrow skull for anything but grief!" and you have condemned him to suffer eternally. You are mistaken; your measurements were wrong; in that brutish head there is a compartment that contains a powerful faculty, that of revenge—an implacable vengeance, horrible but intelligent.[15]

Although some of her manuscript is extremely progressive, it is important to realize that Sedgwick's narrative is not free from the racial prejudice of her day. Comments such as "The climate of Africa is unfavorable to the development of the human capacity" lie side by side with her arguments for equality (16). And at the end of her long argument for racial equality, a margin comment, probably written at a later date, retracts her ideas: "I have changed my opinion. I now believe that there are not merely obvious differences between the races—but that the African is inferior to the Caucasian. But that is no argument for slavery" (21).

The manuscript's third major theme features Duncan Fitzhugh's plan to manumit his slaves. Like Westall in Sedgwick's 1824 novel *Redwood*, Fitzhugh has been preparing his slaves for freedom through education and vocational training. His prospective father-in-law resents his plans and issues an ultimatum: Fitzhugh must discontinue his plans to free his slaves or Cuthbert will prevent his marriage to Augusta. Fitzhugh, of course, chooses "the path of true honor" and refuses these terms (49). While Augusta faints out of pride and grief, Mr. Cuthbert taunts Fitzhugh: "When Augusta comes to her senses she will respect herself better than to care for a fellow who has cast her off [and in a provocative line that Sedgwick added but later deleted] & who may as well take a wife from one of the lovely creatures he prefers to her" (50). In response, Fitzhugh warns Cuthbert that he has not seen the last of him: "I shall not consider myself violating any honorable sentiment in making every effort to evade your tyranny" (51). In all, this *Romeo and Juliet* plot falls flat, perhaps because the character of Augusta is not fully developed, and these comparatively dull characters are overshadowed by Meta, the powerful woman who demands justice and threatens violent self-defense.

What is interesting about this portion of the plot is Fitzhugh's manumission plan. Sedgwick here imagines a model for ending slavery while preserving the Union. Once Fitzhugh informs his slaves about their upcoming freedom,

> He succeeded in inspiring some of them with the honorable ambition of elevating their own condition & that of their race by joining the Colony of Liberia. There were some young men of turbulent spirits who he thought might incite the slaves of the neighboring plantations to rebellion, to their manumission he annexed the condition of their migrating to the Northern States. Some were permitted to establish themselves in Charleston, & a few whose strong affections overcame the impulse of sudden liberty & the natural love of self-direction entreated to remain on condition of receiving their customary support as the equivalent for their labor. To this Fitzhugh consented, taking care to give them such legal securities for their freedom as put it out of his power ever to reclaim a property in them. (40)

This plan offers several alternatives for the newly freed slaves, although it seems chiefly intended to alleviate white fears of black violence, possibly in the wake of Nat Turner's Rebellion. The narrator also conservatively suggests that colonization is an imperfect but efficient remedy for the slaveholder considering manumission, even though "the slaves are themselves prejudiced against immigration to Liberia" (38).

Sedgwick's efforts to portray the issue from all perspectives suggest her desire to unite the nation through her fictional and moral vision. Though her sympathy for the slaves is clear in her Meta character, she also reveals sympathy for the Southern planters. She insists that the North should not demonize the South because of the inherited evil of slavery: "We must beg leave here to deprecate the inconsiderate, unfounded & flippant reproaches which we in the north so liberally lavish on our brethren of the South, for an evil which has been transmitted to them, for which they are no more responsible than a man for a disease born with him, & which they are more anxious to be rid than we are to relieve them" (37). Even Fitzhugh, on the verge of freeing his slaves, insists that slavery is a Southern matter: "The truth is that this is a question that our friends at the north should not interfere with. It is like interposing in the delicate controversies between man & wife" (5–6). The narrator also notes that it is "far above the level of ordinary virtue" to expect slaveowners to act against their "pecuniary interest" by freeing their slaves (37).

The manuscript fragment ends with Fitzhugh finding solace in the happiness of his soon-to-be-freed slaves: "Fitzhugh met his slaves all in their holiday suits and holiday faces—old & young waiting to receive him & eager to express their gratitude & happiness" (51). On the following page, in a different handwriting, lies the enigmatic label, "some pages of a slave story I began & abandoned" (52). And so the reader is left with many questions: When did Sedgwick write this story? Why did she abandon it? Where does this manuscript belong in Sedgwick literary history?

Locating the Manuscript in Sedgwick Literary History

The best working theory is that the manuscript was written in the 1830s, most likely between the years 1833 and 1838. Considering the manuscript as a physical object, Sedgwick's handwriting resembles that of other texts written in the 1830s, and she used the same paper for other 1830s texts. The paper bears the watermark "OH&S"; other extant papers with this watermark all date from the 1820s and 1830s.[16]

Internal evidence and external events also date the manuscript to this time. Elizabeth Freeman died in December 1829, and Sedgwick may have been inspired to create Meta in memory of her surrogate mother. A footnote citing the July 1830 issue of the *Edinburgh Review* also suggests the date of composition.

Sedgwick's treatment of phrenology and a reference to the leading book on the subject also places the manuscript in the 1830s. Phrenologists theorized that "anatomical and physiological characteristics have a direct influence upon mental behavior" and that people had thirty-seven different aptitudes or propensities "localized in different 'organs' or regions of the brain." In 1831, Sedgwick attended a series of phrenological lectures in New York: "They amuse us partly from the originality of the lecturer, & partly from the extravagant pretension & absurdity of the system." In an 1833 letter to her niece Kate, Sedgwick writes that she has been reading George Combe's book, *The Constitution of Man* (1829), and that she strongly agrees with Combe that suffering is the result of "some direct or indirect violation of the laws of Providence." Sedgwick rejects the "phrenological nonsense mixed up with it," but, inspired by Combe's belief in the perfectibility of man, writes that it is "certainly one of the most delightful books I have ever read."[17]

Sedgwick likely incorporated her reading into her antislavery manuscript, where she critiques the use of phrenology to uphold white supremacy through the character of the overseer. She even uses Combe's terminology in the story: Combe categorizes "philoprogenitiveness," or love of offspring, as one of the "Propensities Common to Man with the Lower Animals."[18] In the story, Agar describes his study of the slaves on the plantation: "I have examined every slave's head on our plantation & I find them palpably deficient in every valuable organ excepting philoprogenitive" (26). The overseer acknowledges African philoprogenitiveness even while he argues for black inferiority; he tries to dismiss familial love as evidence of humanity by arguing that the slaves are merely revealing their strong animal instincts.

In addition to her reading, Sedgwick made two trips to the South in the 1830s—one to Washington, D.C., and one to Virginia, where she witnessed slavery firsthand. During her 1831 trip to the nation's capital, she recorded her perceptions of slavery and regional tensions in a flurry of letters written to family and friends. She reported on the workings of the internal slave trade: "Slaves are sent from here to the more southern states. The jail at Alexandria is filled with them during the business season. The servants in the house say they see them chained together like beasts to be sent off!" Though horrified by the slave trade, Sedgwick was willing to consider colonization as a solution to the slavery question; as she notes, "I had quite an effective visit from an Agent for the Colonization Society." Her visit to the nation's capital occurred during the nullification crisis, during which South Carolinians argued that they had the right to nullify federal laws they deemed unconstitutional, and even then Sedgwick worried about antagonizing the South, criticizing Daniel Webster for his militant advo-cacy of protectionist tariffs.[19]

In 1833, Sedgwick traveled to Virginia, where she was invited to tour a plan-tation of 150 slaves. She appreciated the beauty of the rural South, but noted that it was ruined by "this horrid stain—this misery of slavery." She celebrated Independence Day in the South with fellow travelers and a ceremonial reading of the Declaration of Independence. Sedgwick could not help but realize the contradictions inherent within this slave society dedicated to freedom, writing, "I was struck with two slaves who stood on the outside & planting their ears against a broken pane of glass listened intently to declarations as applicable to them as us. One had a lowering brow, & if I mistake not made his own deduc-tions." This anecdote parallels the Freeman story, in that Freeman reported deciding to sue for her freedom after hearing the Declaration of Independence read.[20] In Virginia, Sedgwick also noted color as the basis of social organization: "The Virginians seem content with the Patrician or Aristocratic power that results to them from their being slaveholders. The white is the Patrician color, and there is a much more perfect equality among the whites than with us." But this system of slavery, in Sedgwick's eyes, also hurts the whites: It "keeps back the improvements of society, the betterment of social life."[21]

Even after viewing slavery's evils firsthand, Sedgwick had doubts about the efficacy of immediate emancipation, as well as serious reservations about Garri-sonian methods. Her writings both praise and criticize the radical abolitionists. After spending an evening at Eliza Follen's home "with the chiefs of the Aboli-tion," Sedgwick criticized the "ultraism" of abolitionists but then tempered her criticism with, "we must reverence those who are devoting such energies to the helpless. They are laborers with all their might in the Lord's vineyard, and if they now and then make a false stroke they are still sure of their reward." She made similar comments about the British writer Harriet Martineau: "Her mind . . . is much excited on the AntiSlavery subject & abolition. . . . [S]he sees objects in an exaggerated light. . . . If men must be fanatics, may it be in this most generous of causes."[22]

Sedgwick's letters from the 1830s reveal her search for an appropriate role in the antislavery movement. As she responded to Eliza Follen's entreaties to join her in the movement, "I do indeed *feel* with you—& I would do something more than feel. It is a subject that has much occupied my thoughts."[23] Her reply to Lydia Maria Child's request for a contribution to her abolitionist gift book *The Oasis* provides the most thorough articulation of her caution at this time:

> There is no sorrow of humanity that I have so much at heart as the
> condition of the black race. There are none of my fellow creatures to

whose good I should be more thankful to contribute—your argument for immediate emancipation is a very strong one. Still provided the principle could be established that the blacks might be fitted for freedom and self-government provided it were admitted that they must one day all be free & that their freedom must be effected as soon as compatible with their best good, you take away all apology for keeping them in ignorance & you give the motive & the impulse to their improvement. Slavery as Dr. Follen says is undoubtedly a crime—but having been committed it is the part of wisdom to find it the safest way to escape the consequences. It does not appear to me that immediate abolition is best for the slaves. God only knows what is best. It is a dark & fearful subject. . . . But all this is no answer to your request—If I may be one of your contributors without being considered an advocate of the principles of the abolitionists (which I cannot honestly be), I shall be very happy to fill some of your pages.[24]

Sedgwick's antislavery manuscript echoes these sentiments, especially in Duncan Fitzhugh's plan for gradual emancipation of his slaves.

But Child had no patience for this approach and told Sedgwick, "I cannot accept your friendly proposal. I want none but unqualified Anti-Slavery writers. . . . On this subject I neither have, nor desire to have moderation."[25]

Despite Sedgwick's desire to be a moderate voice of national unity, her moderate antislavery story falls apart, just as the nation would fall apart decades later. She simply cannot craft a satisfactory ending or peaceful resolution that would offer a model for the nation. Her journal entries from 1833 reflect a crisis in her writing, a project that causes her extreme frustration and writer's block. We can only speculate that she was writing about her antislavery manuscript, but the extreme tension makes it a likely candidate. In early February, she was "in absolute despair about my book." By the middle of the month, she doubted "whether at once resolutely to sacrifice my Mss. or to go on & see if I can get a moment of inspiration, a starting point." By mid-April she reported, "I have abandoned my book I am sick of it—I am dreaming over another plan & life is passing!"[26]

In 1834 and 1835, respectively, Sedgwick published "A Reminiscence of Federalism," set in New England during the early years of the Republic, and *The Linwoods; or, "Sixty Years Since" in America*, set in New York during the American Revolution. It is quite possible that Sedgwick began these texts after her antislavery manuscript failed. Unable to write solutions to this brewing regional conflict, she might have looked back to the Revolution and the political controversies of the early period in American history in an effort to remind Americans of their shared heritage, "a union that, as in some chymical combinations, no test could dissolve."[27]

There are some intriguing parallels between the plots of *The Linwoods* and the antislavery manuscript. In both stories, controversial political questions divide families across generations. Just as Duncan Fitzhugh and Augusta Cuthbert reject her father's proslavery toast, "Happy liberty to the master, contented slavery to the servant!" (6), the patriot Herbert Linwood refuses to drink to his father's Loyalist toast, "the king—God bless him" (I, 63). This sympathy for the patriot cause leads Mr. Linwood to banish his son until he swears loyalty to the king. In a similar ultimatum, Mr. Cuthbert insists that Fitzhugh choose between manumitting his slaves and marrying his daughter.

In both novels, there is also a heroic black family servant who serves as a sage and surrogate mother to the family. Meta's protection of her sister takes place in the context of slavery, whereas Rose, the Linwoods' servant, is freed by the love of the child Isabella, who asks her father to free Rose after winning an award at school. Even after her manumission, Rose remains loyal to the Linwoods, and she helps Herbert Linwood escape from a British jail during the war. Rose is an ardent patriot, and she argues that freedom from Britain will lead to freedom for all: "[C]an't you see these men are raised up to fight for freedom for more than themselves? If the chain is broken at one end, the links will fall apart sooner or later" (I, 226).

Despite Rose's prediction, Sedgwick clearly had trouble envisioning a place for freed slaves in the United States. Her antislavery novel breaks off before the planned manumissions actually take place, and the closing scenes of *The Linwoods* reveal that the expanded freedom of the Revolution did not extend to people of color. During the festivities following the British departure from New York, the Linwood family encounters their former servant Jupiter, who tells them he is engaged to dine with General Washington. Mr. Linwood is shocked by this instance of extreme social equality: He "was ready to believe almost any extravagance of the levelling Americans; but the agrarianism that made Jupiter a party at the festive board with the commander-in-chief rather astounded him." But Belle Linwood clarifies matters: "You mean, Jupe . . . that you are engaged to wait on General Washington" (II, 279). People of color are destined to be servants in the new nation, just as Duncan Fitzhugh's slaves are taught work suitable to their station.

In Sedgwick's 1834 story "A Reminiscence of Federalism," yet another tyrannical patriarch lets his political prejudices against Southerners and Federalists disrupt the lives of two generations of his family. Squire Hayford cuts off his daughter when she marries a Southern man, and he forbids the marriage of his grandson Randolph to Fanny Atwood, because her father is a Federalist. As in the antislavery manuscript, when Cuthbert tells Fitzhugh he may marry his daughter if he sacrifices his principles, Randolph's grandfather offers his blessing and a financial incentive if Randolph votes against his conscience in the upcoming election. Fanny, like Augusta, will not hear of her man choosing the path of dishonor. Randolph stays true to himself and votes for the worthy candidate. Unlike the unfinished manuscript, this story has a neat, happy ending: Hayford dies, Randolph renounces his inheritance, and Randolph and Fanny live happily ever after. For Sedgwick, Randolph, a man of Southern blood and New England education, is the hope of the new generation, capable of political compromise and willing to move beyond the prejudices of the past. As Sedgwick's narrator tells us in the beginning of her story, she brings up past political divisions to give current controversies some perspective: Her "vivid recollection of those party strifes . . . should now only be remembered to assuage the heat of present controversies." It was the slavery divide, of course, that made the bitter rivalries between Democrats and Federalists seem like quaint political relics. By the 1850s, Sedgwick's thinking about slavery was still focused on her beloved Union. She valorizes Elizabeth Freeman and Theodore Sedgwick for the suit for freedom in her 1853 article "Slavery in New England." That same year she also contributed to a gift annual produced by the Rochester Ladies' Anti-Slavery Society, in which she appeared alongside such abolitionists as Frederick Douglass, Gerrit Smith, and Harriet Beecher Stowe. Her public affiliation with abolitionists was unusual, since she demurred so many times during her career. More militant editors, such as Lydia Maria Child or Maria Weston Chapman, might have rejected her article, "The Slave and Slave-Owner," which argues that it is much worse to be a slaveowner than a slave. As in her antislavery manuscript twenty years earlier, she makes the "inherited evil" argument that slaveowners are not to blame for their predicament: "Thousands among them are in a false position. They are the involuntary maintainers of wrong, and transmitters of evil. Hundreds among them have scrupulous consciences and tender feelings. . . . But alas! they live under the laws of slave-owners" (25). Focusing on the evil effects of slavery on white domestic life, and perhaps thinking about her friend Fanny Kemble, she asks, "Compared with the miseries of the slave-owner, what are the toils and stripes of the slave?" (26).[28]

Even while outraged by the Fugitive Slave Law of 1850 and the spiraling events of the 1850s, Sedgwick continued to search for compromise and to refrain from vilifying slaveholders, in a last-ditch attempt to save the Union. Just months before the outbreak of war, she wrote, "it is our duty to sacrifice our jealousies, our most indulged hates, & our cherished philanthropies to preserving the great estate with which Heaven has endowed us, an entailed estate which must not be dismembered—if we can help it."[29] The failure of her moderate antislavery manuscript foreshadowed the failure of the moderate course of gradual abolitionism and national unity. Despite—or perhaps because of—this artistic and political failure, the manuscript provides a fascinating glimpse at Sedgwick's struggle with the greatest moral crisis of her time. Although her politics were cautious, her experiments with the genre of antislavery fiction place her on the cutting edge of American literary history.

NOTES

I conducted most of the research for this article as an Andrew W. Mellon Fellow at the Massachusetts Historical Society. Many thanks to the staff at MHS for their support of my project. I'm also grateful to the staff at the American Antiquarian Society and the participants in the Sedgwick Symposium in June 2000 (especially Melissa Homestead, Charlene Avallone, Jenifer Elmore, Lucinda Damon-Bach, and Victoria Clements) for their insights and commentary.

1. Antislavery manuscript, Catharine Maria Sedgwick Papers I, 6.8, Massachusetts Historical Society, Boston, Mass. I will refer to this untitled, undated text as "the manuscript." Page citations will be incorporated into the text. I will refer to Sedgwick by her initials (CMS) in subsequent citations.

2. Carolyn L. Karcher, *The First Woman in the Republic: A Cultural Biography of Lydia Maria Child* (Durham, N.C.: Duke Univ. Press, 1997), 206, 333, 665 n. 34.

3. Catharine Maria Sedgwick, "Slavery in New England," *Bentley's Miscellany* 34 (1853): 421.

Although Theodore Sedgwick did participate in the important case, *Brom and Bett v. Ashley* (1781), his role may not have been as pivotal as Sedgwick contends. The question of how abolition was accomplished in Massachusetts, whether by judicial, economic, or individual means, is a matter of controversy. See Elaine MacEachern, "Emancipation of Slavery in Massachusetts, A Reexamination, 1770–1790," *Journal of Negro History* 55 (1970): 289–306; Arthur Zilversmit, "Quok Walker, Mumbet, and the Abolition of Slavery in Massachusetts," *William and Mary Quarterly* 25 (1968): 614–24; William O'Brien, "Did the Jemison Case Outlaw Slavery in Massachusetts?" *William and Mary Quarterly* 17 (1960): 219–41.

4. H. D. Sedgwick, "The Sedgwicks of Berkshire," *Collections of the Berkshire Historical and Scientific Society* (Pittsfield, Mass., 1900), 97–98; Theodore Sedgwick to Henry Van Schaark, 2 April 1787, Sedgwick III Papers, Box 1.4, Massachusetts Historical Society (MHS hereafter), Boston.

5. Elizabeth Dwight Sedgwick to Kate Sedgwick Minot, 29 Jan. 1852, Sedgwick IV Papers, Box 11.13, MHS.

6. Henry Dwight Sedgwick, *The Practicability of the Abolition of Slavery: A Lecture, Delivered at the Lyceum in Stockbridge, Mass., Feb. 1831* (New York: J. Seymour, 1831).

7. Follen refers to Lydia Maria Child's landmark abolitionist text, *Appeal in Favor of That Class of Americans Called Africans* (1833). Eliza Lee Follen to CMS, 23 Oct. 1831, Catharine Maria Sedgwick Papers III, Box 3.12, MHS; Eliza Lee Follen to CMS, 2 April 1834, Catharine Maria Sedgwick Papers III, Box 4.2, MHS; CMS to Eliza Lee Follen, 15 April 1834, Catharine Maria Sedgwick Papers I, Box 8.8, MHS; CMS to Eliza Lee Follen, 26 Dec. 1836, Catharine Maria Sedgwick Papers I, Box 8.9, MHS.

8. Eliza Lee Follen, "Harshness of Abolitionists," *Liberty Bell* (Boston, 1848), 45–50; CMS to Jane Minot Sedgwick, 28 Dec. 1856, Catharine Maria Sedgwick Papers III, Box 5.2, MHS.

9. Eliza Lee Follen to CMS, Jan. 1860?, Catharine Maria Sedgwick Papers II, Box 4.2, MHS.

10. CMS to Susan Channing, 10 March 1860, *Life and Letters of Catharine Maria Sedgwick*, ed. Mary E. Dewey (New York: Harper, 1871), 377.

11. See Catherine Clinton, *Fanny Kemble's Civil Wars: The Story of America's Most Unlikely Abolitionist* (New York: Simon and Schuster, 2000); CMS to Alice Minot, 10 Aug. 1863, Sedgwick IV Papers, Box 14.8, MHS; CMS to Kate Sedgwick Minot, 29 Dec. 1849, Catharine Maria Sedgwick Papers I, Box 3.16, MHS.

12. Jenifer Elmore, "Parti-Colored Fiction: Political Allegories and National Anxieties in Catharine Sedgwick's *Redwood* and 'A Reminiscence of Federalism'" (paper presented at the Sedgwick Symposium, Stockbridge, Mass., 9 June 2000).

13. Of course, readers of *Hope Leslie* will see parallels between Freeman/Meta and Magawisca, who loses her arm in order to prevent Everell Fletcher's execution.

14. Stephen Jay Gould's *The Mismeasure of Man* (New York: W. W. Norton, 1996) is essential reading on the subject of biological determinism and race science.

15. Gustave de Beaumont, *Marie; or, Slavery in the United States* (Baltimore: Johns Hopkins Univ. Press, 1999), 60.

16. See Thomas L. Gravell and George Miller, *A Catalog of American Watermarks, 1690–1835* (New York: Garland Publications, 1979), 18, 114. The American Antiquarian Society (Worcester, Mass.) has one dated specimen of the OH&S watermark from 1838.

17. John D. Davies, *Phrenology: Fad and Science, a Nineteenth-Century American Crusade* (New Haven: Yale Univ. Press, 1955), 3–4; CMS to Henry Sedgwick, 23 March 1831, Catharine Maria Sedgwick Papers III, Box 3.12, MHS; George Combe, *The Constitution of Man, considered in relation to external objects* (Boston: Carver & Hendee, 1829); CMS to Kate Sedgwick Minot, 13 January 1833, Catharine Maria Sedgwick Papers II, Box 1.9, MHS.

18. Combe, *The Constitution of Man*, 48–49.

19. CMS to Kate Sedgwick Minot, 5 Feb. 1831, Catharine Maria Sedgwick Papers I, Box 1.14, MHS; CMS to Frances Sedgwick Watson, 5 Feb. 1831, Catharine Maria Sedgwick Papers I, Box 1.14, MHS; CMS to Charles Sedgwick, 5 Feb. 1831, Catharine Maria Sedgwick Papers I, Box 1.14, MHS.

20. CMS to Kate Sedgwick Minot, 18 June 1833, Catharine Maria Sedgwick Papers I, Box 1.15, MHS; *The Power of Her Sympathy: The Autobiography and Journal of Catharine Maria Sedgwick*, ed. Mary Kelley (Boston: Massachusetts Historical Society, 1993),

137; CMS to Kate Sedgwick Minot, 2 July 1833, Catharine Maria Sedgwick Papers I, Box 1.16, MHS; Sedgwick, "Slavery in New England," 421.

21. *Power of Her Sympathy*, 137–38.

22. CMS to Jane Minot Sedgwick, 19 March 1834, Catharine Maria Sedgwick Papers III, Box 4.1, MHS; CMS, Journal entry, 16 Mar. 1836, Catharine Maria Sedgwick Papers I, Box 11.10, MHS.

23. CMS to Eliza Follen, 15 April 1834, Catharine Maria Sedgwick Papers I, Box 8.8, MHS.

24. CMS to Lydia Maria Child, 27 May 1834, Stockbridge Library Historical Room, Stockbridge, Mass.

25. Lydia Maria Child to CMS, 31 May 1834, Catharine Maria Sedgwick Papers III, Box 4.2, MHS.

26. CMS, Journal entries, 2 Feb. 1833, 13 Feb. 1833, 13 April 1833, Catharine Maria Sedgwick Papers I, Box 11.8, MHS.

27. Sedgwick, "A Reminiscence of Federalism," *The Token* (1834): 102–43, reprinted in *Tales and Sketches*, Series One (Philadelphia, 1835), 9–43. [Story online] [cited 28 June 2001], available from http://www.salemstate.edu/imc/sedgwick/federalism.html; Sedgwick, *The Linwoods; or, "Sixty Years Since" in America*, vol. 1 (New York: Harper & Brothers, 1835), 163.

28. Sedgwick may also have been influenced by Hegel's discussion of the master-slave relationship in *The Phenomenology of Spirit*.

29. CMS to ?, 21? Jan. 1861, Catharine Maria Sedgwick Papers III, Box 5.6, MHS.

Mrs. Theodore Sedgwick (Pamela Dwight) and daughter Catharine Maria Sedgwick, unidentified artist, ca. 1795. Oil on canvas. Courtesy of Sedgwick Family Society and Trust.

8

🙠 Excerpts from Reviews of *The Linwoods; or, "Sixty Years
Since" in America*

"The Novels of Miss Sedgwick." *American Monthly Magazine* (January 1836):
15–25.

"I should as soon think of galloping through paradise as down one of Miss
Sedgwick's pages," was the reply of a reader of the Linwoods, on being accused
of making slow progress in the book. (P. 15)

North American Review (January 1836): 160–96.

We think this work the most agreeable that Miss Sedgwick has yet published. It is written throughout with the same good taste and quiet unpretending
power, which characterize all her productions, and is superior to most of them
in the variety of characters brought into action and the interest of the fable. . . .

. . . It spreads before us a map of New York, the young emporium of our
western world, now rivaling in wealth, population, splendor and luxury, the
proudest capitals of Europe; as she was in her day of small things, a few Dutch-
built streets interspersed with gardens and grouped round the battery. . . . Miss
Sedgwick has also transported us to the interior of one of the quiet villages of
New England, and has delineated very happily from the living models around
her, the simple virtue, which then as now distinguished their inhabitants, and
at that period were heightened into heroism by a universal, all absorbing devotion to country. Upon this rich canvas of historical fact, our author has embroi-
dered a very ingeniously contrived and pleasantly told story, diversified, as we
have said, with rather more than the usual variety of incidents and characters.
(Pp. 160–61)

Knickerbocker (October 1835): 368–69.

[I]t is with the imaginative creations, —the beings of the writer's mind, —that the unity of the narrative has its connection. The story is made up of their affections, powers, hopes, sorrows, disappointments, and rejoicings, and of the incidents to which these give rise, or by which they are effected: all the rest is incidental, yet so ingeniously commingled with the plot, as to form with it a complete and consistent whole, from which nothing could be spared. (P. 368)

Monthly Review (London), (October 1835): 211–21.

[I]t is much more of a domestic than an historical novel; her aim being to exhibit the feeling of the times she speaks of, which necessarily afford a rich field for the painter of picturesque domestic features. In doing so, by the vividness of her imagination, the truth of her colouring, and the tenderness and gracefulness of her sentiments, she has produced a most fascinating, affecting, and even instructive work. The story abounds with heart-stirring events and incidents, and with a finely varied and contrasted array of characters. (Pp. 211–12)

[Edgar Allan Poe.] *Southern Literary Messenger* (December 1835): 57–59.

[I]n the creation of Bessie Lee, Miss Sedgwick has given evidence not to be disputed, of a genius far more than common. We do not hesitate to call it a truly beautiful and original conception, evincing imagination of the highest order. . . . In . . . the narrative of [Bessie's] singular journey, are some passages of the purest and most exalted poetry—passages which no mind but one thoroughly imbued with the spirit of the beautiful could have conceived, and which, perhaps, no other writer in this country than Miss Sedgwick could have executed.

. . . Kisel, the servant of Eliot Lee, is original, and, next to Bessie, the best conception of the book. . . . While Miss Sedgwick can originate such characters as these, she need apprehend few rivals near the throne. (Pp. 57–58)

The Boston Pearl (12 March 1836): 206–7.

With the characters in the Linwoods we have been truly pleased. There is a rich variety not commonly found in the fictions of the day. We are peculiarly pleased with the high-minded Isabella Linwood, contrasted so strongly as she is with the tender floweret, Bessie Lee. We like not a woman who thinks she has nought to do but to take the events of her life as they come, relying solely upon the more hardy sex for protection, as if convinced that woman's part is merely to obey.—We admire her whose spirit flags not in the hour of trouble—who sinks not beneath the slightest load of adversity, but who meets danger boldly, and like a woman—ready to assume the courage of a man when occasion shall require. . . . (P. 207)

New England Magazine (November 1835): 380–81.

We have whigs and tories, soldiers and clowns, fine gentlemen and fine ladies, coxcombs and true men, most of whom play their parts "excellent well." . . . The subordinate characters are most of them excellent. Kisel, however, we think is a failure—though without him, we should have missed some pathetic scenes. . . .

This novel is full of a most happy and cheerful spirit. It puts one in good humor with himself and the world. (P. 381)

Chapter 8

Mischief, Insanity, Memetics, and Agency in *The Linwoods; or, "Sixty Years Since" in America*

ROBERT DALY

> "I have seen your mind casting off the shackles of early prejudices, resisting the authority of opinion, self-rectified, and forming its independent judgments on those great interests in which the honour and prosperity of your country are involved."
>
> "Then," said Isabella, somewhat mischievously, "I think that you like me for, what most men like not at all—my love of freedom and independence of control."
>
> *The Linwoods* II, 223

> Knowledge and action are the central relations between mind and world. In action, world is adapted to mind. In knowledge, mind is adapted to world.
>
> Timothy Williamson

*T*he Linwoods may be Catharine Maria Sedgwick's bravest book. In it, she put the human and historical complications back into the great icon of the American Revolution, and not everyone was pleased. In her journal entry for 20 November 1835, the year the book was published, Sedgwick scrupulously recorded a negative reaction from someone who could limit her contemporary audience. One Mr. Wells, who kept a school for boys in South Boston, announced that "he had read all my books to them, 'all except the last, and in that were some bad words, some profanity!' "[1]

Slavering after scandal, the degenerate postmodern reader hurries through the text to find the good parts which, strangely enough, have not been dog-eared for us by earlier readers. At good Mrs. Archer's house, the villainous robber, or "skinner," Sam Hewson, addresses his gang, saying, "[W]hat the d—l ails that fellow?" and later expresses frustration: "It's d—d shame."[2] Much later, the British jailer Loring, no one's role model, is described in the book by no less than Ethan Allen as "the most mean-spirited, cowardly, deceitful, and destructive animal in God's creation" (II, 236–37). After that and other careful labeling of him as a villain, Sedgwick finally permits him to tell his American prisoners to go to bed: We overhear him "command the prisoners to get to their beds, in his customary phrase (we retrench a portion of its vulgarity and profanity): 'Kennel, d—n ye—kennel, ye sons of Belial'" (II, 237). And that's about it for profanity, but that was enough for Mr. Wells. Sedgwick's retrenchments and her elision of crucial letters so that only the previously corrupted could even recognize the word were in vain. Mr. Wells was shocked by her contravention of conventional expectations, and he protected his students from Sedgwick's moral decline by reducing her audience.

Risible as this reader response might seem to us, Sedgwick had to take it seriously, recording in her journal: "This is a criticism worth remembering, and in the next edition I will correct, wherever I can, without sacrificing what is essentially characteristic, this fault" (*Life and Letters*, 249). However skittish her readers, and however prudish Mr. Wells's reaction, Sedgwick must have seen it coming. As poor Mr. Wells pointed out in shock and chagrin, this descent into profanity was something new for her.

And profanity is not the only shocking move in *The Linwoods*. Another is the setting out and then almost immediate retraction of quite unexpected sentiments. In a letter to his mother, Eliot Lee, one of our heroes, casually includes this observation: "'Every woman is at heart a rake,' says Pope" (I, 122). He then adds, "[T]hat every man is at heart a coxcomb is just about as true" (I, 122–23), and we are, of course, meant to infer that he believes neither. Yet the occasion, his having a new uniform, hardly requires this strained analogy. We shall later meet Helen Ruthven, a woman who is at heart a rake; she will ensnare Jasper Meredith, a man who is at heart a coxcomb and who has treated Bessie Lee shabbily. When Helen marries Jasper and treats him with the same casual indifference he has shown Bessie, the prose gloats, "Bessie Lee, thou wert then avenged!" But this exuberance simply will not do, and Sedgwick doubles back: "Avenged? Sweet spirit of Christian forgiveness and celestial love, we crave thy pardon!" (II, 273). It is worthwhile to consider why, in 1835 at the height of her powers and fame, that good Christian lady, Catharine Maria Sedgwick, is leading her readers to profanity, Pope's sardonic wit, and *Schadenfreude*.

That she does so in a book on the American Revolution raises the stakes and makes the mystery all the more interesting. What is the relation of all this gleeful skullduggery to Isabella's "casting off the shackles of early prejudices" and "forming . . . independent judgments on those great interests in which the honour and prosperity of your country are involved" (II, 223)? We can begin to address this question by exploring what mischief and madness have to do with the memetics of our culture and with the enabling of our cultural agency.

Writing through the conventions of her day, even as we write through such conventions as writerly transgression and autotelic language, Sedgwick had to educate her readers beyond those conventions without offending them so much that they simply ceased to read her or, worse yet, kept others from reading her. Writings unread do no cultural work.

Though the new edition by Maria Karafilis makes it available once more, *The Linwoods* has long remained largely unread. We now respond well to the Unitarian liberalism and discriminating religious critique of *A New-England Tale*, to the realism of *Redwood*, to the Horatian satire of *Hope Leslie*, and to the more Senecan satire on the worship of wealth in *Clarence; or, A Tale of Our Own Times*. We are, of course, right to do so. The question now is whether we should continue to dismiss *The Linwoods*, as Edward Halsey Foster did: "[T]he romance is not a particularly good one and certainly not worthy of the generous praise that critics gave it in its day."[3]

Tastes change. We may now respond more generously to a novel that tends to confound and revise conventional expectations. As with Hewson's and Loring's profanity, Sedgwick frames carefully her tale of the Revolution and its hero, General Washington, by writing in her preface that she approaches them with "a sentiment resembling the awe of the pious Israelite when he approached the ark of the Lord" (I, xii). One pious Israelite, Uzzah, merely tried to steady the ark of the Lord when "the oxen shook it. And the anger of the Lord was kindled against Uzzah; and God smote him there for his error; and there he died by the ark of God" (2 Sam. 6:6–7). Admittedly, Cooper had survived writing about the Revolution in *The Spy* (1821), but it matters that Sedgwick alludes to Uzzah, the less promising precedent, because her treatment is far less pious than Cooper's.

She assures us of her awe. Yet as soon as we enter the story itself, the pluralistic mischief begins. There is more to the Revolution than perfect English-American heroes united against old England. Several cultures and classes interact in a liminal time, in which power circulates unpredictably and old habits of mind need to be revised. The story opens "just at the close of day" and by implication at the close of a time "of unquestioned aristocracy—(*sic transit gloria mundi!*)" (I, 13). A culture that had seemed stable, even permanent, must now somehow change or die. Throughout the book, comparisons between then and now (Sedgwick's own time) suggest her sense that the hegemony of her own culture of

New England is no more immune to time than is that of old England. Both times are liminal, on the threshold of great change. So she begins her story "[s]ome two or three years before our revolutionary war," among the "Dutch habitations" (I, 14) of New York, then "little more than a village" of "some eighteen or twenty thousand inhabitants" (I, 41), where people can repair to Aunt Katy's garden for "rural recreations," young men bag a "brace of snipe" (I, 20), young women have their fortunes told in a "Dutch parlour" by a mysterious fortune-teller with the decidedly unmysterious name of "Effie" (I, 19).

From the start, though the concerns are serious, the tone is decidedly not reverent. Mrs. Linwood is "a model of conjugal nonentity" (I, 34); her daughter, Isabella Linwood, speaks with "the spirit of mischief playing about her arch mouth" (I, 16), seems "like one who might have been born a rebel chieftainess" (I, 32), and responds to Effie's offer—to tell her fortune together with that of Jasper Meredith and "to ascertain how far she might blend their destinies"— with "Oh, no, no—no partnership for me" (I, 23). Although Isabella's friend, Bessie Lee, "had been bred in the strict school of New England orthodoxy" (I, 15), the book is full of cultural alternatives to New England and quite self-conscious both about its characters' theatricality and about its own. The fortune-teller Effie may well be taken in by her own act, "for it is impossible to say how far a weak mind may become the dupe of its own impostures" (I, 28). Having cast a cold eye upon the theatricality of its characters, the text then places its own narrative in a theatrical context with the following parabasis: "We have thus introduced some of the dramatis personae of the following volumes to our readers" (I, 32). This framing makes the entire story, as Philip Gould has written of Magawisca's narrative in *Hope Leslie*, "self-consciously performative."[4]

The cultural work performed becomes evident in the telling of an unconventional love story in the context of an unconventional history. Sedgwick offers us an American Revolution far more multicultural and humanly complex than the conventional iconicity of her time allowed. Though an extremely good human being, General Washington is human, fallible. Washington trusts his old friend, Mr. Ruthven, who trusts his son, Harry, who plans to kidnap Washington for the British. Timely intelligence from Eliot Lee enables him to avoid capture, but the point is made. Washington himself is not self-sufficient. He needs help, needs to be part of a sustaining network and community. Sedgwick does not undermine the Revolution so much as complicate it, and we may say of *The Linwoods* what Sedgwick wrote of Hawthorne in her reaction to *The Marble Faun*: "He shows to our mind's eye what never of its own power it could see, and he lights up the dim chambers of memory, illuming our faded impressions, putting his own glowing colors on them, and often thrilling interpretation on what to common senses are but blank walls."[5]

Sedgwick's book makes its mischief by beginning with dichotomous prejudices—Whig/Tory, masculine/feminine, New York/New England, aristocratic/
yeoman, urban/rural—then complicating them as different families and cultures
mix and mingle. So, for example, the elder Mr. Linwood of Dutch and English
New York is a thoroughgoing Tory. Yet his son, Herbert Linwood, goes off at
age eleven to school in New England, where he boards with the family of Bessie
Lee and her brother, Eliot. There he catches the Whig Republican virus, so that
when war is imminent, he signs up with the revolutionaries and is promptly
disowned by his father, who will now leave the vast Linwood estate to daughter
Isabella.

Her prospects attract a rich Tory, Jasper Meredith, who feels "his aristocratic
blood tingle in every vein," and takes credit for London in his pride that he is
"a citizen 'of no mean city.'" We are then reminded that these prejudices were
not cured by the Revolution and still need to be mocked and complicated:
"[E]ven now there are young citizens (and some citizens in certain illusions
remain young all their lives) who look with the most self-complacent disdain on
country breeding" (I, 41).

"Self-complacent disdain" is Jasper's stock in trade. He speaks of Herbert
Linwood's time at "farmer Lee's," and he terms young Bessie Lee a "yeoman,"
a "peasant girl," and a bird "of the *basse cour*" (I, 39), or farmyard. He coolly
dumps her to pursue Isabella, and Bessie goes mad.

But madness, like inspiration, enables one to go beyond conformity to local
conventions, and Bessie gains a freedom to wander physically and mentally. Like
many in distress, she travels to New York. The most conventional of the young
friends at the beginning of the book, Bessie moves beyond her earlier limits and
then gets better (no Romantic suicide for Sedgwick). Like Esther Downing in
Hope Leslie, Bessie goes from the completely conventional young life to the
genuinely unconventional decision to live single. Her friends, both the conservative Mrs. Archer and the radical Isabella, have "aided in the entire dissipation
of Bessie's illusions, and no shadow of them remained but a sort of nun-like
shrinking from the admiration and devotion of the other sex" (II, 273).

Needless to say, though Isabella is taken in by Jasper Meredith, and does
love him, she does not do the conventional thing of either marrying Jasper
Meredith or dying for the want of him. Like Bessie Lee, she does an unconventional and rather postmodern thing: She gets over him. She writes the cad a
truly eviscerating Dear John letter, in which she redefines and thereby controls
that early love: "I have loved you, if a sentiment struggling with doubt and
distrust, seeking for rest and finding none, becoming fainter and fainter in the
dawning light of truth, and vanishing, like an exhalation in the full day, can be
called love" (II, 206). And in time she loves again and marries Eliot Lee, one of

Jefferson's natural *aristoi* of talent and merit: "[G]raduated by nature's aristocracy (nature alone sets a seal to her patents of universal authority), he should rank with the noble of every land" (I, 42). Jasper Meredith remains culturally narrow, a victim of unexamined convention, and ends "trapped like a captive insect, paralyzed in the web that enclosed him" (II, 272). He returns to England "now utterly dependent on [his] mother," accompanied by the rakish Helen, a splendidly chilling creation. Now his unloved and unloving wife, she announces that his mother's "governing principle" is "that 'appearances must be managed'" and that "'I shall convince her that I am one of the managers, and the *prima donna* in this drama of appearances'" (II, 272).

In "this drama of appearances," theatricality is a given, and insanity and paralysis are real dangers, particularly for those who choose only one class or culture and choose it entirely. The mischief and pluralism of a mind open to the bits and pieces of many cultures—choosing and then choosing again, continually "self-rectified" (II, 223), open to inherited conventions and to the viruses of cultural cross-pollination, and willing to love and then love again and this time do it better—are the virtues in which the book most heavily invests. Sedgwick, always surefooted among conventions, foregrounds this unconventional view: "We are aware that the champions of romance, the sage expounders of the laws of sentiment, maintain that there can be but one love. We will not dispute with them, though we honestly believe, that in the capacities of loving, as in all other capacities, there be diversities of gifts" (II, 285).

In this book, happiness does not depend upon choosing the right person or culture or category. It depends rather more on developing a repertoire of virtues or strengths in which no one virtue or Aristotelian excellence (*areté*) trumps any of the others. Sedgwick's families, nations, classes, genders, races, and massive intertextuality (both her text and her characters are constantly allusive) are a huge resource, what Pierre Bourdieu calls an "inexhaustible toolbox"[6] from which to draw whatever one needs at the time.

One term for these bits of culture is "meme," which the *OED* now defines as "an element of a culture that may be considered to be passed on by non-genetic means, esp. imitation."[7] To extend a familiar homology, if the gene is the atom of biology, the atom of culture is the meme. Sedgwick's central characters start out with their cultures and conventions preselected for them.

Some, like Jasper Meredith, engage with others and toy with alterity but only for a time. "Meredith's deluded vanity" (II, 165) causes him to dismiss the rich cultural alterities he is offered and to retreat into a familiar self. The novel reaches its conclusion about him long after we have: "Meredith was a self-idolater" (II, 189). Others, like Helen Ruthven, Jasper's manipulative flame and later wife, invoke the *ignava ratio*, the argument from determinism, and apply it to both themselves and others: "I am but the passive subject of an irresistible power" (I, 200) and "I judge others by myself" (II, 4). But this synecdochic view, that society is merely the individual self writ large and that all the world is or should quickly become Britain, is severely undermined and then complicated. Several other characters and the book itself incorporate linguistic alterities. The Tory Mr. Linwood at first objects to Lady Anne Seton's habit of "interlarding your English with French" (II, 170), but no one else does, and the book itself has the same habit of including French along with English. Indeed, French is associated with freedom. Isabella negotiates with her father for a favor if she wins the prize in French. He agrees. She wins it and demands that he set Rose free from slavery. Though he keeps his other eleven African Americans enslaved, he does free Rose, who later returns the favor by helping his son, Herbert Linwood, escape from a British prison. In nation as well as family, French augurs freedom. French allies show up and, understandably, speak French (II, 123), and in the epigraphs Montaigne is quoted without translation.

But French is not the only alterity folded into family and nation: "Our revolutionary contest, by placing men in new relations, often exhibited in new force and beauty the ties that bind together the human family" (I, 163), and the best of Sedgwick's characters learn from several roots, branches, and rhizomes of that larger family. They reach out past local convention to other languages, cultures, skills, and options. Master Hale quotes Virgil. Eliot Lee quotes Pope, though he does not, of course, agree with Pope's misogyny, especially not in a letter to his mother. Aged twelve and ten respectively, Isabella Linwood and Bessie Eliot consult a Dutch fortune-teller named Effie. Isabella grows up to have a "Grecian outline" (I, 193), to wear her dark hair "contrary to the fashion of the times (she was no thrall of fashion)" (I, 192), and to be beautiful without being conventional: "Her person was rather above the ordinary height, and approaching nearer to *embonpoint* than is common in our *lean* climate" (I, 193). Bessie Lee takes lessons in Italian, and Sedgwick's occasional epigraph in Italian (II, 192) makes clear that she has, too. Jasper Meredith has taught Bessie Lee "the Persian language of flowers" (II, 183), and she is able to quote it back to him in embarrassing circumstances. These characters learn and use memes from languages and cultures outside their own.

This habit of reaching out and folding in is habitual, not calculated. It confers advantage and enables agency, but in ways not easily predictable. In crises, moreover, unexpected help comes from unconventional persons. Having grown up with the "habits of a boy" (II, 246), Lizzie Bengin is a good mariner and can escape, along with Isabella Linwood and Lady Anne Seton, from the British soldiers, who brim with force but lack the skill and practice for navigation. Eliot Lee befriends little Lizzie Archer out of habitual kindness and fellow feeling. Yet her blindness does not reduce her to merely a sentimental object of pity or pious declamation. She can navigate in the dark as skillfully as Lizzie Bengin can on water. She alone can lead Eliot Lee through the darkness to the skylight without lighting any candles or lamps, whose light would give them away to the British soldiers. And Rose, far stronger than expected, can beat up, hold down, and terrorize the British Provost-Marshal, Cunningham. She can literally make him take his medicine and allow Herbert Linwood to escape from prison. All reach out beyond convention to alterity; link themselves to other races, classes, genders, times, places, and people; and benefit from a multiplicity that gives them more options and greater collective agency.

What the Revolution has done for them the book will, *mutatis mutandis*, do for us. It will put the human complications and the multiplicity of cultural memes back into the icon of the Revolution. It will shock. It will, by placing us "in new relations," exhibit "in new force and beauty the ties that bind together the human family" (I, 163). In doing so, it will present radical transgression, even as the Revolution itself did, as a conservative act, a Machiavellian *ricorso*, a return to first principles.

In that context, Sedgwick presents the Revolution as the natural outgrowth of the Pilgrim settlement: "It has been justly said, that the seeds of our revolution and future independence were sown by the pilgrims" (I, 67). She presents her own portrayal of a social sense of self as merely an homage to George Washington, since she portrays him as "alive to social virtues and affections" (II, 257). And she can even use him to justify her own less-than-pious approach to the Revolution, since she has Washington himself say "that flattery corrupts the giver as well as the receiver" (I, 145). Modeling himself on Cincinnatus, Washington insisted on absolute honesty, on receiving and delivering the bad news with the good, the profane with the sacred. Invoking him, Sedgwick can do the good work that Tzvetan Todorov considers the only ethical use of history and that he calls, appropriately, sacrilege, the history in which the sacred and the profane are inextricably interwoven.[8] A history of paper saints and perfect heroes cuts off the imperfectly good living generation from any connection with its past. A history of scandal and scoundrels cuts off the imperfectly bad living generation. Only the sacrilegious mix gives us a history we can use.

In a letter to Bessie Lee, the young Isabella Linwood argues that all narratives, fictive and historical, are fashioned, constructed, not simply recorded passively and objectively: "If history then is mere fiction, why may we not read romances of our own choosing?" (I, 64). Though we may wish to maintain the distinction, both history and fiction are shaped by and for the present culture. Sondra Smith Gates suggests that historical unity is retrospectively constructed through a process of inclusion and exclusion. Gilles Deleuze argues that the

"One is always the index of a multiplicity."[9] What Sedgwick restores to the American Revolution is a good deal of the individual and cultural multiplicity that drove it. For Deleuze, "[T]he American Revolution continues to send out its fragments . . . always trying . . . to take up the experiment once again, to find a brotherhood in this enterprise, a sister in this becoming, a music in its stuttering language, a pure sound and unknown chords in language itself."[10] Sedgwick's fictive narrative of the Revolution gives us an America that is not pure and monotone, but symphonic. In her America, fragments are shaped into structures, individual voices into contrapuntal harmonies. America becomes politically independent by making good use of its cultural interdependence.

In short, we move ahead by going back. Sedgwick could bring together her own time with that of the Revolution to create what Wai Chee Dimock calls "temporal hybridity,"[11] the bringing together of different times. For Dimock, "such temporal heresies are the largest gifts poetry has to offer, to reader and writer alike," and such literature is not timeless, but "time*ful*. It is full of time, densely populated, home to each of the centuries bearing signs of human life."[12] Such incorporations of alterity can free us from the delusion that the fashions of any one time and place are universal. They can focus our attention on other times and other people and so enlarge our sense of options in present.

They do as much for Sedgwick's wiser characters. The "self-rectifying power" (I, 105), (II, 44–45) of their minds is enabled by their interactions with others. Through plot machinery that links each to others, they are exposed to foreign modes of perception and discourse. They pause, misinterpret, and suffer. But they don't romantically kill themselves or die of broken hearts. They're resilient. They recover. They learn. Through learning, they adapt mind to world; through agency, they adapt world to mind. And they secure their own agency, neither by subsumption within a single hegemonic discourse nor by rejection of it, but by selective alliances with many discourses. Indeed, they frequently seek out multiple alterities in order to learn more in an active form of cultural shopping. Such active selection and combination, rather than creation *ex nihilo*, stand behind Barbara Herrnstein Smith's observation that "those with cultural power and commonly other forms of power as well" are those "with competence in a large number of cultural codes."[13]

Like the country, Sedgwick's protagonists become independent by first being interdependent. While splendidly individual, they are not individualists, "for this detestable selfishness dulls a man's perception of the rights of others . . . while it makes him keenly susceptible to whatever touches self. He resembles those insects who, instead of the social senses . . . are furnished with feelers that make their own bodies the focus of all sensation" (I, 246). It is no surprise that Jasper Meredith, whose complacency leaves him, like his mother, "spell-bound within a narrow circle of selfish interests" (II, 67), ends "trapped like a captive insect" (II, 272).

Isabella Linwood, on the other hand, allies with many alterities and becomes, like Eliot Lee, an agent of the new America, "an agent, who might, as the exigency should demand, be prudent or bold, wary or decided, cautious or gallant, and self-sacrificing" (II, 211). Indeed, when they marry, they help to create and recreate, as many readers have recognized, both a family and nation. As Shirley Samuels observes, "Isabella's marriage, like that of other characters in the novel, involves her discovery of self in a political world, a founding of the family that is a founding of the state."[14]

Isabella secures agency by being an agent of many things larger than herself—family, friends, nation, world, and history. She does so by learning and making "the ties that bind together the human family" (I, 163). Cultural theory and memetics enable us to understand how Isabella Linwood can secure an agency that is Dutch, English, French, African, New English, and other, but also her own.

NOTES

1. *Life and Letters of Catharine Maria Sedgwick*, ed. Mary E. Dewey (New York: Harper and Brothers, 1871), 249. Hereafter cited in the text as *Life and Letters*.

2. Catharine Maria Sedgwick, *The Linwoods; or, "Sixty Years Since" in America* (New York: Harper and Brothers, 1835), I: 262, 268. Hereafter cited in the text with volume number.

3. Edward Halsey Foster, *Catharine Maria Sedgwick* (New York: Twayne, 1974), 107.

4. Philip Gould, "Catharine Sedgwick's 'Recital' of the Pequot War," *American Literature* 66 (December 1994): 653.

5. *The Power of Her Sympathy: The Autobiography and Journal of Catharine Maria Sedgwick*, ed. Mary Kelley (Boston: Massachusetts Historical Society, 1993), 103.

6. Pierre Bourdieu, *In Other Words: Essays Towards a Reflexive Sociology* (Stanford, Calif.: Stanford Univ. Press, 1990), 103.

7. Susan Blackmore, *The Meme Machine* (Oxford: Oxford Univ. Press, 1999), viii.

8. Tzvetan Todorov, "History and Ethics" (paper presented at Cornell Univ., 24 March 1997).

9. See Gates' essay in this volume. Gilles Deleuze, *Pure Immanence: Essays on a Life,* trans. Anne Boyman (New York: Zone Books, 2001), 30.

10. Gilles Deleuze, *Essays Critical and Clinical,* trans. Daniel W. Smith and Michael E. Greco (Minneapolis: Univ. of Minnesota Press, 1997), 89.

11. Wai Chee Dimock, "Non-Newtonian Time: Robert Lowell and Temporal Hy-

bridity" (paper presented at the twelfth annual Comparative Literature Symposium, Buffao, N.Y., 31 March 2001).

12. Wai Chee Dimock, "Literature for the Planet," *PMLA* 116 (January 2001): 182.

13. Barbara Herrnstein Smith, *Contingencies of Value: Alternative Perspectives for Critical Theory* (Cambridge, Mass.: Harvard Univ. Press, 1988), 51.

14. Shirley Samuels, *Romances of the Republic: Women, the Family, and Violence in the Literature of the Early American Nation* (New York: Oxford Univ. Press, 1996), 64.

9

✍ Excerpts from Reviews of *Tales and Sketches*

"Catharine M. Sedgwick." In *The National Portrait Gallery of Distinguished Americans*. Ed. James Herring, James B. Longacre, and American Academy of the Fine Arts. Vol. 1. New York: Monson Bancroft, 1834, 1–8.

While we are talking of this beautiful tale ["Le Bossu"], we may be permitted to say, that a collection of Miss Sedgwick's contributions to the Souvenirs would form two delightful, and, we doubt not, popular volumes. (P. 6)

H. M. [Harriet Martineau]. "Miss Sedgwick's Works." *The Westminster Review* (October 1838): 42–65.

It has occurred to us that a glance at the course of a thorough-bred popular American writer may throw some light on the state and prospects of American literature. In the pursuit of our object we shall say nothing of Irving, because he is not a fair instance, being a mixture of the American of the present day and of the Englishman of the last century. Neither shall we refer to Cooper, because he is not a very popular author at home, his works having met with a less favourable reception there than abroad. Miss Sedgwick is our subject. She suits our purpose in every way. She is the most popular writer, we believe, in the United States. Her later works have met the national mind, and warmed the national heart; and, while her education has made her as well acquainted with the literature of the Old World as those of her countrymen who have been able to do nothing better than imitate it, she is thoroughly American in her principles, her intellectual and moral associations, and in her more recent productions. (P. 42)

We refer to the volume of Tales and Sketches for the purpose of mentioning that it contains a dialogue, perhaps the most beautiful of the author's single pieces, on OLD MAIDS. We have never before happened to see the subject expressly treated of in the right spirit, except perhaps in a well-known glorious passage of Jean Paul; and it is remarkable that the first essay on this condition of modern human life should reach us from a country where the condition is supposed to be almost unknown. (P. 58)

The truth of the pictures Miss Sedgwick gives in her Essay is manifest, and the stories themselves are touching; but there is something higher than this—a moral dignity, united with a mournful pathos, which raises this piece above all the many beautiful expressions of individual opinion and feeling which are scattered through her novels. (P. 59)

Southern Literary Messenger (January 1836): 167.

This volume includes—A Reminiscence of Federalism—The Catholic Iroquois—The Country Cousin—Old Maids—The Chivalric Sailor—Mary Dyre—Cacoethes Scribendi—The Eldest Sister—St. Catharine's Eve—Romance in Real Life—and the Canary Family.

All of these pieces, we believe, have been published before. Of most of them we can speak with certainty—for having, in earlier days, been enamored of their pervading spirit of mingled chivalry and pathos, we cannot now forget them even in their new habiliments. Old Maids—The Country Cousin—and one or two others, we have read before—and should be willing to read again. These, our ancient friends, are worthy of the pen which wrote "Hope Leslie" and "The Linwoods." "Old Maids," in spite of the equivocal nature of its title, is full of noble and tender feeling—a specimen of fine writing, involving in its melancholy detail what we must consider the beau-ideal of feminine disinterestedness—the *ne plus ultra* of sisterly devotion. "The Country Cousin" possesses all the peculiar features of the tale just spoken of, with something more of serious and even solemn thought. . . . "The Reminiscence of Federalism" relates to a period of thirty years ago in New England—is a mingled web of merriment and gloom—and replete with engrossing interest. . . . "Cacoethes Scribendi" is told with equal grace and vivacity. "The Canary Family" is a tale for the young—brief, pointed, and quaint. But the best of the series, in every respect, is the sweet and simple history of "The Eldest Sister."

While we rejoice that Miss Sedgwick has thought proper to condone into their present form these evidences of her genius which have been so long floating at random before the eye of the world—still we think her rash in having risked the publication so immediately after "The Linwoods." None of these "Sketches" have the merit of an equal number of pages in that very fine novel—and the descent from good to inferior (although the inferior be very far from bad) is most generally detrimental to literary fame. (P. 167)

Chapter 9

The Collection as Literary Form:
Sedgwick's *Tales and Sketches* of 1835

JOHN AUSTIN

For many antebellum writers, the publication of a collection was a necessary first step, often after a long apprenticeship in the field of periodical writing, in their development as a professional author: Nathaniel Hawthorne, Edgar Allan Poe, Harriet Beecher Stowe, William Leggett, Eliza Leslie, and James Hall each commenced their careers as professional authors of fiction with single-author collections. Hawthorne's career is perhaps most representative; only after the publication of *Twice-Told Tales* and *Mosses From an Old Manse* was he able to amass enough cultural capital to attract a major publisher, Ticknor and Fields, and launch himself as a novelist. Sedgwick's career reverses this pattern. By 1835, the year she published *Tales and Sketches*, Sedgwick was already, with Cooper, one of America's most popular and critically successful novelists. One is tempted to conclude that the publication of this volume was merely an attempt by the publisher, Cary, Lea & Blanchard, to turn a quick profit on the success of Sedgwick's novel *The Linwoods*, published by Harper & Brothers just months earlier. (The title page of *Tales and Sketches* presents "Miss Sedgwick" as the author of "'The Linwoods,' 'Hope Leslie,' &c. &c.") Yet the publication of this volume is as important to the meaning and shape of Sedgwick's career as the publication of *Twice-Told Tales* was to Hawthorne's. In selecting which stories would be republished (and equally important, which would not), arranging the order in which those stories would appear, and collecting them under a title of her own choosing, Sedgwick reinvents herself as a professional author and creates from an extensive body of periodical writing a distinct oeuvre, a canon upon which she imprints her own authority. Stories and sketches published in a range of literary annuals (mostly *The Atlantic Souvenir* and *The Token*, where they appeared as single elements of a larger, often more eclectic, textual program) are, in this, the first book of Sedgwick's to appear in her own name, unified under the signature of her authorship. Works that may have been read one way in the context of first publication are given new force and meaning through their republication in book form.

In *Tales and Sketches* Sedgwick uses the expressive potential of the collection form to redirect her career and redefine her authorial vocation. *Tales and Sketches* appeared at a moment of radical change in the structure of the literary field and the profession of female authorship. As magazines and annuals proliferated in the late 1820s and 1830s, more and more women appeared in print. These women experimented in a variety of narrative, poetic, and historical forms, spoke on a range of issues of national importance, and established female authorship as a respectable and profitable profession. Of central importance here is the work of Sedgwick's friend and colleague, Lydia Maria Child, and the three books she published between the years 1832 and 1834: *The Coronal*, a collection of her stories, sketches, and poems fashioned as a literary annual; *An Appeal in Favor of That Class of Americans Known as Africans;* and *The Oasis*, an abolitionist annual edited by Child. Sedgwick was both inspired and repulsed by Child's aggressive move into the public debate over slavery, and her collection is shaped by this ambivalence. In *Tales and Sketches* Sedgwick responds to the conservative polemics against "bluestockingism" advanced by the literary establishment and, at the same time, subtly checks the abolitionism of Child—a move that, in the end, strained their friendship to the breaking point. Child came to view Sedgwick as "very deficient in moral courage." Sedgwick, Child wrote, "sincerely wished well to the negroes, but she could not bear to contend for them, or for anything else."[1] Over time, then, Child and Sedgwick staked out in their collections very different positions in the literary field—Child as an abolitionist and Sedgwick as a propagandist for Christian virtue opposed to both slavery and abolitionism. But as Sedgwick and Child matured and grew apart, the sphere of female engagement enlarged, and, as their very different uses of the collection demonstrate, the possibilities for female accomplishment diversified in scope, range, and depth.

The emergence of the annual offered unprecedented access into the literary field for aspiring women authors, helped popularize the short forms of the tale and sketch, and created conditions favorable to the publication of single-author collections. Sedgwick quickly availed herself of the opportunities the new form of the annual offered, contributing to *The Legendary*, *The Atlantic Souvenir*, *The Token*, and *The Youth's Keepsake*. Indeed it was in the pages of *The Token* that Sedgwick first emerged from anonymity—one reason, it seems, why *Tales and Sketches* was published in her own name, one of the few books of Sedgwick's attributed to her in her lifetime. Samuel Goodrich, the savvy editor of *The Token* who insisted that many of his contributors, including the young Hawthorne, publish anonymously, frequently placed Sedgwick's name at the head of his table of contents. As he recognized, the name of one of America's most prominent and popular novelists lent considerable prestige to his volume and guaranteed it a certain success. For Sedgwick to have retreated behind the veil of anonymity, when a number of the works appearing in *Tales and Sketches* had already been attributed to her upon their first publication, would have been senseless, even for as self-effacing an author as Sedgwick.

Sedgwick's success—and the increased access to the literary field the annuals offered to all women—spawned angry and often hostile reactions on the part of male authors. It was not long before the female annualist became herself a fictional subject. *The Token* for 1832, for instance, though best known as the volume in which Hawthorne's "Roger Malvin's Burial," "The Gentle Boy," and "My Kinsman, Major Molineux" were first published, contains two contrasting stories on the question of female authorship, "My Wife's Novel," a tale believed to have been written by Edward Everett, and Sedgwick's "A Sketch of a Bluestocking."[2] At stake in these stories is nothing less than the scope and nature of female authorship itself. "My Wife's Novel" expresses male anxieties typical of the period and plays off a type—the assertive, reckless, outspoken "bluestocking"—that would haunt the male literary imagination throughout the nineteenth century. This tale details the hardships that befall a young bluestocking who, inspired by Scott (and the three thousand pounds he reportedly received for the *Waverly* novels), embarks on a career as a professional author. Encouraged by her writer husband who believes his wife to be "too exclusively domestic in her character," Lucinda subscribes to the leading journals, contributes to the annuals, publishes a novel, *The Pleasures of Sentiment,* and finally assumes responsibility for the "literary tone of the household," even adventuring a "criticism of her [husband's own] literary compositions."[3] Personal embarrassment, near bankruptcy (as her husband attempts to buy up the remaining copies of his wife's novel), and emigration westward to Ohio follow in turn. Chastened, Lucinda cancels her various subscriptions and returns to her needlepoint.

"My Wife's Novel" illustrates the animosity women authors excited in men. But the tale has a further interest in that it also appears to have been a satire on the efforts of Lydia Child, written by Edward Everett, a man who would soon become one of Child's most outspoken and hostile critics. Its publication in *The Token* of 1832 coincides with the appearance of Child's first antislavery writings, and Lucinda bears a resemblance to Child in more than one way. Like Lucinda, Child was a frequent contributor to the annuals. Lucinda's essay, "Characteristics of the Female Mind," published in the fictitious annual *The Anodyne,* recalls Child's piece on the same subject, "Comparative Strength of Male and Female Intellect," published in *The Massachusetts Journal* of 1829. Their first names, Lucinda and Lydia, bear a phonetic resemblance which, given the similarities of their literary careers—like Lucinda, Child's first novel was a failure—seems more than accidental. Lucinda's marriage to her husband, moreover, resembles that between Lydia and David Child. David Child encouraged Lydia's literary efforts, and his career as an author and abolitionist was eventually eclipsed by that of his gifted wife. To this extent, "My Wife's Novel" is as much about the dangers of ineffectual, if well-meaning, men who fail to establish an appropriate hierarchy within their own households as it is about women who trade their needles for pens.

Sedgwick's "A Sketch of a Bluestocking" implicitly answers "My Wife's Novel," defends the efforts of women like Child, and offers a compelling rationale for the presence of women in the literary marketplace. This tale, one of three Sedgwick wrote on the subject of female authorship in the early 1830s, contrasts two women: Mrs. Rosewell, the bluestocking of the title, and Mrs. Laight, a newly widowed mother of twelve and aspiring author. Sedgwick's narrator tells her story from the perspective of a group of young men and women who eagerly await the arrival of this "literary amazon," a woman they assume to be bookish, immodest, and "mannish."[4] Everything about Mrs. Rosewell disabuses them of these assumptions. Unlike Lucinda, Mrs. Rosewell effortlessly combines motherhood with the demands of professional authorship. She is not only a successful author, but also the agent who resolves the romantic conflicts that constitute this story's subplot; her most important "plots" are those involving her friends and relatives. Mrs. Rosewell "authors" the marriage on which the tale concludes, marrying Mrs. Laight's daughter to the unlettered but virtuous Clay. But she is also an agent of censorship, for she suppresses the publication of a metaphysical essay that Mrs. Laight hopes to see published—an act Mrs. Rosewell believes to be her greatest accomplishment. In this tale, then, writing, censorship, and matchmaking are coextensive and mutually supporting activities. Women writers, Sedgwick suggests, must police their wayward sisters—as well as themselves: Women become authors not by unsexing themselves in the literary marketplace but by embracing and, when necessary, enforcing gender identity through their literary activity.

Child's first collection, *The Coronal*, published just months after *The Token* for 1832, conforms to the model of female authorship advocated by Sedgwick in "A Sketch of a Bluestocking." Although by the time *The Coronal* appeared on the market Child had abandoned the annuals as a vehicle for her work for more politically radical journals like *The Massachusetts Journal,* where she had begun to articulate the antislavery ideas she would soon publish in *An Appeal in Favor of That Class of Americans Called Africans* (1833), there is little hint of this more radical Child in the pages of *The Coronal.* Child includes sketches, essays, tales, short fables, and poems, alternating prose works with poetry in the manner of an annual. Child includes in this volume an early antislavery story, "Stand from Under!" first published in *The Massachusetts Journal* and later reprinted in *The Liberator*, but its polemical force is muted by its placement between two more conventional pieces, an allegorical dialogue on art, "Fable of the Caterpillar and Silk-Worm," and "The Adventure of a Rain Drop," a sentimental sketch in the tradition of Hawthorne's "A Rill from the Town Pump" that was at one point attributed to Hawthorne. Although Child could have confined her first collection to prose—in which case the distinctiveness of her work and her fondness for the historical tale would have been in clear evidence—no single genre is allowed to dominate. The poetry and short sketches balance the longer tales and give this volume a lightness of tone, comparable to its diminutive size. Tellingly, Child dedicates the volume to Sedgwick, humbly presenting herself as a protégé to an older and more accomplished author known for her grace, elegance, and tact.

In *An Appeal,* Child announces a very different sort of literary vocation from the one staked out in *The Coronal.* She challenges the conventional notion that women should confine their work to the familial and domestic sphere by engaging an issue—slavery—upon which few women had dared to speak, and she does so in a recognizably masculine form: the polemical essay. Here she symbolically unveils herself, demanding, somewhat sensationally: "Read it, from sheer curiosity to see what a woman (who had much better attend to her household concerns) will say upon such a subject." Nor does she spare the sensibilities of her readers, warning: "We must not allow our nerves to be more tender than our consciences."[5] The whole of *An Appeal* is written in what David Reynolds calls the spirit of "immoral didacticism"—a fictional idiom in which the sensational—in Child's case, descriptions of mutilation, flogging, and torture—is exploited for genuinely reformist ends.[6]

In *The Oasis* Child comes before her public not as a woman who has abandoned her "household concerns" but as the editor of an annual to which other more important figures have contributed. Throughout the volume Child aligns herself with—and invokes the authority of—notable men like the Rev. Samuel May, to whom *The Oasis* is dedicated, the English abolitionist William Wilberforce, the subject of the opening sketch, and the popular John Greenleaf Whittier. By including the work of her husband, Child reminds her readers that she is a wife as well as an author, neatly reconciling roles that were increasingly seen as incompatible. This strategy is reinforced by the different genres in which Child and her husband work: David contributes essays on historical, political, and legal issues ("Henry Diaz," "Three Colored Republics of Guiana," and "Judicial Decisions in Slave States"), whereas Lydia, when not translating or compiling excerpts from other sources—as she does in "Joanna," "Scipio Africanus," "Opinions of Travelers," and "History of Mr. Thomas Jenkins"—contributes fiction.

In the early 1830s, Child wrote to Sedgwick asking her to contribute to *The Oasis*. Sedgwick politely demurred, explaining that she did not wish to be viewed as an "advocate of the principles of the abolitionists":

> There is no sorrow of humanity that I have so much at heart as the condition of the black race. There are none of my fellow creatures to whose good I should be more thankful to contribute—your argument for immediate emancipation is a very strong one. Still[,] provided the principle could be established that the blacks might be fitted for freedom and self-government[,] provided it were admitted that they must one day be free & that their freedom must be effected as soon as compatible with their best good, . . . you give the motive & the impulse to their improvement. . . . It does not appear to me that immediate abolition is best for the slaves. God only knows what is best. It is a dark and fearful subject.[7]

Sedgwick's nervous and equivocal answer to Child is typical of someone who opposed slavery but who found abolition unimaginable, and it reveals a powerful tension in Sedgwick's sense of her own vocation. On one hand, she wishes to participate in the debate—indeed she has passionate, if conflicted, views on the subject. On the other, she shrinks from the emotions this subject excites in others, particularly Aurthur and Lewis Tappan, whom she describes as "doubtful zealots." In the end she offers to fill up some pages—"I should like to illustrate the Metayer principle—almost a theory (not quite) as applied to Slavery"—though she knows Child cannot and will not accept a contribution on those terms. (The Metayer principle refers to a system of farming, common in Western Europe, in which the farmer pays a proportion of the produce to the landowner.) So troubling was this "dark and fearful subject" that Sedgwick was unable to finish the only story (perhaps the above-mentioned tale in imitation of Martineau "illustrat[ing] the Metayer principle") that directly grappled with it.[8]

Tales and Sketches is conditioned by Child's advocacy for abolitionism and the discomfort it engendered in Sedgwick, but it also allows Sedgwick to master and shape this discomfort. Though miscellaneous in structure, the ordering of the tales within this volume is artful and strategic, and it furthers Sedgwick's project of authorial self-definition. Her dedication to Martineau, and her decision to begin this volume with a leading tale, "A Reminiscence of Federalism," that surreptitiously warns against the dangers of sectional conflict, allow Sedgwick to speak on the question of slavery and answer Child. Sedgwick's omission of "A Sketch of a Bluestocking" from her 1835 collection in favor of two other stories on the question of female authorship, grouped as a diptych in the center of the volume, "Cacoethes Scribendi" and "Mary Dyre," works to a similar end and represents on her part a strategic attempt to redefine her authorial vocation. In *Tales and Sketches* Sedgwick speaks on the question of slavery and female authorship but she does so obliquely, brilliantly mobilizing the expressive potential of the compilation form.

Of particular importance here is Sedgwick's dedication to Martineau, the first "work" in the volume. The form of Sedgwick's "Dedication" is as significant as the dedication itself. Not only does this dedication appear on a separate page, but it also appears as the first entry in the table of contents. That is, the dedication is given to us not as something external to the book itself, but as an essential component of it. Given Sedgwick's reluctance to support the cause of abolition, her decision to dedicate *Tales and Sketches* to Martineau, an outspoken opponent of slavery who played a pivotal role in the abolition of the British slave trade, may come as a surprise. Yet although Sedgwick may not have shared Martineau's political views, she clearly admired the way Martineau combined authorship with a committed interest in larger social issues, investing the literary vocation with moral and political significance. Sedgwick sympathized with Martineau's efforts to fashion a career that combined literature with a commitment to what Sedgwick called, in reference to Martineau, the "general good." As Sedgwick explained in an 1834 journal entry after a visit from Martineau, Martineau crafted a career as a professional author "devoted . . . not to the intellectual amusement or advancement of the gifted and educated, but to make bread more plentiful in the husbandman's dwelling, and to still the cry of hunger forever in the poor man's cottage."[9]

Sedgwick's decision to begin *Tales and Sketches* with her most autobiographical and political tale, "A Reminiscence of Federalism," emphasizes the connection between her and Martineau and also clarifies it. On the surface, "A Reminiscence of Federalism" is a conventional tale of courtship in which the grandson of the town's most prominent Democrat, the noble and selfless Randolph, seeks the hand of the daughter of the town's most prominent Federalist. Yet on a deeper level and when placed in the context of Child's and Sedgwick's rivalry, "A Reminiscence of Federalism" is the very slavery story Sedgwick seems to have been unable to write. "A Reminiscence of Federalism" offers a critique of abolition and warns of the dangers this debate poses to national union. As Sedgwick explains in the opening paragraphs, she wrote this tale of political rivalry, one detailing "party strifes" between Democrats and Federalists in a small New England village at the turn of the century, as a way "to assuage present political controversies," an allusion to the increasingly acrimonious debate surrounding slavery and abolition. By transposing present controversies to the past, a strategy Sedgwick later employs in "Mary Dyre" as well, Sedgwick is free to explore an issue on which she was otherwise uncomfortable speaking. And by reconfiguring one conflict (slavery) in terms of another (party rivalry), Sedgwick is able to finesse (much as she does in her letter to Child) the troubling realities of the problem.

"A Reminiscence of Federalism" describes a village—not unlike a typical 1830s American town—riven by deep-rooted political differences between Jeffersonian Democrats and Federalists. The Democrats and their leader, Squire Hayford, a fierce republican and opponent of slavery, occupy the hill; the Federalists and their leader, Doctor Atwood, "parson Fed," the vale. The central conflict of this story turns on the question of slavery. The story begins with Squire Hayford disinheriting his daughter after her marriage to a slaveholding Southerner. He adopts his grandson Randolph, at the dying request of his daughter, only on condition that Randolph renounce the name of his slaveholding father, take the name of Hayford, and pledge his loyalty to the Democrats—a demand to which Randolph reluctantly acquiesces. Randolph thus finds himself in an impossible situation: loyal to the name of his father, pledged to the antislavery Democrats of his grandfather, and in love with the daughter of "parson Fed," Fanny Atwood. These conflicts come to a head at the conclusion of the story when Randolph must publicly cast the deciding vote in the local congressional election. Rather than vote for an unprincipled Democrat, Randolph defies his grandfather and votes for an honest Federalist. This act infuriates his grandfather, who promptly and publicly disinherits him, but it so impresses Doctor Atwood that he crosses party lines and votes Democratic, thereby forcing a runoff, which the Democratic candidate wins.

Unlike Child and Martineau, who advocated direct political intervention, "A Reminiscence of Federalism" counsels what Sedgwick calls in "The Country Cousin," another story in *Tales and Sketches*, Christian republicanism—a belief in Christian virtue as a positive moral force that transcends party politics and factional interests.[10] In the end, Fanny's desire for a world "where all was hope and friendship and no politics" is realized, and the political and familial conflicts at the center of the tale are neatly resolved. Hayford welcomes his grandson back into the family (as Doctor Atwood hoped he would) only to die in the resulting celebration of excessive food and drink. Randolph reassumes the name of his father, the Southern slaveholder, and marries Fanny. And the abolitionist Democrat is sent to Congress—all because Randolph and Atwood ultimately reject party loyalties in favor of the higher principle of Christian virtue.

The diverse stories that follow "A Reminiscence of Federalism" further illustrate, in different contexts, Sedgwick's belief in Christian virtue as a positive moral force. Although Sedgwick could easily have offered a more homogeneous volume, she chose instead a representative and diverse selection of her work. Sedgwick follows "A Reminiscence of Federalism" with an Indian tale set in French Canada, describing the martyrdom of a young Iroquois convert to Christianity ("The Catholic Iroquois"); a "ghost story" set during the American Revolutionary War ("The Country Cousin"); a dialogue between an older and younger woman on the theme of unmarried women ("Old Maids"); a naval adventure, also set during the Revolutionary War ("The Chivalric Sailor"); a historical tale of religious persecution and martyrdom set in seventeenth-century Boston ("Mary Dyre"); a contemporary story of female authorship ("Cacoethes Scribendi"); a satire on dandyism ("The Eldest Sister"); another tale of religious martyrdom set in thirteenth-century France ("St. Catherine's Eve"); a story of a young French foundling adopted into an American family who grows up to marry the French ambassador to America ("Romance in Real Life"); and a children's fable ("The Canary Family"). Like Hawthorne, Sedgwick had a fondness for the historical tale, but she does not allow these works to dominate the volume; rather, she intersperses them throughout, alternating them with other forms. The overall effect of the volume is that of a miscellany. In casting *Tales and Sketches* as a miscellany, Sedgwick appeals to as wide an audience as possible, a strategy that governed Hawthorne's selection of tales two years later. And by including a range of forms—political satires, comic sketches, historical tales, juvenile stories—she establishes her versatility as an author. In this way she champions an enlarged sphere for female authorship and extends the expressive range of the collection form.

Two pointedly juxtaposed stories at the center of the volume deserve special attention, since they speak directly to the question of female authorship, "Cacoethes Scribendi," perhaps the best known of Sedgwick's short works, and "Mary Dyre," a historical tale in the tradition of Hawthorne's "The Gentle Boy" and "Mrs. Hutchinson." The republication of "Cacoethes Scribendi" in *Tales and Sketches* suggests the truth of Roger Chartier's claim that "a text, stable in its letter, is invested with new meaning and status when the mechanisms that make it available to interpretation change."[11] Together these tales complement one another, offering a model of female authorial engagement that furthers the project inaugurated by Sedgwick's dedication and opening tale. As its title suggests, "Cacoethes Scribendi" (Latin for "writer's itch") imagines professional authorship as a sort of disease, and the cast of characters is neatly divided into those who succumb to this itch, like Mrs. Courland, and those who do not, like Mrs. Courland's daughter, Alice. Throughout this story Sedgwick contrasts Alice's humility—her steadfast refusal to appear in print—with Mrs. Courland's ambition and brazen self-assertion. The tensions between mother and daughter reach a climax after Mrs. Courland, now an established contributor to the annuals, submits to *The Anodyne* a story Alice had written as a child. Alice reacts to this breach of her private feeling by throwing the book in which her sketch appears into the fire. It takes the intercession of Mrs. Courland's nephew, Ralph, to "cure" Mrs. Courland and reconcile her with her daughter. He offers to write Mrs. Courland and Alice a "true" story. His story takes the form of a marriage proposal that he writes on a piece of paper and gives to Alice. The effect on Mrs. Courland is immediate, and dropping a tear upon Ralph's missive, she embraces Alice and Ralph, forever renouncing her ambitions for her daughter's authorial career.

If "Cacoethes Scribendi" explores and in the end proscribes one particularized and limited view of the female literary vocation—that embodied by Mrs. Courland, who writes out of vanity and self-interest, and whose contributions to the annuals (unlike Sedgwick's) are unprincipled and invasive—"Mary Dyre" offers a positive model of female public engagement. Religious martyrs like Mary Dyre were figures of considerable interest to authors of this period, functioning as metaphors through which the question of female authorship was sometimes routed. In "Mrs. Hutchinson," one of his first published works, Hawthorne used a brief historical sketch to decry the feminization of the literary marketplace. Sedgwick wrote a number of stories about female martyrs, a number of which appear in *Tales and Sketches*, including "The Catholic Iroquois" and "St. Catherine's Eve." Sedgwick appears to have been drawn to these figures because of their courage, selflessness, and sense of mission, qualities that no doubt appealed to Sedgwick's essentially Christian sensibility. They offered clear analogies to her own situation as a public woman. In considering Dyre's history, Sedgwick considers her own position as a professional author.

In "Mary Dyre" Sedgwick uses the medium of a historical fiction, not, as Hawthorne did, to denounce public engagement on the part of women, but to offer an exemplary instance of it. Her treatment of Dyre is revisionary in two ways. Like recent social historians, she rewrites Dyre's story from "below," supplementing William Sewel's *History of the Rise, Increase and Progress of the Christian People called Quakers*, the source from which she works, with original research of her own. She reproves "the historian of the people called Quakers" for "having given very slight notice of Mary's private life" (152) and speaks unflatteringly of his "stinted curiosity" (153). To correct this bias Sedgwick quotes at length Mary's "Appeal to the Rulers of Boston," written during Mary's first imprisonment, as well as a letter from Mary's husband William written in defense of Mary at the time of her second imprisonment. In writing her tale Sedgwick focuses exclusively on Dyre, abstracting her story from that of the other martyrs (William Robinson and Marmeduke Stevenson) with whom she appears in Sewel's account. Like Hawthorne (who, in writing "The Gentle Boy," also drew material from Sewel's history), Sedgwick enters into creative dialogue with her historical sources.

Just as Sedgwick seeks to revise Sewel, so too does she challenge the established conventions of romantic fiction. Dyre, she writes, "may appear to be a very unfit personage to be introduced into the romantic and glorious company of lords and ladye loves; of doomed brides; and all-achieving heroines" (151), and she informs her readers that in choosing to write Dyre's history "she [has not] selected the most romantic heroine that might be found in the annals" (151). Sedgwick's disagreements with Sewel and the literary romancers to whom she alludes, moreover, echo Mary's differences with Governor Endicott. Just as Mary repeatedly challenges the governor's authority by reappearing in Boston and publishing her complaints, so too does Sedgwick pit herself against the historical and literary establishment.

Tales and Sketches announces a shift in Sedgwick's literary intentions; henceforth she worked almost exclusively in the short forms of the tale and novella. She did not write another novel until 1857, publishing instead three domestic novellas (the first for Henry Ware's Sunday Library), dozens of tales and sketches in a range of periodicals, and, in 1844, a second collection of short fiction.[12] If *Tales and Sketches* signals a turning point in Sedgwick's career, it also marks the emergence of a new and distinctly American genre: the miscellaneous collection. Most authors of this period eschewed the loose organizational structure of the miscellany, crafting more integrated and thematically homogenous volumes. Sarah Hale published *Sketches of American Character* (1829), a work unified by its emphasis on native materials and themes; Caroline Kirkland published *A New Home—Who'll Follow? or, Glimpses of Western Life* (1839), a series of interrelated sketches set in Michigan; and a number of authors published, like Child, collections masquerading as annuals. Henry Wadsworth Longfellow (*Outre-Mer*, 1833) and Henry T. Tuckerman (*The Italian Sketchbook*, 1835) published "sketch books" in imitation of Irving, whereas Irving himself turned to collections (*Bracebridge Hall; or, the Humourists*, 1822; *Tales of a Traveller*, 1824; *The Alhambra: A Series of Tales and Sketches of the Moors and Spanish*, 1832) that employed a variety of framing devices. Sedgwick's more miscellaneous *Tales and Sketches* provided an alternative generic model to these other forms—one widely emulated by a later generation of classic American authors. Two years after the publication of Sedgwick's *Tales and Sketches* Hawthorne would follow Sedgwick's example and publish his first collection of fiction, *Twice-Told Tales;* it, too, is structured as a miscellany. Poe and Simms followed with miscellaneous collections of their own: Poe in 1840 (*Tales of the Grotesque and Arabesque*) and 1845 (*Tales*), and Simms in 1845 (*The Wigwam and the Cabin*). That the miscellany, a form pioneered by Sedgwick, would be taken up by the same literary establishment against which Sedgwick found herself fighting remains one of the ironies of American literary history, but it is also a testament to Sedgwick's lasting influence.

NOTES

1. Quoted in Carolyn Karcher, *The First Woman of the Republic: A Cultural Biography of Lydia Maria Child* (Durham, N.C.: Duke Univ. Press, 1994), 192.

2. Ralph Thompson attributes this story to Everett in *American Literary Annuals & Gift Books, 1825–1865* (Archon Books, 1967), 70.

3. "My Wife's Novel," in *The Token, a Christmas and New Year's present* (Boston: Gray and Bowen, 1831), 285, 287.

4. Catharine Sedgwick, "A Sketch of a Bluestocking," in *The Token, a Christmas and New Year's present* (Boston, Gray and Bowen, 1831).

5. Lydia Child, *An Appeal in Favor of That Class of Americans Called Africans* (1833; reprint, ed. Carolyn L. Karcher, Amherst: Univ. of Massachusetts Press, 1996), 5, 12.

6. David Reynolds, *Beneath the American Renaissance: The Subversive Imagination in the Age of Emerson and Melville* (Cambridge, Mass.: Harvard Univ. Press, 1988), 54–91. In *An Appeal* Child describes a slaveowner, who, having cast the feet of a boy of seventeen into a fire, "proceed[s] to cut off the limbs below the knees. The sufferer besought him to begin with his head. It was all in vain—the master went on thus, until trunk, arms, and head were all in the fire" (25–26).

7. Letter from Sedgwick to Child, 27 May 1834, Catharine Maria Sedgwick Papers, Massachusetts Historical Society.

8. This untitled, unfinished fragment remains in manuscript form in the Sedgwick collection at the Massachusetts Historical Society; See Karen Woods Weierman's essay in this volume.

9. *Life and Letters of Catharine M. Sedgwick,* ed. Mary E. Dewey (New York: Harper, 1871), 241.

10. In "The Country Cousin" Sedgwick asks rhetorically: "Is not Christianity the foundation, the essence of republicanism?" *Tales and Sketches* (Philadelphia: Carey, Lea, and Blanchard, 1835), 69. All subsequent references to *Tales and Sketches* will be given parenthetically.

11. Roger Chartier, *The Order of Books: Readers, Authors, and Libraries in Europe between the Fourteenth and Eighteenth Centuries*, trans. Lydia Cochrane (Stanford, Calif.: Stanford Univ. Press, 1994), 3.

12. Sedgwick wrote the first narrative for the Sunday Library, described by Ware as something "between a formal tale and a common tract" and illustrating the "practical character and influences of Christianity." *Life and Letters,* 239. The second and third were published with Harper's, but the three were nevertheless regarded as a series; they became Sedgwick's most popular and reprinted works.

IO

❧ Excerpts from Reviews of *Home, The Poor Rich Man and the Rich Poor Man*, and *Live and Let Live*

The Boston Observer (30 April 1836): 142–43.

This is one of those books which are alike the admiration of readers and the despair of critics, and which deserve only "large draughts of unqualified praise." [*Home*] is a perfect gem, without flaw or blemish. . . .

We think this book will do a great deal of good. Its literary merit is so high, its story so well conducted, the style so beautiful, and the fine touches of genius are so plentifully scattered over its pages, that those who seek in books merely the gratification of taste or a relief from the vacuity of idleness, will be eager to read it; and it is so full of moral and religious truth that no one can read it without catching some good influences.

American Quarterly Review (March 1837): 18–28.

[Of *The Poor Rich Man*:] A full appreciation by the poorer and humbler classes (we of course use this latter term in no invidious sense) of their proper station in the social economy, their responsibilities and advantages, is what is needed. In them a spirit of contentment, not of ambition, should be fostered. . . . (P. 20)

We have formally noticed this little book, and made these extracts, for the purpose of doing what in us lay to aid in its dissemination. We would, if we could, send it to every fireside in our land—of the rich as well as the poor—though to the last we especially commend it. (P. 28)

New York Review (October 1837): 447–57.

Having expressed ourselves so strongly in praise of [*Live and Let Live*], we shall speak with equal frankness of two faults in it. The first is one common to

171

all the late writings of Miss Sedgwick: it is a leaning to the side of *ultra-democratic* sentiments, which are neither wise nor salutary. It is far more important, it is doing much more for social virtue and welfare, to instruct the people in the *duties,* and to warn them of the *dangers,* of liberty, than to minister continually to that overweening sense of rights, which, by an easy transition, in this country, passes into the licentious spirit of *Liberty above Law,* begetting discontent with established and necessary distinctions and subordinations, and hatred towards the richer classes. . . . Miss Sedgwick need not trouble herself to spread among the people of this country a sense of social equality and popular rights. The democratic element in our social system is in no danger of being overborne and weakened by any antagonist force. It will take care of itself on this side. She would exert herself far more wisely and beneficently in restraining, purifying, and guiding it in safe and rational channels, in administering needful warnings and cautions.

The other fault of this book is, that it is too partial, one-sided a view of the subject. The author says, indeed, in her preface, that it has been "her business to illustrate the failures of one party in the contract between employers and employed." We should not quarrel with this if the book were to be confined to the party whose failures are described. But it will be extensively read on the other side; and in its present form it is precisely the book we should wish to keep out of the hands of a numerous class of servants. (Pp. 456–57)

"Miss Sedgwick's Tales." *North American Review* (October 1837): 475–81.

Miss Sedgwick knows perfectly well what she is about, in what she has now undertaken. She surveys her whole ground; she is full of resource; she understands the place and the power of every spring that she touches. She knows our people. . . . And she uses her power in the spirit of a generous humanity. She has found out the secret of *leveling upwards.* (Pp. 475–76)

In speaking of the great worth of Miss Sedgwick's writings [*The Poor Rich Man* and *Live and Let Live*], in a moral and political point of view, as inculcating and exciting the self-respect and mutual respect, which make the distinctive nobility of the republican character . . . we have implied our sense of their high literary excellence; since if her pictures were not radiantly true and vivid, they would not charm and move readers as they do. We remarked that, in this series of tales, she was working the true vein of her own power. She has also, we believe, fallen upon the vein, from which the treasures of our future literature are to be wrought. A literature, to have real freshness and power, must be moulded by the influences of the society, where it had its origin. (Pp. 480–81)

Sedgwick's American Poor

SONDRA SMITH GATES

I n 1834, the prominent Unitarian Henry Ware Jr. requested that Catharine Sedgwick contribute to a series exhibiting "the practical character and influences of Christianity."[1] Sedgwick complied the following year with *Home* (1835). In the ensuing years, she published two similar tales with Harper's, *The Poor Rich Man and the Rich Poor Man* (1836) and *Live and Let Live* (1837). As reviews reprinted in this volume make clear, Sedgwick's series of didactic tales were some of the most popular and critically acclaimed works of her career. Each of the short novels focuses on America's poverty and class divisions, subjects that had long concerned their author. In her first novel, *A New-England Tale* (1822), Sedgwick had critiqued her country's bourgeoisie by opposing hypocritical, wealthy characters with a host of the virtuous poor.[2] In *Clarence* (1830), a novel that depicts with alarm New York City's growing commercialism, the wealthy heroine masquerades as a poor girl to ensure that her lover is attracted to her and not to her money.[3] In Sedgwick's domestic trilogy, however, the protagonists do not merely appear to be poor but actually are so. Sedgwick explores through these three novels how the presence of poor people in America, a matter of national concern in the 1830s, could be compatible with the nation's claims to freedom and equality. The different fortunes of Anglo-American and Irish American poor characters, furthermore, reveal how poverty had become inextricably intertwined with ideas of race. The didactic series demonstrates the importance of the poor—that is, the inclusion of some poor people and the exclusion of others—in an image of America as an independent and virtuous nation.

America's Humble Roots

Since colonial days, writers obsessed with distinguishing America from England had celebrated the country's common people to de-emphasize America's reliance on Old World wealth and ancestry. Sedgwick's third cousin, Timothy Dwight, expressed a dominant sentiment in his epic poem *Greenfield Hill* (1794):

> *Not here how rich, of what peculiar blood,*
> *Or office high; but of what genuine worth,*
> *What talents bright and useful, what good deeds,*
> *What piety to God, what love to man,*
> *The question is.*[4]

In order to prove that in America "the question" truly does have to do with a person's merits rather than with wealth, blood, or position, the swains of Dwight's poem must begin life on "little farms" rather than in "bloated pomp" and earn any prosperity they acquire.[5] Similarly, Thomas Jefferson's vision of America depended upon yeoman farmers, each subsistence-farming his own small plot of land. Even the quasi-mythical Daniel Boone and other American folk heroes who followed him take as their starting point an existence unencumbered by material possessions, eating only what they can hunt or gather and existing purely by their own ingenuity.

Convinced of the exceptional nature of the United States' national structure, early Americans saw their nation's growth as "the unfolding realization of its inherent form and meaning," explains Myra Jehlen, and not the result of a long history of European involvement.[6] From Samuel Danforth's sermon "New England's Errand into the Wilderness" (1670) to Abraham Lincoln's Gettysburg Address (1863), we hear the refrain, "our fathers brought forth on this continent a new nation," emphasizing the role of America's founders in building the United States from the ground up, with God's blessing. Lincoln's famous phrase draws our attention to a familiar narrative of American development, in which the country begins as a primitive, natural land and is transformed into a civilized nation by the industry, labor, persistence, and faith of early forebears.[7] Theorists of national identity, including Benedict Anderson and Immanuel Wallerstein, have suggested that nationalism consists in the recognition of such a shared history, created in hindsight by choosing some past events to incorporate into a national history while excluding others. Such "inventions of pastness" give a heterogeneous set of people the sense of having something in common.[8]

As they struggled to win first political and then cultural independence from England, Americans frequently imagined for themselves a past characterized by independence. Hawthorne, for example, describes the Puritan colonists of "Endicott and the Red Cross" (1838) as defiant precursors of the American Revolution.[9] Although the founding fathers were often depicted as heroes or geniuses, a countervailing and equally enduring viewpoint located America's independence in its simple, humble roots. There is nothing necessarily "American" about the happy, bucolic labor and bountiful scenery that *Greenfield Hill* depicts. Dwight borrows the conventions of British pastoral to describe the Connecticut setting. His opening descriptions of the various seasons in the village and its surrounding farms would have brought to mind James Thomson's widely read poem *The Seasons* (1726–30). Yet Dwight proclaims these scenes intrinsically American, offering up the flourishing village as a contrast to Oliver Goldsmith's *The Deserted Village* (1770), which laments the decline of such rural idylls in England. The narrative of development that ends with America's unparalleled ability "[t]o rein, protect, employ, and bless mankind" must logically begin in simple self-sufficiency, if those achievements are to be attributed to the virtues of the new nation's laws and citizens and not to its Old World predecessors.[10]

Greenfield Hill and similar epic poems, such as Joel Barlow's *The Columbiad* (1807), take as their mission the public definition and dissemination of American character. But the interlocking narratives of national and personal development they depict are no less important to texts whose setting is domestic. Amy Kaplan has drawn attention to the double entendre of the term "domestic"; it is the counterpart not only of "the market," but also of "the foreign": "*domestic . . .* links the familial household to the nation but also imagines both in opposition to everything outside the geographic and conceptual border of the home."[11] The poem "Connecticut River" (1834) by popular sentimental poet Lydia H. Sigourney closely resembles the language and sense of *Greenfield Hill*. Sigourney's "farmer" and his "thrifty mate," domestic residents of the idyllic Connecticut River valley, owe their happy virtues to democratic institutions: "On equal laws their anchor'd hopes are stay'd." Even the nation-building "patriot sires" of the poem are depicted as lowly laborers, defending "threaten'd Liberty" with "hands with toil embrown'd."[12] Sigourney's selective history of the region overlooks those "patriot sires" and "mighty statesmen" who owed their political influence to money carried with them from England and instead lauds Revolutionary heroes who were both "Firm at the plough, and glorious in the field."

A review included in the publisher's notice for Sigourney's *Select Poems* (1856) articulates the connections among humble simplicity, domesticity, and nation in a comparison between Sigourney and Felicia Hemans, the "English Sappho." Though the review acknowledges that both poets write of "cottage" and "hearth" and finds "something kindred in their spirits," it claims that Hemans's version of domesticity is affected by her citizenship in a "state whose associations are of aristocracy": She is the "high-souled and delicately proud poetess of an old dominion; . . . the asserter of hereditary nobility." But Sigourney is "the Hemans of a republic": "[I]f she rather delights to dwell in the hamlet, to muse over the birth of the rustic infant, or the death of the village mother, it is, that such is the genius of her country,—the boasted associations of her land, are simplicity and freedom;—and as befit the muse of such a land, so are her meditations fain to celebrate the Virtues of her country's children."[13] The reviewer sees rustic humility as a virtue that distinguishes the United States from England. Hemans may write of cottage and hearth, but only Sigourney is permitted to claim them as "the genius of her country." The sentiment extends to the most canonical works of the midcentury literary renaissance. Walt Whitman confidently proclaimed that "the genius of the United States is not best or most in its executives or legislatures, nor in its ambassadors or authors or colleges or churches or parlors, nor even in its newspapers or inventors . . . but always most in the common people."[14]

The Riches of America's Poor

Sigourney's near contemporary, Catharine Maria Sedgwick likewise locates America's "genius" in its common people. The three domestic novels she wrote following Ware's request feature protagonists who resemble their self-sufficient, hardworking literary predecessors, but with one crucial difference: They are explicitly identified as *poor*. By incorporating the poor into an earlier nationalist discourse, Sedgwick sought to validate America's claims to unlimited opportunity and equality, even in the context of newly apparent social problems. Expanding urbanization and industrialization made poverty more visible in the 1830s than it had been in the early national period. In Sedgwick's novels, the problem of poverty is transformed into merely the initial stage of a narrative of progress that confirms America's exceptional status. At least for characters who are not hampered by their own vices or the racial prejudices of others, a period of poverty can serve as proof that both citizen and nation deserve the illustrious future to which they are destined.

Written explicitly for "farmers and mechanics," the first novel of Sedgwick's trilogy, *Home*, illustrates the promises that America makes and fulfills for its virtuous poor.[15] Its protagonist, William Barclay, loses his father and then grandfather when he is only a few years old, which leaves him and his mother penniless. Regretting the strain that dependency on friends causes his mother, Barclay vows to support himself and his family through his own labor as soon as he is able. Before the close of the first chapter, he moves to New York, obtains a position in a print shop (with the possibility of future partnership), marries for love, and buys a new house.

Barclay's past in poverty is brief in terms of narrative pacing, occupying only the first five pages of the book. Yet the novel's didactic message and view of American identity depend upon it. Because Barclay began life with no material advantages, Sedgwick can attribute his amazing and rapid change of condition to democracy. She asserts that only in America can men like Barclay marry young. Across the Atlantic, she writes, "the working man, be he 'capable, diligent, and frugal,' has an alms-house in his perspective, or the joyless alternative, a life of safe and pining singleness" (*Home*, 4). Barclay's past in poverty thus sets up a framework in which any success he achieves in the novel, whether it be in love, child-rearing, philanthropy, or business, will confirm the virtues of both American institutions and American citizens. Whereas poverty is portrayed as a structural flaw in England, in America it is simply the ground floor upon which the industrious can build happy homes, given the tools of democracy.

Following Barclay's speedy establishment in New York, the plot slows almost to a standstill to focus attention on the protagonist's child-rearing practices. Numerous lectures and exemplary scenes involving the Barclay children take precedence over the narrative, which had progressed so quickly in the opening pages of the book: A new story line has begun, that of the Barclays' middle-class children. In the Barclay children, the past and the future of America meet; they embody the future the virtuous poor can look forward to, as well as the past in poverty that wealthier Americans can claim. Though the Barclay children grow up in material comfort (if not abundance), the text insists that their past is well rooted in poverty, and that "the question," to invoke Dwight's terminology, is still "what genuine worth" citizens possess and not "how rich" they are or "of what peculiar blood, / Or office high."

The situation of the Barclay children is particularly significant for democratic ideology since so many Americans, Sedgwick included, could not claim a personal past in poverty like William Barclay's. The Barclay children are a product of what Lauren Berlant describes as nationalism's collective subjectivity. Berlant shows that a national culture makes the nation's history a part of the history and identity of each individual person. Acquiring the collective history of the nation, the individual becomes a "*collective* subject, or citizen."[16] Through their collective citizenship, people of differing economic status are able to play a role in the narrative of national development, even if they have not personally experienced all the events comprising that plot. Americans who are not poor can, paradoxically, inherit their past in poverty and thus merit the ensuing rewards.

In *The Poor Rich Man and the Rich Poor Man* published the following year, Sedgwick halts the trajectory toward prosperity she had developed in *Home* in order to examine more closely the plight of the American poor. The condition of New York in the 1830s convinced many that America had failed to fulfill its post-Revolutionary promise, articulated by Dwight, to "rein, protect, employ, and bless mankind." A substantial portion of "mankind" in the country's largest and most rapidly growing city lived in severe poverty, with many of the decade's four hundred thousand European immigrants settling in crowded, cholera-infected slums.[17] If the country's democratic idealism were to survive, it had to address the problem of urban poverty. In *The Poor Rich Man,* Sedgwick delays the protagonist's rise into the middle class until the very end of the novel, thereby emphasizing the dramatic effects of democracy on the lives of the poor. Harry Aikin, the "rich poor man" of the novel's title, begins life in happy poverty in the country, marries, and moves to New York, much like Barclay—but he does not find the same financial success there. Aikin's "shoe concern" fails, and due to his "broken-down constitution" he is unable to "perform half the labour of a sound man."[18]

With his poor health and ever-growing family, Aikin is something of a worst-case scenario. The novel recounts how the family is able to survive through patience and frugality, and once again Sedgwick attributes this ability to American democracy. As in *Home*, she contrasts Aikin's condition in the United States with what it might have been in England: "What could Aikin have been in [England] with his shattered health, his children, and helpless father-in-law, and invalid sister? [They] would have been tenants of the almshouse . . . and his children supported by the parish" (*PRM*, 154). Whereas English society forces its deserving poor into pauperism, the novel contends, America provides opportunities for even its most disadvantaged citizens—for those who have not yet achieved the success of William Barclay. The weakness of Aikin's "constitution" is remedied by the strength of his nation's Constitution. And, in turn, Aikin's ability to feed and clothe his family reflects favorably upon the United States: "A country may well boast its equality . . . that has such families as this in it" (*PRM*, 153).

The nationalist implications of the rich poor man and Sedgwick's other virtuous poor characters were not lost on their contemporary readers. An article published in the *North American Review* called Sedgwick's domestic series a "service of patriotism . . . in which the upright genius of Miss Sedgwick has kindled the sympathy of readers in the virtues that benefit the American citizen and awakened their veneration and love for that essential dignity and charm which every man and woman in this nation may aspire to wear."[19] Personal virtues like "dignity" and "charm" carry particular nationalist significance—they "benefit the American citizen." Just as Aikin's characteristics of "affection, intelligence, temperance, contentment, and godliness" (*PRM*, 75) make him "rich" despite his outward poverty, so the existence of citizens like Aikin bespeaks the great riches of American democracy, which make a noble character attainable by all. Yet though "every man and woman in this nation may aspire to wear" those national virtues, one begins to suspect as the paragraph continues that such moral attributes pertain specifically to the lower classes. Books like Sedgwick's, the article explains, "[instruct] the common mind of this nation to appreciate its privileges—forming it to discharge, and winning it to love, the duties of its position." This familiar attempt to regulate the morals of the working classes may have had little effect upon the behavior of poor people themselves, but it certainly influenced the way wealthier Americans imagined their national character.[20]

Reshaping the imagination of America's ruling classes is the central purpose of Sedgwick's third didactic tale, *Live and Let Live*, which addresses the condition of America's domestic servants. To teach mistresses that servants are in fact their equals under the tenets of democracy and should be treated with respect, the novel features a heroine who fits the pattern of the previous two novels. Lucy Lee is forced to go into service at a young age to keep her family from starvation. After several years of patience and honest work, she marries a baker's son and settles comfortably into the middle class. As in *The Poor Rich Man*, the extended period of hardship endured by the protagonist has national significance. The inequality and poverty that seem permanent to the characters are in fact temporary, a characteristic only of the young nation's "transition state" from Old World to New World social structures.[21] Sedgwick projects: "Surely the time will come in this country, where the elements of general prosperity have not been destroyed by the foolish combinations and wicked monopolies of men, . . . when physical, intellectual, and moral education will have raised the level of our race, and brought it to as near an approximation to equality of condition as it is capable of in its present state of existence" (*LLL*, 72).

Statements like these no doubt fueled the fears of conservative reviewers, who labeled the novel "*ultra-democratic*" (emphasis in original) and a threat to order should it fall into the hands of the lower classes.[22] Sedgwick contends that such aristocratic prejudices are precisely what prevent the nation from fulfilling its promises to the poor. *Live and Let Live* teaches those who have not yet learned to "relish the freedoms of democracy" that they must treat all people as equals, anticipating and hastening the time when equality will exist in fact and not just in theory.[23]

The novel foreshadows this imminent "equality of condition" through the experiences of the model employer Mrs. Hyde, who explains that she learned to value her servants when she temporarily came to occupy their position. Upon moving to the frontier, Mrs. Hyde had to perform all domestic duties herself, with mixed results. When her nurse Clara Lane later rejoined her, Mrs. Hyde replaced the language of hierarchy with that of friendship: Clara was "my friend—my *help* in all things, and I treated her accordingly" (*LLL*, 88). Conservative reviewers may fear the egalitarianism of this "ultra-democratic" sentiment, but in fact Mrs. Hyde's efforts to understand her employees and treat them "as if" they were her equals helps to ensure that they never will be her equals. Due to the affectionate treatment Clara receives, she stays with the Hydes even though "[t]he money we paid her could have been far more easily earned elsewhere" (*LLL*, 88). Sedgwick's great faith that in America mistresses and servants do at heart have the same rights, abilities, and opportunities leads her to promote understanding as the solution to class divisions. Yet in the case of Mrs. Hyde, understanding only strengthens the status quo. She explains, "There will seldom be occasion for a lady to perform drudgery herself who thoroughly understands it, for this very knowledge will enable her to direct the services of others" (*LLL*, 91).

Poverty's Racial Identity

Sedgwick's admonition to treat servants as friends sidesteps more than economic differences between people. Though the connections were rarely mentioned overtly, issues of race and ethnicity played into Americans' conceptions of poverty in the early national and antebellum years. Eric Lott has found that for Northern urban workers, "[i]t was through blackness that class was staged."[24] The reverse was also true. In Sedgwick's novels, depictions of class relations provided space for addressing obliquely the specter of racial division that haunted white Americans' construction of national identity.

The loyal servant who joins Mrs. Hyde on the frontier in *Live and Let Live* is referred to as "Clara Lane" only once; thereafter she is called "Mammy," a term used specifically for black women who cared for white children.[25] Sedgwick narrates Mammy's domestic servitude without mentioning the part race might play in the events; yet surely Mammy's decision to stay on with the Hydes in gratitude for their kind treatment, despite more lucrative opportunities elsewhere, would have brought to mind the "grateful Negro" stories popularized by plantation fiction. By her name, intrinsically connected to the plantation house-slave, Mammy acquires a history not just of poverty, but of slavery. As was the case for Sedgwick's own nurse Elizabeth Freeman, domestic servitude represents the end of a journey for Mammy—from slavery to freedom—rather than just the beginning, as it is for Lucy Lee. By conflating race with class in the figure of the virtuous servant, Sedgwick implies that in the United States people of color, like the Anglo-American poor, will soon receive the full benefits of democracy. But by avoiding overt discussion of race, she sidesteps the abolitionist implications of that assumption.

Such ambivalence about race characterizes much of Sedgwick's work. While there exists a strong resemblance between Sedgwick's descriptions of Elizabeth

Freeman and the virtuous servant Mary Hull in *A New-England Tale*,[26] yet Sedgwick never explicitly portrays Hull as black, just as she does not explore the significance of race for Clara Lane. Judith Fetterley calls Sedgwick's *Hope Leslie* (1827) "a text that potentially argues for the equality of race" through its favorable portrayal of the Indian Magawisca but observes that the novel "ultimately abandons that potential."[27] In an unpublished, unfinished manuscript discussed by Karen Woods Weierman in this volume, Sedgwick began an antislavery story but was never able to complete it. Weierman speculates that the manuscript was written between 1833 and 1838, which would suggest that the slavery question was on Sedgwick's mind as she wrote her domestic trilogy during those years.

Similarities in how poverty and race were conceptualized made the "virtuous poor" a character type particularly suited to discussing the volatile issue of race relations without mentioning it directly. Americans and their British counterparts in the age of industrialization were perplexed by the origin and nature of poverty: Is it a temporary condition or, as Thomas Malthus claimed, a more essential part of one's identity? Similar concerns surrounded Americans' troubled definitions of race. Shirley Samuels explains that antebellum representations of slaves tended either to fix identity in the slave's body or to "unfix" it by understanding identity as something that transcends the body.[28] Parallels between class and race remain tacit in Sedgwick's oblique treatment of the black character Clara Lane, but her descriptions of the virtuous poor deal directly with another subjugated group, the Irish. Though Irish Catholics and Scots-Irish were distinct, oppositional social groups in Ireland, upon immigrating to the United States they were lumped into a single racial category.[29] Anti-Irish sentiment was particularly strong in New York following the massive cholera epidemic of 1832 that began in the Irish-populated slums.[30] In her sympathetic descriptions of Irish domestic servants and laborers, Sedgwick shows deep concern for the immigrants' plight. Yet she is unable to imagine any kind of solution to Irish Americans' poverty. Poor Irish characters appear in all three novels of Sedgwick's trilogy, but despite moral virtue and hard work, they do not once participate in the American narrative of progress. Irishness and poverty are inextricably intertwined, and both fix themselves permanently in the identities of immigrant characters.

Sedgwick attempts to overturn anti-Irish prejudice in *Live and Let Live* through the introduction of the Irish American servant Bridget. By depicting Bridget as "a woman of great strength, capacity, and industry" who "accomplished more work than two ordinary women," the text challenges the stereotypes propagated by her employer. Mrs. Broadson believes that "those Irish are so sluttish and hard to teach," but she undermines her own observation by paying Bridget above-average wages for her invaluable service (*LLL*, 57–58).

The text further attempts to generate sympathy for Irish Americans by relaying Bridget's traumatic family history. Her father, brother, and brother-in-law all died tragically; her sister died giving birth to Bridget's niece Judy; and her mother passed away shortly thereafter. Bridget had come to America to make enough money to send for Judy (the sole remaining member of her family), but she had encountered harsh and unfair employers. Once she finally did earn enough to pay Judy's passage, she had been unable to find her a servant's position, and Judy was now dying in a "cold garret" (*LLL*, 67). Though Bridget's history is pitiful, it generates less respect for Irish immigrants than it might due to the way Sedgwick frames it. Bridget relates her history to account for her moral failings. The story is meant to explain why she had treated Lucy so coldly when the girl had come to work for Mrs. Broadson—taking the position already promised to Judy. Bridget's resentment contrasts with Lucy's sweetness. Far from behaving uncharitably in response to mistreatment, Lucy promptly resigns her position when she learns it had been previously promised to Judy, even though her own family is also starving.

An explanatory passage appended to Bridget's history likewise turns swiftly from indicting Anglo-Americans for their prejudice to explaining the sources of Irish inferiority. "[L]est the effect of our humble friend Biddy's autobiography should be lost by a [careless] mode of reading," the passage begins, "we would venture to ask whether the right principles and feelings . . . are in exercise in relation to Irish domestics." The ensuing text, however, does not discuss mistresses' failings. Instead, it explains why the Irish are just what Mrs. Broadson thinks—"sluttish and hard to teach":

> The abuses of government have left them ignorant, degraded them, and deprived them of their birthrights as members of the human family. They have been bred in miserable dirty cabins, where they had *no* means of learning the arts of domestic economy. . . . The Irish come to us with their habits formed. They require knowledge, energy, and patience on the part of their employers. Some of them may be unteachable and irreclaimable; but, for the most part, do they not repay *real* disinterested kindness with fidelity and affection? . . . Is an Irish person less docile than any other who has arrived to maturity in ignorance? (*LLL* 71)

Since Sedgwick attributes the poor habits of the Irish to "abuses of government," one might expect people of Irish descent born in America to escape the problems of their ancestors—but such is not the case. Poverty and Irishness remain fixed in the identities of even those characters born on American soil and blessed with its virtues.

Home introduces a poor Irish immigrant who seems to have all the necessary ingredients for an American success story. John Phealan is industrious, intelligent, virtuous, and charitable. A widower with three children, he marries a widow with four children, fathers two more, and even adopts an orphan, yet—like the poor rich man—is able to provide for the large family by his hard work. In contrast to the Aikins, however, no prosperous or even comfortable future awaits this Irish American family. Indeed, no future awaits them at all. Both parents die, and nine of the ten children soon disappear from the novel.

Only the adopted orphan, Biddy, remains a part of the story. Striking parallels between Biddy and another orphan—as well as inexplicable differences between them—suggest the ethnic dimensions of poverty in American understanding. At age seven, Biddy is too young for domestic service when her adoptive parents die and so is taken in by the Barclays. In the following chapter, a similar fate befalls motherless Emily Norton, the granddaughter of William Barclay's business partner. When Emily's father and grandfather die, she too is taken in by the Barclays. The similarities in the orphans' situations make the differences in their fate all the more conspicuous. Before accepting Biddy into their fold, the Barclays consult with their cook, Martha, who will be responsible for Biddy's upbringing. Before welcoming Emily, they consult with Mrs. Barclay herself, since the burden of increased family size will fall on her (*Home*, 74, 96). Biddy's training in the kitchen equips her for a life of domestic service with the Barclays, in keeping with the common practice of "bringing up" a poor girl for service. Emily's education takes place not in the kitchen but in the nursery, where she learns how someday to manage a household of her own. Without national or racial characteristics to hamper Emily's progress from poverty to wealth, her integration into the Barclay family is complete with a marriage to one of the sons at the novel's end.

Despite the striking similarities between Biddy's and Emily's situations, the text never compares the two orphans or so much as draws them into the same scene. Either the ethnic dimensions of the virtuous poverty Sedgwick praises are completely invisible to her, or she chooses to portray the troubling inequalities realistically for readers' own consideration, without interpretation from the didactic voice that explains other moral dilemmas in the book. For Anglo-American Emily, poverty serves as a ritual purification, signifying America's freedom from inherited fortune and aristocratic vice. Her temporary period of poverty ensures that she will merit the middle-class domesticity she eventually enjoys. For Irish-descended Biddy, though, no future exists save economic dependence on the Barclays.

Sedgwick's domestic series demonstrates how difficult it was for an industrializing nation to claim the poor as its "genius." Beyond the pastoral confines of

Greenfield Hill or Sigourney's Connecticut River valley, America can confer happiness and prosperity on all its virtuous poor only by excluding some people from citizenship: Poverty that cannot be domesticated, made to serve national ends, must be expelled from the national character by being attributed to individuals' own vice or to the collective character of a group excluded from full citizenship through prejudice. *Home* concludes with the Barclay family's return to idyllic country life, where the association between deprivation and foreignness becomes explicit. William Barclay observes with satisfaction, "We have not here [in the country] the abject poverty and brutish ignorance that exist among the foreigners in the city, but 'the poor we have always with us'; the poor, whose condition may be raised; the sick, whose sufferings may be alleviated; the ignorant, who may be instructed; the idle and vicious, who may be reclaimed" (*Home*, 118). Here even the "idle and vicious" can be counted among those redeemed by American values, for the tangible evils of poverty are borne in full by "foreigners in the city." Because Sedgwick wrote repeatedly and at length about the virtuous poor during years when Americans were consciously trying to distinguish themselves from England, her work provides a valuable case study of how narratives of poverty make possible a narrative of nationhood, with all its accompanying complications.

NOTES

1. *Life and Letters of Catharine Maria Sedgwick*, ed. Mary E. Dewey (New York: Harper, 1871), 239; quoted in *The Power of Her Sympathy: The Autobiography and Journals of Catharine Maria Sedgwick*, ed. Mary Kelley (Boston: Massachusetts Historical Society, 1993), 39.

2. Victoria Clements notes that with some "notable exception[s]," all characters who practice a "Christian ethic of social love" in the novel are members of the "lower classes." Introduction to *A New-England Tale* (New York: Oxford Univ. Press, 1995), xxv–xxvi.

3. See Patricia Kalayjian's discussion of these issues in "Disinterest as Moral Corrective in *Clarence*'s Cultural Critique," included in this volume.

4. Timothy Dwight, "Greenfield Hill: A Poem in Seven Parts," in *The Major Poems of Timothy Dwight* (Gainesville, Fla.: Scholars' Facsimiles and Reprints, 1969), 1:52–56. Sedgwick is related to Dwight through her mother, Pamela Dwight. Catharine Maria Sedgwick and Timothy Dwight share the same great-great-grandparents, Timothy and Anna (Flint) Dwight. Rossiter Johnson, ed., *The Twentieth Century Biographical Dictionary of Notable Americans,* vol. 3 and vol. 9 (Boston: Biographical Society, 1904). Thank you to Victoria Clements for discovering this connection.

5. Dwight, "Greenfield Hill," 1:140, 143.

6. Myra Jehlen, "The Novel and the Middle Class in America," in *Ideology and Classic American Literature*, ed. Myra Jehlen and Sacvan Bercovitch (Cambridge: Cambridge Univ. Press, 1986), 127–28.

7. For a thorough investigation of this view of American history, see Perry Miller, *Errand into the Wilderness* (Cambridge, Mass.: Harvard Univ. Press, 1956); and Sacvan Bercovitch, *The American Jeremiad* (Madison: Univ. of Wisconsin Press, 1978). See also Houston A. Baker Jr., "Figurations for a New American Literary History," in *Ideology and Classic American Literature*, 147–48.

8. The phrase "inventions of pastness" is Immanuel Wallerstein's. "The Construction of Peoplehood: Racism, Nationalism, Ethnicity," in *Race, Nation, Class: Ambiguous Identities*, ed. Etienne Balibar and Immanuel Wallerstein (London: New Left Books and Verso, 1991), 78.

9. See Terence Martin, *Nathaniel Hawthorne*, rev. ed. (Boston: Twayne, 1983), 49.

10. Dwight, "Greenfield Hill," 7:129. The most thorough account of the role of pastoralism in American consciousness is Leo Marx, *The Machine in the Garden: Technology and the Pastoral Ideal in America* (New York: Oxford Univ. Press, 1964). Marx believes that though many societies yearn for pastoral ideals, "our experience as a nation unquestionably has invested them with peculiar intensity" (6).

11. Amy Kaplan, "Manifest Domesticity," *American Literature* 70 (September 1998): 581.

12. Lydia H. Sigourney, "Connecticut River," in *Select Poems* (Philadelphia: Parry and McMillan, 1856; electronic edition, Univ. of Michigan Humanities Text Initiative, 1999), 77, 79.

13. Quoted in Sigourney, *Select Poems*, i.

14. Walt Whitman, Preface to *Leaves of Grass* (1855; electronic edition, the Walt Whitman Hypertext Archive, ed. Kenneth M. Price and Ed Folsom, 1998), iii.

15. Catharine Maria Sedgwick, *Home* (Boston: J. Monroe, 1835), Dedication. Subsequent references to this text will be cited parenthetically by title and page number.

16. Lauren Berlant, *The Anatomy of National Fantasy: Hawthorne, Utopia, and Everyday Life* (Chicago: Univ. of Chicago Press, 1991), 21; emphasis in original.

17. See Carroll Smith Rosenberg's detailed account of immigration and living conditions in New York City of the 1830s in *Religion and the Rise of the American City: The New York City Mission Movement, 1812–1870* (Ithaca, N.Y.: Cornell Univ. Press, 1971), 30–43.

18. Catharine Maria Sedgwick, *The Poor Rich Man and the Rich Poor Man* (New York: Harper, 1836), 113. Subsequent references to this text will be cited parenthetically by page number with the abbreviation *PRM*.

19. [J. G. Palfrey], "Petition of certain Legal Voters of Boston and its Vicinity to the Honorable Senate and House of Representatives in Congress assembled, praying for the Passage of an International Copyright Law," *North American Review* 55 (1842): 245–64. I learned of this article from Melissa J. Homestead, "Suited to the Market: Catharine Maria Sedgwick, Female Authorship, and the Ante-bellum Copyright Debates" (paper presented at the Catharine Maria Sedgwick Symposium, Stockbridge, Mass., June 2000).

20. Paul Lewis discusses the moral reforms attempted through antebellum middle-class benevolence as well as other complex goals of charitable visiting, from effecting social change to celebrating the charitable impulse. Of particular relevance to the present study is his treatment of *The Rich Poor Man and the Poor Rich Man.* "'Lectures or a Little Charity': Poor Visits in Antebellum Literature and Culture," *New England Quarterly* 73 (June 2000): 246–73.

21. Catharine Maria Sedgwick, *Live and Let Live; or, Domestic Service Illustrated* (New York: Harper, 1837), 73. Subsequent references to this text will be cited parenthetically by page number with the abbreviation *LLL*.

22. *New York Review* (October 1837): 456.

23. Sedgwick uses the phrase to describe her aristocratic father, who was "born too soon to relish the freedoms of democracy." Mary Kelley, "Negotiating a Self: The Autobiography and Journals of Catharine Maria Sedgwick," *New England Quarterly* 66 (September 1993): 371.

24. Eric Lott, *Love and Theft: Blackface Minstrelsy and the American Working Class* (New York: Oxford Univ. Press, 1993), 64.

25. *Oxford English Dictionary*, 2nd ed., s.v. "mammy," sense 2.

26. See *Power of Her Sympathy*, 70.

27. Judith Fetterley, "'My Sister! My Sister!': The Rhetoric of Catharine Sedgwick's *Hope Leslie*," *American Literature* 70 (September 1998): 513; contained also in this volume.

28. Shirley Samuels, "The Identity of Slavery," in *The Culture of Sentiment: Race, Gender, and Sentimentality in Nineteenth-Century America*, ed. Shirley Samuels (New York: Oxford Univ. Press, 1992), 157.

29. David Noel Doyle, *Ireland, Irishmen, and Revolutionary America, 1760–1820* (Dublin: Mercier Press, 1981), 93, 101. In *How the Irish Became White* (New York: Routledge, 1995), Noel Ignatiev argues that the oppression of Irish Catholics was specifically racial rather than ethnic or national.

30. Smith-Rosenberg, *Religion and the Rise of the American City*, 34, 136–37.

Photograph of a portrait of Catharine Maria
Sedgwick by Charles Cromwell Ingham
(likely 1836). Originally published in Nathalie
Sedgwick Colby's *Remembering* (Boston:
Little, Brown, 1938). Courtesy of Stephen
Delafield.

II

❧ Excerpts from Reviews of *Means and Ends, or Self-Training*

"American Women." *United States Magazine and Democratic Review* (August 1839): 127–42.

We do not know but this little volume, unpretending as it is, pleases us best of all of Miss Sedgwick's writings. . . . [W]e take most pleasure in regarding . . . its thoroughly *American* and *Democratic*—words that we regard as altogether synonymous—character.

An enlightened attention has not yet been sufficiently directed to the proper principles on which the education of American women should be conducted, with reference to the great principles of public policy on which our whole system of institutions is founded, and to the entirely peculiar state of society naturally growing out of them. (P. 128)

It is a lamentable fact, that with the other numerous and formidable obstacles with which the cause of democracy has to struggle amongst us, is to be reckoned the anti-democratic spirit that pervades the great majority of that sex which exerts the powerful influence over the opinions and character of men, involved in the relations of mother, wife, and sister.

Miss Sedgwick does not hesitate to attack these false notions and habits, point blank, with downright simplicity and earnestness. (P. 130)

[T]he concluding chapter touches slightly on a subject which is now rising into prominent interest among the many social reforms called for by the awakened philanthropy and intelligence of the age—the rights of women. Upon this she speaks certainly very sensibly. . . . (P. 136)

How far they ought to take part in the public movements of society, in our political action, &c., is a point upon which more disagreement may arise among those who are favorable to a great extension of the rights of women. . . . Miss Martineau and her "School" claim the elective franchise on the ground of the principles of liberty; and quoting the proposition of our Declaration of Independence, that the free consent of the governed is the sole rightful source of public authority. . . . As a perversion of the obvious meaning of the proposition . . . , this authority for the claim is not entitled to serious notice. Nor can we really see how it is involved, as a right, in the theory of democratic liberty and equality to which we profess attachment. . . . It will not be difficult, at a probably not distant day, to obtain from the sense of justice and affection of fathers, husbands, sons and brothers, enlightened by the civilization of which christianity is the animating principle, those reforms in legislation, in favor of the rights of women, which do in fact constitute a worthy and rightful object of pursuit. . . . [W]e cannot too much approve of the good sense of Miss Sedgwick's advice to her young friends, which is, so to qualify themselves for the exercise of the rights from which they are now excluded, as to make manifest to all eyes the injustice of their exclusion. . . . (Pp. 138–39)

[W]e are tempted to conclude with a slight sketch of a little society existing in a New England country village, to which it would be improper to refer by name. . . .

. . . All are highly educated and refined—many cultivated by foreign travel, by much intercourse with intelligent foreigners, and familiarity with the treasures of other languages and literatures as well as their own—and for the most part early accustomed to the associations and habits of aristocratic life, whether abroad, or in those circles and families among ourselves to which the term may be applied in a social sense as far as possible removed from the contemptuous one in which we have before employed it. In no place does a higher tone of true refinement and elegance pervade the whole society . . . fully equal to that of the most polished circles of the highest aristocracy of any foreign country. (P. 140)

Such a society as this must necessarily be totally distinct from all surrounding it not placed by education—we do not say on the same level—but within the same orbit of social life. . . . Yet is this no artificial exclusiveness. It is the mere spontaneous action of natural affinities—the voluntary mutual attraction and adaptation of congenial elements. It is quite independent of either wealth, or of rank, as the latter is commonly classified. . . . (P. 141)

Christian Examiner (September 1839): 134–35.

A Boston Review thinks it not democratic enough,—a New York Review thinks it too democratic, much too radical. For ourselves, we were not troubled with either quality. . . . It is an agreeable, plain, matter-of-fact, truth-telling book. (P. 134)

Chapter 11

Catharine Sedgwick and the "Art" of Conversation

CHARLENE AVALLONE

Critics have traced the interweaving of rhetorical tradition and literary form in the work of antebellum male authors, following reminders from historians and New Critics that oratorical conventions and standards informed that body of writing.[1] Rhetorical criticism, however, in emphasizing prohibitions on women's public speech or the influence of male rhetoricians on the exceptional woman, silences women or downplays their creative agency. Further, focus on traditional forms of men's oratory mutes the era's range of oral genres and the extent to which antebellum discourse evolved gendered patterns or what Carroll Smith-Rosenberg calls "dialect[s]."[2] Such critical strategies perpetuate assumptions that "eloquence was basically masculine," and such presumptions continue to sustain claims for male ascendancy in the fields of both rhetorical and literary accomplishment. We have yet to reconstruct the ways that the conversational "eloquence" which contemporaries credited to nineteenth-century women informed the oral and written culture of their time.[3]

Feminist theorizing of the social sphere has worked to recenter women's discourse in "the heart of civil society," as Carole Pateman writes, enabling us to hear more of it, including conversational forms, in public as well as private registers.[4] Attention to ways the antebellum United States valorized both female conversation and male oratory as gendered dialects of "eloquence" shows a strand of conversation becoming as conventional a literary discourse and as removed from the vernacular as the oratory against which it was defined. Divisions that now discriminate literary, polite, and political discourses from each other were then less firmly drawn in the field of female eloquence, so that "literary" in antebellum usage might signify either oral or written discourse that was highly literate or informed by textual tradition. In the historical separation of "spheres," conversation developed into a womanly art of speaking and writing, with political, moral, intellectual, and aesthetic functions equivalent to those of the "manly" art of oratory, its countergenre. Nationalist rhetoric attributed to women's talk a power over the commonweal, making women's conversation more an alternative public-sphere discourse than a private one, even as ideology positioned it outside the public sphere of men. The political and social influence of the female conversationalist accrued from an ethos linked to the gender ideology of woman's supposed moral superiority to men, whereas artistry was judged by linguistic facility and the capacity to be agreeable and instructive. Even though such expectations of refined conversation led to socializing women to reproduce culture—including its hierarchies of gender, class, and ethnicity—rather than to produce it, women singly and collectively found ways to turn conversation to literary accomplishment and transgressive or transformative social power. American men, unable to converse as well as their female compatriots in the opinion of such cultural critics as Tocqueville, ceded conversation to women as the single art in which they might excel and as the discourse of woman's unique "influence."[5] Conventions of conversation came to inform not only women's private and public speech, but also many women writers' forms, styles, and poetics, much as critics have shown oratory informed the literature of canonical male writers.

Catharine Sedgwick was immersed in this culture of conversation, in its instruction, practices, and communities. Her writing, through narrative and thematic development, structures, and characterization, engages the forms of the "art" and enters as well into discussions then defining the ideals of discourse. Studying her elaboration of the art can illuminate not only her accomplishments, but also the "entanglement" of her achievement with systemic classism and racism that Judith Fetterley holds makes Sedgwick's work "worth recovering."[6] In part because American literary study has developed few critical paradigms that comprehend the value of women's writing, such as the antebellum model of conversational art might afford, Sedgwick's oeuvre and that of other women remain understudied and underestimated. Sedgwick as case history suggests the applicability of such a paradigm, demonstrating how historical and textual analysis of conversational culture can show something of the aesthetic and ideological complexity of antebellum women's "eloquence."

Along with other theorizers and practitioners of conversation, including such later notables as Margaret Fuller, Sedgwick defines a middle-class model following moral writers like Hannah More and Maria Edgeworth, who promoted women's education to the end of highly literate conversing that yet avoided the display epitomized for Americans by Madame de Staël and her fictional Corinne. Like other writers trained in the womanly art, Sedgwick often values conversation over androcentric rhetorical and literary modes; she indicts the irrational, heated rhetoric of party politics through a female character's rational converse and describes women's talk as "as good as a preached sermon" and offering "more of true philosophy and political economy . . . than . . . volumes of dull treatises."[7] Although Sedgwick usually advances conventions of literary converse, she also satirizes its tendencies to ostentation or to coercion of women's speech in the name of liberalism. She expresses nostalgia when practice of the emergent advanced literacy makes a drawing room a gathering place for pretenders to literary criticism or transforms a parlor from "a sort of village exchange" for "innocent gossips" into a factory of women writers who "fancied no conversation could be . . . improving that was not about books."[8] When she revives an older model of conversation under the direction of a paterfamilias, however, thereby endorsing lesser female influence and eloquence, she intends it for the laboring classes.

Sedgwick's development of conversational ideals defended social hierarchy,[9] advocating middle-class values and Anglocentric cultivation. Still, she represented modifications of the art that contravened some contemporary presumptions of class and racial superiority. The conversational model of the plebian Mrs. Barclay's domestic sabbath observances, depicted as better than learned preaching, won approval from a "factory girl."[10] Conservatives, on the other hand, worried that Sedgwick threatened "almost all the conventional forms" in promoting the "mingling of all classes." Poe charged that her making "graceful eloquence . . . proceed from the mouth of a negro woman" violated otherwise excellent verisimilitude in *The Linwoods*. In *Hope Leslie,* a Native American character embodies both hegemonic conversational ideals (Magawisca participates in mutually instructive literary conversation, exchanging her "traditionary tales" for the hero's readings of Spenser) and conversational discourse elaborated beyond prescribed confines, evoking Native American traditions of women's authoritative speech, as Magawisca dialogues in public space and calls upon the "name" of the mother to conjure the Puritan governor, with whom she converses, to keep his word. Women of color could find access to conversational culture through Sedgwick's work, as Sarah Forten apparently did before taking the pen name "Magawisca" to publish poetry that deploys its conventions to abolitionist ends.[11]

The Culture of Conversation

Like other girls of the elite classes at the time, Catharine was schooled in an intellectual and social discipline of literary conversation. Tutored by her sister to read as a base for conversation and offered a pattern for turning education to conversing in evening soirées of "intelligent people" at Mrs. Bell's Albany adventure school, Sedgwick would count among the "rare advantages in my school days—the elevating society . . . of [that] superior woman and cultivated companions . . . who enriched my mind."[12] Sedgwick's training less typically included the models of her Federalist legislator–father in "conversation with his political friends" ("Autobiography," 63) and her mother, who was recognized publicly in circles of the "Republican Court," keeping "open house" when he was at home.[13] Sedgwick herself contributed to the conversational pedagogy at the Lenox school for young ladies kept by her sister-in-law, Elizabeth, with "occasional lectures and readings," likely in social interaction with her "Dear Young Friends." The school gained a reputation for turning out "girls . . . always afterwards known in society by their conversation."[14] Catharine's works stress "conversation [as] one of the most effective means of education, attractive and instructive" and offer multiple models of educative converse (*Home*, 41–42). Her writings served as textbooks in extending cultural literacy and oralcy to middle- and laboring-class pupils at Sunday schools, as well as at New York public schools, and, sanctioned by the Massachusetts Board of Education, appeared in the School Library series for self-improvement. The "influence" in the common schools of *Means and Ends, or Self-Training* (1839), for example, her advice manual for young women, attracted public remark.[15]

Sedgwick further cultivated conversation, again like other women, by criticizing and paraphrasing talk in her diary and letters, noting "vapid" chat at Saratoga, a gay Berkshire "*soirée*," an "agreeable" evening at Anne Lynch's salon, "conversation half sentimental and half religious" aboard a steamboat.[16] Harriet Martineau conversed on the widest "variety of topics" and avoided "pedantry [and] display"; Fanny Kemble exhibited extraordinary "eloquence in conversation"; and actress Ellen Tree was "perfectly frank and natural" (*Life*, 240, 287, 264); but Anna Jameson was "the best talker" ("Autobiography," 109–10). Sedgwick registers the criticism of her own talk and writing that came to her through social intercourse, noting that her propriety in discussing her own writing drew censure and savoring "bonbons" of praise, particularly from readers of the laboring classes (*Life*, 248; and see 295–96, 203; Kelley, *Private Woman*, 400). Although Sedgwick anguishes over possible detraction against a sister writer and joins in the universal deprecation of gossip, her diary quotes "clever thing[s]" men said against other women and women's rights (some of which she repeats in *Means and Ends* in cautioning schoolgirls how best to achieve rights).[17] A more mature letter esteems Lucy Stone's conversational ability (marred only by reformist "slang") and admires her hermeneutics for refuting the stereotype of women's "jabber," thereby authorizing their more public speech (*Life*, 319). Sedgwick records particular delight at the discussion in Boston's Unitarian circles, its moral and intellectual character "more like what I have read of than any thing I have before seen," and she encourages Susan Higginson Channing that "a little occasional lay-preaching from you might produce great effect" on clergy in her "sphere" (*Life*, 181, 146).[18] Philadelphia, though, appears possessed of "a more genial influence"—"delightful" for "cultivation of mind, . . . ease, facility, and grace"; Philadelphians, unlike Bostonians, "do not seem to be afraid to speak lest they should commit themselves for life" (*Life*, 203).

Sedgwick's published criticism of conversation aims to instruct the nation in conversational art. She sketches receptions featuring Anne Lynch and Frederika Bremer to critique Americans' mores and cult of celebrity.[19] "Leisure Hours at Saratoga" in the *Democratic Review* (1838) advances the magazine's positions on states' rights and the elevation of the masses, praising the model of eloquent conversation that she represents as raising Americans at the spa above "'sectional prejudices.'" *Letters from Abroad* (1841) extends travelogue conventions of reporting the talk of luminaries to construe conversing as a national discourse: The book praises Americans for listening abilities that help them avoid Britons' ostentatious conversational competition and for a class structure that favors the dissemination of cultivated conversational practices, yet also advises adopting some refinements from the British "art of conversation."[20]

Conversation Communities

Sedgwick's participation in interrelated conversation communities in Europe, the Berkshires, New York, Boston, Washington, and Saratoga brought her into divers literary, political, and reform circles. Such circles, often noted briefly as social context, should be considered also as opportunities for professional exchange and various forms of influence. As Sedgwick moved among conversation communities, she talked with a multitude of other women (and some men) who were also developing conversational art, in a wide range of modes—fictional, poetic, epistolary, dramatic, oratorical, pedagogical, and reformist. Much might be learned from her interactions with those such as Margaret Bayard Smith, Eliza Cabot Follen, William Ellery Channing, Nathaniel Willis and Sarah Willis/Fanny Fern, Caroline Kirkland, Elizabeth Oakes Smith, Frances Osgood, Eliza Robbins, the Grimké sisters, Abby Hopper Gibbons, Julia Ward Howe, Susan Warner, Fanny Kemble, Ellen Tree, Robert Sands, Anne Lynch, Jane Johnston Schoolcraft, Bayard Taylor, Orville Dewey, Lucy Stone, Henry Ward Beecher, and Elizabeth Sedgwick. Contemporaries remarked Catharine's wit made her "the centre and soul" of "delightful intercourse" and especially appreciated the extraordinary "intellectual cultivation" of her female circle in the Berkshires. Assemblies of female writers there posed enough threat to androcentric power that the *North American Review* felt compelled to sneer at one Sedgwick gathering as a "Blue Congress."[21]

Sedgwick extended her literary intercourse beyond the literati, albeit patron-izingly. Her "lectures" (conversational readings) with women clients in her prison reform work sought "to mingle some social pleasure with the elements of moral teaching" (*Life*, 309; cf. 420). In entertaining the daughter of her black nurse on "Sunday visits," Sedgwick found in Betty's "dramatic gossip" and ghost tales details that "would not be bad for a German story" (*Life*, 326–27). Sedgwick's condescension in such confabs complicates profiles of her as a "high-bred" conversationalist: literary and cordial, if prone to haughtiness or flattery and constrained by fear of gossip.[22]

Writing Conversation

Like other women, Sedgwick self-consciously exploited conversation to sup-ply both devices for writing and "raw material for my humble craft." Her work incorporates actual conversations or "ingraft[s]" fiction upon them (*Letters from Abroad*, 2: 280). She structures sketches and chapters on represented conversa-tion,[23] develops the narrative or instructive ends of fiction as much through conversations among characters as through narration or exposition, employs dialogue as a code of characterization, advances plot and thematics through devices of gossip and reported or overheard conversation, models interpretive paradigms for readers through characters' dialogue,[24] and produces generic inno-vations through the introduction of conversational features. And she does so effectively, as detailed textual analysis demonstrates. Sedgwick drew on the ge-neric repertoire of middle-class conversation, which was spelled out in etiquette and advice books, rhetorical instruction, and cultural criticism, and which de-fined conversation on one border by its openness to the resources of oral culture, yet on its opposite border by an openness to features of artful discourse that removed it from "mere talking."[25] Characteristically, her texts draw colloquial-isms and dialect into their more literary foundational discourses, opening the way, with others such as Caroline Kirkland, for more radical experiment in the next generation of regionalists. Her writings generally exhibit the elevated moral tone, the allusion, and the mild wit that comprise the style recommended for oral literary conversation. Her characteristic mix of morals with fiction accords with the aesthetic requirement that conversation be both entertaining and in-structive, and she often manipulates conversational devices to maintain the req-uisite difference from rhetorical persuasion while nevertheless producing as po-tentially effective a discourse of influence.

Although accounts of American fiction of manners omit Sedgwick's oeuvre while treating less accomplished work by men, conversational features in most of her writing signal some degree of participation in the genre.[26] Cooper ad-

mired her depiction of "our domestic manners, the social and moral influences
. . . in common intercourse," and the first full history of the American novel
finds "her greatest success [in] the historical romance crossed by the novel of
manners."[27] Sedgwick reworks such features in original plot and thematic patterning, introduces them into other genres, and puts them to metalinguistic
purposes as well. She understood the network of speech, letters, and fiction that
sped new fashions in conversing around the nation, with "every circle . . .
correspondent to the remotest . . . town,"[28] and her fiction of manners aims to
shape Anglo-American conversational culture, with early work depicting a middle-class New England ideal, later novels satirizing New York elites, and conduct
books urging the laboring classes and schoolgirls to cultivate the art, as well as
with her ambitious historical novels "crossed" with the genre.

A New-England Tale; or, Sketches of New-England Character and Manners
represents the way co-ed academies increasingly taught the rhetorical arts in
gendered countergenres of oratory and conversation to the end of public exhibition. The narrative voice, however, promotes conversational "eloquence" like
the heroine's, which—though fit for a public forum—exercises its influence in
domestic social space, a preference consistent in Sedgwick's writings.[29] *Redwood*
weaves into a novel of regional manners elements of *bildungsroman*, romance,
and conversion narrative to illustrate ways for Americans to appropriate European modes of intercourse, yet to avoid their purported dangers. The title character, seduced by skepticism at college and in Parisian "highest literary circles"—where conversation intoxicates as "strong liquors"—is led to religion
in part through his daughter's conversation (1: 70–71). The contrast between
Redwood's Southern daughter, trained to social display by a French governess,
and his New England daughter, trained to literary conversation and domestic
management by the combined efforts of surrogate mothers—an English gentlewoman and a "Pilgrim" farm wife—stresses social and moral ends of intercourse, but Sedgwick's expansive discursive ideal permits the New England
heroine to discuss her reading in Italian romance and French drama, shine in
spa talk, and acquire associates of "the first class," in addition to winning a
husband and redeeming her father (2: 85).

Clarence, in a story of the "difficult art [of] select[ing] our society" (2: 285),
satirizes New York's institutions of conversation—the matinées imported from
Europe, the college lyceum, trade in gossip as a livelihood and trade in political
favors, and "that most vapid of all modes of human congregating—tea-parties"
(2: 65; cf. 2: 160). The ideal of literary conversation embodied by the heroine
and Julia May, the "prima donna" of their circle (2: 285), along with the maternal and pedagogic model of the hero's mother, contrasts with several abuses of
it—the pretensions of fashionable "aspirants to the reputation of *fine women*"

who read only European novels (2: 155; emphasis in original); the limited rural model that the heroine outgrows; and the "eloquent" but ethically impoverished conversation of Grace Layton, who would imitate de Staël's *Corinne* (2: 146; cf. *Life*, 266).[30] *Married or Single?* is invested in regulating the economy of conversation—exchange in the social "market," the "supply" and "demand" for gossip, the "intellectual capital" of the talented (1: 197, 190, 160). The novel shows the heroine's talents wasted "in our American Paris," represented as mediocre because its social competition lacks stable class distinctions like those of Europe. Alternatively, the novel promotes the worth of literary conversation, such as the heroine and hero's courtship talk of Anna Jameson and William Cullen Bryant (1: 170, 2: 199).

The conduct tales encourage development of literate conversation in the laboring classes at the table, in sabbath observances, and through such mutual-improvement societies as "*sociable*[s]" (a domestic adaptation of the lyceum).[31] The centerpiece conversation on the servant problem in *Live and Let Live* presents to listeners of both "fashionable" and serving classes a paradigm of service as training for the role of wife and mother, including conversation (174). The "great privilege" conferred on the serving-girl heroine of admission to the Hyde family's instructive table conversations is contrasted with the "sterile talk" of economic matters and gossip, the "vitiating influence of unprincipled servants," and mistresses' tendency to "talk to" women in "a menial condition," all of which displace domestic social intercourse elsewhere (196–97, 26). The tale endorses admitting the laboring classes into the pleasures and instruction of the culture of conversation, but not into the New York society of their employers; the characters who rise through self-improvement are sent to the Ohio frontier.

The advice book *Means and Ends*, greeted on its appearance as "a contribution to 'American *Literature*,'"[32] combines elements of fiction and dialogue with exposition in counseling the extension of female cultivation and rights through the art of conversation. Sedgwick, having tutored her young audience in conversational etiquette and the importance of reading American history so they can breach separate sphere divisions of social circles where men dispute party politics and women gossip, represents women's rights as the central subject in the field of conversation that girls enter when they are old enough to "mingle in society" (250). While Sedgwick discourages her "dear young friends" from becoming "bold assertors of your own rights and the noisy proclaimers of your own powers," she urges, "you cannot too early take into your serious consideration" the issue of women's rights (250). Avoiding polemics herself, she instead evokes the chorus of voices "you will hear" discoursing on the subject, responds to each, and states her own belief (250). Sedgwick rejects as "bigoted" separate sphere discourse that disclaims women's rights, yet she rejects as well the liberal dis-

course of equal rights circulated by such contemporaries as Fanny Wright and
Sarah Grimké, appropriating the discourse of natural rights instead to describe
an agenda for particular claims (rights to education, work preparation, property,
and divorce and custody in an abusive marriage) that she labels "more moderate" but that would still seem radical to many when repeated six years later in
Fuller's *Woman in the 19th Century* (250). Where Sedgwick finds men's political
sphere characterized by "collision and noise . . . folly and corruption," women's
political conversation promises reform; not because of innate moral superiority,
but because women's intellectual and moral development through education
can prepare them differently so that together, through "more communion . . .
on their great social duties," men and women can generate improvement (253–
54).[33] Although *Means and Ends* promotes women's "independent position"
with more stress on gender difference than is desirable today (252), Sedgwick's
effort "to reconcile theories of equal rights with cultural concepts of sexual
difference"[34] could help advance discussion in 1839, and the advice to girls aged
ten to sixteen to prepare for access to more rights and power through education
and self-improvement in conversation can still seem progressive. Sedgwick's
equation of Americans with the "well-bred" and the "Saxon" "race" (133, 134),
however, limits her claims for women, and it remained for others, such as Forten, Grimké, Lydia Maria Child, Harriet Jacobs, and Fuller, to point up the
class and racial exclusions embedded in the prevailing ideology of "woman."

Preoccupation with powers and conventions of speech, especially women's
conversation, informs the text of *Hope Leslie* as a metalinguistic motif. The
narrative voice strains against "laws of decorum" that bind speech (143); conversational traits demarcate each female character; the title character's "freedom of
speech" (177) is at issue in conversations throughout the narrative; and the
climactic chapters play out fantasies of women violating prescribed conversational decorum in hopes of access to freedom or power. Magawisca, jailed to
control her speech, dialogues in a public forum despite a chorus of male voices
attempting to discipline her utterance. She refuses the terms and forms of speech
prescribed by the Anglo male judicial system; neither will she be silent in public
nor will she plead in the binary of judicial discourse, a discourse she shows is
inadequate to express her truth. Instead, she persists in conversing in a forum
where some judge it "indecorous" (294). Hope Leslie employs her conversational art to deceive and manipulate the jailer, thereby gaining Magawisca's
liberation and the hero's admiration. Although her transgressive use of conversation is tantamount to treason, she meets only a private reprimand from authorities. By contrast, the servant Jennet's report of an overheard conversation precipitates the thwarted rape plot that ends in her own demise. Her death by
explosion exhibits the intensity of the era's anxieties about the power of women's

speech, combined in Jennet's case with a threat to class prerogatives. The end meted out to Jennet displaces readers' attention from the more political transgressions of Magawisca and Hope Leslie, which are represented as noble exercises of conversational powers, perhaps what a *Lady's Book* commentator had in mind in protesting that all Sedgwick's heroines defy "all the ordinary rules of propriety."[35] Although the novel can imagine that the conventions of conversation might be turned to radical ends, it finally—through fantasies of removal and violence—reserves that prerogative for the middle-class white woman and premises its exercise only in individual instances, not to effect structural change in existing power relations.

Conversation in *The Linwoods* functions as a synecdoche of national sociopolitical formation. In reaction to Jacksonian ideologies of upward mobility and separate spheres, the novel introduces into a romance rehearsal of Revolutionary history discursive types from the comedy of manners—the disingenuous, social-climbing coquette and coxcomb, the "tedious" meddler, the gossiping servant, and a hero and heroine who can "play citizen of the world," yet prefer to shine in the domestic "circle".[36] The hybrid romance remarks not only how forms of government shape social speech, but also how the right formation of the social sphere and right government of individual speech within it are foundational to national commonweal. Against the regime of the "aristocratic and feudal" English, in which both public and private speech are "governed by policy" that distorts truth for political, sexual, and economic self-interests (1: 68, 2: 14), Sedgwick's heroine prophesies a superior American alternative grounded in the domestic: The "religious obligations of truth . . . in . . . intercourse . . . which rule us in our homes and at our firesides . . . will be the basis of government, and of public, as well as of private intercourse" and will entail "equal rights and equal duties" (2: 15). The vision of a Christian republic recognizes no significant divisions among state, public, and private—whatever the stations defined by gender and rank—and narrative intrusions dialogue with "those who deem political subjects beyond the sphere of a woman's mind," urging that knowledge of "political institutions" enhances women's social intercourse (2: 259–60). The novel's conception of republican equality based in religion and domesticity, however, assumes hierarchies and exclusions that impair its discursive ideal. The heroine and hero demonstrate republican superiority to the British court circle in part by outperforming the English in their own conversational arts, distinguishing their talk by the bluestocking standard invoked through the volumes of More and Johnson on the governor's library table, in contrast with the insinuating gossip, flattery, and political intrigue of the British elite and their sympathizers. Yet the cosmopolitan conversation of the heroine and hero also demarcates class and racial differences within America, represented through the conversational inferiority of other characters. The novel delineates the intercourse of the patriot yeomanry as limited—"dull," "monoton[ous]," lacking refinement and domestic privacy—and its participants, like Bessie Lee, vulnerable to manipulation through more polished conversation (1: 70; and see 1: 83–96). The conclusion, wherein the African American Jupiter struggles to "'spress" himself in a dialogue with his former master, dismisses the anxious fantasy that a "levelling" democracy would put blacks and whites in social interaction as equals, instead serving up in its two marriages a republican meritocracy—the "true *American order of merit*" (2: 275)—remarkably like the traditional elite, comprising only the old colonial "aristocracy," English nobility, and a single self-made exception descended from "pilgrim fathers," an "aristocracy of our own" (1: [13], 42).

Readerly and Critical Reception

The reception of Sedgwick's writing, like that of other antebellum women, is embedded in the culture of conversation. Contemporaries discussed her fiction in venues that cultivated literary talk, from the celebrated Berkshire fêtes of notables like Hawthorne, Melville, and Sedgwick herself, to the "reading parties" of Boston Unitarians and the Maternal Association meetings of orthodox missionary women in the Sandwich Islands.[37] A Boston teenager, noting in her journal that Sedgwick's "fictional daughters . . . conversed . . . on a model far superior to the standards set by society," worked to make her own and her friends' conversation embody such an ideal and to reform the censorious standards of her minister. Ralph Waldo Emerson's diary also admires Sedgwick's fiction for its conversational ideals, finding in them inspiration not to reform but to decry, "How we drivel . . . in real life!"[38]

Critics evaluated Sedgwick's works in terms of the perceived woman's art. Reviewers routinely observe her "colloquial" style and "eloquence," marked by the "ease" and naturalness esteemed in the conversational standards for prose set by Addisonian criticism.[39] They praise the "spirited" dialogue of her characters; some cite such conversation among the most "valuable" aspects of her writing. Critics appreciate conversational attributes of her characters, whether as indicative of their exemplary nature or of her originality and artistry, capable of creating a character who "speaks for himself [*sic*], and not the author, for him" and "people—such as a man of taste likes to read of, and still more to visit."[40] One reviewer held that her writing had more impact than did men's political dispute because she did not antagonize her audience with polemics, but instead focused the "power" of her "patriot's work" on representing "the sphere of her strength . . . [i.e.,] society, . . . where thought and feeling are educated for more public action."[41] Negative appraisals, too, appeal to conversational standards, observing that her American propensity to gossip deprives her of the "delicacy" expected of a female moralist, objecting to "conversations" in *Redwood* as "strained and pedantic, like those of all the young ladies in Cooper's novels," and protesting the "effort to give to every sentence which is spoken the instinctive character of the individual speaking."[42] Reviewers make gender and ethnic norms function as aesthetics to police her variations from their standards of feminine conversation or cultivated English: They reprimand vulgar slang or fashionable French in the mouth of a lady and "negro jargon" in that of a black character. A review charged *Clarence* with improbability for depicting a lady of the heroine's "delicacy" conversing at midnight with "an utter stranger." Poe censored "the vulgarity of such a phrase as 'I put in my oar'—meaning 'I joined in the conversation'—especially in the mouth of so well-bred a lady."[43]

Later literary histories commend Sedgwick's exceptional achievement in writing dialogue. Current criticism locates a strength of Sedgwick's narrative technique in her development of characters' conversation through complex dialogic interplay with her own narrative voice(s).[44] Sustained critical attention to her oeuvre as a whole—something now wanting—might build on this critical tradition to elaborate alternative aesthetics capable of reevaluating her work from the depreciation and displacement it suffered when romance and renaissance theories of American literature were formulated to redeem the work of male peers from charges of shortfall of classic forms.

Just as More, de Staël, Elizabeth Freeman, and many others informed Sedgwick's conversational artistry, her own talk and writing stand behind others' development of the art, such as the fiction and journalism of Fanny Fern (who visited in Berkshire circles), the novels of Susan Warner (who met Sedgwick in Unitarian Boston circles) and of Maria Cummins (a pupil at the Lenox school), and the essays and conversation classes of Margaret Fuller, who cites her in *Woman in the Nineteenth Century* as the "wisest" of Americans writing on female self-cultivation.[45] Conversational texts like *The Linwoods*, with its influence on later works such as William Wells Brown's *Clotelle*, stand at crucial junctures of traditions that contribute to the cultures of the United States—women's and men's, Afro-American and Anglo-American, oral and written, formalist aesthetic and socially engaged aesthetic.[46] To assess Sedgwick's success and that of other writers within conversational traditions can give an expanded sense of their significance for their own time and their potential value to ours.

NOTES

Thanks to Paula Bernat Bennet and the editors of this volume for their thoughtful comments and enthusiasm about this essay.

1. See, e.g., William Charvat, *The Origins of American Critical Thought, 1810–1835* (Philadelphia: Univ. of Pennsylvania Press, 1936); F. O. Matthiessen, *American Renaissance: Art and Expression in the Age of Emerson and Whitman* (London: Oxford Univ. Press, 1941), esp. 14–24.

2. "Writing History: Language, Class, and Gender," in *Feminist Studies/Critical Studies*, ed. Teresa de Lauretis, Theories of Contemporary Culture Series (Bloomington: Indiana Univ. Press, 1986), 38. See Lawrence Buell, *New England Literary Culture: From Revolution through Renaissance* (Cambridge: Cambridge Univ. Press, 1986); Gregg Camfield, "The Moral Aesthetics of Sentimentality: A Missing Key to Uncle Tom's Cabin," *Nineteenth-Century Literature* 43 (Dec. 1988): 319–45; David Leverenz, *Manhood and the American Renaissance* (Ithaca, N.Y.: Cornell Univ. Press, 1989); David S. Reynolds, *Beneath the American Renaissance* (Cambridge, Mass.: Harvard Univ. Press, 1989). Such tendencies cramp even efforts to examine women's speech, e.g., Annette Kolodny, "Inventing a Feminist Discourse: Rhetoric and Resistance in Margaret Fuller's Woman in the Nineteenth Century," *New Literary History* 25 (1994): 355–82; Sandra M. Gustafson, "Choosing a Medium: Margaret Fuller and the Forms of Sentiment," *American Quarterly* 47 (March 1995): 34–65; Caroline Field Levander, *Voices of the Nation: Women and Public Speech in Nineteenth-Century American Literature and Culture,* Cambridge Studies in American Literature and Culture, ed. Eric Sundquist (Cambridge: Cambridge Univ. Press, 1998). But see Joanne Dobson, "Sex, Wit, and Sentiment: Frances Osgood and the Poetry of Love," *American Literature* 65 (1993): 631–50; Joan D. Hedrick, "Parlor Literature: Harriet Beecher Stowe and the Question of 'Great Women Artists,'" *Signs* 17 (winter 1992): 275–303; David S. Shields, "British-American Belles Lettres," in *Cambridge History of American Literature*, vol. 1., ed. Sacvan Bercovitch (Cambridge: Cambridge Univ. Press, 1994), 307–44 and *Civil Tongues and Polite Letters in British America* (Chapel Hill and London: The Institute of Early American History and Culture and Univ. of North Carolina Press, 1997); and Nicole Tonkovich, "Writing in Circles: Harriet Beecher Stowe, the Semi-Colon Club, and the Construction of Women's Authorship," in *Nineteenth-Century Women Learn to Write*, ed. Catherine Hobbs, Foreword by Carroll Smith-Rosenberg, Afterword by Joan Campbell (Charlottesville: Univ. of Virginia Press, 1995), 145–75.

3. Kenneth Cmiel, *Democratic Eloquence: The Fight Over Popular Speech in Nineteenth-Century America* (New York: W. Morrow, 1990), 71. On "eloquence," see, e.g., Daniel Chandler, *An Address on Female Education Delivered Before the Desmosthenian and Phi Kappa Societies . . . in the University of Georgia* (1835; reprint, History of Women Microfilm series, New Haven: Research Publications, 1975), reel 944.

4. "Feminist Critiques of the Public/Private Dichotomy," in *The Disorder of Women: Democracy, Feminism, and Political Theory* (Cambridge, Eng.: Polity, 1989), 118–40. See also Lori D. Ginzberg, *Women and the Work of Benevolence: Morality, Politics, and Class in the Nineteenth-Century United States* (New Haven: Yale Univ. Press, 1990).

5. Alexis de Tocqueville, *Democracy in America*, (1840; ed. and rev. trans. Phillips Bradley, New York: Knopf, 1945), 1: 250 and see 2: 199. Of course men conversed, but women (especially white, elite, or middle-class women) were recognized as better

conversationalists and given more training and practice in conversational rhetoric and etiquette.

6. "'My Sister! My Sister!': The Rhetoric of Catharine Sedgwick's *Hope Leslie*," *American Literature* 70 (Sept. 1998): 493. Contained in this volume.

7. *Redwood: A Tale*, 2 vols. (New York: Bliss and White, 1824), 2: 284 and cf. *Live and Let Live; or, Domestic Service Illustrated* (New York: Harper, 1837), 87; *Clarence; or, A Tale of Our Own Times* (Philadelphia: Carey and Lea, 1830), 2: 87; and see "Second Thoughts Best" (1839; reprint, in *Tales and Sketches*, Second Series, New York: Harper, 1844), 2: 340–42.

8. "Cacoethes Scribendi" (1830; reprint, in *Provisions: A Reader from Nineteenth-Century American Women*, Bloomington: Indiana Univ. Press, 1985), 52–53.

9. E.g., "A Reminiscence of a Foreign Celebrity's Reception Morning," *Harper's New Monthly Magazine* 14 (April 1857): 658.

10. *Life and Letters of Catharine M. Sedgwick*, ed. Mary E. Dewey (New York: Harper, 1871), 248; see *Home* ([1835], 15th ed., 1841; reprint, History of Women Microfilm, New Haven: Research Publications, 1975, reel 1504), chap. 6.

11. Rev. of *Means and Ends, New Yorker* 7 (20 July 1839): 285; rev. of *The Linwoods, Southern Literary Messenger* 2 (Dec. 1835): 58; *Hope Leslie; or, Early Times in the Massachusetts* (1827; reprint, edited and with an introduction by Mary Kelley, New Brunswick, N.J.: Rutgers Univ. Press, 1987), 32, 293; Forten, "The Abuse of Liberty," *Liberator* (26 March 1831). Rose's speech, however, could reflect the dialect that distinguished some "Black Yankee" women; see William Dillon Piersen, *Black Yankees: The Development of an Afro-American Subculture in Eighteenth-Century New England* (Amherst: Univ. of Massachusetts Press, 1988). Sedgwick's own nurse, Elizabeth Freeman (Mumbet), although illiterate, was noted for "conversation [that] was instructive"; Henry Sedgwick, *The Practicality of the Abolition of Slavery: A Lecture Delivered at the Lyceum in Stockbridge, Massachusetts, Feb., 1831* (New York: J. Seymour, 1831), 18.

12. "Autobiography," in *The Power of Her Sympathy: The Autobiography and Journal of Catharine Maria Sedgwick*, ed. Mary Kelley (Boston: Massachusetts Historical Society and Northeastern Univ. Press, 1993), 105–6; and see Mary Kelley, *Private Woman, Public Stage: Literary Domesticity in Nineteenth-Century America* (New York: Oxford Univ. Press, 1984), 63.

13. Rufus Wilmot Griswold, *The Republican Court; or, American Society in the Days of Washington* (1864; reprint, New York: Haskell House, 1971), 326; Elizabeth F. Ellet, *The Court Circles of the Republic; or, The Beauties and Celebrities of the Nation* (Hartford, Conn.: Hartford Publishing Co., 1869), 74, 93; Sarah Cabot Sedgwick and Christina Sedgwick Marquand, *Stockbridge 1739–1939: A Chronicle,* with a foreword by Rachel Field (Great Barrington, Mass.: *Berkshire Courier*, 1939), 173.

14. Richard D. Birdsall, *Berkshire County: A Cultural History* (New Haven: Yale Univ. Press, 1959), 128; Dedication, "Eighteen Hundred Thirty-Eight's Farewell," in *Stories for Young Persons* (New York: Harper, 1840), 39–51, offers a fictional account of the literary social interaction at the Lenox school; *The Letters of Ellen Tucker Emerson*, ed. Edith E. W. Gregg, foreword by Gay Wilson Allen, vol. 1 (Kent, Ohio: Kent State

Univ. Press, 1982), 34. See Mrs. Charles [Elizabeth] Sedgwick, *A Talk with My Pupils* (New York: Hopper, 1863), "a sort of résumé of oral lessons [on] topics not found in our school-books" (ii); and see schoolgirls' conversation represented in *Means and Ends*, 4th ed. (Boston: Marsh, Capen, Lyon, and Webb, 1839), including institutions such as the literary sewing circle, e.g., 204–6, 216–17.

15. "C. M. Sedgwick," in *Homes of American Authors* (New York: Putnam, 1853), 162. "The School Advertiser" in the endmatter of books issued by Marsh, Capen, Lyon, and Webb lists *Means and Ends* by Caroline [*sic*] Sedgwick (e.g., at the end of Elizabeth Ellet, *Scenes in the Life of Joanna of Sicily* [Boston: 1840], 15). Sarah Robbins's work in progress, *Mothering Literacy, Managing America*, discusses Sedgwick and what Robbins calls "the domestic literacy narrative," that is, representations of mothers teaching in conversations that extend maternal ideology to the "managing" of literacy to social and moral ends with effects on nation making (Kennesaw State Univ.).

16. *Life*, 240; Birdsall, 350; *Life*, 352, 164. See also Kelley, *Power of Sympathy*, 133–37.

17. See Bertha Monica Stearns, "Miss Sedgwick Observes Harriet Martineau," *New England Quarterly* 7 (Sept. 1934): 539; *Means and Ends*, 253.

18. A "meeting [of] ladies and gentlemen learning to read" (*Life*, 182–83) was likely a Unitarian "reading party" where educator William Russell led conversational exercises in elocution; see Louise Hall Tharp, *The Peabody Sisters of Salem* (Boston: Little, Brown, 1950), 42–43, and Bruce A. Ronda, *Elizabeth Palmer Peabody: A Reformer On Her Own Terms* (Cambridge, Mass.: Harvard Univ. Press, 1999), 71.

19. See John S. Hart, *The Female Prose Writers of America; With Portraits, Biographical Notices, and Specimens of Their Writings*, 3d. ed. (Philadelphia: E. H. Butler, 1857), 345–47.

20. "Leisure Hours," *United States Magazine and Democratic Review* 1 (Jan. 1838): 202; *Letters from Abroad to Kindred at Home* (New York: Harper, 1841), 1: 106, 118. Brigitte Bailey notes the original combining of elite women's transnational political discussions with aesthetic motifs, in "Tourism and Visual Subjection in *Letters from Abroad* and 'An Incident at Rome'" (contained in this volume).

21. Fanny Kemble in *Life*, 417; Frederika Bremer, *The Homes of the New World; Impressions of America*, trans. Mary Howitt (1853; reprint, New York: Johnson Reprint, 1968), 2: 596; rev. of *The Linwoods, North American Review* 42 (Jan. 1836): 194. See also "Caroline [*sic*] Maria Sedgwick," *American Ladies' Magazine* 8 (Dec. 1835): 659; Mary Dewey in *Life*, 330. Karen Woods Weierman shows Follen's efforts to draw Sedgwick into abolitionist conversation and Sedgwick's use of conversation in an uncompleted fiction to represent positions on slavery, in "'A Slave Story I Began and Abandoned': Sedgwick's Antislavery Manuscript," contained in this volume. Jenifer Banks notes connections with Gibbons and Kirkland, in "Catharine Maria Sedgwick, First Directress of the Women's Prison Association of New York" (paper read at the Second Catharine Maria Sedgwick Symposium, Stockbridge, Mass., June 2000).

22. Edgar Allan Poe, *The Literati of New York City* (1846), in *Edgar Allan Poe: Essays and Reviews*, ed. G. R. Thompson (New York: Library of America, 1984), 1204; cf. Martineau in Stearns, 533, 536.

23. See, e.g., "Cacoethes Scribendi," 41–59; "A Sketch of a Blue-Stocking," *The Token*, ed. S. G. Goodrich (Boston: Gray and Bowen, 1833), 334–46; "Old Maids" (1834; reprint, in *Old Maids: Short Stories by Nineteenth-Century U.S. Women Writers*, comp. Susan Koppelman, Boston: Pandora, 1984), 8–26; "Society," *Ladies' Companion* 19 (June 1843): 93–94; *Home*. Koppelman explains that "oral and written traditions co-existed among women writers for longer than among other groups," shaping conversational devices of storytelling (10); Bailey ("Tourism") notes that the thematic development in both *Letters from Abroad* and "An Incident at Rome" (*Graham's*, 1845) is structured as "an implied conversation between intimates who share a class identity and who participate in 'culture.'"

24. See, e.g., "Old Maids"; *Redwood*, 1: 256–58; *Hope Leslie* glosses Jennet as a conversational type "in every class of life"—the bore (141).

25. Eliza Farrar, *The Young Lady's Friend* (1836; reprint, Women in America Series, New York: Arno, 1974), 386. And see, e.g., George Winfred Hervey, *The Rhetoric of Conversation; or, Bridles and Spurs for the Management of the Tongue* (New York: Harper, 1853); *Means and Ends*, esp. chaps. 17 and 18.

26. See James W. Tuttleton, *The Novel of Manners in America* (New York: Norton, 1972).

27. Rev. of *A New-England Tale*, in *The Literary and Scientific Repository* (1822; reprint, *Early Critical Essays, 1820–1822*, ed. James F. Beard Jr., Gainesville, Fla.: Scholars Facsimiles and Rpts., 1955), 97; Alexander Cowie, *The Rise of the American Novel* (New York: American Book, 1948), 207.

28. *Married or Single?* (New York: Harper, 1857), 1: 186.

29. 1822; reprint, ed. Victoria Clements, foreword by Cathy N. Davidson (New York: Oxford Univ. Press, 1995), 115; see esp. 51–53.

30. The heroine has a statue of Fénélon, whose work, the *locus classicus* on conversational literacy for girls, was translated by Follen, *Selections from the Writings of Fenelon. With a Memoir of His Life*, 2nd ed. (Boston: Hillard, Gray, Little, and Wilkins, 1829).

31. *The Poor Rich Man and the Rich Poor Man* (New York: Harper and Brothers, 1836), 104; see *Home*, chaps. 3, 6, and 13; *Morals of Manners; or, Hints for Young People* (New York: Putnam, 1846), 53–54; *The Boy of Mount Rhigi* (Boston: Peirce, 1848), 222.

32. "American Women," *United States Magazine and Democratic Review* 6 (Aug. 1839): 128, emphasis in original.

33. Sedgwick's own conversation with her brothers forwarded laws favoring women; *Life*, 442, Birdsall, 312. On Sedgwick's conservative gender politics see Deborah Gussman, "Sedgwick's *Married or Single?* and Feminism," contained in this volume.

34. Joan W. Scott, "Deconstructing Equality-versus-Difference: Or, The Uses of Poststructuralist Theory for Feminism," *Feminist Studies* 14 (1988): 48; Scott argues all (proto)feminist arguments need to negotiate this dilemma.

35. Rev. of "Memoir of Lucretia Maria Davidson," *Lady's Book* (August 1837): 61.

36. *The Linwoods; or, "Sixty Years Since" in America* (1835; reprint, New York: Harper and Brothers, 1873) 2: 198, 1: 215, 2: 63.

37. See Patricia Grimshaw, *Paths of Duty: American Missionary Wives in Nineteenth-Century Hawaii* (Honolulu: Univ. of Hawaii Press, 1989), 77.

38. Sarah Ann Wider, *Anna Tilden, Unitarian Culture, and the Problem of Self-Representation* (Athens, Ga.: Univ. of Georgia Press, 1997), 97; *The Journals and Miscellaneous Notebooks of Ralph Waldo Emerson,* vol. 4, ed. William H. Gilman *et al.* (Cambridge, Mass.: Belknap and Harvard Univ. Press, 1960), 458.

39. Rufus W[ilmot] Griswold, *The Prose Writers of America* (Philadelphia: Carey and Hart, 1847), 385; rev. of *Redwood, U.S. Literary Gazette* 1 (1 April 1825): 101; rev. of *Clarence, North American Review* 32 (Jan. 1831): 75; and rev. of *The Linwoods, Southern Literary Messenger* 2 (Dec. 1835): 57.

40. Rev. of *The Linwoods, New England Magazine* 9 (1 Nov. 1835): 380; "Miss Sedgwick," *Southern Literary Messenger* 3 (May 1837): 334; rev. of *Clarence, North American Review* 32 (Jan. 1831): 89, and see 74; "Caroline [*sic*] Maria Sedgwick," *American Ladies' Magazine* 8 (Dec. 1835): 600; *New England Magazine,* 380.

41. "Miss Sedgwick's Tales," *North American Review* 45 (Oct. 1837): 480–81.

42. Rev. of *Letters from Abroad,* London *Athenaeum,* cited in Sister Mary Michael Welsh, "Catharine Maria Sedgwick: Her Position in the Literature and Thought of Her Time Up to 1860" (Ph.D. diss., Catholic Univ. of America, 1937), 15; Harriet Martineau, "Miss Sedgwick's Works," *The London and Westminster Review* 28 (Oct. 1838): 49–50, 58; rev. of *The Linwoods, New England Magazine* 9 (1 Nov 1835): 381.

43. Rev. of *The Linwoods, The Boston Pearl* 5 (12 March 1836): 207; rev. of *The Linwoods, North American Review* 42 (Jan. 1836): 162; rev. of *Clarence, North American Review* 32 (Jan. 1831): 85; rev. of *The Linwoods, Southern Literary Messenger* 2 (Dec. 1835): 58, cf. *The Literati,* 1203.

44. Cowie, 208; see also Ernest E. Leisy, *The American Historical Novel* (Norman: Univ. of Oklahoma Press, 1950), 71. Patricia Larson Kalayjian, "Revisioning America's (Literary) Past: Sedgwick's *Hope Leslie,*" *NWSA Journal* 8 (fall 1996): 68; historical or textual contextualizing could avoid overstating Sedgwick's progressivism.

45. Henry D. Sedgwick, "Reminiscences of Literary Berkshire," *Century Magazine* 26 (1895): 559; Anna B. Warner, *Susan Warner* (New York: Putnam and Knickerbocker, 1909), 251–52; Birdsall, 349; *Woman in the Nineteenth Century* (1845; reprint in *Margaret Fuller: Essays on American Life and Letters,* ed. Joel Myerson, New Haven: College and University Press, 1978), 196. Young Susan Warner observed, "I did not find other people anything particular. I did however enjoy my own . . . conversability."

46. On Brown, see Ann duCille, *The Coupling Convention: Sex, Text, and Tradition in Black Women's Fiction* (New York: Oxford Univ. Press, 1993), 17–29 and "Where in the World Is William Wells Brown? Thomas Jefferson, Sally Hemings, and the DNA of African-American Literary History," *American Literary History* 12 (fall 2000): esp. 452.

12

🐦 Excerpts from Reviews of *Letters from Abroad to Kindred at Home*

Literary Gazette (London), (July 1841): 433–36.

Miss Sedgwick has produced a lady-like and amiable book—observant, and marked by good feeling throughout. . . . [I]t is the impressions made by a visit to the mother country on her cultivated and intelligent children of the New World, that give the chief . . . value to descriptions of this nature. (P. 433)

Roberts' Semi-Monthly Magazine (August 1841): 600–604. Reprinted from *London Examiner*.

Miss Sedgwick . . . [is] the most popular native writer in America, and she deserves to be so. . . . It was . . . a remark of Miss Martineau's . . . that in such books as *Hope Leslie* . . . there was [the] vigorous beginning of a national literature. . . . [W]e think it a great charm that she is thoroughly republican and New-World-ish in her way of looking at the Old World. She sticks to the stripes and the stars. Where she subjects her own countrymen to disadvantageous comparisons, it is in matters wherein . . . they fall short of their own institutions. She gives no quarter to the aristocratic spirit. . . . Even her American forms of speech she is proud of exhibiting, and "realizes" at a prodigious rate. Nor is she an exception to the American habit of leaving open after her the doors of private houses into which she may have entered. Her errors of judgment seem to be such as a clever critic out of a provincial place would most easily tumble into in this great metropolis of ours. . . . [W]hen she has seen very little, [she] is apt to think that she has seen everything. And truly England covers so small a space of ground in comparison with her own *Favored Land* . . . that it is a natural mistake to suppose it explorable in a month or two, manners and all. She forgets what a great many centuries have passed over it. (Pp. 600–601)

Ladies Companion (September 1841): 255.

This is just such a work as might have been expected from the pen of Miss Sedgwick, characterised by liberal opinions and sound judgment. . . . She looks upon humanity with the eye of a philanthropist. . . . We know of no traveller who has ever written a more graphic, just and intelligent work upon Europeans and their institutions, than this gifted lady; a work which we would be inclined to regard as more sound on matters of vital interest to both countries, than . . . the sophistical reasoning of political diplomatists. (P. 255)

North American Review (October 1841): 529–32.

We yield to none . . . in admiration for Miss Sedgwick's genius. . . . [I]t would be a high gratification to receive from a personal friend a series of such letters. . . . But when one takes up a printed book of the kind, it is with expectations, such as we fear this falls short of satisfying. . . . (P. 529)

There are remarks of a more general character, which a "sober second thought" might have induced her further to weigh. Excellently educated in some much better things, but . . . not at all in art, she, like too many weaker people among our travellers, falls to criticizing its masterpieces at first sight, with a confidence equally misplaced in commendation as in censure. (P. 531)

Godey's Lady's Book (November 1841): 239–40.

[T]hese charming volumes . . . are composed of a record of the faithful impressions called forth fresh and glowing from a highly cultivated and watchfully observant mind. But more than this, they are the record of a mind capable of disengaging itself from the thraldom of local prejudices, and of soaring to an elevation, from which it can take a clear and unembarrassed view of the scenery, natural and moral, mapped out before it. . . . (P. 239)

Christian Review (December 1841): 631–32.

Miss Sedgwick . . . had no panting after the celebrity of authorship, . . . nor is there in the charming volumes any of the . . . ambition for reputation which spoils many such works. On the contrary, the impressions of a mature and highly cultivated American mind, and a generous female heart, are impressed on these pages in a manner so fresh, truthful, and with all the gushing sympathy befitting each relation and circumstance which passed before her, that it would belie human nature, to suppose they would not touch chords that will vibrate in harmony with these impressions in every intelligent and virtuous bosom. . . . [T]hese volumes [are] among the most pleasant and useful of the light reading which our mothers and daughters can procure. (P. 632)

Chapter 12

Tourism and Visual Subjection in *Letters from Abroad* and "An Incident at Rome"

BRIGITTE BAILEY

In 1845, five years after her European tour, Sedgwick published a tale about touring Italy in *Graham's Lady's and Gentleman's Magazine*. "An Incident at Rome" recapitulates a myth in nineteenth-century culture about the interaction of northern and southern Europe, one that recounts a threat to the northern tourist's visual and economic domination of southern Europe: the myth of Italy's seduction and emasculation of the northern male traveler.[1] The female American narrator hears the story from an English aristocrat, "Lady C—," as they make a day trip outside Rome. A middle-class English widow encourages her son, Murray Bathurst, in "the study of antiquities" until his antiquarian obsession turns him away from wholesome present interests, such as sex and money; his mercantile uncle wants him to marry his daughter, inherit his money, and take up a "manly career," but Bathurst wants six months in Italy instead.[2] During the trip, Italy comes to feel like his "lover," and Bathurst loses his sanity in a fever, disappears into the Italian landscape, and wanders as a beggar. His mother finds him "groping" among the ruins; the shock of recognition restores him to rationality. The tale ends with his return to England, his marriage to his cousin, "a more fitting mistress than Italy," and his restoration to healthful striving in the world of the present: the world of the British bourgeoisie.

This tale illustrates the function of tourism in the production of the modern national subject and so serves as a commentary on the tradition of masculine tourist writing.[3] Successful tourism entailed an excavation of and libidinal engagement with nationally suppressed traits in the self—traits associated with the feminine, with affect and aesthetic susceptibility, and with a premodern lack of political or commercial pursuits—that were experienced as inhering in foreign scenes. This engagement ideally functioned as a pleasurable disciplining of the self, a subordinating of "othered" aspects of human experience through the aesthetic embrace of these aspects.[4] Northern European and American male tourists, who defined themselves and their nations through language, through "*logos*,"[5] located these "othered" aspects in the visual image and in destinations, such as Italy, that represented the visual. As language's "unspeakable other," the image evoked attempts to incorporate it in language even as it resisted such incorporation.[6] "An Incident at Rome" associates Bathurst's antiquarian impulses with the excavation of un-English characteristics in himself; his temporary succumbing to these characteristics, rather than completing the ritual of subordination and integration, signals the touristic enterprise gone awry and the risk (usually treated comically in travel books) of a reversal in power relations, of the subordinated icon and its associated traits overwhelming and silencing the spectator. Here, the term "Rome" conflates a pagan classicism with Catholicism and associates both with the regressive power of the visual, which must be superseded yet contained by the self-determining rationalism of the Protestant, republican subject.

The tale is a useful gloss on the Italian half of Sedgwick's travel book. *Letters from Abroad to Kindred at Home* (1841) participates in the nationalizing project of tourism, even as it projects a distinctly gendered tourist consciousness. In her reading of British women travel writers, Elizabeth A. Bohls argues that the double position of these women, participants in the tourist gaze by virtue of class but its objects by virtue of gender, creates "the intimate distance that fractures the female subject."[7] As I will argue below, Sedgwick creates a scene in her travel book that enacts this fracture, that positions her as the observer of aesthetic response as it unfolds in a male alter ego. This scene has the effect, on one hand, of displacing her subjectivity from center stage and, on the other, of giving her the ultimate supervisory position: the spectator of elite male consciousness. This and other scenes also shed light on the role of women in binding the republican nation—and a republican brotherhood—together through acts of witnessing and representation and through the articulation of an ideal masculine aesthetic response. Read together, Sedgwick's book and her tale comment on the cultivation of the elite male and illuminate the function of elite women in the construction of a normative national subjectivity.

Like many such accounts, *Letters from Abroad* is informed by the tension between the pleasurable visual submission to the foreign scene and the need to put the "spectacle" of otherness into the service of American ideology.[8] Sedgwick says that what she will miss most when she goes home is the explicitly aesthetic experience of Europe, and especially Italy, and that this experience constitutes the chief risk to Americans: "I would advise no American to come to Italy who has not strong domestic affections and close domestic ties, or some absorbing and worthy pursuit at home." Otherwise, one might feel on returning home "as one does who attempts to read a treatise on political economy after being lost in the interest of a captivating romance."[9] For both women and men the visual and feminine scene of Italy can thwart the formation of republican subjects by drawing tourists away from the symbiotic and nation-constructing activities of "domestic" pursuits and "political economy" back into a premodern, prelinguistic past in which the image dominates and, therefore, renders a rational citizenry impossible.[10]

Her language here, with its opposition of domesticity, commerce, and politics on one hand, to "romance" on the other, and its half-humorous warnings of being "lost" in a captivity of the senses, has connections with the oppositions that structure her historical romance of the Massachusetts frontier, *Hope Leslie; or, Early Times in the Massachusetts* (1827).[11] As Jenny Franchot argues, Americans of Sedgwick's era were engaged with two problematic sites of national identity: the American frontier, with its possibly "contaminat[ing]" native cultures, and an aesthetically imagined but "tainted" European—and especially Catholic—past.[12] As did many of her contemporaries, such as Caroline Kirkland, Margaret Fuller, Washington Irving, James Fenimore Cooper, Nathaniel Hawthorne, and Grace Greenwood, Sedgwick wrote both about the incipiently national community on the frontier and about Europe.[13] Through its doubled captivity narratives, in which both whites and American Indians repeatedly are held prisoner by the other culture, *Hope Leslie* imagines various approaches to intimacy across racial and cultural lines, but the novel finally reinforces racialized national boundaries between English settlers and Native American tribes. This segregation is secured apparently in spite of—but also, I would argue, by means of—its development of elective affinities between white and native protagonists.[14] As does the novel, Sedgwick's travel book instates a national subjectivity by means of a temporary affective engagement with the representatives or the scene of an "other" nation, or rather, as with the Pequots in the novel, with what Anglo-Americans would have designated a proto- or non-nation.

Bathurst's captivation by the Italian visual space of prebourgeois values signals Sedgwick's sense of the greater vulnerability of men and of the rising middle class to the image. Sedgwick's status as upper-class woman, on the other hand, enables her to pursue the cultivation that a visual exposure to "Italy" offers through a more sophisticated encounter with the positions of submission and dominance assumed by tourists. Her framing of the story is a strategy that, in effect, shapes the travel book as well. The American narrator and the English teller of the story form a compact of elite women who, themselves apparently immune to Italy's dangers, preside over and interpret the extreme version of tourism Bathurst represents. By implication, they extend this compact to the middle- to upper-class readers of *Graham's Magazine*, one of the leading monthly magazines in the 1840s.[15] This interpretive community is asked to consider the problem of tourism as simultaneously a formative influence on a governing, managing elite and a threat to the self-possession of the members of this elite. By displacing the dialectic between the rational and the affective self onto English characters and Italian landscapes, where it is performed for the benefit of her American readers of both sexes, Sedgwick gives her tale a pedagogical function; American readers are asked to see the English characters as near equivalents to themselves, as relevant case studies of the promise and pitfalls of tourism in the creation of a national identity.

The promise and threat of Italy involve the whole complex of Anglo-American middle-class identity. While Italy threatens manliness, defined as the ability to act decisively in the public sphere, it also threatens femininity and domesticity; it warps Mrs. Bathurst's mothering and almost denies Murray the chance to start his own family and thus ensure the continuity of the middle-class home. By the same token, Italy is able to enrich the private, interior life of the tourist by providing opportunities to practice bringing marginalized values into the service of dominant ones: the spectacles of the senses, of antiquity, and of Catholicism into the service of the rational, Protestant, and domestic self. Bathurst's Philistine uncle embodies the expansionist, entrepreneurial qualities Sedgwick would have seen as defining the rising wealthy classes in Jacksonian America; his wealth is founded in imperialist activities in India but remains unaccompanied by the cultural knowledge and sensibilities of the older elite. He represents the new male elite's liability of a "thoroughly *mercantilized*" mind, convinced of the "unproductiveness of all learning" (105). But his nephew is able to achieve the potentially higher, more influential status of the cultured man through his temporary submission to Italy and his return to England, one of the sites of political and economic agency. Having recognized the power of Italian scenes, he has learned to manage his response to them through the distancing conventions of poetry and the picturesque; Sedgwick ends the tale with a quotation that reencloses Italy within English verse: Mother and son can now "look back with tranquil minds, to that 'beautiful region' where 'A spirit hangs o'er towns and farms, / Statues and temples, and memorial tombs'" (108).[16]

In her tale, Sedgwick examines the uses masculine texts found for the Italian tour in addressing a central problem of the modern nation.[17] To recapitulate the logic of this body of texts, if the nation-state, especially the United States, defined itself as historical, linguistic, and characterized by manly agency, it nevertheless depended on what its culture defined as oppositional traits, especially aesthetic response and affective bonds, to keep its self-regulating and individualized subjects together.[18] The Italian tour particularly was an engagement with the American dreamscape of the feminine, visual, silent, posthistorical, noncommercial, and prenational.[19] The resources this tour provided became available for binding an increasingly widening middle class to the nation via "culture," that is, literature and art, disseminated by an elite. Opening oneself to "Italy's" influence, cultivating "feminine," aesthetic, and affective aspects of the self, prepared an elite to guide the nation culturally.[20] Sedgwick's two texts create a critical distance between the reader and this training process, the tale through its ironic treatment of male acculturation and the travel book, paradoxically, through its sympathetic viewing of the cultured man's gaze. *Letters from Abroad* posits the elite woman both as a participant with male elites in aesthetic tourism and as the especially insightful spectator of this practice in male elites. This sympathy assumes both identification and difference and brings into play what critics have argued is the "relational self" so often evident in nineteenth-century women's writings; what Anne Mellor has called "a self built . . . on a model of affiliation rather than a model of individual achievement."[21] With such an affiliated, communally defined self as its narrative voice, Sedgwick's text opens the opportunity for understanding the tourist gaze as a social product, an effect of multiple social relations.

Sedgwick represents her tourist experience and gaze as emanating out of and sustained by a web of tightly interrelated interpretive communities; she traveled with one brother, Robert Sedgwick, and his family, and cast her travel book in the form of a journal addressed to another brother, Charles. Like the tale, *Letters from Abroad* contemplates Italy and tourism through the medium of an implied conversation between intimates who share a class identity and who participate in the ongoing creation and regulation of "culture":

> My Dear C., . . .
> Would that I could surround you with the . . . balmy atmosphere of this most delicious place and transport you to its orange bowers! but since that cannot be, pray, the next time you pass by my bookcase, take down a certain yellow-covered book, "Kenyon's Poems," and read the few last lines of "moonlight," and you will find the poet doing for you what I cannot. (*Letters* II, 228)

The sensual and visual experience of Naples is multiply mediated: through her relationship with her brother, through literary representations of such scenes, and, at this stage of the trip, through the literal presence of the English poet John Kenyon, whose work Sedgwick cites and who is a companion of the Sedgwicks.

Such passages reveal the complex relationship between gender and class in the role of the elite woman tourist, a role Sedgwick occupied, I would argue, fairly consciously. As Mary Kelley has shown, in Sedgwick's generation, her socioeconomic class sought to recuperate the political power they had lost in the more egalitarian Jacksonian period by transferring their guardianship of the nation from the political to the cultural field. This shift permitted elite women—excluded from the overt political arena—to join their brothers in "ruling" the nation, to be "participant[s] in the construction of culture."[22] But her "letters" to Charles also illuminate the function of women as the aesthetic principle itself—as ceaselessly constituting the national brotherhood by modeling, evoking, and witnessing aesthetic and affective engagement.[23] This letter brings into conjunction the (male) poet, who can best incorporate into language the Italian image and the emotions it evokes, and the brother at home; her own aesthetic response, which she codes as less articulate, is the medium of exchange.[24] What Terry Eagleton has argued in discussing late-eighteenth-century aesthetic theory often seems embodied in Sedgwick's writing: In their capacity to ground ideological order—especially for male citizens—in feeling rather than force, "Woman, the aesthetic[,] and political hegemony are . . . in effect synonymous."[25] Kelley has described Sedgwick's unusually intimate and mutually sustaining relationships with her four brothers;[26] I suggest Sedgwick's *Letters* are further addressed to a national fraternity, whom she engages in a cultural conversation and whose subjectivity her discourse seeks to mold.[27] Her "relational self" is, then, also an ideologically functional self, necessary to the union of the nation.

However, Sedgwick extends this openness to emotion from the aesthetic to the social, so that her text at once supports the aesthetic project of evoking and managing feeling on behalf of the nation and partially undermines the national distinctions on which the tourist gaze depends. Her travel book models scenes of sympathy that clearly locate national identity in affective attachments but that also ask her American readers to identify with (elite) Italian subjects; she describes social contacts with a series of Italian elites, especially women. The Sedgwicks were connected with upper-class circles of resistance to the Austrian occupation of northern Italy through Italian exiles in the United States (*Letters* II, 31). The letters of introduction they carried from Italian political refugees gave them entrée into Italian society in a number of places; Sedgwick's descriptions of what she sees are often linked with an account of the person showing them the sights and her comments on their host's sensibility and political views.[28] Her conflation of aesthetic touring and political discussion is unusual in travel books on Italy in this period and results in an equally unusual sense of a shared class perspective across national lines;[29] Sedgwick presents a transnational vision of stewardship among the elite with respect to their nations or "the people." She assigns different functions to upper- and lower-class Italians; the philanthropic, aesthetic, and supervisory gaze is shared across national lines by a mobile elite that trains this benevolent gaze on a fixed, picturesque lower class.

One effect of this shared elite perspective is Sedgwick's emphasis on cross-national sympathetic alliances—sympathetic "looking relations"—between elite women.[30] In two scenes especially she shows herself in intimate contact with Italian women who pour out their grief at the loss of exiled, imprisoned, or deceased family members in Sedgwick's sympathetic presence. Here she counters standard tourist definitions of Italy by extending domestic space into Italy as the basis for and as connected to patriotic and revolutionary activity. Sedgwick, like Margaret Fuller, who wrote about Italy during a more active phase of the *risorgimento* in 1848–49, asks her readers to visualize Italy as a potential nation-state.[31] She at once remasculinizes Italian elite men by comparing them to American revolutionaries and evokes the republican connection between domesticity and national agency.[32] These domestic moments modify her aesthetic response to Italian sights and emphasize the connections between political oppression and domestic distress. After touring the exquisite estate of a Milanese woman, Sedgwick remarks to her hostess: "'What a happy woman you must be!' said I . . . , 'to be mistress of this most lovely place!' . . . ; her face changed, her eyes filled with tears, and after alluding to repeated afflictions from the severance of domestic ties by death, and to the sufferings of her friends for their political opinions, she concluded, 'you know something of the human heart—judge for me, can I be happy?'" (*Letters* II, 63). She describes another "scene," as she calls it, by quoting from her niece Kate's journal a description of herself listening to the sister of an Italian political exile in New York: "'I came into the drawing room to find . . . Aunt K. [Sedgwick] holding the hand of a lady in black, who . . . was pouring out a rapid succession of broken sentences.'" In this strongly gendered scene of intimacy and reciprocity, Sedgwick nevertheless emphasizes the intersection of politics and domesticity by describing the pain that one sphere can inflict on the other: here the ability of Austrian repression to turn "the sweet streams of domestic love into such bitter, bitter waters" (*Letters* II, 121–22).[33] And through the evocation of the sentimental, she also seeks to forge affective ties between her American readers and these middle- to upper-class Italian citizens and citizens' wives, sisters, and mothers.[34]

Nevertheless, such antitourist sections coexist with conventional responses to Italy as a non-national aesthetic space. In Sedgwick's *Letters*, as in travel writings from Addison to Goethe to James, the destiny of "Italy" is to evoke an aesthetic response in the cultivated man.[35] The class and gender structures of the tourist gaze surface most fully in a scene she composes, near Naples, which combines two of the most popular visual forms in the antebellum United States: genre and landscape images. As Elizabeth Johns defines it, genre painting depicted characteristic "scenes of everyday life" that enabled middle-class and elite Americans to engage in "typing," to "assert, parcel out, and deny power" to various figures in the creation of social order.[36] Sedgwick sets a genre scene of dancing peasant girls within a large backdrop that is meaningful to the tourist (but not to the girls); its "materials" are an epitome of the romantic Italian landscape and, therefore, part of the American unconscious imaginary (signaled by the "dream[iness]" of the scene): ruined temples and villas, Vesuvius, the wide expanse of the Bay of Naples, and the island of Capri "far off in the bay, so soft and dreamy that it seemed melting away while we were gazing at it." A group of children and "Moorish-looking" teenage girls surround the tourists, trying to sell them souvenirs; their lower-class status, gender, and racialized identity make them available for the tourists' aesthetic gaze. Sedgwick locates the significance of the episode not only in the scene itself but also in the response of the man of sensibility, in this case, the poet Kenyon.[37] Her description of his response becomes a case study of the role of cross-racial and cross-gender gazes in the formation of subjectivities:

Our merry followers were joined by an old woman, . . . the living picture of Raphael's Cumean Sibyl . . . holding . . . a tamborine, on which she was playing [a] wild air . . . and accompanying it with her cracked voice. To this music [a] gleeful bare-legged girl . . . was dancing a tarantella around K—n, who, though far enough from a Bacchus or Faun, has in his fine English face much of the joyousness of these genial . . . worthies. [The] girl danced and shouted like a Bacchante . . . ; there were children with tangled locks of motley brown and gold, and eyes like precious stones, leaping and clapping their hands. . . . [A]nd we pilgrims from the cold North were looking on. K—n . . . [gave] himself up to the spirit of the scene. The floodgates of poetry, and of sympathy with these wild children of the South, were opened; and over his soul-lit face there was an indescribable shade of melancholy, as if by magic he were beholding the elder . . . time, and that were an actual perception which before had been transmitted by poetry, painting and sculpture. He threw a shower of silver among the happy creatures, and we drove off. (*Letters* II, 267–69)

This scene echoes standard antebellum representations of Italy. Johns has argued that American genre paintings of United States subjects, such as George Caleb Bingham's *Jolly Flatboatmen* (1846), focused on the lower-class male figures with whom the middle-class viewer was increasingly asked to share power in Jacksonian America. Italian genre scenes, on the other hand, often placed lower-class women and children, tokens of the lack of political or economic agency, in the foreground and moved the ruined traces of an active, masculine history—of empire, technological transformations of the environment, or cities—into the background. Engravings in English and American gift books, annuals, and other publications of the 1830s present a timeless, feminized world without modern forms of labor and without access to the transformations of contemporary history; ruins here come to signal not only the history that originally produced them but more fully the pastoral world—the "elder time"— which supposedly preceded and followed this history. J. D. Harding's "Tivoli," published in *The Landscape Annual* (1832), positions, typically, a contadina with two children in the foreground, as a conceptual threshold that defines the tourist's perspective on the Roman ruins behind them; the male figures in the middle distance are upper-class tourists, the current possessors of the scene(s) of history and pre- and post-history through their presumed knowledge and connoisseurship, a knowledge which does not draw them into the scene or subject them to its power, as it does Bathurst, but which affirms their self-possession. Thomas Stothard's "The Fountain" appeared in a book with which Sedgwick was familiar: Samuel Rogers's *Italy, A Poem* (1830); as did so many touring American writers, Sedgwick had breakfast with its author in London (*Letters* I, 78). This image rehearses the tourist's sense that this feminine, "elder" world has superseded the masculine one of military activity, just as the hero's tomb has been turned into a fountain that supports a timeless, nurturing activity—a sister, the poem tells us, giving her brother a drink.

On the other hand, J. M. W. Turner's print of Florence for *The Amulet* (1831) depicts a space in which both male and female figures are subsumed by forms of leisure and piety and class behavior that separate them from tourists and make them available to the traveler's aesthetic gaze. The crosses and procession in the middle distance serve as tokens of the distance between the mobile and historically viable Protestant tourists, who are not pictured within the scene but who define its point of view and consume this "picturesque" world as an aesthetic object, and its Catholic inhabitants, who are contained and determined by it.[38] If scenes with ruins ask modern national subjects to reflect on the passage of empire and the loss of history, such images as Turner's view of Florence offer an encounter with the "archaic" traits whose imagined loss underwrites modern identity. By showing the losses incurred by the emergence of the rational self, and by at once inviting recontact with the "lost" characteristics of the visual and controlling this contact through the distancing conventions of the tourist gaze, they replicated the process by which tourism ordered affect in order to produce the modern national subject.

In her own "scene" of the dancers surrounding Kenyon (*Letters* II, 267), Sedgwick is the sympathetic spectator of the elite male tourist's sensibility at work. If "Italy" stimulates an engagement with those nationally suppressed traits in the self labeled archaic, childlike, or primitive, then the cultivated male tourist is the site on which these "faunlike" traits are "remembered" and reintegrated into the self-governing modern citizen, whose pleasurable "melancholy" marks

J. D. Harding, "Tivoli," title page of *The Landscape Annual* (London: Jennings and Chaplin, 1832). Courtesy of the President and Fellows of Harvard College.

Thomas Stothard, "The Fountain," in Samuel Rogers, *Italy, A Poem* (London: T. Cadell and E. Moxon, 1830). Courtesy of the President and Fellows of Harvard College.

the distance in his own internal landscape between the childlike past and the mature present. The paid performance of archaic identities, safely distanced via the mechanisms of nostalgia and aesthetics, is one of the means by which the tourist purchases a modern subjectivity. Sedgwick constructs an epitome not only of "Italy" here but also of the erotics of tourism. The desire of the tourist is not simply for the teenaged dancing girl, whose tarantella affords him the opportunity to integrate the primitive intoxication of a Bacchus and the lasciviousness of a faun into "his fine English face," but more fully for the entire

J. M. W. Turner, View of Florence, *The Amulet*, ed. S. C. Hall (London: Westley and Davis, 1831). Courtesy of the President and Fellows of Harvard College.

panorama of the "elder . . . time," a scene which simultaneously evokes a sense of loss and offers the occasion for aesthetically experiencing, ordering, and managing the emotions bound up with this imagined loss. The slippage between identification and difference in the spectator's relationship with Kenyon, who is English yet also part of the "we" of the passage, signals Kenyon's function as an exemplary male subject from whom the American middle-class reader can learn, but it also matches the slippage in Sedgwick's simultaneous identification with and sense of difference from this male other self. The difference submerged in the travel account is accentuated in the tale, which separates male and female travelers and which creates a mirror image, at once comic and bathetic, of the poet's aesthetic response.

"An Incident at Rome" supplies a more detached reading of the spectacle of the cultivated English man submitting himself to the influences of "Italy." Bathurst possesses in an exaggerated sense the latent capacities to which "Italy" speaks in all modern tourists. He is actually already Catholic, Italian in appearance, and fluent in the language; he has "large dark melancholy eyes, . . . and tangled long dark hair." This feminized self—indicated by his "unEnglish person"—is the nonproductive self that needs at once to be acknowledged and disciplined. His "love" for Italy is figured as a narcissistic passion that prohibits the development of his heterosexual, reproductive, commercial self—the self-regulating, self-reproducing, and future-oriented citizen necessary to the vigor of the modern nation. When he loses his reason in Italy, he moves from being a subject (a tourist) to being an object, from independent traveler to dependent beggar, from the surveyor of the scene to a figure in the landscape. He disappears from police and consular records, forms of surveillance that authenticate middle-class status, and appears instead in tourist observations, a form of surveillance that denies it. His immersion into his own delusional world of wandering and ruin-hunting parodies the tourist's proper cultivation of interiority. In this respect the tale is a parable of a national "brother" becoming an "other," a warning to emerging American republicans—displaced onto an English character—about the necessity of maintaining the boundaries of identity.[39]

Through its American and English frame narrators, however, Sedgwick's tale also opens up a gap between the spectatorship of elite women and that of men. These female narrators contemplate the emergence of a money-based ruling class via the acculturating mechanism of tourism; caught between his mother's "enthusiasm" for things Italian and his commercially successful but boorish uncle, the protagonist has to forge a properly elite identity composed both of "learning" and of money. Sedgwick prevents this fusion from becoming entirely naturalized by creating a disjunction between the languages associated with these two identities in the tale. Mrs. Bathurst speaks in a heightened sentimental discourse that indicates her own passionate engagement with classical antiquities, as well as her remorse at having impelled her son on this less than "natural" path: "'I developed prematurely, and most unwisely, his taste. . . . Thus I fed the flame that was to consume my poor boy'" (105). Sedgwick treats the uncle as a comic figure, and so the tone of the tale itself becomes comic as Bathurst moves into the uncle's sphere of influence at the end. The uncle comments that the immersion in Italy has turned out to be the antidote for Murray's love of Italy, "saying, somewhat coarsely, that to be sure the hair of the same dog would cure the bite, if you ate hide and all" (108). The mother's "enthusiasm" for Italian ruins makes her a pathetic figure of the feminine middle-class susceptibility to the values Italy represents and contributes to her son's feminization, insanity, and temporary plunge out of the bourgeoisie, whereas the uncle would block the acculturating process of the Italian tour altogether. Sedgwick's use of two separate linguistic registers prevents the reader from identifying with their point of intersection and common heir—Murray Bathurst—as Sedgwick identifies with Kenyon in her Neapolitan scene. This strategy also creates an ironic distance between her pair of narrators (with whom the reader *is* asked to identify) and the subject matter of the story: the education through tourism of male elite sensibility.

In her study of British women travel writers, Sara Mills emphasizes the tension between "feminine and colonial discourses," a tension which results in "heterogeneous" narratives that reinforce the dominance of the imperial gaze even as they subvert it.[40] By reading these two tourist texts together, I have argued that Sedgwick similarly reinforces the project of shaping a masculine republican subject while creating the conditions for elaborating a critique of this project. In doing so, she suggests that elite women have access to multiple and possibly contradictory cultural functions, which include both an identification with the aesthetic and the analysis of republican subjectivity. As in her novels, her concerns are ultimately national ones; and, as in her novels, Sedgwick's central concern is to trace the interplay between national boundaries and the boundaries of the normative subject, between gender formations and the formation of citizenship.

NOTES

Thanks to Rachel Trubowitz and Mary Rhiel for their critically astute reading of a draft of this essay and to the participants of the Sedgwick Symposium for their conversation and suggestions.

1. See James Buzard on Italy as feminized—cast as a seductive woman—in English and American male tourist writing in *The Beaten Track: European Tourism, Literature, and the Ways to "Culture," 1800–1918* (Oxford: Oxford Univ. Press, 1993), 132–39, and Kenneth Churchill on the pattern of attraction and disappointment, "ennervation" and even death, in English and American literary treatments of Italy: *Italy and English Literature, 1764–1930* (New York: Macmillan, 1980), 3, 23, 58, 159.

2. Miss C. M. Sedgwick, "An Incident at Rome," *Graham's Lady's and Gentleman's Magazine* 27 (1845): 104–8. Sedgwick seems to name her character "Murray" to indicate, jokingly, his degree of immersion in tourism; John Murray of London published a popular series of guidebooks, a series the Sedgwicks used and to which Sedgwick refers in her travel book.

3. In thinking about the modern subject, I am drawing on Catherine Belsey's useful survey of ideological and linguistic theories of the "cultural construction of subjectivity" (593), based on Althusserian and Lacanian perspectives: "Constructing the Subject: Deconstructing the Text," *Feminisms: An Anthology of Literary Theory and Criticism*, ed. Robyn R. Warhol and Diane Price Herndl (New Brunswick, N.J.: Rutgers Univ. Press, 1991), 593–609. Belsey highlights the ambiguity of the term "subject" in this context as at once an agent (the "grammatical subject" of sentences and actions) and a *subjected being*," interpellated into the social order through language (596). This complex under-

standing of modern subjectivity is especially helpful in reading women's writings, which, as Sedgwick's texts do, embody a range of subject positions.

4. I have argued that this is especially true of tourist writings on Italy: Brigitte Bailey, "'The Protected Witness': Cole, Cooper, and the Tourist's View of the Italian Landscape," in *American Iconology: New Approaches to Nineteenth-Century Art and Literature*, ed. David C. Miller (New Haven: Yale Univ. Press, 1993), 94–96. See John Urry for a discussion of "the tourist gaze," a "socially organized" gaze "constructed through difference" that reinforces the normative identities of tourists: *The Tourist Gaze: Leisure and Travel in Contemporary Societies* (London: Sage Publications, 1990), 1–2.

5. Buzard, 134.

6. Gilman, 23. In discussing the ideological relationship between word and image in the nineteenth century, I draw on Ernest B. Gilman's "Interart Studies and the 'Imperialism' of Language" (*Poetics Today* 10 [1989]: 5–30) and W. J. T. Mitchell's historical discussion of this relationship in aesthetic theory in *Iconology: Image, Text, Ideology* (Chicago: Univ. of Chicago Press, 1986).

7. Elizabeth A. Bohls, *Women Travel Writers and the Language of Aesthetics, 1716–1818* (Cambridge: Cambridge Univ. Press, 1995), 16.

8. Neil Harris, *The Artist in American Society: The Formative Years, 1790–1860* (Chicago: Chicago Univ. Press, 1982), 146–48.

9. [Catharine Maria Sedgwick], *Letters from Abroad to Kindred at Home*, 2 vols. (1841; reprint, New York: Harper and Brothers, 1845), II, 193.

10. Amy Kaplan has persuasively argued for "the relationship of domesticity to nationalism and imperialism" (582) in antebellum American culture. See her article for readings which illustrate the mutual reinforcement of the "separate spheres" in these projects: "Manifest Domesticity," *American Literature* 70 (1998): 581–606.

11. Catharine Maria Sedgwick, *Hope Leslie; or, Early Times in the Massachusetts*, ed. Mary Kelley (New Brunswick, N.J.: Rutgers Univ. Press, 1987).

12. Jenny Franchot, *Roads to Rome: The Antebellum Protestant Encounter with Catholicism* (Berkeley: Univ. of California Press, 1994), 19.

13. Relevant titles indicating this double focus of the period include (this is of course a small selection of possible titles): Irving's *The Sketch Book* (1819–20) and *A Tour on the Prairies* (1835); Cooper's Leatherstocking novels and his series of travel books, *Gleanings in Europe* (1836–38); Kirkland's *A New Home—Who'll Follow? or, Glimpses of Western Life* (1839) and *Holidays Abroad; or, Europe from the West* (1849); Hawthorne's *The Scarlet Letter* (1850) and *The Marble Faun* (1860); Fuller's *Summer on the Lakes* (1844) and her dispatches from Europe to the *New-York Tribune* (1846–50); Greenwood's *A Forest Tragedy; or, The Oneida Sisters* (1855) and *Haps and Mishaps of a Tour in Europe* (1854).

14. See Judith Fetterley's analysis of the complexities of race and "Republican Sisterhood" and Brotherhood in *Hope Leslie*: "'My Sister! My Sister!': The Rhetoric of Catharine Sedgwick's *Hope Leslie*," *American Literature* 70 (1998): 491–516, also in this volume.

15. See Edward E. Chielens's discussion of the reputation and popularity of *Graham's* in the 1840s in his edited volume, *American Literary Magazines: The Eighteenth and Nineteenth Centuries* (Westport, Conn.: Greenwood Press, 1986), 157. John Tebbel

and Mary Ellen Zuckerman point out that "while a rather wide range of people read the women's journals [such as *Graham's*] of the antebellum period, they were bought primarily by economic elites": *The Magazine in America, 1741–1990* (Oxford: Oxford Univ. Press, 1991), 38.

16. I have not yet found the source of this quotation; I speculate, without much evidence, that it may be from one of John Kenyon's poems, although I did not find it in the book Sedgwick cites: his *Poems*. It is possible that Sedgwick made it up.

17. Examples of such male-authored travel books include James Fenimore Cooper's *Gleanings in Europe: Italy* (1838) and George Stillman Hillard's *Six Months in Italy* (1853).

18. Critics who examine the role of affect in constituting self-regulating, modern subjects in this period include Terry Eagleton, in *The Ideology of the Aesthetic* (Oxford: Blackwell, 1990), and Benedict Anderson, in *Imagined Communities: Reflections on the Origin and Spread of Nationalism*, rev. ed. (London: Verso, 1991).

19. Bailey, 94.

20. Harris, 159–68.

21. Mary Kelley, Introduction to *The Power of Her Sympathy: The Autobiography and Journal of Catharine Maria Sedgwick* (Boston: Massachusetts Historical Society, 1993), 26–27. Anne K. Mellor, *Romanticism and Gender* (New York: Routledge, 1993), 166.

22. Kelley, 32.

23. Melissa Homestead has, in conversation, pointed out Sedgwick's complex allusions to Germaine de Staël's novel, *Corinne, or Italy* (1807), influential for tourists, in Sedgwick's novel, *Clarence* (1830). Sedgwick tends to identify de Staël and her heroine, an *improvisatrice*, with the socially disruptive egotism of another female character and to characterize her own heroine, Gertrude Clarence, as facilitating, by contrast, male aesthetic response in cultivated conversations, much as Sedgwick defines the feminine role in her letter to Charles. But it also seems as though the novel suggests, more surreptitiously, some parallels between Gertrude and Corinne, perhaps in their capacity for connoisseurship.

24. I am thinking here, generally, of Eve Kosofsky Sedgwick's discussion of women as the medium of exchange between men in the formation of homosocial bonds and the maintenance of patriarchal power: *Between Men: English Literature and Male Homosocial Desire* (New York: Columbia Univ. Press, 1985).

25. Eagleton is using "hegemony" here in Gramsci's sense of domination through culture rather than physical coercion, 59.

26. Kelley, 17–18, 24–31.

27. Charlene Avallone has illuminated Sedgwick's highly conscious participation in the intergender nineteenth-century conventions of cultural discussions in her paper given at the 2000 Sedgwick Symposium: "Catharine Sedgwick and the 'Art' of Conversation," also in this volume.

28. See, for example, her description of meetings with Milanese contacts: *Letters* II 31–68.

29. See William W. Stowe for a description of the normative tourist's lack of im-

mersion in the political issues of tourist (desti)nations, as well as of the tourist's customary othering of both upper- and lower-class inhabitants of these sites: *Going Abroad: European Travel in Nineteenth-Century American Culture* (Princeton: Princeton Univ. Press, 1994), 45–48.

30. I draw here generally on E. Ann Kaplan's discussion of "looking relations," shaped by gender, race, and national identity, in films about travel: *Looking for the Other: Feminism, Film, and the Imperial Gaze* (New York: Routledge, 1997).

31. Margaret Fuller, *"These Sad But Glorious Days": Dispatches From Europe, 1846–1850*, ed. Larry J. Reynolds and Susan Belasco Smith (New Haven: Yale Univ. Press, 1991). See Larry J. Reynolds on American responses to the Risorgimento (*European Revolutions and the American Literary Renaissance* [New Haven: Yale Univ. Press, 1988]) and William L. Vance for a reading of Sedgwick's responses to the social inequalities of Rome (*America's Rome*, 2 vols. [New Haven: Yale Univ. Press, 1989], II, 116–17, 169–70).

32. Sedgwick extrapolates a national masculine political agency from the example of the Italian revolutionaries who were imprisoned by the Austrians following a failed 1821 revolt: "I wish that those who ignorantly think lightly and speak disparagingly of 'Italians' could know these men. . . . We honour our fathers for the few years of difficulty through which they struggled; and can we refuse our homage to these men, who sacrificed everything . . . that man holds most dear, to the sacred cause of freedom and truth? and let me ask, what should we in reason infer of the nation whence they came? surely that there are many ready 'to go and do likewise'" (*Letters* II, 31–32).

33. Sedgwick's recourse to her niece's journal raises provocative questions about her authorial strategies: in this case her highlighting the mediated or perhaps communal nature of such scenes of sympathy.

34. See Mary Suzanne Schriber for a discussion of the relationships of separation and identification, "difference and doubling," in American women's travel narratives: *Writing Home: American Women Abroad, 1830–1920* (Charlottesville: Univ. Press of Virginia, 1997), 81–89.

35. See Joseph Addison's *Remarks on Italy* (1705), Johann Wolfgang von Goethe's *Italienische Reise* (1829), and Henry James's *Italian Hours* (1909).

36. Elizabeth Johns, *American Genre Painting: The Politics of Everyday Life* (New Haven: Yale Univ. Press, 1991), xi–xii.

37. As in the writings of most American tourists (Stowe, 13), another English poet, Byron (especially *Childe Harold*), was Sedgwick's frequent touchstone in her responses to Italy.

38. Franchot argues that the American "Protestant gaze on Rome . . . celebrated Catholicism as a spectacle, and fantasized the consumption of this foreign substance rather than conversion to it" (234).

39. Thanks to Mary Rhiel and Rachel Trubowitz for this point.

40. Sara Mills, *Discourses of Difference: An Analysis of Women's Travel Writing and Colonialism* (London: Routledge, 1991), 106.

Silhouette of Catharine Maria Sedgwick, cut by August Edouart. Caption reads:
Miss Catharine M. Sedgwick   Authoress of Stockbridge, Mass.   Saratoga   16th
Augt. 1842. Courtesy of Sedgwick Family Society and Trust.

13

🌱 Letters and a Sketch of Sedgwick's Prison Work

Excerpts from *The Life and Letters of Catharine M. Sedgwick*. Ed. Mary Dewey. New York: Harper & Brothers, 1871.

Miss Sedgwick to Mrs. [Frances] Watson
Albany, March 25, 1816
. . . The great disadvantage and the only reproach of a single life is, that we poor spinsters are generally condemned to uselessness, and Satan, availing him-self of his prerogative, "finds mischief still for idle hands to do." It has always, and I pray it may ever be my happy destiny to have employment enough to keep me out of danger of falling into the folly of repining or the meanness of envying. (Pp. 102–3)

Miss Sedgwick to Mrs. K. S. [Katharine Sedgwick] Minot
New York, May 21, 1848
. . . I have yet a great deal of duty to do in our Prison Society, and for the last month, with the exception of a week at Lenox, it has occupied me for three days in the week. . . . I think the favored class of society owe an immense debt to Providence, which can only be discharged by attempting to rescue the vicious and ignorant from misery and degradation. But it seems to me they must be saved, and *can not* be *rescued*, and we remain as if there were a palsy on us. With the means of universal education and sustenance, we see creatures with the powers and faculties out of which heroes and martyrs have been made, covered with bruises and putrefying sores. My whole soul is sickened, and today, when I went into our church filled with people in their fine summer clothes, and

heard a magnificent sermon from Mr. Dewey, and thought of the streets and dens through which I had just walked, I could have cried out, "Why are ye here?" Some good is achieved—I see that—but the work is struggling and inefficient. If the sea were to roll over the adults and leave the children, we could devise a future, perhaps attain it for them. (Pp. 306–7)

Miss Sedgwick to Mrs. Susan Channing
Lenox, October 21, 1849

. . . I believe that the little charity work I do is conservative in its tendency. It takes me out of doors, and is solacing to the heart, after the heavy disappointments, and amidst the wearing small trials of life. Dear Susan, while I fully realize the shortness of life, and do sometimes ardently desire to do two days' work in one, I feel its value more than I ever did, and take far more pains to nourish it than when I was younger and happier, and it seemed fairer. The transition from "beauty to duty," if it takes from its loveliness, gives it an infinite value. (P. 318)

Mrs. James S. Gibbons
"Sketch of Miss Sedgwick's Connection with the Women's Prison Association of New York"

We were soon brought into close companionship by visits to the prison, and kindred institutions, especially the Tombs, Blackwell's, and Randall's Island. The hospital claimed much of her interest, perhaps because there her tenderest sympathies were enlisted. In her visitations she was called upon to kneel by the bedside of the sick and dying. The sweetness of her spirit, and the delicacy of her nature, felt by all who came within her atmosphere, seemed to move the unfortunate to ask this office from her, and it was never asked in vain. So tenderly shrinking was she that she sought opportunities for such ministrations when no ear heard, no eye beheld her, and many an erring sister was soothed and comforted as she passed through the dark valley by the heavenly voice of this angel of mercy.

At the Isaac T. Hopper Home she labored faithfully for this class of humanity, and for many successive years during her sojourn in this city, attended by her niece Helen, with her favorite dog, she devoted Sunday afternoons to a Bible-class, and sometimes to the reading of such books as met the needs of the inmates. Sometimes the hours were passed in conversation, one and another relating their sorrows and misfortunes, and receiving in their turn the balm which flowed from a heart touched with a sense of their infirmities, and accepting the lesson that "to cease and do evil and learn to do well" was the way to a new and better life. (Pp. 419–20)

Chapter 13

"From Home to Home": Sedgwick's Study of Deviance

JENIFER BANKS

I knew I was disgraced, but I did not feel wicked, Mother. It seemed to me that my Father in heaven looked down on me in pity, not anger" (*Married*, 2: 23). In asserting her right to define her own sense of self, Jessie Manning—seduced, abandoned, and the mother of an illegitimate child (now dead)—authorizes herself to challenge the prevailing bourgeois social ethic by which she is condemned and socially "exiled." In distinguishing between religious and social judgments she privileges sympathy over punishment and thus reverses the prevailing social attitude toward the "fallen woman." This exchange in Catharine Sedgwick's last novel represents the culmination of her critical analysis of the culturally sanctioned bourgeois "cult of true womanhood," an interrogation informed by her career in benevolent work among poor, criminal, and sexually "fallen" women of New York. Here Sedgwick confirms themes she has been exploring throughout her fiction: women's search for personal liberty and their right to define "respectability" and "virtue" for themselves, and thus to determine what should constitute membership in the domestic world which had been identified as their proper sphere.[1]

Sedgwick's publishing career extended from 1822 to 1858, her career in benevolent work from 1835 to 1863, a period when the essentially exclusionary and restrictive elements of the white bourgeois ideology of the "cult of true womanhood" were promoted by advice books, gift books, prescriptive literature, and mass-circulation newspapers and magazines. This was also a period, however, when many best-selling novels and short stories, and the rhetoric of women involved in evangelical, charitable, and reform causes such as abolition and temperance showed how the tenets of that ideology—piety, purity, submissiveness, and domesticity—could be used to do the cultural work that empowered rather than restricted women.[2] Although she opposed the more "zealous" public actions of the women's rights activists, through both her writing and her work with the poor and with discharged female convicts Sedgwick was one of the first and most steadfast critics of the confining elements of the conservative ideology of "true womanhood." Her resistance, however, is expressed in terms of inclusion rather than of empowerment.

Sedgwick's private correspondence suggests that a philosophy of inclusion, designed to make the spiritual, economic, and/or domestic worlds of America more available to the "unfortunate," informed all her benevolent work. Initially focused on the "deserving poor," such as impoverished Sunday school children, homeless orphans, and poor women seeking employment through the House of Industry, her work culminated in her service as First Directress of the Home for Discharged Female Convicts (subsequently incorporated as the Women's Prison Association and Home) from 1848 to 1863, helping released women prisoners reenter society.[3] The last, which included finding work for these "fallen" women, often as domestic help in private homes—including her own—was the most radical, because admitting such women required breaking down the defensive distinction between public and private, the marketplace and the home, so carefully constructed by the idealized domesticity inherent in the "cult of true womanhood."

The restrictive nature of these social ideals also excluded from "respectability" and true womanhood those who actively sought autonomy and personal fulfillment beyond the socially defined boundaries. Indeed, those whose elimination was so necessary to the plot of "respectability" were, Deborah Anne Logan has argued, "more normative than the legitimated angels of the reigning ideology." Thus, when defined in opposition to such a narrow ideal, "the compelling image of the deviant woman," Logan suggests, "is the richest and most conflicted site of nineteenth-century social ideology."[4]

As she interrogates cultural constructions of women in her fiction Sedgwick features women who deviate in a variety of ways from rigid social ideals. Positive models of such deviant women include her heroines Hope Leslie, Gertrude Clarence, and Isabella Linwood, who challenge submissiveness by voicing and acting on their own beliefs to effect some social change and who are willing to postpone marriage as they pursue self-development (*Hope, Clarence, Linwoods*). Similarly, Esther Downing and Julia Travers, "deviant" as voluntary lifelong spinsters, challenge traditionally defined domesticity by finding satisfaction in performing good works outside of the established woman's sphere (*Hope, Married*). Those who perhaps most clearly reflect the impact of Sedgwick's benevolent work on her fiction are Fanny McDermot and Jessie Manning, who, although seduced, refuse to define themselves exclusively in terms of chastity ("Fanny," *Married*). They suggest that Sedgwick's work with such women profoundly changed her attitude from pity for the fallen woman—the "other"—to respect for her inner dignity, a revised definition of virtue, more expansive than mere chastity.

In contrast, through minor characters such as Crazy Bet, Rosa, and Bessie Lee, who define themselves exclusively in terms of their love for men, Sedgwick dramatizes the loss of self-mastery and of personal identity inherent in the ideal submission (*New-England, Hope, Linwoods*). Through her images of women who deviate, in various ways, from the ideals of True Womanhood, but who are still restored to a place in the home or their mother's arms, Sedgwick projects her vision of a more inclusive society. Such restoration requires a reconfiguration of family based on nurturing and an understanding of women's shared values and emotional experiences, rather than on male-dominated, marketplace, and legal definitions.

Sedgwick's developing articulation in her fiction of "the compelling image of the deviant woman" coincides with other contemporary voices for reform. The New York Female Moral Reform Society, for example, which was founded in 1834, sought to close down New York City brothels, publish the names of men who frequented them, and reform the prostitutes. Central to their reform program was their resolution, "That the licentious man is no less guilty than his victim, and ought, therefore, to be excluded from all virtuous female society."[5] Sedgwick almost certainly heard of the society's controversial efforts both during her annual visits to New York and during its missionaries' visits to Stockbridge beginning in 1835.

Two women whose voices resonate on behalf of women's restoration into their society in terms Sedgwick particularly advocated were Margaret Fuller and Elizabeth Gaskell. Sedgwick admired Fuller because "her truth was exemplary."[6] Fuller praised Sedgwick as "a fine example of the independent and beneficial existence that intellect and character can give to Woman."[7] Particularly in her 1845 journalism "Our City Charities: Visit to Bellevue Alms House, to the Farm School, the Asylum for the Insane, and Penitentiary on Blackwell's Island . . ." and "Asylum for Discharged Females," as well as in *Woman in the Nineteenth Century*, Fuller enunciates ideas Sedgwick advocated. These works emphasize that economic and social forces and not innate weakness cause the poverty that pushes women into prostitution; that unmarried women who lose their chastity should not be condemned for life; that rehabilitation rather than punishment could help reduce crime; and that the wealthy had an obligation to help the poor without condescension.[8] Sedgwick also particularly admired the British author Elizabeth Gaskell's novel *Ruth*, because it advocates forgiveness for the penitent "fallen" woman and shows the positive service she can offer her community.[9] As an act of appreciation Sedgwick proffers "all honor, praise, and love" to Gaskell in her preface to *Married or Single?*

Between the publication of *Clarence* and *Married or Single?* Sedgwick undertook the benevolent work which I suggest informed her increasingly inclusive vision. This work revealed the ways women were victimized by the socioeconomic system and by an inequitable moral code which condemned the sexually active woman but not her seducer. Just as her sympathy for these women grew, so grew her frustration with "respectable" women who, eager to exile the wronged woman, welcomed her male seducer into their homes.

Sedgwick's private correspondence reflects the way her sense of Christian redemption informed all her benevolent work. This, however, is increasingly complemented by her awareness of socioeconomic realities. Initially she was heavily invested in helping impoverished children enter into the fold through both religious and practical education. On 14 February 1835 she writes to her favorite niece Kate Minot: "I had to scamper off to my Sunday School . . . those poor little barren fields in which scarcely a seed has ever been cast, interest me mightily."[10] She expresses a more practical note a couple of years later: "All my spare time yesterday was spent on concocting a report for remodeling of society & I found it more difficult than writing a novel. . . . We have come to a sensible resolve to have a school to teach little girls to sew, darn their socks etc. instead of a parcel of gossiping women meeting to corrupt the 'less favored orders' by supplying them with ready-made garments."[11]

Sedgwick's direct contact with the poor forced her to face the myopia central to the upper classes' definitions of virtue, morality, and respectability. By 1848 she is outraged at both the church's failure to address social problems and the complacency with which church members assumed their virtuous superiority:

> I think the favored class owe a great deal to Providence. . . . With the means of universal education and substance, we see creatures with the powers and faculties out of which heroes and martyrs have been made, covered with bruises and putrefying sores. My whole soul is sickened; and today, when I went to our church filled with people in their fine summer clothes . . . and thought of the streets and dens, through which I had just walked, I could have cried out, "Why are ye here?"[12]

Her private correspondence also reflects her growing appreciation of the economic realities governing the lives of the lower classes: Few opportunities for "honest" work were available to the poor, and economic circumstances drove many poor women to "go public" by seeking work outside of their homes. Writing to Kate about the House of Industry, Sedgwick expresses her appreciation that virtue is often distinct from wealth: "I received about 200 registered names etc., poor women, eagerly seeking the boon of fifty cents' worth of work, on which, by their account, a sick husband and any number of orphan children are to be supported." Although writing as a privileged upper-class woman, Sedgwick also emphasizes the gendered significance of women helping women. "The best of it all," she continues, "is to see the ladies whose splendid equipages stand at the door in close contact with these exuberant daughters of Erin, earnestly devoting themselves to the relief of their wants."[13]

Just how jealously women guarded this opportunity to act as co-partners with men in the construction of a new and godly world, even in the face of male opposition, is exemplified in Sedgwick's encounter with the New York Prison Association (NYPA). In December 1844 a group of men established NYPA to help male ex-prisoners reenter society by finding them jobs or vocational training. Shortly after this they also authorized a Female Department, whose members raised enough money to open the Home for Discharged Female Convicts on 12 June 1845 as a refuge and training center until work and a home were found for the women.[14] Sedgwick, like members of the Ladies' Prison-Discipline Society, resented the men's assumption that the NYPA was authorized to determine how the Home should be run. In fact, she reported that after "a committee from the men's society appeared to remind the women that they were but a department . . . [s]ome of [the] *collaborators* were disposed to stand upon their reserved rights," and, convinced of their own authority, they resolved the impasse by incorporating their own Women's Prison Association and Home in May 1854.[15]

This conviction that women have special gifts for helping other women is evident in *The Helping Hand*, published as a fund-raiser for the Home. In this book Caroline Kirkland articulates a prevalent cultural model: "Woman is the natural and God-appointed aid of woman in her needs; the woman that feels not this, has yet to learn her mission aright." By conflating ideas about femininity with ideas about morality, she argues that virtue is more pronounced in women than in men, and that this virtue could be a force behind a moral transformation of society at large. More subversive, however, is her rallying cry that women cross from class to gender identity: "It is time that women . . . should consider themselves as a community, having special common needs and common obligations, which it is shame to them to turn aside from, under the pleas of inability or distaste."[16] Sedgwick often dramatizes such capacities in her fictional women (e.g., Hope Leslie, Isabella Linwood, Gertrude Clarence, and Rose) by featuring them as the agents of rescue and prison escapes, and by emphasizing the beneficial quality of the domestic home.

A far more punitive approach to the moral transformation of society is reflected in the particularly repressive judicial system introduced by Jacksonian male reformers for whom, Estelle Freedman has argued, sexual pollution was a central symbol for their "deep fear of social disorder."[17] Under this system the law was extended to include a stricter code of female morality: Abortion was defined as a "crime against a person," and women could be arrested, even imprisoned, for crimes against chastity or decency, such as disorderly conduct, lewd and lascivious carriage, vagrancy, and even stubbornness. Such indiscriminate labeling of these women together with hardened criminals as "fallen" often forced first offenders into a vicious cycle which led to a life of crime and debauchery. Moreover, the assumption that by acting "unnaturally" these women had permanently fallen to some "lower order" meant they could never be reformed to reenter the home or society. Thus, even though models were developed as early as 1815 for spiritual redemption and/or job training for male prisoners, an 1849 report from the Prison Association of New York still claimed that a "fallen" woman "has sinned away her right to return to her friends at home."[18] The same attitude followed her after her release. No conventionally respectable women would hire her into their homes, and few respectable men would hire her outside of theirs. To admit such women back into the domestic sphere was to blur the distinction between private and public so central to domestic ideology.

Sedgwick, however, was in advance of her day in her confidence that these women could be reformed and reestablished within society. "I went to the 'Home,'" she wrote Kate Minot, where "the outstretched hands and brightened eyes of these poor Creatures spoke to me as assurances that they have that in them which will finally be worked out of the dismal swamp of circumstances."[19] Moreover, she acted on her beliefs by taking some of these women from the Home into her own home and by persuading members of her family to do so also. In a letter encouraging her niece Kate to persevere with one such young woman, Sedgwick shows her appreciation of the probable horrifying alternative:

> It seems to me there is no sin so dreadfully punished in this world as the frailty of a poor girl like Ellen—according to the common course that follows from the first "misfortune" as it is called by the vulgar with better justice than other moralists mete to it. To have some notion of what "the city vice" entails one need make but a single visit to the hospital for women of a certain class on Blackwell's Island and see there physical and mental wretchedness in their extremist degree which is the *certain* fate of these wretched people. The only alleviation is their short lives—not averaging more than thirty years.[20]

Later in this letter she emphasizes that frailty, not wickedness, characterizes these women, and that the healing power of the home is helping a girl she has taken in: "I wish you could see the little damsel with a round florid fair contented face who is sitting by my window sewing for me— She comes from the storehouse of Frailty, the Home—18 or 19 years old—She 'met with a misfortune'—concealed it like Effie Deans—had a dead baby and locked it up in her trunk. After a short residence in the Tombs she was acquitted and is now repairing damages in our leaky arms." Central to Sedgwick's moral vision is her confidence in the essential virtue, dignity, and worth of many so-called fallen women. This requires a redefinition of virtue, such as Lori Ginsberg attributes to moral reformers who

> asserted their common difference from men, not because they identified with all women (poor, prostitutes, etc.), but because they understood worth by a different standard from that presumably adhered to by men. By defining women as victims of a lustful society, and men as the personification of that lust, they sought to define respectability not by wealth (tenuous under men's control) but by women's own virtues.[21]

In a letter to Kate discussing *Ruth*, however, Sedgwick excoriates both men and women for their hypocritical emphasis on the importance of female chastity.

> The absolute necessity of chastity in a woman, as far as the certain transmission of property goes, has given legal sanction to this blinding of the eyes and hardening of the heart. Women who violate every duty . . . to the utter degradation of the soul, ride in the world's chariots . . . and in men the *permitted* grossness in thought, word, and deed, can't be spoken of, but a poor girl, ignorant of her own nature, with opportunity thrust upon her, and love blinding her, is the victim through life of a single offense.[22]

Margaret Fuller's experiences with women inmates, like Sedgwick's, revealed a profound difference between the inmates' understanding of themselves and that imposed on them by the upper classes. In a letter to Georgiana Bruce, Fuller observes that for the inmates of the women's prison in Sing Sing, New York, chastity was a "circumstance of condition" that fallen women apparently found meaningless. "You say few of these women have any feeling about chastity. Do you know how they regard that part of the sex who are reputed chaste? Do they see any reality in it; or look on it merely as a circumstance of condition, the possession of fine clothes?"[23] In her more mature works Sedgwick gives the fallen women their own voices to tell their own stories and project their own sense of dignity, and thus introduces far greater realism into her fictional world.

All of Sedgwick's novels reflect the various ways she imagined women could be integrated more fully into their society. The changing images in her work of women who have deviated or fallen from the rigidly defined appropriate women's sphere are of particular interest because they suggest the impact that her

direct contact with such women had on her fiction. Just as she came to understand the complex relationships between these women's economic and moral
lives, so she imagined in her novels increasingly complex identities for her deviant or fallen women, as well as ways for them to be redeemed. In doing this
Sedgwick aligns herself with practitioners of "domestic" fiction, which Elizabeth
Barnes has argued largely replaced the seduction novels of the early Republic.
This change, she claims, "signals a radical shift in the representation of affective
bonds. . . . Whereas seduction fiction depicts the middle-class family as a collection of shared values and emotional experiences, these stories emphasize nurture
over nature, the *act* of familying over the fact of it."[24]

A comparison of Crazy Bet (*New-England*) and Bessie Lee (*Linwoods*) reflects Sedgwick's growing resistance to submission as a defining trait of the True
Woman and her argument for the greater inclusion of women in the Republic.
Both Crazy Bet and Bessie Lee identify themselves as suffering from thwarted
love, and as long as their sense of self is so totally identified with submission to
a man's "memory," they remain "outsiders," wandering between communities.
Crazy Bet acts as a guide to the heroine Jane, and shares with her and other
"outsiders" a "reconstituted family" formed from common values and feelings.
But she never finds a still center in herself or in the community. This highlights
her limitations in a novel where the trope of the home takes on special significance: The heroine marries a father figure, the man who has purchased her
childhood home.

In contrast, Bessie Lee, who regains her sense of personal identity, and exercises her "self-rectifying power," returns to serve her community (*Linwoods*, 2:
145, 273). Initially, abandoned by her lover Jasper Meredith, Bessie claims that
her love is so excessive that she has none for anyone else, not even her family.
If, as Barnes argues, in the domestic novel, "sentimental politics [were] designed
to make familial feeling the precondition for inclusion in the public community," Bessie's alienation had been absolute.[25] After she takes the initiative to
return Meredith's love tokens, however, she moves toward becoming "mistress
of herself again" (*Linwoods*, 2: 218). Through Bessie's restoration, Sedgwick
counters the fears expressed in the current political debates of her day about
expanding the rights of the democracy to a broader population, including
women. "Eager spirits," Stephanie Smith has argued, "like inordinate ardency
. . . were the particular dangers that an American mother, and America as a
nation, faced."[26] In learning to control her emotional excesses and to channel
that energy into positive community service, Bessie represents what Barnes defines as the "early national culture's attempts to reconcile conservative republican values of duty to others with a liberal agenda of self-possession."[27]

A comparison of Sedgwick's portraits of fallen women in *A New-England*

Tale, *Hope Leslie*, *Clarence*, "Fanny McDermot," and *Married or Single?* reveals Sedgwick's growing appreciation of their essential dignity and virtue. The impact of her benevolent work is reflected in her movement from pity for the "other" to respect for fellow women. Mary Oakley, the "giddy and credulous . . . victim" of the "depraved" David Wilson, dies declaring, "I am guilty, and must not go" to heaven, even though those around her believe that God, who inspires them to pity her, must himself pity her (*New-England*, 91–93). Similarly, Rosa, although more self-conscious and self-punishing, is victim of her obsessive love for Sir Philip Gardiner. Despite Hope Leslie's encouragement to "leave this wretched man, and trust thyself to heaven," Rosa declares, "but the guilty must forsake their sinful thoughts, and I cannot. My heart is steeped in this guilty love" (*Hope Leslie*, 244). Unable to conceive of an identity other than as his mistress, she cannot regain emotional control of her own life. Because Rosa accepts society's condemnation of her sexual license, and cannot conceive of any way to be redeemed, she remains outside the pale.[28]

In *Clarence* Sedgwick critiques the construction of woman as sexual property. She includes three examples of parents who willingly sell their daughters into marriage to pay off their debts or otherwise gain material profit. By highlighting such economic exchange she likens many nineteenth-century American marriages to legalized prostitution. Her most sustained portrait of parental pandering is the story of Emilie Layton. Her parents, "degraded far below the level of those pagan parents who abandon their children to the elements or sacrifice them to their divinities," promise her to Pedrillo as payment of her father's debts (*Clarence*, 135). Emilie, however, rejects the ideal of submission and dramatizes women's powers of self-assertion. During a trip to see the falls at Trenton, just as Rudolph Marion has declared his feelings for her, Emilie catches sight of her fiancé, Pedrillo, spying on them and, guided by a strong "instinct of self preservation," she "abruptly" springs from Marion's side to escape Pedrillo. Both her vulnerability and her self-assertion are dramatized as, falling from the cliff, she grasps a "hanging cedar that depended over the cliff," and, "with heavenly instinct," finds her footing over "the foaming abyss" (*Clarence*, 259–60). She hangs there, a female body exposed to the public gaze, victim of the marketplace mentality driving her parents' plans. In her flight Emilie has literally and figuratively *fallen* from the path her parents decreed. The narrator tells us she has "*unconsciously* deviated" (emphasis mine) from the "one safe path" (*Clarence*, 258), which convention would dictate to be obedience to her parents. But Emilie, who has *unconsciously* fallen in love with Marion (*Clarence*, 270), finds safety in another path. As Pedrillo retreats in fear, Marion, under the supervision of the heroine, Gertrude, rescues her. So, an independent-minded, sympathetic woman, Gertrude, masterminds a plan which restores Emilie to the "one safe path," marriage to Marion.

Perhaps the most progressive theme in Sedgwick's novels is the essential virtue and dignity to be found in so-called fallen women. Sedgwick dramatizes this by allowing them to speak for themselves and thus to authorize a female definition of virtue. This understanding of worth informs much of Sedgwick's writing from the 1840s and is epitomized by her short story "Fanny McDermot." Fanny, an honest orphan, turns to Russell Sydney for help in supporting her dying great-aunt. After Sydney seduces and abandons her, Fanny looks for work but is rejected because of her immoral past. Meanwhile, Sydney courts the wealthy Augusta Erly. Although her mother encourages his suit, Augusta holds him in contempt as dissipated. Finally, Fanny is committed to the Tombs, a New York City jail, where she and her baby die.

Three sequences suggest that Sedgwick understood the limitations inherent in the failure of the current domestic ideology to encompass a community of sympathy between women. When Fanny is thirteen she is knocked down by a passing carriage. Russell Sydney jumps out, wipes the blood from her cheek, kisses her, and cuts off a lock of her hair. Sydney's act of aggression anticipates both his abuse of Fanny and the cruelty of the magistrate who imprisons her for stealing a shawl to wrap around her dying baby. The Law of the Father is associated with violence; it fails to protect her, instead readily condemning her as a social criminal.

In the second sequence, Fanny, although qualified for several positions, is repeatedly rejected in the name of middle-class respectability and the sanctity of the home—that is, because of her illegitimate baby. Mrs. Erly argues, "No respectable lady would take a person of that kind into her home." But Augusta, who appreciates the community of sympathy that should exist between women, asks, "Then what is respectability worth, mama, if it cannot give help to a weak fellow creature? . . . As women, as professed followers of Christ, my dear mother, ought we not to help her out of the pit into which she has fallen?" ("Fanny," 368, 372).

Sedgwick contrasts Fanny's probity with society's hypocrisy. Although her friends advise her to pretend to be a young widow, as a way to gain sympathy and thus a job, Fanny has a strong sense of self, and she rejects all attempts to preempt it. She insists on telling her own story her own way. She explains to Mrs. Erly, "I never had a husband. I have been betrayed and forsaken—I am no farther guilty—no more innocent" ("Fanny," 367–68). Sedgwick further dramatizes the inadequacy of the domestic ideology that pits the Angel of the House against the Fallen Woman in the name of the sanctity of the home, in a scene in which Mrs. Erly dismisses Augusta's objection that Sydney has a dissipated past. "So have forty other men," she argues, "who are good husbands now, or whose wives are too prudent to make a fuss about it if they are not" ("Fanny," 370). When Augusta exclaims, "Monstrous, monstrous, monstrous. That he, loaded with God's good gifts should make a prey and victim of a living, trusting, defenseless woman, and she should be cast out of humanity," Mrs. Erly does acknowledge, "There does seems to be inconsistency, but it appears different when one knows the world" ("Fanny," 386). Sedgwick emphasizes that women like Mrs. Erly are complicit in their own oppression. In the name of social propriety they remain silent and allow promiscuous men to remain in society.

Finally the alignment of Fanny, the Fallen Woman, and Augusta, as an enlightened Angel of the House, is vividly dramatized at a fashionable party. Fanny has followed Sydney into the house, and in an attempt to avoid the public gaze, has taken refuge behind a screen in the ladies' cloakroom. Subsequently, Augusta also retreats there to escape Sydney's unwelcome advances. As he pursues her—invades her space just as he had invaded Fanny's—the screen falls to reveal a tableau vivant: two young women, both victims of a lustful and greedy society. This identification of Fanny and Augusta serves to show not only how close Augusta is to Fanny as a victim of male exploitation, but also how close Fanny is to Augusta in her understanding of true virtue.

A woman's sense of dignity and of the limits of her culpability is further developed in Sedgwick's *Married or Single?* Jessica (Jessie) Manning, an innocent young girl, is seduced by Horace Copley, the son of a wealthy woman who has taken Jessie into her home as a servant. Mrs. Copley fails Jessie by ignoring her and, almost certainly, turning a blind eye to her son's behavior. Very much the victim of a man of the world, Jessie still maintains a sense of her own worth and dignity. First, she refuses to stay in the house of ill repute to which he has sent her, and she leaves there the money and gifts he has given her. After her baby is born dead, she succumbs to consumption and is taken to Blackwell's Island, with "wretched women from wretched places" (*Married*, 2: 24). There Sedgwick enacts a reconciliation scene that secures Jessie's reentry into the woman's world. She is reunited with her long-lost mother, and confides in her, "I knew I was disgraced, but I did not feel wicked, Mother" (*Married*, 2: 23). The narrator confirms this by describing her as "this victim of a man of the world, degraded—not *corrupted*—a beautiful flower ruthlessly crushed" (*Married*, 2: 26).

Sedgwick's opposition to the more zealous public actions of the women's rights activists is well known, but her commitment to defending women's worth through her fiction and her benevolent work reflects a lifelong appreciation of female potential. In taking to task the domestic ideologies of her day, she worked to include white members of all classes of women in her expansive vision of the

Republic—a vision limited, of course, by its omission of black and Irish women. By interrogating the concept of "respectability" and revising the image of the sexually "fallen" woman, though, Sedgwick promoted women's "self-rectifying" powers. Self-respect was central to her vision, and she increasingly emphasized this in her portraits of deviant and fallen women. Although all of her fallen characters do finally die, perhaps because the shrewd authoress judged her readers not yet ready to practice the tolerance that she herself did, the impact of Sedgwick's benevolent work on her writing is nevertheless clear, shown in the way she gives these characters their own voices, allowing them to tell their own stories and to proclaim their own dignities. A quiet activist, Sedgwick blurred the distinction between public and private that so often kept the "unfortunate" in social exile, by taking women from the Home into her own home. For her, activism was a domestic affair, based in a community of sympathy that both her fiction and her benevolent work sought to advance.

NOTES

Sedgwick's works are cited parenthetically in the text with the following abbreviations:

Married	*Married or Single?* (New York: Harper and Brothers, 1857).
Hope	*Hope Leslie; or, Early Times in the Massachusetts* (1827; reprint, ed. Mary Kelley, New Brunswick, N.J.: Rutgers Univ. Press, 1987).
Clarence	*Clarence; or, A Tale of Our Own Times* (New York: George P. Putnam, 1849).
Linwoods	*The Linwoods; or, "Sixty Years Since" in America* (New York: Harper and Brothers, 1835).
New-England	*A New-England Tale; or, Sketches of New-England Character and Manners* (1822; reprint, ed. Victoria Clements, New York: Oxford Univ. Press, 1995).
"Fanny"	"Fanny McDermot," first published in *Godey's Lady's Book* 30 (1845): 13 and 75. Citations from *A New England Tale and Miscellanies* (New York: Putnam, 1852).

1. My discussion is informed by Carroll Smith-Rosenberg's question: "To what degree did women collaborate with the emergence of a restraining bourgeois 'discourse'?" in "Writing History: Language, Class, and Gender," in *Feminist Studies; Critical Studies* (Bloomington: Indiana Univ. Press, 1986), 31–54, hereafter, "History." It is also informed by Lora Romero's contention that "Ideologies . . . become popular . . . not because they provide the masses with a finite and orderly set of beliefs relieving them

from the burden of thinking but instead because they give people an expansive logic, a meaningful vocabulary, and rich symbols through which to *think* about their world." Ideology is "both contested and always under construction" (19). Lora Romero, *Home Fronts: Domesticity and Its Critics in the Antebellum United States* (Durham, N.C.: Duke Univ. Press, 1997). Mary Kelley defined such "contest" and "construction" in her pioneer study, *Private Woman, Public Stage: Literary Domesticity in Nineteenth-Century America* (New York: Oxford Univ. Press, 1984). Sedgwick's *A New-England Tale* is the earliest novel she cites.

2. Barbara Welter introduced this term in her article, "The Cult of Womanhood: 1820–1860," *American Quarterly* 18 (summer 1966): 151–74. Quotations cited from pp. 154, 137, 141. For studies of antebellum texts that interrogate Welter's paradigm see Mary Kelley, "Beyond the Boundaries," *Journal of the Early Republic* (spring 2001), and Laura McCall, "'Shall I fetter her will?' Literary Americans Confront Feminine Submission, 1820–1860," *Journal of the Early Republic* (spring 2001): 95–113. Further studies of ideological shifts concerning the role of women include: Gerda Lerner, "The Lady and the Mill Girl: Changes in the Status of Women in the Age of Jackson, 1800–1840," in *A Heritage of Her Own: Toward a New Social History of American Women,* ed. N. F. Cott and E. H. Pleck (New York: Simon and Schuster, 1979), 182–97.

3. Margaret Hope Bacon, *Abby Hopper Gibbons: Prison Reformer and Social Activist* (Albany: State Univ. of New York Press, 2000), 57.

4. Deborah Anna Logan, *Fallenness in Victorian Women's Writing: Marry, Stitch, Die, or Do Worse* (Columbia: Univ. of Missouri Press, 1998), 189.

5. Carroll Smith-Rosenberg, *Disorderly Conduct: Visions of Gender in Victorian America* (New York: Oxford Univ. Press, 1985), 111–12.

6. To Mrs. Channing (1852), in *Life and Letters of Catharine Maria Sedgwick,* ed. Mary E. Dewey (New York: Harper and Brothers, 1871), 341. Hereafter Dewey.

7. Margaret Fuller, *Woman in the Nineteenth Century* (New York: W. W. Norton, 1971), 163.

8. *Margaret Fuller's New York Journalism,* ed. Catherine C. Mitchell (Knoxville: Univ. of Tennessee Press, 1995), 88–96.

9. Elizabeth Gaskell, *Ruth* (London: Chapman and Hall, 1853).

10. To Kate Minot, 14 February 1835, Catharine Maria Sedgwick Papers 1, box 1, folder 17. Massachusetts Historical Society. Hereafter CMS/MHS.

11. To Kate Minot, 24 April 1837, Dewey, 264–65.

12. To Kate Minot, 21 May 1848, Dewey, 307.

13. To Kate Minot, 3 June 1850, Dewey, 322. See also Gates in this volume.

14. Bacon, 54–55. *The Life of Abby Hopper Gibbons Told Chiefly Through Her Correspondence,* ed. Sarah Hopper Emerson (New York: G. P. Putnam's Sons, 1897), 1: 252–53.

15. To Kate Minot, 2 March 1845, Dewey, 292–93.

16. Caroline Kirkland, *The Helping Hand* (New York: Scribners, 1853), cited in Bacon, 58. See also Logan's discussion of "the curious collapsing of class between women where appropriate and inappropriate sexualities were concerned," 6, 15, and Carroll Smith-Rosenberg, *Disorderly Conduct,* 21–22, 109–28.

17. Estelle B. Freedman, *Their Sisters' Keepers: Women's Prison Reform in America* (Ann Arbor: Univ. of Michigan Press, 1981), 14, 19.

18. *Ibid.*, 25.

19. To Kate Minot, 28 July 1846, Dewey, 297.

20. To Kate Minot, 11 April 1852, CMS 1, box 4, folder 23, MHS.

21. Lori Ginsberg, *Women and the Work of Benevolence: Morality, Politics, and Class in the Nineteenth-Century United States* (New Haven: Yale Univ. Press, 1990), 6.

22. To Kate Minot, 20 March 1853, Dewey, 346.

23. *The Letters of Margaret Fuller*, ed. Robert N. Hudspeth (Ithaca, N.Y.: Cornell Univ. Press, 1984), 3, 236.

24. Elizabeth Barnes, *States of Sympathy: Seduction and Democracy in the American Novel* (New York: Columbia Univ. Press, 1997), 15. See also Lora Romero, "Domesticity and Fiction," in *The Columbia History of the American Novel*, ed. Emory Elliott (New York: Columbia Univ. Press, 1991), 110, and Karol L. Kelley, *Models for the Multitudes: Social Values in the American Popular Novel, 1850–1920* (New York: Greenwood Press, 1987), 38.

25. Barnes, 3.

26. Stephanie Smith, *Conceived by Liberty: Maternal Figures and Nineteenth-Century American Literature* (New York: Cornell Univ. Press, 1994), 49.

27. Barnes, 11–12.

28. See Fetterley in this volume.

14

9• Excerpts from Reviews of *Married or Single?*

Gentleman's Magazine (August 1857): 188.

"*Married or Single*," by Miss Sedgwick . . . is the London reprint of an American work which is disfigured by more than the usual number of faults of style peculiar to novels emanating from the pens of transatlantic ladies. (P. 188)

The Albion (15 August 1857): 393.

Miss C. M. Sedgwick, long silent, has resumed her pen; and in Married or Single, (2 vols. Harpers), again tries her hand at the lesson of life. The personages and scenes are borrowed from New York city and New England villages—principally the former; and judging from the Preface, the tale was designed to plead the cause of Spinster-hood. If this were so, the cause is not well pleaded: in fact this object is well-nigh lost sight of. Here and there may be found a didactic page or two in praise of "maiden meditation, fancy free"; but the old subject of marriage and giving in marriage is the staple of this as of ninety-nine out of a hundred kindred works. If some of the leading female characters exemplify the emptiness and the wretchedness that attend ill-assorted unions, there is not one that markedly vindicates the soundness of St. Paul's advice, as quoted by Miss Sedgwick—"I say therefore to the unmarried and widows, it is good for them if they abide." (P. 393)

The Athenaeum (London), (22 August 1857): 1057.

The women of America have been for some time trying their best to make men of the world avoid their confections in print; and we have not seen a success much more complete than this. . . . But what is there *not* in this novel?—Simply not a spark, not a syllable, not a sentiment, such as remind us of the *right* Miss Sedgwick, whom English readers have long ago learnt to love. (P. 1057)

Ladies Repository (September 1857): 564.

It is the most thoroughly American, and the most *real* book I have read in a long while. The time is the present. The place New York and New England. The people such as probably cross your path each day you go down Broadway. The beginning of the volume gives one an idea that the authoress is about to insist upon the reality of single female blessedness. But the moral—was it accidental and inevitable, or done of a forethought?—is strongly in favor of married life. I must say that I have no where seen the joys and sorrows of American married life in its really best phases, so accurately and naturally drawn. Nor do I know of a single book in all my reading, written with so much evident feeling, even fervor, yet displaying so little exaggeration in either statements or deductions. "Married and Single" [*sic*] is a book which old people will read with delight, and from which I opine young folks will get as much profit as pleasure. (P. 564)

Harper's New Monthly Magazine (September 1857): 549.

The present work is of a similar character to that of her previous stories. The plot is free from complicated details, though rich in impressive situations. It is marked throughout by the fine discriminations of personal traits, which is a never-failing feature of her productions. The scene is laid in no far distant period, and presents a living picture of the prevailing manners and humors of fashionable life at this moment. She paints in real colors the weaknesses of the day, mingled with the characteristic virtues which are never entirely lost even in the most frivolous and the most corrupt times. Her pen has lost none of its elasticity with the lapse of years; her eye sends as keen a glance as ever into the recesses of the human heart; her feelings are fresh and youthful as when she first depicted the experiences of young lovers; and her latest work exhibits all the vitality, shrewdness of observation, delicacy of moral tone, warmth of affection, and sweet religious wisdom which marked the promise of her prime. (P. 549)

North American Review (October 1857): 562–63.

The author's prime aim is to exhibit, as parallel with the holy and benign ministries of the true wife and mother, the no less sacred and lofty sphere of service open to self-respecting and voluntary maidenhood. But to enumerate all the moral axioms and postulates which the story illustrates and defends with explicitness and power, would be to give titles for a tolerably complete treatise of moral philosophy. While we find it hard to use, with regard to the author, degrees of comparison short of the superlative, this seems to us, both in artistical and an ethical point of view, the best of the series that bears her name. (P. 563)

"Equal to Either Fortune": Sedgwick's *Married or Single?* and Feminism

DEBORAH GUSSMAN

atharine Maria Sedgwick's novel *Hope Leslie* (1827) ends somewhat
atypically for a work of nineteenth-century women's fiction. Rather
than conclude with a romantic picture of the newly married Hope and
Everell Fletcher, Sedgwick provides a view of Esther Downing, happily single,
along with the narrator's admonition that "marriage is not *essential* to the contentment, the dignity, or the happiness of woman."[1] Thirty years later, Sedgwick
returned to that point as the focus of her final novel, *Married or Single?* The
question that is her title reveals the novel's theme: the right of a woman to
"shape [the] course" of her life, and to "force her separate sovereign way."[2] The
question is decidedly not a rhetorical one to Sedgwick: In her novels, journal,
and autobiography, she explored both statuses and the compromises they entailed for women. Her writing about the emotional and material realities of
marriage is largely unromantic, and her discussions of the challenges of being
single and without a household of one's own are unflinchingly honest. Sedgwick
emphasizes in the novel, and in her personal writings, that marriage is usually
preferable to a single state (indeed the novel's heroine Grace Herbert, while
putatively "equal to either fortune" [II, 284], does in the end choose marriage);
at the same time, she asserts that a single life can and should be considered
respectable for women. Sedgwick's answers to her novel's provocative question
about women's place in society raise larger questions about the relation of her
ideas and writing to the nineteenth-century women's rights movement, and,
more generally, to feminism. *Married or Single?,* seen in relation to women's
rights and the rhetorics with which the movement engaged, chiefly republicanism, liberalism, domesticity, and Christianity, provides a clearer understanding
of how Sedgwick used narrative to negotiate the complex discursive terrain of
the late antebellum United States.

In 1853, four years before Sedgwick published *Married or Single?* Elizabeth

Cady Stanton reflected on the political significance of marriage, in a letter to Susan B. Anthony: "I do not know whether the world is quite willing or ready to discuss the question of marriage. . . . I feel, as never before, that this whole question of women's rights turns on the pivot of the marriage relation, and mark my word, sooner or later it will be the topic for discussion. I would not hurry it on, nor would I avoid it."[3] Whether the world was ready or not, women, throughout the nineteenth century, identified marriage as a key component of their oppression. Women's rights activists such as Stanton and Anthony gave speeches and organized campaigns aimed at reforming the laws affecting married women's property rights.[4] Lucy Stone included a written protest of existing marriage laws in her 1853 wedding ceremony to Henry Blackwell and retained her own name after marriage.[5] Ernestine Rose characterized marriage as a form of bondage, declaring at the Syracuse convention, in 1852, "Woman is a slave, from cradle to grave."[6]

Nineteenth-century women novelists, regardless of their political affiliations, also made marriage central to their works, exploring not only the emotional dimensions of courtship and conjugal relations but the economic and political dimensions as well. Feminist critics have disagreed, however, about the extent to which women novelists' treatments of marriage subverted or transformed conventional ideas and practices. Rachel Blau DuPlessis has argued against seeing this body of writing as transgressive: "In the nineteenth-century narrative . . . any plot of self-realization was at the service of the marriage plot and was subordinate to, or covered within, the magnetic power of that ending."[7] Susan Harris sees the marriage plot as more strategic, arguing that it enabled women writers to "cover—or cover up—for a far more radical vision of female possibilities embedded in the texts."[8] Karen Tracey, emphasizing the role of the heroine in deciding her fate, suggests that "novelists used their heroines' power of choice among suitors to give those characters some agency within the restrictive ideology of marriage."[9]

By shifting the focus of her novel away from the choice of one suitor over another to the necessity of marriage altogether, Sedgwick took this cultural debate a step further. The preface to *Married or Single?* provides the novel's most explicit statement regarding women and marriage: "[W]e raise our voice with all our might against the miserable cant that matrimony is essential to the feebler sex—that a woman's single life must be useless or undignified—that she is but an adjunct of man—in her best estate merely a helm to guide the nobler vessel" (vi). Her insistence that such a choice might exist at all for women was still progressive in the nineteenth century, when, as Mary Kelley notes, nine out of ten women married.[10] Indeed, the critical reception of the novel, though mostly positive, suggests that Sedgwick's propositions, like those of her more activist contemporaries, posed a threat to the status quo. Only the *North American Review* acknowledged Sedgwick's stated agenda, noting that the "author's prime aim is to exhibit . . . [the] sacred and lofty sphere of service open to self-respecting and voluntary maidenhood" and lauding the novel as "the best of the series that bears her name."[11] *Harper's New Monthly Magazine* managed to avoid any mention of the novel's plot or themes, praising instead Sedgwick's "vitality, shrewdness of observation, delicacy of moral tone, warmth of affection, and sweet religious wisdom."[12] And the *Ladies' Repository*, while calling *Married or Single?* "the book of the season," rejected outright Sedgwick's opening propositions, reassuring readers that "[t]he beginning of the volume gives one an idea that the authoress is about to insist upon the reality of female single blessedness. But the moral—was it accidental and inevitable, or done of a forethought?—is strongly in favor of married life."[13] Perhaps out of deference to Sedgwick—still clearly recognized, at the age of sixty-eight, as an author of national prominence, the reviews tended toward the vague but respectful, focusing on the novel's realism, Americanness, and moral wisdom.

Despite the revival of interest in Sedgwick at the turn of the twentieth century, critics have paid less attention to *Married or Single?* than to her other works.[14] Certainly this critical inattention stems, in part, from the novel being so lengthy and so long out of print, but it derives also, perhaps, from Sedgwick's discomfort with women's rights activism. Sedgwick's attempts to negotiate between repressive models of women's role and duty and radical mid-nineteenth-century interrogations of those models are reflected in the "distinctly ambivalent presentation of the struggle for women's social and political rights" that Victoria Clements and others have identified in Sedgwick's writing.[15] Much Sedgwick criticism, even that which acknowledges the conservative themes in her work, has tended to highlight the ways that Sedgwick challenged the status quo and to minimize the extent to which she reproduced it in her novels.[16] *Married or Single?* does exemplify some of the progressive ideas about women's rights as well as the indirect approach to social change reflected in Sedgwick's previous writings, and it registers a concern with women and marriage shared by women's rights activists. However, it is neither a feminist, nor even a protofeminist, text.[17] As several recent critics have noted, we need to be cautious in ascribing the term "feminist" to Sedgwick; as more of her work comes to be reread and interpreted, it becomes increasingly clear that this is not a term she would have chosen for herself (had it been available to her), despite the many unconventional, active, and assertive female characters she invented and the creative way she lived her life as a single woman and a writer.[18] *Married or Single?* provides us with a clearer understanding of the development of Sedgwick's ideas about women's place in society as well as a fuller sense of Sedgwick's place on the continuum of nineteenth-century feminist thought. Neither a classic republican nor a liberal feminist, Sedgwick occupied the slippery terrain between those two poles. Selecting and inventing from the ideological maps provided by republican, liberal, domestic, and Christian discourses, Sedgwick created an alternative route for American women to traverse as they attempted to find their place in this world. At the same time, Sedgwick attempted to assure women that their efforts would find them a secure place in the next world, too.

Few contemporary readers are familiar with the novel, which centers on a young woman, Grace Herbert, and her sister Eleanor, living in the New York household of their deceased father's second wife. Grace and Eleanor are both part of and somewhat removed from New York society, having the requisite social credentials but only a modest income. On the threshold of marriage (they are eighteen and twenty-two, respectively, at the beginning of the novel), they serve, as do Hope Leslie and Esther Downing, as foils for one another. Sedgwick uses a letter from their late Aunt Sarah to contrast the two women:

> Grace is a tropical plant, capable of rich growth and marvelous beauty but exposed to volcanic perils. . . . She is capable of soaring higher than my Eleanor, and will always be capable of feats, but never of Nelly's patient continuance in well-doing. . . . Eleanor will inherit the earth, which I take to mean the spiritual harvests that life yields. . . . Poor Grace will reach heaven at last, but through much tribulation. (I, 34)

Aunt Sarah's letter, of course, turns out to be prophetic. Eleanor becomes a minister's wife, bears three children and her share of trials, but her solid marriage and religious devotion sustain her throughout.[19] Grace, on the other hand, becomes secretly engaged to Horace Copley, a rich and worldly man, who, despite his engagement, is also devoted to Mrs. Tallis, a beautiful married woman. Grace's preoccupation with Copley prevents her from noticing, until it is almost too late, the man who is devoted to her and whom she is destined to marry. Archibald Lisle, a young, honest lawyer from a modest but worthy New England family, also happens to be the favorite of Walter, Grace's uncle and surrogate father. After a series of trials and mishaps, as well as a serious flirtation with the idea of remaining single, Grace rediscovers Archibald, falls in love, and, we are given to understand, marries him.

Surrounding the main plot are a series of subplots peopled by characters who represent almost every type of marriage or relationship imaginable in the nineteenth century. Mrs. Tallis, the vain, married society woman, who neglects her husband and child, typifies the effects of a loveless marriage; Jessie Manning, the innocent servant girl, who is seduced and abandoned by Horace Copley (a plot Sedgwick presents with variations in *A New-England Tale*, *Hope Leslie*, and

Redwood),[20] exemplifies the dangers of female beauty and virtue in the hands of corrupt males; Walter Herbert and Helen Dale, the true lovers forbidden by their parents to marry, illustrate the ill-fated consequences of arranged matches; and Anne Carleton, Grace's calculating stepsister and rival, who eventually marries Horace Copley for his money and position, suggests the callous and materialistic attitudes toward marriage Sedgwick associates with liberal society. These and other characters provide cautionary tales to Grace, and to the reader, about the consequences of immoral, ill-fated, or otherwise improper relationships.

The many plots and the language of *Married or Single?* illuminate the relation of Sedgwick's political ideas to those of late-eighteenth- and early-nineteenth-century advocates of women's rights, such as Hannah Mather Crocker, Emma Willard, and Judith Sargent Murray, who appropriated republican discourse to argue that women's influence, women's virtue, and domestic life in general had a primary role in shaping society.[21] The features of classic republicanism were commonly understood as the sacrifice of individual interests to the public good, the idea that politics transcended (rather than reconciled) differing interests, the subordination of individual liberty to civil liberty, the rejection of luxury, and the exaltation of independence, reason, benevolence, and public virtue.[22] Both nineteenth-century and contemporary feminist critics have noted that these features, particularly the notion of public virtue expressed as active, disinterested service, were also specifically understood to be possessed by men.[23]

In *Married or Single?,* as in many of her other writings, Sedgwick suggests that the discourse of republicanism need not be reserved for men, and uses it to promote her views of the relation of both men and women to society and to one another.[24] The republican presumption of natural rights made available to Sedgwick a vocabulary that enabled her to reformulate female identity as consistent with republican identity. Blending the discourse of republicanism with domestic and Christian ideas, Sedgwick imagined a revisionary republicanism that would bridge the gap between the roles and responsibilities of men and women as citizens, while resisting the more radical implications of Jacksonian democracy, liberalism, and feminism. Sedgwick's focus on marriage—not just as the conclusion of the plot, but as the novel's controlling idea—exemplifies the republican ideals that infuse the novel. The novel's exploration of marriage enables Sedgwick to theorize about political relations in familial or domestic terms.[25] In keeping with the republican emphasis on the importance of marriage, Sedgwick rarely criticizes or advocates against marriage per se. Rather, by juxtaposing good and bad unions, Sedgwick instructs readers on how to achieve the ideal.

Eleanor's union with Frank Esterly offers an intimate look at the idealized republican union. The Esterlys' is not a fairy-tale marriage, and Sedgwick describes this husband's sometimes petulant behavior toward his wife in ways many readers might still recognize: "Eleanor, do I own a pocket handkerchief? There's not one in my drawer" (151); "I am not sure I shall return to dinner. You may wait for me till five, Eleanor" (152). Far from living happily ever after, Eleanor and Frank suffer the loss of their first-born son, as well as loss of status and income when Frank resigns his ministry. This contrast between the small, daily conflicts of married life and the significant mutual support that emerges during the large and life-changing events illustrates to Grace (and, once again, to the reader, as Grace rehearses her lesson in a letter) "how [marriage] gives strength to weakness, how it takes the bitter from disappointment, the sting from sorrow . . . how it helps the loving pilgrims heavenward, how . . . it is heaven" (I, 243).

By contrasting the hellish relationships depicted in the novel and the heavenly marriage of Frank and Eleanor, the novel questions the commonplace assumption that any marriage is preferable to a single life for women, and intersects with the discourse of women's rights. Discussing Grace's engagement to Horace Copley, Frank asserts that "most marriages . . . are compromises," and Eleanor explains why she thinks Grace is making a mistake by offering her "theory of marriage" (II, 78, 79). According to Eleanor, an ideal marriage requires "a mutual dependence, and an individual freedom springing from reciprocal faith, love and charity; each a life apart, and a life together" (II, 79). For Eleanor, "individual freedom" is inseparable from "mutual dependence," and the foundation for both statuses is a decidedly Christian one: "faith, love and charity." For Eleanor, a marriage without these qualities is worse than a single life. Frank disagrees, stating, "[I]t is never wise to run counter to the institutions of Providence. Marriage is the first and greatest of these, the central point, whence all the relations of life radiate, the source of all political and social virtue" (II, 81).

Eleanor's response to Frank's rather conventional argument is an interesting example of Sedgwick's revision of republican rhetoric. First, Eleanor appears to agree with Frank and then subtly turns the table by suggesting that the "low rate of conjugal virtue" must be directly responsible for the lack of virtue in political and social life—blaming, in other words, corrupt private relations for corrupt political ones. Next, she admonishes him to

> teach my doctrine in simplicity and godly sincerity. Don't go on in the common rut and multiply these miserable matings (not unions), by saying "women must be married." If a woman misses her highest destiny . . . counsel her to try "that other fate." Teach her that she can prepare her soul for its eternal destiny without marriage—that she can be sister, friend, and benefactor; and that to do her duty within the wide compass

of these relations is far more honorable in the judgment of man, than to
be a mismated wife and incompetent mother, condemned to stagnation
instead of progress. (II, 82)

The rhetoric of this passage relies on a complex blend of discourses. The allusions to "doctrine" and the soul's "eternal destiny" suggest the spiritual consequences of married and single life, whereas the appeal to "duty," honor, and
"progress" point to the social and political consequences of choice within a
republican framework. The mention of "mismated" wives and "incompetent
mother[s]" reveals the flip side of the ideal of the republican wife and mother.
Notably, Eleanor does not mention freedom, independence, or self-sufficiency
in relation to a single woman's life, but rather suggests that such a life is to be
carried out in service to others.

Sedgwick's revision of republican ideals is further illustrated as the novel
traces Grace's journey toward adulthood. Grace initially seems less qualified to
be a republican heroine than some of Sedgwick's previous characters. In *Hope
Leslie*, for instance, Sedgwick suggests that republican virtue comes naturally to
both Hope and Magawisca, as their many acts on behalf of the public good, and
their oratorical skills, demonstrate. Grace is, arguably, Sedgwick's most flawed
and, in some ways, most realistic heroine. Early in the novel, she is presented as
vain and self-centered. Her first lesson in humility comes when she discovers
that Frank Esterly, whom she had assumed to be her suitor, is in love with her
sister Eleanor (I, 83). Grace's relationship with Horace Copley provides her next
object lesson in virtue. Uncle Walter warns Grace about Copley's character:

[He] is undoubtedly the glass of fashion, and a most sweet-spoken and
plausible young gentleman . . . he drives four-in-hand admirably; he
rides almost as well as the gentry of the circus; he is the lover of married
women, and the flatterer of young ladies. And yet, Grace, when he has
contested for three years—point by point—a property that I believe in
my soul rightfully belongs to us, and has been so ruled by three successive decisions, from which he has appealed, I can not—quite—trust him
Grace, when he assures you at a "matinee musicale," that he is indiffer-
ent to the results. (I, 46)

Copley is the antithesis of republican manhood and the embodiment of aristocratic luxury, licentiousness, and self-interest. Ambitious, but above honest
work, he uses the legal system to steal property from Grace's family by producing in court surprise "evidence" of a prior claim that trumps Uncle Walter's
understanding of a gentleman's agreement and Archibald Lisle's "admirable"
efforts to represent the Herberts as their attorney (I, 56–57). Copley's ability to

manipulate the law for personal gain, his association with "fashion," and his general lack of either public or private virtue strongly link him to liberalism.[26]

Learning of Copley's relationship with Mrs. Tallis forces Grace to examine her own character. Grace discovers the affair on the night of her engagement party, which is interrupted by the delivery of a package containing all of Copley's gifts to Mrs. Tallis: "fans, rings, bits of fantastical jewelry, a splendid opera glass, a certain delicately-carved cigarette case, and a *diamond bracelet*" (Sedgwick's emphasis, II, 90). The package includes a letter from Mrs. Tallis detailing how her obsession with Copley and her jealousy over his engagement to Grace led to the neglect and the subsequent death of her daughter Elise. The letter also exposes Copley's reasons for marrying Grace: "[H]is incentive in the pursuit of you had been the difficulty of attaining you" (II, 93). The packet of valuables, which Mrs. Tallis refers to as "trinkets" and "witnesses of my vanity" (II, 94), illustrates the dangers of luxury, not only to individuals but to the foundation of civic life, the family.

In classic republican terms, women represented, at worst, the indulgence of passion and luxury which, if unchecked, destroyed the very fabric of republican governments.[27] Grace's response to Mrs. Tallis's surprise package revises this stereotype. Grace receives the information as an act of "the beneficent Providence that has saved me from perdition" (II, 94). She not only rejects Copley, vanity, and luxury, the obstacles to her progress as a heroine, but also turns from her own humiliation to comfort Mrs. Tallis and to reclaim her as a virtuous wife. Grace goes immediately to Mrs. Tallis, and helps her to reconcile with her husband, advising her, "Feeling as you do, this bereavement, you will know what he feels, and from your infinite pity for him, affection must spring up; not a girlish love, but the affection of a steadfast friend" (II, 101–2). Grace's words reflect her internalization of the republican ideal of marriage, one based on what Judith Sargent Murray described as "[m]utual esteem, mutual friendship, mutual confidence, begirt about by mutual forbearance."[28] Further, Grace's act of "private" service exemplifies her personal development, leading to a new understanding of her role in society, one that combines republican and Christian values, such as living a "responsible life" with experiencing "penitence" (II, 103), and working toward "virtue" (II, 104) with comprehending "humility, love, and fidelity" (II, 105).

Archibald Lisle must go through a similar transformation. Though Uncle Walter sees in Archibald's disdain for fashion and high culture the "true faith of a republican by conviction, as well as by birthright" (II, 173), Archibald's character is changed by his relations with women. Like Grace, Archibald must learn to be more virtuous. Though he is generous to his kin, he becomes, in the initial flush of his education and success in New York social circles, condescending toward them, leading the narrator to reflect that "Lisle was but a man" who was "now deeper in the world" (II, 147). Like Grace, Archibald makes two significant errors: The first is not admitting that his seemingly benevolent relationship with Letty, his stepmother's niece and a girl whom he does not consider his social equal, has compromised her happiness and reputation, rather than helped her. The narrator tells us that though Archibald was "aware that he might become the idol to her" and "guarded against the danger," his "devotion" to Letty was not "self-denying" (II, 53). Letty's accidental death leaves him with "bitter, vain, regrets" and questions about his own integrity (II, 59). His effort to repair the damage to his self-image leads him to woo the sister of a childhood friend, Alice Clifford, despite the fact that he is still in love with Grace. Alice, rejecting his marriage proposal, tells him, "My dear Archy . . . you have wronged me and wronged yourself" (II, 241), thereby forcing him to examine his actions and his heart. Nevertheless, as Uncle Walter predicts early on, though Archy loses several battles, he finally wins the war (I, 57). The union of Archibald and Grace at the novel's conclusion is described in language reminiscent of the colonial "discovery" of America: "They were like two beatified spirits on the threshold of another world—behind them darkness, entanglement, and obstruction, before them a land of promise, bright with love and faith, lights now glowing in their firmament, and there to shine forever and ever" (II, 283). Their union not only exemplifies the course of true love, but is the fulfillment of the American dream, a dream destined for the republican stewards of the promised land.

Although the novel's conclusion satisfies the demands of the romance plot, it radically undercuts Sedgwick's efforts to legitimate single life and reveals more fully her distance from women's rights advocates and their critical analyses of marriage. Though the novel holds out the possibility of Grace trying "that other fate," the conclusion reverts to the anachronistic idealization of republican marriage. Grace chooses to not be an "old maid," and Sedgwick provides the reader with few positive illustrations of a single woman's life.[29] The two most favorable examples of unmarried women are Martha Young, the poor seamstress whose generosity includes an ailing father and the destitute Jessie Manning; and "good Cousin Effie" (II, 38), who cares for Eleanor's children when she decides to become a schoolteacher. Both women are significantly beyond childbearing years, devoted to the children of others, and utterly selfless. No model emerges in the novel of a young and/or independently single woman, or of a woman like Sedgwick herself, who had something akin to an independent life within the "wide compass" of her family, including travel, private rooms within her brothers' homes for entertaining and for writing, and a public career as an author.[30] Letty, who is earning her living as a governess, suggests one possibility for a single woman. However, her unrequited love for Archibald, and the potential she presents for sexual feelings outside of marriage problematize her singleness, and she is literally purged from the narrative in the fire which takes her life (II, 57). Another alternative to married life might be that of Julia Travers, the "saint and vestal" who ministers to poor and homeless women (II, 29). Yet Julia's susceptibility to her cousin Horace Copley's logical but self-serving rhetoric, as well as her decision not to act on her better impulses (to tell Grace what she knows of Horace's character), imply that even the most well-meaning and intelligent single woman may require protection from the corrupting influences of liberal society. Thus the novel endorses the idea of a single life as an acceptable alternative to marriage but fails to present a character who could be said to embody that idea wholly successfully.

Yet to critique Sedgwick for failing to represent in idealized terms a status that she knew to be less than ideal is to miss the novel's efforts to paint a realistic picture of women's limited choices. In general, the novel's ambivalent endorsement of single life (and its efforts to present fairly the challenges of marriage) is consistent with the views Sedgwick offered in her journal. Reflecting, in an 1828 entry, on the pain of being "first to none," she concluded: "[I]t is the necessity of a solitary condition—an unnatural state. . . . I would not advise anyone to remain unmarried—for my experience has been a singularly happy one."[31] Two years later, she returned to the theme of being "second best," a problem magnified by her "hanker[ing] after the independence and interests and power of communication of a home of my own. . . . I know what reason— what religion demands of me—and I pray to God to give a spirit of humility, of submission, of resignation."[32]

Given Sedgwick's reluctance to endorse single life fully in her writings, it may be worth considering the parameters of choice in the context of the mid-nineteenth century. Nancy Cott notes that "nineteenth-century marriage policy made an obvious and positive connection between Christian morals and stable government," and this connection is clearly articulated throughout the novel, as Frank and Eleanor's comments (discussed above) about the relation of marriage to social and political virtue suggest.[33] Cott notes that marriage operated as a civil and a religious institution, with forms and obligations that were "created and regulated by public authority."[34] Throughout the nineteenth century, federal and state-sponsored policies were developed to endorse public authority and to encourage intraracial, Christian marriages. These policies included allowing a greater variety of individuals to perform marriages, removing complicated procedures and expensive fees associated with licenses, and enabling more common-law marriages to be validated.[35] The conclusion of *Married or Single?* registers the constraints of public authority upon a woman's choice to remain single. The novel implies, perhaps inadvertently, that Grace has less choice than she thinks.

The novel also suggests Sedgwick's identification with some traditional forms of public authority that were, perhaps, beginning to erode. In a comic subplot, the rich, vulgar, childlike Adeline Clapp attempts to entrap Archibald Lisle into marriage with a complex legal maneuver and the lure of her money. Though her efforts fail, she soon finds another man and ends up happily wed. Adeline Clapp's ultimate "success" and the narrator's reluctant acceptance and corresponding fear that her type will be seen as an illustration of "the social results of democratic institutions" by the "European reading public" reflect Sedgwick's sense of the impending social and moral erosion of liberalism (II, 278). Indeed, the name "Clapp" suggests a fear of infection from the democratic masses who were beginning to press for rights.[36] Adeline Clapp's story suggests that Sedgwick wants simultaneously to affirm this marriage and to warn of dangers that will ensue in a more egalitarian society. Thus, though Sedgwick's rhetoric regarding unmarried women initially points toward a possible feminist reordering of society, the overall resolution of the novel's various plot lines reinforces the nineteenth century's gendered public order in relation to marriage, and along rather conservative lines.

The public authority of Christianity is also clearly in evidence in *Married or Single?* The novel's revisionary republicanism is not just feminized, but Christianized, as well. Sedgwick presents a humane Christianity as an alternative to the free-market capitalist and egalitarian impulses of liberalism. The narrative is replete with references to New York City as "Vanity Fair." Several subplots represent the follies of the newly rich; the power of unchecked wealth to corrupt both the elite and working classes; the need for civic, religious, and vocational training for the masses in general, and Irish immigrants in particular; and the dangers to young women of worldly pleasures. More centrally, *Married or Single?* incorporates elements of the conversion narrative into its romance plot. It is no coincidence that the heroine of the novel is named Grace. Grace's choice between being a "Christian" or "heathen" (II, 105) is as important to the novel's purpose as her choice between being married or single. Arguably, the climax of the novel comes when Grace, saved from marrying Horace Copley by the death of Elise Tallis, has a conversion experience. Grace reflects on her narrow escape from the world in a letter to her sister:

> I have gifts that compel the world to admire me . . . but what use have I made of them, Eleanor? I have been one of the veriest idlers in that wide harvest-field, where the laborers are few and the harvest still plenteous. I have made myself my own centre; I have studied art and literature as ends, not means; I have fretted in the harness of the frivolous society in which my lot was cast, but I have not thrown it off; I craved, and

expected—as I believe most young women do—an adoring, exclusive love, as if we came into this working world merely to worship idols, and be idols in turn; in short, Eleanor . . . I sought for peace everywhere but where it is to be found, and where, being found, all pure human affections, all gifts and graces, all diversities of attainments, are its gracious accessories, *never its substitutes.* (II, 104)

Sedgwick shows us, in no uncertain terms, what Grace's sins have been—not just vanity, but also indolence, greed, and idolatry. Her salvation comes not from marriage, but from conversion—indeed, she must be a worthy person, a Christian, before her "choice" can be meaningful. Grace vows to become a respectable old maid, to leave social obligations behind, and to live for others, even moving to the country to help support Eleanor's family by going to work as a music teacher.[37] That she ultimately ends up with Archibald is represented more as an act of Providence than a choice. As Alice Clifford puts it, "You would have made a splendid old maid, but one can't shirk one's destiny" (II, 269).

Grace's near fall and eventual salvation support the novel's revisionary republican agenda. Just as Grace saves herself from moral corruption through the practice of virtue, duty, sacrifice, and restraint, so can the nation save itself from political corruption by rejecting the temptations of liberalism and reexamining its republican roots. The novel's emphasis on the advantages of country life and the excesses of the city—seen in Grace's rejection of New York City; in the contrast between Archibald Lisle's "country-bred" morality and work ethic (II, 144) and Horace Copley's inherited "fortune," worldly "appetite," and "love of pleasure" (II, 33); in the narrator's description of the "human depravation" that leads people to the "Tombs" (II, 123–27); and in the New England matron Mrs. Clifford's understanding of "the fashionable society of New York" as an "infected district" (II, 203)—illustrates Sedgwick's concern about the liberal direction the nation was taking and a desire to keep it from further "contagion" (II, 203).

Sedgwick's description of the novel's agenda was conventionally modest. In a letter of 1857, Sedgwick described *Married or Single?* as "a novel without any purpose or hope to slay giants, slavery, or the like, but only to supply mediocre readers with small moral hints on various subjects that come up in daily life."[38] She made her distance from women's rights activists explicit in the novel by including derogatory asides, such as Grace's declaration, "I do not like women publicly to champion *women's rights.* The Madame George's, and our own prize-fighters in women's conventions have made the very phrase odious" (I, 153). The novel's promotion of an idealized, Christian form of republican marriage as a solution to the problems it acknowledges—such as married women's rights to children and property, or young unmarried women's economic and sexual vulnerability—is a far cry from the critique of marriage as a form of slavery or civic death being voiced by Sedgwick's more radical contemporaries.[39]

Still, Sedgwick's rejection of women's rights activism should not blind us to the "interventionary value," to use Lora Romero's phrase, of her work.[40] One such intervention is that, in asserting that the choice to marry or not to marry is a woman's prerogative rather than a moral or social imperative, Sedgwick attempted to revise the social order without rejecting it entirely. Also, by combining the republican and Christian meanings of virtue, and by locating virtue in both men and women, Sedgwick made more visible the political nature of the so-called private sphere. Another intervention is the novel's participation in a public, literary discussion about the exchange of women within patriarchal marriage, one that would be pursued and enlarged by women writers such as Alice Cary, Emily Dickinson, and Edith Wharton.[41] If this is less than we wish Sedgwick could have done, it may be more than we might have expected. And a more careful look at her whole body of work, and its conservative as well as its liberal implications, may provide us with a more comprehensive and complex understanding of Sedgwick as a writer and as a woman in nineteenth-century America.

NOTES

1. Catharine Maria Sedgwick, *Hope Leslie; or, Early Times in the Massachusetts* (1827; reprint, New Brunswick, N.J.: Rutgers Univ. Press, 1990), 350.

2. Catharine Maria Sedgwick, *Married or Single?* 2 vols. (New York: Harper and Brothers, 1857), vi. All future references are to this edition and will be cited parenthetically in the text.

3. Stanton qtd. in Miriam Schneir, *Feminism: The Essential Historical Writings* (New York: Vintage, 1972), xvii.

4. For overviews of the early women's rights movement see Jean V. Matthews, *Women's Struggle for Equality: The First Phase, 1828–1876* (Chicago: Ivan R. Dee, 1997), and Sylvia D. Hoffert, *When Hens Crow: The Women's Rights Movement in Antebellum America* (Bloomington: Indiana Univ. Press, 1995).

5. For the text of Stone and Blackwell's statement see Schneir, *Feminism*, 103–5.

6. Ernestine Rose qtd. in Hoffert, *When Hens Crow*, 55.

7. Rachel Blau DuPlessis, *Writing Beyond the Ending: Narrative Strategies of Twentieth-Century Women Writers* (Bloomington: Indiana Univ. Press, 1985), 6.

8. Susan Harris, *Nineteenth-Century American Women's Novels: Interpretive Strategies* (Cambridge: Cambridge Univ. Press, 1990), 12–13.

9. Karen Tracey, *Plots and Proposals, American Women's Fiction, 1850–90* (Urbana: Univ. of Illinois Press, 2000), 29.

10. *The Power of Her Sympathy: The Autobiography and Journal of Catharine Maria Sedgwick*, ed. Mary Kelley (Boston: Massachusetts Historical Society, 1993), 22.

11. Review of *Married or Single?*, *North American Review* 88 (October 1857): 562–63.

12. Review of *Married or Single?*, *Harper's New Monthly Magazine* 15 (September 1857): 549.

13. Review of *Married or Single?*, *Ladies' Repository* 17 (September 1857): 564.

14. Sister Mary Michael Welsh, *Catharine Maria Sedgwick: Her Position in the Literature and Thought of Her Time up to 1860* (Washington, D.C.: The Catholic Univ. Press, 1937), and Edward Halsey Foster, *Catharine Maria Sedgwick* (New York: Twayne's, 1974), essentially dismissed the novel, finding value only in the light it shed on prevailing social concerns. Barbara Bardes and Suzanne Gossett discuss the novel briefly in *Declarations of Independence: Women and Political Power in Nineteenth Century American Fiction* (New Brunswick, N.J.: Rutgers Univ. Press, 1990), 34.

15. *A New-England Tale; or, Sketches of New-England Character and Manners* (1822; reprint, ed. Victoria Clements, New York: Oxford Univ. Press, 1995), xxvi. See also Dana D. Nelson, *The Word in Black and White: Reading "Race" in American Literature, 1638–1867* (New York: Oxford Univ. Press, 1992), 65–89, and Judith Fetterley, "'My Sister! My Sister!': The Rhetoric of Catharine Sedgwick's *Hope Leslie*," *American Literature* 70 (September 1998): 496. Also in this volume.

16. Fetterley offers a cogent analysis of this trend in "My Sister!" (493).

17. Competing definitions of feminism abound in reference to both nineteenth- and twentieth-century writers. Nancy Isenberg, noting that some historians believe the word "feminist" should be limited to a twentieth-century perspective, argues that the "theoretical framework of feminism has a larger history" which includes the ideas of antebellum women's rights activists (*Sex and Citizenship in Antebellum America* [Chapel Hill: Univ. of North Carolina Press, 1998], 206, n. 3). Sara M. Evans describes the concerns of antebellum feminists as "full participation in public and civic life for women, [and] a challenge to the separation of spheres" (*Born for Liberty: A History of Women in America* [New York: The Free Press, 1989], 102). Sedgwick's rejection of politics and public activism, despite her clear concern with issues of women's rights, distinguishes her ideas from those of liberal feminists.

18. David S. Reynolds, in 1989, identified Sedgwick as a "moderate feminist in advance of her times" (*Beneath the American Renaissance: The Subversive Imagination in the Age of Emerson and Melville* [Cambridge, Mass.: Harvard Univ. Press, 1989], 348), and other critics continue to discuss Sedgwick in this vein. Cheri Louise Ross posits that Sedgwick "offer[s] a covert feminist message critical of both Puritan and nineteenth-century society's treatment of women" in "(Re)Writing the Frontier Romance: Catharine Maria Sedgwick's *Hope Leslie*," *College Language Association Journal* 39.3 (1996): 339. Stacy Alaimo argues that Sedgwick's representations of nature, in *Hope Leslie*, create a feminist space (*Undomesticated Ground: Recasting Nature as Feminist Space* [New York: Cornell Univ. Press, 2000]). For more nuanced discussions of Sedgwick's politics, see Dana Nelson, "Sympathy as Strategy in *Hope Leslie*," in *The Culture of Sentiment*, ed. Shirley Samuels (New York: Oxford Univ. Press, 1992), and Fetterley, "My Sister!" in this volume.

19. The character of Eleanor Herbert Esterly bears resemblance to Sedgwick's sisters Frances and Eliza; see Kelley, *Power*, 22–24; and *Life and Letters of Catharine Maria Sedgwick*, ed. Mary E. Dewey (New York: Harper and Brothers, 1871), 110–11.

20. Catharine Maria Sedgwick, *Redwood: A Tale* (1824; reprint, New York: Garrett Press, 1969).

21. See Evans, *Born for Liberty*, 67–92, and Fetterley, "My Sister!" in this volume.

22. See Robert E. Shalhope's influential essay, "Toward a Republican Synthesis: The Emergence of an Understanding of Republicanism in American Historiography," *William and Mary Quarterly* 29 (1972): 49–80, and, more recently, Daniel T. Rogers, "Republicanism: The Career of a Concept," *Journal of American History* (1992): 11–38. Feminist scholars have demonstrated the possibilities and the limits of republicanism in helping women to construct a political identity; see Nancy Cott, *The Bonds of Womanhood: Women's Sphere in New England, 1780–1835* (New Haven: Yale Univ. Press, 1977); Linda Kerber, *Women of the Republic: Intellect and Ideology in Revolutionary America* (New York: Norton, 1980); and Joan Hoff, *Law, Gender, and Injustice: A Legal History of American Women* (New York: New York Univ. Press, 1991).

23. Patricia Kalayjian makes a similar point about Sedgwick's concern with civic virtue; see "Disinterest as Moral Corrective in *Clarence*'s Cultural Critique," in this volume.

24. For more extended discussions of Sedgwick's writing in relation to republicanism, see Fetterley, "My Sister!" 495–99; Philip Gould, *Covenant and Republic: Historical Romance and the Politics of Puritanism* (New York: Cambridge Univ. Press, 1996), 61–132; and Deborah Gussman, "Remembering Plymouth Rock: The Making of Citizenship in Nineteenth-Century Narratives of Colonial New England" (Ph.D. diss., Rutgers University, 1993), 161–211.

25. See Susan Harris, "The Limits of Authority: Catharine Maria Sedgwick and the Politics of Resistance," in this volume, for an analysis of Sedgwick's use of familial discourse to discuss politics.

26. Morton J. Horowitz argues that liberalism "had to create a new analysis [of society] that could justify the possible existence of freedom in a large state. . . . Liberals were thus compelled ultimately to break with the concept of the virtue of their citizenry" ("Republicanism and Liberalism in American Constitutional Thought," *William and Mary Law Review* 29 [fall 1987]: 72).

27. See Ruth Bloch, "The Gendered Meanings of Virtue in Revolutionary America," *Signs* 13 (1987): 37–58.

28. Murray qtd. in Evans, *Born for Liberty*, 63.

29. For a discussion of the "old maid" in Sedgwick's other works, see Mary Kelley, *Private Woman, Public Stage: Literary Domesticity in Nineteenth-Century America* (New York: Oxford Univ. Press, 1984), 240–41.

30. See Kelley, *Power*, 117, 122–23, 128, 137–38, 151–52.

31. *Ibid.*, 122, 123.

32. *Ibid.*, 127.

33. Nancy F. Cott, "Giving Character to Our Whole Civil Polity: Marriage and the

Public Order in the Late Nineteenth Century," in Linda K. Kerber, Alice Kessler-Harris, and Kathryn Kish Sklar, eds., *U.S. History as Women's History: New Feminist Essays* (Chapel Hill: Univ. of North Carolina Press, 1995), 107.

34. *Ibid.*, 107.

35. *Ibid.*, 114–20.

36. "Clap" has been used as a synonym for gonorrhea since the late sixteenth century, and that usage was in evidence during the nineteenth century. *Oxford English Dictionary*, 2nd ed., s.v. "clap."

37. We see a similar pattern in *A New-England Tale* in which Jane Elton almost marries a nonbeliever, experiences earning her own living, and seriously considers spinsterhood before consenting to marry (103–4, 106–36, 158–65).

38. *Life and Letters of Catharine Maria Sedgwick*, ed. Mary E. Dewey (New York: Harper and Brothers, 1871), 369.

39. Sedgwick's concern over married women's property rights is made explicit in chapter 1, where Grace learns, by reading old letters, that her aunt chose to stay in a "bankrupt marriage" rather than risk losing legal access to her children (I, 19). Kelley notes that Sedgwick wrote to her sister Eliza regarding their sister Frances's similar marital dilemma (*Power*, 23).

40. Lora Romero, *Home Fronts: Domesticity and Its Critics in the Antebellum United States* (Durham, N.C.: Duke Univ. Press, 1997), 20.

41. See Reynolds, *Beneath*, 421–25, for a discussion of Cary and Dickinson on marriage. Critics have not generally connected the writing of Sedgwick and Edith Wharton. There are interesting parallels between Grace Herbert and Lily Bart in *The House of Mirth* (1905), though Wharton is clearly rejecting the optimism and sentimentality of novels like *Married or Single?*

15

Excerpts from Reviews Addressing Sedgwick's Politics

"The Novels of Miss Sedgwick." *American Monthly Magazine* (January 1836):
15–25.

[Sedgwick] has embodied, as no other of our writers has, the spirit of her
native soil; a spirit evolved so inevitably out of the elements of human nature,
as it has been peculiarly nurtured and inwardly restrained in this section of our
country [New England]. . . . (P. 15)

It was not, however, merely to vindicate the unrulableness in which Miss
Sedgwick sometimes indulges her heroines, who are ever "pure in the last recesses of the heart," that these remarks have been made on New-England society
and its literature. Miss Sedgwick's works begin to claim a higher place than that
of elegant literature. She is evidently a republican writer, in a department which
has hitherto been devoted to glorifying the spirit of feudalism, and its consequent false views; and which has certainly never before been made a refracting
atmosphere to diffuse the light of our institutions over the whole surface of our
society, though so admirably adapted to this purpose. (P. 20)

[H]ow is all "Liberator" vituperation put to shame by the genuine argument
to the heart and understanding that goes forth from the faithful services of the
freed-negro Rose! Even when Miss Sedgwick seems to take the least pains to
inculcate a moral, a moral spirit breathes from all her pages: and it is a beautiful,
glowing, creative, moral spirit, that not only goes back to repent with Redwood
over the past, but with Elliot Lee and William Barclay, goes forward to sanctify
the new forms of political and social condition in which it finds itself. (P. 22)

It is true, our political writers, from the high-souled, pure-hearted, con-
science-clear Quincy, down through all who have written in the various depart-

269

ments of Political Economy and Legislation, even to Webster . . . have been most truly inspired with an ever-present aim of making political constitution and legislative enactment "coincident with the moral code."* But these works are such pure reasonings from first principles, that they are too hard reading to be the popular recreation of our community, who generally take up books only as a pastime. Therefore, although the duties of republicans to the constitution and laws which secure their rights, have been reasoned on and set forth by the framers of our government and their successors in the judicial and legal profession, in lucid arguments . . . the mass of our population is growing up ignorant of the true views which should possess a professedly self-governed nation. Never, therefore, was the feminine genius, whose nature it is to apply principle to domestic and social action, and, like spring and summer, to breathe beauty into and over the sublime but wintry outlines of the political system drawn over by masculine power;—never, we repeat, was feminine genius before called to a work of such far-reaching beneficence as this one, [*Home*]—to accomplish which Miss Sedgwick has given us by her two last works [*Clarence* and *The Linwoods*] an earnest of her power.

*This fine expression is taken from the Report of the Massachusetts Legislature on Insolvent Debtors, 1835. [Reviewer's footnote.] (P. 24)

"Miss Sedgwick's Tales." *North American Review* (October 1837): 475–81.

What a power is that of an intellectual woman over the condition of a people, if she does but understand the sphere of her strength; moving as she does everywhere in the recesses of society; privileged to observe the operations of thought and passion, in the scenes where thought and feeling are educated for more public action; necessarily disconnected from those parties, which make men distrust and refuse instruction from one another. Who would venture to say, that there is a man in this nation, with any genius, or in any place, who is doing a patriot's work more effectively, than [Sedgwick]. . . . (P. 480–81)

"Art. VIII. Petition of certain Legal Voters of Boston and its vicinity to the Honorable Senate and House of Representatives in Congress, assembled, praying for the Passage of an International Copyright Law." [*Boston Daily Advertiser*, 4 June 1842.] Reprinted in the *North American Review* (July 1842): 245–64.

. . . In our opinion there is scarcely a better service of patriotism than is to be rendered by the multiplication of works in this department, in the tone of some of those, in which the upright genius of Miss Sedgwick has kindled the sympathy of readers in the virtues that befit the American citizen. . . . Works in this tone,—the more abundant and more highly wrought the better,—instructing the common mind of this nation to appreciate its privileges,—forming it to discharge, and winning it to love, the duties of its position,—will go further than any parchment Bill of Rights to perpetuate our political blessings. . . . (Pp. 261–62)

Chapter 15

The Limits of Authority: Catharine Maria Sedgwick and the Politics of Resistance

SUSAN K. HARRIS

hat are the limits to legitimate authority? When is it appropriate to defy king, magistrate, father?

*W*Americans passionately debated these questions in the period before and after the Revolutionary War. As early as 1743 Samuel Adams argued for the affirmative in a Harvard debate on the question "[I]s it lawful to resist the Supreme Magistrate, if the Commonwealth cannot otherwise be preserved?"[1] In 1750 Jonathan Mayhew, minister of Boston's West Church, asked, "[W]hat reason is there for submitting to that government, which does by no means answer the design of government?"[2] And in 1767 John Dickinson, writing the third of his otherwise conservative *Letters from a Farmer in Pennsylvania*, noted that English history was replete with instances of "resistance by force" when the people's applications for a redress of grievances had failed.[3]

As historians have frequently pointed out, by the eighteenth century the English political system had become essentially contractual, despite the continuing existence of a hereditary kingship.[4] In the American colonies, where grievances were magnified by the difficulty of communicating with Parliament and king, and where one of the legacies of Puritanism was a valorizing of the individual conscience, resistance to legitimate authority attained the status of a moral duty. As Bernard Bailyn pointed out in his classic study, *The Ideological Origins of the American Revolution*, the colonists' sense of grievance inspired them to read all discussions of disagreement and resistance as "a general injunction against uncritical obedience to authority in any form."[5]

That this issue preoccupied Americans across all ranks and conditions is evident in the writings of the period, from the thousands of political pamphlets that brought the debates within the purview of anyone capable of reading or being read to, to the fiction and poetry that flowed from those determined to produce a uniquely American literature. Catharine Sedgwick was one of these latter; daughter and sister to statesmen and lawyers in the new Republic, her work was thickly imbricated in the public debates over the limits of legitimate authority, the character of the new citizen, and the moral behavior of the new man. Proudly claiming in her autobiography that "a love of freedom, a habit of doing their own thinking, has characterized our clan,"[6] Sedgwick carried her family legacy into the thematic heart of much of her writing. In this essay, I will argue that *Hope Leslie, The Linwoods, A New-England Tale, Redwood,* and *Clarence,* all novels that Sedgwick published between 1822 and 1838,[7] not only engaged contemporary debates over race, gender, and class, but also intervened in that most privileged debate of the period, the debate about resisting legitimate authority—when resistance is appropriate, who has the "right" to undertake it, and what its limits and consequences should be.[8]

Sedgwick's work is still in the process of recovery, and Sedgwick's themes, and their relative weights against one another and against those of her contemporaries, are still being debated. In her own time and again in ours, Sedgwick has been compared to James Fenimore Cooper. Many recent readers have suggested that Sedgwick dealt more forthrightly and radically with issues of freedom, race, and gender than did Cooper; most of these readers are, rightly, thinking of Sedgwick's treatment of women, Native Americans, and interracial marriage in *Hope Leslie* in comparison to Cooper's treatment of the same issues in *The Last of the Mohicans.*[9] But the most appropriate Cooper novel to compare with Sedgwick's work is *Home As Found* (1838), Cooper's most curmudgeonly novel of manners. *Home As Found* and Sedgwick's *Redwood* and *Clarence* (not to speak of the didactic novels, *Home, The Poor Rich Man and the Rich Poor Man, Live and Let Live,* and even *Married or Single?*) all examine new world manners, especially in New York City, and both authors find fault with their countrymen's aggressiveness, materialism, and coarseness. But for Sedgwick, these faults are remediable, glitches in a social program that will eventuate in the well-being of all; whereas for Cooper, the fault lies in the basic freedoms assumed by citizens in a democratic system. For Cooper, American society had been all downhill since the Revolution.

In contrast, for Sedgwick the Revolution laid the basis for a society in which social and political relationships would eventually lead to the perfectibility of man. Robert Ferguson has argued that American defenders of the early Republic saw their fledgling civilization in terms of a Kantian dialectic, where the process was to be valued despite the uncertainty of the result.[10] In Sedgwick's writings, dialectical formulations are evident in her juxtapositions of character types and moral issues as her novels struggle to envision the ideal citizen. Anterior to these dialectics, however, the question of freedom appears as *the* ideological ground for all other issues. That is, for Sedgwick, the right to resist lawful authority when it exceeded moral boundaries was the starting point for all subsequent debates. For this reason, an examination of those novels that highlight exploration, both of the nature of resistance and of those individuals who dare to enact it, seems an appropriate foreground for subsequent inquiry into Sedgwick's work.

Like Cooper, Sedgwick uses family and social relationships as models for political relationships. In this, both writers reflected a common configuration. In her study of patriarchal language in the early Republic, Cynthia S. Jordan has noted how, in the wake of Locke's writings on both government and education, Anglo-Americans of the eighteenth and early nineteenth centuries began to see the relationship between fathers and sons in the same vein as the relationship between sovereigns and subjects: first, as contractual, and second, as positing the father's role as guide and loving friend, rather than as absolute authority.[11] In the literature of the fledgling Republic, this transformation frequently was represented in terms of family plots. Like her contemporaries, Sedgwick uses the trope of the family to compare the duties of children to their parents (and vice versa) to the duties of subjects to their king (and vice versa).

If we order Sedgwick's novels not according to their dates of publication but according to the historical periods with which they are concerned, we see Sedgwick locating both the question of resistance and the familial and civil ·relationships through which the question was debated as they were formulated in each period.[12] This is especially evident in the two novels set before the national era—*Hope Leslie* (1827), set during the Pequot Wars, and *The Linwoods* (1835), set during the Revolution.[13] In *Hope Leslie*, the political topography is dominated by resistance; the novel opens on the issue, figured as the tension between William Fletcher, a young Englishman and Puritan sympathizer, and his uncle, a Loyalist. In the first chapter Fletcher relinquishes his inheritance and loses his beloved because he refuses to acquiesce to his uncle's demand that he "abjure . . . in the presence of witnesses . . . the fanatical notions of liberty and religion with which [he had] been infected," or to "pledge [him]self, by a solemn oath, to unqualified obedience to the king, and adherence to the established church" (*HL*, 10). By opening with scenes of resistance Sedgwick signals her major theme; by placing her novel two hundred years before her own time, she creates a lineage for the American's desire to determine his or her own loyalties.

Like all of Sedgwick's novels, *Hope Leslie* works out its ideas through marriage plots and family tensions, probing relations of power and authority within the complexities and tangents of those plots. In this novel, Sedgwick foregrounds her concerns by alternately examining authority as it is exercised by parents, magistrates, sovereigns, and religious divines, and suggesting that in this new society, all hierarchical relationships are open to challenge. As Digby, a former servant to the Fletcher family, avers,

> [T]his having our own way . . . is the privilege we came to this wilderness world for . . . there are many who think what blunt Master Blackstone said, "that he came not away from the Lords-bishops, to put himself under the Lord's brethren." . . . [T]here is a new spirit in the world—chains are broken—fetters are knocked off—and the liberty set forth in the blessed word, is now felt to be every man's birth-right." (*HL,* 225)

As Judith Fetterley notes, Sedgwick is not unambiguously enthusiastic about this "new spirit"; her limning of her headstrong protagonist Hope shows that there are, or should be, limits to Americans' insistence on their right to determine their own way.[14] Like Thomas Jefferson, who cautioned that governments "should not be changed for light and transient causes,"[15] Sedgwick recognizes that mere individual dissatisfaction with the prevailing order or a hotheaded, rebellious temperament are not sufficient to justify acts of resistance. Despite this caveat, Sedgwick pursues the issue throughout both *Hope Leslie* and *The Linwoods,* laying out the ideological differences between those characters who hold it their duty to submit to authority and those who hold it their duty not to do so.

In many of her novels, Sedgwick's primary vehicle for demonstrating the issue of resistance is a father-son dyad, where an older man, very much the patriarch, attempts to force a younger man to submit to his authority and through him, to a higher power. Like *Hope Leslie, The Linwoods* opens with the tension between a father who declares for the king, swearing that "I hate a Whig as I do a toad, and if my son should prove a traitor to his King and country, by George, I would cut him off forever!"[16] and a son, Herbert Linwood, who declares for the rebels. As was common in Whig writing of the period, the tyrannical father here is constructed as bombastic and somewhat comic. Like many of Sedgwick's father figures in particular, he is also ill—a physical manifestation of his unbalanced political judgments. In *The Linwoods,* Isabella Linwood, daughter to the Tory father and sister to the Whig son, stands between the two men, negotiating compromises. Although she is overtly loyal to her parents' politics, she nevertheless signals her own independence by admiring her brother for "honestly and boldly [clinging] to his opinions" (*L,* 40), and she eventually comes to stand with the rebel side. In part because of Isabella's urging, Mr. Linwood finally pardons his son, and they are reconciled. Despite the happy outcome, the fractures and healings resulting from the alienation of father and son are a model in miniature of the conflicts and resolutions Sedgwick saw emerging from the "family conflict" of the war, a domestic version of the dialectic of process that informs much of these works. As her narrator maintains, "Our revolutionary contest, by placing men in new relations, often exhibited in new force and beauty the ties that bind together the human family" (*L,* 100). As Gordon Wood notes, the familial metaphor dominated New World Englishmen's understanding of their quarrel with England.[17]

In *The Linwoods*, not surprisingly, the dominant trope for political difference is the father-son dyad. In *Hope Leslie*, the dyads are as often female as male. *Hope Leslie* features numerous pairings, some dialectical and constituted on political questions, others more conventionally created to facilitate plot details. Hope Leslie, an Englishwoman, and Magawisca, a Native American captured by the English in adolescence, are the dual heroines of this novel, posed not against each other but as English and Native American spokespersons against both narrow-minded religion and overweening imperialism. Both are fearless and independent, and both are torn between loyalty to beloved father figures and their understanding of the compromises necessary to facilitate the new order. Together, they constitute Sedgwick's trope for the independent New World woman, especially in contrast to the more commonly valued woman who submits to male authorities. At one point in the novel Magawisca has been imprisoned by Boston authorities, and Hope, convinced of her innocence, plots to rescue her. She tries to enlist the help of Esther, a recent immigrant from England. Unlike Hope or Magawisca, Esther does not question legitimate authority, at least as it exists within the Puritan community. She refuses Hope's request, arguing for submission as a religious duty. "'We are commanded,'" she avers, to "'submit ourselves to every ordinance of man, for the Lord's sake: whether it be to the king, as supreme; or unto governors, as unto them that are sent by him for the punishment of evil doers, and for the praise of them that do well.'" Articulating the novel's dominant position, Hope disagrees, arguing in return that "surely, Esther, there must be warrant, as you call it, for sometimes resisting legitimate authority, or all our friends in England would not be at open war with their king" (*HL,* 278). Here, the position represented by Hope, Magawisca, and their friend Everell is dialectically juxtaposed to the position represented by Esther, a model Puritan maiden. Sedgwick makes the political ramifications of this plot explicit through Hope's reference to the English Civil War.[18]

In addition to explicitly political formulations of the question of resistance to legitimate authority such as we have seen in *Hope Leslie* and *The Linwoods*, Sedgwick also approaches the issue through investigation into gender hierarchies. In fact one thematic link between Sedgwick's two historical novels and those set in Sedgwick's own time is a continued inquiry into the contradiction between a society that valorizes resistance for men but insists on submission for women.[19] Here, the dialectic constructed is between activity and passivity. Across Sedgwick's writings, the words "submission" and "passivity" occur time and again, usually, though not always, in relation to women. She was extremely interested in the ramifications of passivity, along both political and gender lines. One of her favorite vehicles for examining this question was to pair a beautiful, virtuous, and passive young woman with an equally beautiful and virtuous but strong-minded one, and to create a plot in which the happiness of the first depends on the activities of the second. Such pairs play a major part in the debates Sedgwick sets up concerning resistance in *Clarence, Hope Leslie, Redwood*, and *The Linwoods*. The frequency and centrality of this dyad in these novels indicates that she wanted this question debated: Her basic implication was that celebrating passivity was tantamount to celebrating the absence rather than the presence of a virtue. In *Hope Leslie*, for instance, the adult William Fletcher and Governor Winthrop debate female merits, the governor valuing "that passiveness, that, next to godliness, is a woman's best virtue," and Fletcher crisply responding that "I should scarcely account . . . a property of soulless matter, a virtue" (*HL*, 153).

Although Sedgwick clearly supports Fletcher's argument here—essentially Milton's contention that emptiness and purity are not equivalents—passive women abound in her novels. In keeping with her insistence that her characters be plotted along more than one grid, Sedgwick's passive women are neither unlikely nor unlikeable characters. Her young passive women are often warm and loving, a bit naive, and generally in some bodily or spiritual danger because of their inability to protect themselves. Through them, Sedgwick holds up a cultural ideal and, though rarely criticizing it overtly, nevertheless undermines it, especially as it relates to useful qualities for the republican woman. In *Hope Leslie*, for instance, Esther is not the only passive vessel. Hope's sister Faith, who we first see as a clinging child, reappears as an equally dependent adult. Even though she passionately wants to return to her Native American husband after her "rescue" by the white community, Faith is incapable of acting on her own behalf, instead waiting listlessly until her husband can steal her back. In *The Linwoods*, Bessie Lee, sister to the male protagonist Eliot Lee, becomes a New World Ophelia when she realizes the villain Jasper Meredith's perfidy; making her crazed way into British-held New York City, she lives just long enough to demonstrate the perils of emotional dependency. In *Redwood*, a novel that implicitly argues for a moderate republican religion by examining two extremes— the fanatical Shakers on one hand and French atheism on the other—passivity is represented by Emily Allen, a young woman who has followed her aunt into the Shaker community because "she was glad to be saved from the efforts of self-dependence."[20] Emily Allen is less sympathetically projected than most of

Sedgwick's passive young women: When she is introduced the narrator describes her as having features that "would have rendered her face insipid, but that it was rescued by an expression of purity and innocence, and a certain appealing tender look" (*R*, I: 90), and her role in the novel's plot is first to be virtually imprisoned in the Shaker community and then to be kidnapped and almost forced into marriage with a corrupt elder who plans to steal the community's savings. Finally, in *Clarence,* Emilie Layton—sweet, flighty, and seventeen—is almost forced into a miserable marriage by parents who care more for their own reputations than for their daughter's welfare. In both cases, the passive parties are incapable of action on their own behalf; they are dependent on their active counterparts for their rescue and subsequent happiness.

Although she delineates passivity in young women more frequently than in older ones (perhaps because the melodrama of forced marriage and seduction plots gives her a ready vehicle), Sedgwick also takes the question of passivity into the realm of married women. Sedgwick routinely celebrates the good woman who follows her husband and carries out his wishes (*Hope Leslie*'s Mrs. Fletcher is the model wife in this regard), but she also undermines this figure through the fates meted out to her (Mrs. Fletcher is scalped early in the novel). In *A New-England Tale*, as in most of the novels, the wife who passively submits to her fiscally irresponsible husband finds her virtue rewarded by poverty and calumny; after her death, her twelve-year-old daughter is handed over to a tyrannical guardian. Throughout her novels, Sedgwick treads a fine line between representing the submissive woman as a culturally valorized figure and showing how her passivity inevitably results in her being manipulated by others for their own gain. In Sedgwick's work, passive submission by women to male authority may result in harmonious families, but it almost inevitably ends in the destruction of the passive party, generally as a result of her partner's irresponsibility. Sedgwick suggests that the new woman has to be an active participant in her own destiny, a citizen able not only to enter into contractual relationships, but to renegotiate them when events do not transpire in her favor.

Sedgwick's New World citizen is an early-nineteenth-century version of the New Woman, described in political rather than explicitly feminist terms. In contrast to the passive woman, all of Sedgwick's novels feature at least one female protagonist who not only resists, rebels, and controls her own destiny, but whose resistance is described in terms explicitly reflective of the larger Republican context. *Hope Leslie* features two: Hope and her Native American friend Magawisca. Unlike her sister Faith, who finds her identity through her husband, Hope battles her way through rules and regulations both legal and theological, sure—sometimes too sure—of her own rectitude. Magawisca, a Native American who, because she was captured during the Pequot Wars, has lived in both the Indian and white communities, figures as the rebel chieftainess who articulates her people's case to the blindly prejudiced English community. Both protagonists represent Sedgwick's ideal citizen: rational, articulate, and self-confident, not only able but eager to act on her own initiative—not always right (in Kantian terms, she is part of the *process* of moving toward perfection) but representative of a necessary and very positive stage in the evolution of the Republic.

Similarly, the heroine of *The Linwoods* trusts her own judgment and makes her own decisions. In contrast to Bessie Lee, whose "destiny were passive obedience," "Isabella [Linwood] seemed like one who might have been born a rebel chieftainess" (*L*, 18). When Bessie observes that as women, neither she nor Isabella are obliged to take sides in the Revolutionary conflict, Isabella retorts that "your vocation it may be, my pretty dove, to sit on your perch with an olive-branch in your bill, but not mine" (*L*, 36). Isabella and her Aunt Archer,[21] both of whom come to sympathize with the Whigs, think through political positions and act with decisive courage in tight situations. As such, both become models for Republican Womanhood. So, too, does Gertrude Clarence, protagonist of the novel *Clarence*, who uses her authority to arrange for Emilie's rescue and her inheritance to buy her friend out of her odious engagement. And in *A New-England Tale*, Jane Elton's resistance to both oppression (in the form of her aunt) and persuasion (in the form of an unscrupulous fiancé) makes her the perfect combination of capable, upright woman and knowledgeable, resistant citizen.

These dyads—the pairing of older and younger males over the question of resistance to political authority, and the pairing of passive and active females over the question of submission to familial or community authority—are gendered forms of the same debate. Not only do both dyads raise the question of resistance to legitimate authority; in the end, both reflect the larger epistemological question of the relation of the individual to the state and to the local community. As the dialogue between Governor Winthrop and William Fletcher shows, spokesmen for the dominant community (here, the Puritan hierarchy in America) value passivity among the subordinate parties in any hierarchically arranged relationship: woman to man, son to father, subject to sovereign, human to God. But as Fletcher points out, submissiveness implies lack, absence; in these relationships, men must complete women, fathers must complete sons, kings must complete subjects, God must complete humankind.

If this patterning were carried through consistently, there would be no tension between participants in the hierarchy. As we have seen, however, in the new world Sedgwick represents, men no longer stand in relation to their sovereign as humankind stands to God, or, as those male characters insist, as women should stand to men. As Digby puts it in *Hope Leslie*, in this new world "thought and will are set free" (*HL*, 225). When men in the new country insist on their rights as individuals, they knock the whole chain of hierarchical relations out of sync, implicitly challenging the legitimacy of the chain's other dyadic relationships. As a woman and a patriot, Sedgwick wants to extend the limits of this dismantling; for her, women, like men, have the right to challenge lawful authority. If men are no longer subjects but citizens, if young men need no longer obey their fathers, why should women obey their fathers or their husbands? The discrepancy between Americans' insistence on independence for men, and their equal insistence on dependence for women, establishes an ironic juxtaposition that reverberates throughout Sedgwick's work, reflecting the passionate debates of the first generation of Americans over who, exactly, merits citizenship, and to whom, exactly, the privilege of rebellion belongs.

Which is not to assume that Sedgwick did not classify her countrymen and discriminate between them. With her contemporaries, she was ambivalent about which categories of Americans should possess the rights of citizenship, especially the right to resist lawful authority. As Robert Ferguson notes, for the new Americans "the question is not so much 'What is an American?' . . . but, rather, 'Who will be allowed to act as one?' "[22] Even when Sedgwick theoretically supported the "right" of one group to freedom, as she did, for instance, on the question of black slavery, she did not necessarily assume that full citizenship should follow. In large part this was because she shared her contemporaries' conviction that even if all (white, propertied) men were created equal, not all ethnic groups were. In her work, Sedgwick reflects many, even most, of the popular prejudices of her day: Although she wrote warmly of Mumbet, the Sedgwick family servant and guide in her childhood, and portrays a few black women (such as Rosa in *The Linwoods*) as intelligent and capable people, most of her black characters are lazy, rude, and untrustworthy.[23] Her portrayal of the Irish is relentlessly negative: Some Irish characters are warm-hearted, but they are also either shifty or gullible, and far too vulnerable to the persuasions of alcohol. Within her own ethnic group, Sedgwick's class biases are manifested by her portrayals of American yeomen; although they have admirable qualities of independence and honesty, they are also provincial and rough, subjects for comic treatment rather than figures of the new man. She also shared her contemporaries' distrust of Roman Catholics. Although few Catholics figure as major characters in her novels, those that do either have questionable morals or else have been so robbed of independent reasoning by their Catholic training that they cannot think for themselves. Sedgwick's construction of Catholics, in fact, may well be influenced by her ambivalence about passivity; in *Hope Leslie*, Faith's lack of personal agency is first signaled by the crucifix around her neck, evidence of her conversion to Catholicism. Like other Protestant Americans, especially descendants of the Puritans, Sedgwick sees the Church as an authoritarian structure and the faithful as dupes of a crafty priesthood. Similarly, Sedgwick's construction of Shakers emphasizes the authoritarian structure of that society, with the subsequent loss of personal agency among its members. Throughout her work, prevalent caricatures of rural and lower-class whites and of Americans and immigrants of color narrow the range of candidates for a truly democratic citizenry.

Rather than serving as evidence of Sedgwick's marginality to the American literary tradition, these attitudes indicate her intense involvement in the political debates of her time. In fact, if we weighted her characters for class and ethnicity, and charted them as potential citizens of a democratic republic, we might well produce an index for early-nineteenth-century anxieties about class distinction in the new society. Certainly, Sedgwick's novels set in her own time are intensely concerned about class and manners; her New York settings in particular give scope for many narratorial comments about the shortcomings of the local parvenus. But as the narrator of *Clarence* notes toward the end of the novel, class discriminations have their "source in man's natural love of distinction."[24]

Here Sedgwick reflects the conundrum facing her generation as it tried to hew order out of what many saw as social chaos. If, as Sedgwick's two historical novels show, it is legitimate to resist lawful authority, and if in the process of establishing a new nation in which "all men" are considered equal, inherited rank is abolished, what kinds of distinctions *are* operative for the new society? Although Sedgwick herself focuses on class issues within white Protestant society, the marginalization of Catholics and people of color in her work suggests that, unconsciously, she was reflecting the form of distinction that the new culture would take. In the United States as it evolved, the genetic, that is, the "inherent," distinction of racial and ethnic difference substituted for the socially "inherited" distinction of class; unlike the relative homogeneity of European cultures, where foreigners could potentially be absorbed into standing class structures, in the United States ethnicity displaced class as the means of discriminating between "natural" (or inherent) differences. Sedgwick's writings show the early stages of these evolving distinctions.

At least five of Catharine Maria Sedgwick's novels, then, were active players in the literary reproduction of the debates about the nature and limits of resistance in early American culture. Assuming, with her contemporaries, that the freedom to challenge existing authority was the ground of all civil and moral rights, she actively intervened in discussions about the qualifications for American citizenship and the proper manners and class distinctions for the new society. With this, she explicitly and implicitly centered white Protestant women in the new order, celebrating their activity, intellectuality, and capability. Self-consciously patriotic, she did not hesitate to criticize her countrymen (and -women) on everything from political behavior to taste. Nevertheless, as she notes in her preface to *Redwood,* the nation formation that she and her contemporaries had undertaken was not only a challenge, it was a *process*, one that would not be accomplished quickly but that clearly was headed for success. "We have indeed little sympathy with that narrow-minded patriotism which claims honors that are not yet merited," her authorial voice claims.

> Our republicanism is founded on a broad and general principle, which is opposed to all coronations. We cannot, therefore unite in hailing our country the "queens of the earth:" . . . but we have a deep and heart-felt pride . . . in the increasing intelligence, the improving virtue, and the rising greatness of our country. There is something which more excites the imagination and interests the affections in expanding energy and rapid improvement, than even in perfection itself . . . therefore we will ask, what country there is, or has been, whose progress towards greatness has been in any degree correspondent with our own? Our change is so rapid that the future presses on our vision, and we enjoy it *now*. . . . The future lives in the present. What we are, we owe to our ancestors, and what our posterity will be, they will owe to us. (NY, June, 1824). (*R,* xi)

NOTES

1. Robert A. Ferguson, *The American Enlightenment, 1750–1820* (Cambridge, Mass.: Harvard Univ. Press, 1997), 2.

2. Edmund S. Morgan, ed., *Puritan Political Ideas, 1558–1794* (New York: The Bobbs-Merrill Company, 1965), 306.

3. Walter H. Conser Jr., Ronald M. McCarthy, David J. Toscano, and Gene Sharp, eds., *Resistance, Politics, and the American Struggle for Independence, 1765–1775* (Boulder, Colo.: Lynne Rienner, 1986), 536.

4. C. C. Bonwick, "English Radicals and American Resistance to British Authority," in Conser et al., *Resistance, Politics,* 403–15. The contractual nature of the eighteenth-century British political landscape is noted frequently in writing about the American Revolution, from Bernard Bailyn's classic study *The Ideological Origins of the American Revolution* (Cambridge, Mass.: Harvard Univ. Press, 1967) to the present. Historians also note the eighteenth-century tendency to frame subjects-ruler relationships in familial terms. One of the most lucid recent accounts of this process occurs in Wood's chapter on "Enlightened Paternalism," which examines the erosion of both monarchical and parental authority in the seventeenth and eighteenth centuries in conjunction with

the rise of contractual ideologies of governance. The result, Wood notes, was a situation in which "it was natural for Americans to turn their familial relationship to the crown into a contractual one, for this merely substituted one personal relationship for another; but this substitution also made it easier for them to take the awful step of rebelling against their own parents." Gordon S. Wood, *The Radicalism of the American Revolution* (New York: Vintage Books, 1991), 164–65. See also Pauline Maier, *From Resistance to Revolution: Colonial Radicals and the Development of American Opposition to Britain, 1765–1776* (New York: Alfred A. Knopf, 1972); Robert E. Shalhope, *The Roots of Democracy: American Thought and Culture, 1760–1800* (Boston: Twayne, 1990); and Bailyn, *The Ideological Origins of the American Revolution*.

5. Bailyn, *The Ideological Origins of the American Revolution*, 305.

6. *The Power of Her Sympathy: The Autobiography and Journal of Catharine Maria Sedgwick*, ed. Mary Kelley (Boston: The Massachusetts Historical Society, 1993), 45. Hereafter abbreviated *POS*.

7. Of course, Sedgwick published many other novels beyond the five I list here, most notably *Home* (1835), *The Poor Rich Man and the Rich Poor Man* (1836), *Live and Let Live* (1837), and *Married or Single?* (1857). Whereas I have chosen to focus on her more overtly political works, that is, novels that examine resistance to authority on a national scale, a similar investigation could be fruitfully carried out on the domestic novels, where Sedgwick probes questions of authority on a more personal and familial level.

8. At the date of this writing, spring 2002, only four Sedgwick texts are in print, *A New-England Tale; or, Sketches of New-England Character and Manners,* ed. Victoria Clements (New York: Oxford Univ. Press, 1995), hereafter abbreviated *NET; Hope Leslie; or, Early Times in the Massachusetts,* ed. Mary Kelley (New Brunswick, N.J.: Rutgers Univ. Press, 1991); hereafter abbreviated *HL; The Power of Her Sympathy;* and *The Linwoods; or, "Sixty Years Since" in America,* ed. Maria Karafilis (Hanover, N.H.: University Press of New England, 2002), hereafter abbreviated *L.*

Not surprisingly, most recent critical writing on Sedgwick has focused on *Hope Leslie,* a novel that easily lends itself to late-twentieth-century interests in race, class, and gender issues. Writers in the 1980s, especially Nina Baym's *Novels, Readers, and Reviewers: Responses to Fiction in Antebellum America* (Ithaca, N.Y.: Cornell Univ. Press, 1984) and Mary Kelley's *Private Woman, Public Stage: Literary Domesticity in Nineteenth-Century America* (New York: Oxford Univ. Press, 1984), discuss more than one novel, but like later critical overviews, they tend to project Sedgwick as a writer of domestic novels first and a commentator on the political scene second. Most subsequent critics, such as T. Gregory Garvey, in "Risking Reprisal: Catharine Sedgwick's *Hope Leslie* and the Legitimation of Public Action by Women" (*ATQ* 8:4 [December 1994]: 287–98), acknowledge Sedgwick's interest in "the foundations on which legitimate authority ought to rest" (290), but few pursue the subject from cultural-political rather than cultural-feminist approaches, and nearly all restrict their examination to *Hope Leslie*. Philip Gould's *Covenant and Republic: Historical Romance and the Politics of Puritanism* (New York: Cambridge Univ. Press, 1996) comes closest to my concerns in its examination of

Sedgwick's focus on civil ethics (92) and his observation that we should not underestimate "the political significance" of "rebellious daughters, tyrannical fathers, convoluted marriage plots" in women's fiction of the the republican era (93); but he, too, focuses on *Hope Leslie*. Maria Karafilis, in "Catharine Maria Sedgwick's *Hope Leslie:* Fostering Radical Democratic Individualism in the New Nation" (*ATQ* 12:4 [December 1998]: 327–44), frames her investigation into the novel in terms of a tension between "Sedgwick's desire to offer an alternative model of governance and citizenship appropriate for members of a democratic republic and her desire to foster a fledgling domestic national literature" (328). Gustavus Stadler, too, recognizes that Sedgwick's work "was situated within current public debates over the shape of the nation, of where it began and ended, of who belonged and who didn't," but his article focuses on corporeality in *Hope Leslie*. See Stadler, "Magawisca's Body of Knowledge: Nation-Building in *Hope Leslie*," *Yale Journal of Criticism: Interpretation in the Humanities* 12:1 (spring 1999): 41–56. In short, although many critics acknowledge the political framing of Sedgwick's writing, only a few focus on its manifestations, none foreground the question of resistance to legitimate authority, and very few examine more than one or two of Sedgwick's works.

9. Susanne Opfermann is one of the most recent of the commentators on the connection between Sedgwick and Cooper. In "Lydia Maria Child, James Fenimore Cooper, and Catharine Maria Sedgwick: A Dialogue on Race, Culture, and Gender" (*Soft Canons: American Women Writers and Masculine Tradition*, ed. Karen L. Kilcup [Iowa City: Univ. of Iowa Press, 1999] 27–47), Opfermann compares Child, Cooper, and Sedgwick on race, culture, and gender, arguing that even if the three writers had never met, "it seems safe to assume that [they] had read and reacted to each other's texts" (31). Opfermann's article, however, focuses on *Hope Leslie*, *Hobomok*, and the Leatherstocking books, rather than Cooper's and Sedgwick's novels of manners.

10. Ferguson, *The American Enlightenment*, 25.

11. Cynthia S. Jordan, *Second Stories: The Politics of Language, Form, and Gender in Early American Fictions* (Chapel Hill: Univ. of North Carolina Press, 1989), 19–23. Jordan's study, which focuses on specifically republican language, reflects the assumptions about political relationships detailed by recent historians. See note 4.

12. Philip Gould tackles the question of Sedgwick's historicity and revisionism in "Catharine Sedgwick's 'Recital' of the Pequot War" (*American Literature* 66:4 [December 1994]: 641–62). Reprinted in *Covenant and Republic*.

13. Although recent critical readings of *Hope Leslie* have focused, rightly, on race and gender issues, these readings are weighted by late-twentieth-century preoccupations more than they reflect the relative importance of race and gender issues in the early-nineteenth-century political landscape. This is not surprising, given the scarcity of Sedgwick texts. As note 4 indicates, however, few of the recent articles on Sedgwick, even on *Hope Leslie*, have dealt specifically with the question of resistance to legitimate authority. Unfortunately, spatial considerations prevent me from acknowledging critical works not directly relevant to my own interests here.

14. Judith Fetterley, " 'My Sister! My Sister!': The Rhetoric of Catharine Sedgwick's *Hope Leslie*," *American Literature* 70:3 (September 1998): 499–500; included in this volume.

15. Thomas Jefferson, from "A Declaration by the Representatives of the United States of America, in General Congress Assembled." See Giles Gunn, ed., *Early American Writing* (New York: Penguin Books, 1994), 433.

16. Catharine Sedgwick, *The Linwoods; or, "Sixty Years Since" in America,* ed. Maria Karafilis (Hanover, N.H.: University Press of New England, 2002), 18.

17. Wood, *The Radicalism of the American Revolution*, 157.

18. The colonists' struggle with the Pequot Indians began in 1636, when John Endecott led a contingent against them in reprisal for the murder of John Oldham. In 1637, the Pequots began attacking settlements along Long Island Sound. Later that year, Connecticut troops destroyed the main Pequot village, the event that is told—and retold—in *Hope Leslie.*

Meanwhile, back in England, the Civil War was beginning. In 1629 Charles I had dissolved Parliament; the war officially began in 1642. In 1649–50 England was declared a Commonwealth and Cromwell took over. Sedgwick was clearly composing *Hope Leslie* with these contemporaneous events in mind.

19. In colonial New England and the early Republic, women, at least publicly, were valued for their passive acquiescence to the patriarchy. Taking their text from the Apostle Paul, most Americans believed that wives should "submit [them]selves unto [their] husbands, as unto the Lord. For the husband is the head of the wife, even as Christ is the head of the church. . . . Therefore as the church is subject unto Christ, so let the wives be to their own husbands in every thing" (Eph. 6.22–24). Here, as in the relationship of subjects to sovereign, normative family governance is modeled from Christian conceptions of divine governance, with clearly demarcated rankings intended to minimize friction by dictating lines of authority. Women were frequently referred to as "the weaker vessel," a phrase that occurs satirically in scores of women's writings, private and published, during the century.

20. [Catharine Maria Sedgwick], *Redwood: A Tale* (New York: E. Bliss & E. White, 1824), I: 93. Hereafter abbreviated as *R.*

21. Could Henry James have taken the name Isabel Archer from these two independent American women?

22. Ferguson, *The American Enlightenment*, 152.

23. I'm thinking especially of Lilly, in *Redwood,* but black characters play minor roles throughout Sedgwick's work, usually as comic stereotypes.

24. [Catharine Maria Sedgwick], *Clarence; or, A Tale of Our Own Times*, 2 vols. (Philadelphia: Carey and Lea, 1830), II: 197. Hereafter abreviated as *C.*

Chapter 16

Rediscovery

DANA NELSON

I encountered Catharine Maria Sedgwick in graduate school, through two of her works, *Hope Leslie* and a short story called "Old Maids."[1] This reading opened up an imaginative world that countered and complicated the unrelenting if liberally romantic racism of Cooper's Natty Bumppo ("a man without a cross") and the far less liberal racism of frontier writers such as William Gilmore Simms, Robert Montgomery Bird, and Francis Parkman. Some white people in the early nineteenth century could, judging from the popular success of *Hope Leslie*, imagine a world without Indian hating. They could envision, contra Hawthorne's *Scarlet Letter*, a world with strong women who go unpunished, unmarked, unfettered. They could, in the face of everything I'd been taught about the cult of true womanhood, imagine a single life—an unmarried life—for interesting women.

The opening of the canon, the rediscovery project that introduced me to Sedgwick, shaped my critical imagination in its earliest professional moments. I was caught up in the energy of feminist scholars such as the Australian Dale Spender, who wrote books with fabulous titles like *Women of Ideas (and What Men Have Done to Them)* and *Mothers of the Novel: One Hundred Good Women Writers Before Jane Austen*. American feminists such as Joyce Warren, Elaine Showalter, and Deborah McDowell were, like Spender, reprinting women writers and analyzing their importance to American literature. Just as exciting as the newly discovered were the new insights they forced from old texts. I and many others were profoundly motivated by the critical reexaminations of canonical writers that this wave of canon expansion encouraged, in books such as Judith Fetterley's *The Resisting Reader: A Feminist Approach to American Fiction* and Annette Kolodny's *The Lay of the Land: Metaphor as Experience and History in American Life and Letters*, and articles such as Nina Baym's "Melodramas of Beset Manhood: How Theories of American Fiction Exclude Women Authors" and Henry Louis Gates's "Editor's Introduction" to the 1985 *Critical Inquiry* special issue on "'Race,' Writing and Difference."

Rediscovery shook up critical paradigms, and it promised a whole new way to understand not just literary history in the United States, but American history more broadly. Writers had imagined a far wider variety of political expression and social being than I had recognized, and had done it in captivating literary forms that I had been encouraged to ignore. Exploring our literary record more widely and bringing important work back into print meant expanding our notion of literary possibility, democratic vitality, and egalitarian vision in the early United States, broadening our ideas about what had been possible then, and what could be possible now.

How Do You Solve a Problem Like the (1950s) Canon?

The Americanist rediscovery project is now more than a quarter of a century old. What have we learned in over two decades of "rediscovery"—of busting a canon only instantiated some thirty years before the initiation of its counterproject? Quite a bit, judging by the reprint series and the new critical series devoted to analyzing the plethora of new texts and writers that have come under study since the 1970s. When you take the time to look at what has been brought into print since 1985, it's purely breathtaking. It's easy to think that we have the best of the long-overlooked writers and writing back in print, that our proper task now is to celebrate our accomplishment in the abundance of materials we have available.

This volume shows us how wrong that assumption is. In fact, precious little of the work by Sedgwick that scholars analyze in this volume is easily accessible: Up to the time that this volume went to press, only two of Sedgwick's novels were readily available in print: *Hope Leslie* and *A New-England Tale*. A third, *The Linwoods*, only just became available in 2002 and will thus be entirely new and unfamiliar to most Americanists. The reprint of a third Sedgwick novel is quite an achievement—and not just for Sedgwick scholars but for all Americanists: To have a new edition of any unreprinted novel appear, let alone a third novel by a rediscovered writer, is almost surprising these days—it has become a rare event.

Why has recovery slowed to a near halt when there's so much left to do? It's tempting to just blame it on the new obsession with profits that fuels the megaconglomerate publishing industry these days. But is that correct? I'm not sure that it is. Presses print what critics, scholars, and teachers create a critical and pedagogical demand for. If we expect presses to aid us in critical recovery, we need to document that we study, write about, and teach all the materials we bring into print. We don't really need sales figures to show us the way here: MLA citation tallies are illuminating. From my recent survey of the PMLA index, it seems our profession continues to fuel canon logic. According to my figures,[2] when we write about nineteenth-century women authors, we write about, in this order:

1. Emily Dickinson (1538/64)
2. Kate Chopin (471/16)
3. Harriet Beecher Stowe (375/39)
4. Charlotte Perkins Gilman (235/28)
5. Margaret Fuller (220/27)
6. Sarah Orne Jewett (220/5)
7. Harriet Jacobs (124/10)
8. Mary Wilkins Freeman (115/5)
9. Phillis Wheatley (96/4)
10. Rebecca Harding Davis (65/6)

We encounter Frances Ellen Watkins Harper (59/7) at number eleven. Catharine Maria Sedgwick (50/3) and Susan Warner (41/4) come in twelfth and thirteenth. These totals are either laughable or shocking alongside a more recognizably canonical male list:

1. Melville (2839/76)
2. Hawthorne (2173/62)
3. Poe (1879/61)
4. Whitman (1772/63)
5. Thoreau (1345/59)
6. Emerson (1313/58)
7. Cooper (542/12)
8. Irving (294/12)
9. Douglass (211/10)

It takes the most canonical of women writers to break into the top five. If we went by pure numbers for nineteenth-century authors, there would be three white women on the top-ten list, and no black writers at all. The anti-multiculturalist screeds and the rediscovery backlash have worked to divert us from a crucial fact: Rediscovery—so-called canon busting—has not in fact busted the canon. It has hardly slowed it down at all.

Clearly, we need to get better at resisting and interrogating our own trained anxieties that the work of many rediscovered writers does not "stand up" against the Dickinsons, Douglasses, and Melvilles. We cannot learn enough about them to make sophisticated arguments on their behalf until we treat them with the same care and respect we were trained to give Emerson and Melville (can you imagine what the critical consensus around the "transparent eyeball" passage might have been if it had been written by, say, E.D.E.N. Southworth?). These rediscovered texts are not inadequate; our tools for describing them are.

Harriet Wilson's *Our Nig* (which in my unofficial survey comes in at number fourteen on the women's list, at 30/3) makes a productive case in point for arguments about the value of pursuing the time-consuming project of critical analysis. When Henry Louis Gates, one of the most prolific citizens of the recovery project, reprinted *Our Nig* in 1983, he presented it as a literary artifact—the first published novel by an African American woman writer.[3] At first, scholars viewed the novel simply as an autobiographical window into the life of Harriet Wilson, who succeeded at her novelistic project only insofar as she adhered closely to the painful factual details of her life. Early scholars like Gates and Blyden Jackson apologized for the novel's simplicity, "inevitable sentiment," and "stock devices," as well as for the character Frado's false consciousness.[4]

But the novel was incorporated into our courses, even if, as I suspect, we lacked good ideas for teaching it. Critics such as Hazel Carby, Gabrielle Foreman, Harryette Mullen, and Claudia Tate amplified our critical appreciation over the next few years. And now, just less than twenty years after its "recovery," we are witnessing an amazing burst of approaches to *Our Nig*, from the careful biographical excavation of Barbara White, to Eric Gardner's careful reconstruction of the book's circulation, to Cynthia Davis's elegant reading of the way the novel works metonymically to displace cultural stereotypes of black women as sexualized bodies, to Julia Stern's insistence that *Our Nig* offers up so powerful a critique of domestic motherhood that critics have literally been unable to read it as such.[5] Or consider R. J. Ellis's stunningly concise analysis of the narrative's "'two-story' rhetoric": "[R]epeatedly, sentimentalism's characteristic rhetorical hyperbole is deployed when describing the experiences of white characters in the book . . . whereas Frado's experiences recurrently draw on . . . silences and restraints [that] tropically replicate the constrained silences imposed on Frado."[6] It has taken over a decade for the recovery of *Our Nig* to begin really flowering. Just as important as reprinting the physical text was the long and demanding process of learning *how* to read it—registering the challenges it offered to extant critical paradigms and changing our own strategies in order to treat it with the seriousness it deserves.

Harriet Wilson, as far as we know, wrote just one novel, so we can speak confidently about her contributions to antebellum literary, social, and political discourses on the basis of a single text. How much longer might it take adequately to assess the position and contributions of someone like Sedgwick, author of more than ten novels and dozens of short stories, tales, and sketches, in her historical and literary time? Though she was one of the first nineteenth-century women writers recovered in the 1980s, her reputation rests largely—and misleadingly—on a single novel, one that, as Susan Harris points out in this volume, is not characteristic of her larger oeuvre.

The Continuing Work of Rediscovery

How did *Hope Leslie* come to stand for Sedgwick? The initial stages of the rediscovery project were fueled by ethical and political imperatives growing out of the civil rights and feminist activism of the 1960s and 1970s. Recovered writers were heralded because they resisted ruling-class hegemony, like Martin Robinson Delany's *Blake; or, the Huts of America*, like Harriet Ann Jacobs's *Incidents in the Life of a Slave Girl*, or Fanny Fern's *Ruth Hall*. Countering a canon that insisted that art transcended politics, recovery scholars heralded a new canon, one that embraced political struggles and provided readers with strategies for resisting injustice, inequality, and oppression.

Scholars proceeded therefore by concentrating on texts that explicitly addressed injustice. It's no accident that Sedgwick returned to popular critical attention as the author of *Hope Leslie*. This novel, with its spunky, resourceful, and compassionate heroine, spoke powerfully to a white, middle-class feminist project in antebellum America and in the American 1980s. It seemed radical in its openness to Native America, its willingness to make a Native American woman, Magawisca, a co-heroine with its Puritan exemplar, Hope Leslie. But more careful study began to destabilize critical admiration. Indeed, when the scholarly community was reminded that Lydia Maria Child had a falling-out with Sedgwick over her refusal to contribute to an abolitionist gift book, and had, late in life, explicitly condemned Sedgwick for her lack of political resolve on the slavery question, Sedgwick fell somewhat in the ranks of the rediscovery canon.[7]

As critics reassessed their estimation of Sedgwick's politics, *Hope Leslie* remained front and center. Not only was it one of the earliest frontier novels, it stood conveniently alongside *Hobomok*, Child's own early contribution to the genre. Critics now heeded the way its initial cross-racial pairing of heroines eventually narrowed to the single (white) heroine of its title. This new assessment joined in a new wave of scholarship that had begun investigating women writers' complicity with, not resistance to, bad politics. *Hope Leslie* proved useful for such inquiry, as scholars now debated its racial and class politics and Sedgwick's ideological support for white nation-building.[8]

As the recovery project continued developing in the 1990s, though, critics began to interrogate their own expectations for these texts. Lora Romero neatly encapsulated the critical problems that developed from rediscovery's early implicit assumption that literature, like culture, "either frees or enslaves."[9] In our critical desire to counter the transcendent art of the canon, we had embraced an ideal that required recovered artists to stand not just against but above the social and political powers and ideologies of their time: This was an attitude that had fueled both celebratory and reactively critical treatments of recovered authors. As Romero puts it, "[S]tudy of nineteenth-century culture seems to have consistently organized itself around binarisms (dominant/marginal, conservative/countercultural, unconscious/self-reflexive, active/passive)." Romero urged critics to see politics not as a "monolith," but as a web of overlapping, competing, and interconnecting relations. The advantage to such a reconceptualization, she argues, is that "we can better understand the seeming incommensurability of political visions represented in early nineteenth-century texts—and perhaps temper our disappointment when we realize authors have not done the impossible, that is, discovered the one key for the liberation of all humankind."[10]

After an initial stage of recovery, then, fueled by what Romero calls "surplus binary energies" that were valuable for opening up many texts and writers to critical scrutiny but that may have had the unintended effect of flattening the corpus of what was recoverable along with the texture of what was recovered, scholars are now returning to many understudied authors and texts and studying them in new ways.[11] These newer studies, more invested in exploring the nuances of history, the density and porosity of writers' and texts' social embeddedness, and the complexity of personality, are quietly uncovering a wealth of literary engagement, of social and literary impact, and of revealing humanity for our critical project.

The essays in this volume are exemplary of such work. At the same time, they epitomize the very best of the early recovery spirit. As Susan Koppelman observed very early in the recovery project, women and minority writers were habitually misrepresented in twentieth-century anthologies. They tended to be represented by the same short story, stories not characteristic of the larger career of the writer in terms of style, range, or thematic concerns.[12] Recovery critics had set out to remedy such misrepresentation. But despite the amazing energy and corrective aims of that movement, Sedgwick's popular and critical reputation ironically continued trapped in such bad practice, limited largely to readers' interpretations of a single novel, *Hope Leslie*. This volume remedies that, with a range of careful explorations of the full array of Sedgwick's literary production. Essays explore the dynamics of her authorial anonymity and the rhetorical aims of her literary craft; they examine the national implications and (the limits of) political resistance in Sedgwick's work. Other essays examine Sedgwick's understanding of transracial sisterhood, the developing significance of recurring character types, and, going beyond *Hope Leslie*, Sedgwick's personal and authorial relationship to abolition as well as to other social manifestations of otherness such as poverty, insanity, and deviance. Together, these critical essays ably document the range and innovations of Sedgwick's literary craft, political interests, and career. This volume decisively establishes Sedgwick's centrality to our current study of early national literature as it forwards the most important energies of critical rediscovery. May it inspire its readers to more such work!

NOTES

1. Catharine Maria Sedgwick, *Hope Leslie; or, Early Times in the Massachusetts* (New Brunswick, N.J.: Rutgers Univ. Press, 1987); "Old Maids" (1834; reprint, in *Old Maids: Short Stories by Nineteenth-Century U.S. Women Writers*, ed. Susan Koppelman, Boston: Pandora Press, 1984).

2. The first number represents a twenty-seven-year total of MLA database listings of articles on a given author since 1975—what we might think of as the "take-off" date for publications on recovered texts; the second number represents total articles published since 2000—to gauge what has happened recently with these various authors.

3. Harriet Wilson, *Our Nig; or, Sketches from the Life of a Free Black* (1869; reprint, ed. Henry Louis Gates, New York: Oxford Univ. Press, 1983).

4. See Jackson's *A History of Afro-American Literature* (Baton Rouge: Louisiana State Univ. Press, 1989), esp. 360–61.

5. Barbara White, " '*Our Nig*' and the She-Devil: New Information about Harriet Wilson and the 'Bellmont' Family," *American Literature* 65.1 (March 1993): 19–52; Eric Gardner, " 'This Attempt of Their Sister': Harriet Wilson's *Our Nig* from Printer to Readers," *New England Quarterly* 66.2 (June 1993): 226–46; Cynthia Davis, "Speaking the Body's Pain: Harriet Wilson's *Our Nig*," *African American Review* 27.3 (fall 1993): 391–404; Julia Stern, "Excavating Genre in *Our Nig*," *American Literature* 67.3 (September 1995): 439–66.

6. R. J. Ellis, "Body Politics and the Body Politic in William Wells Brown's *Clotel* and Harriet Wilson's *Our Nig*," in *Soft Canons: American Women Writers and Masculine Tradition*, ed. Karen L. Kilcup (Iowa City: Univ. of Iowa Press, 1999), 113; 109.

7. In a letter dated 7 May 1872, Child acknowledges the receipt of Sedgwick's memoirs from her friend Sarah Shaw and promises to read and return the volume, "as it is not the kind of book I care to keep." Elaborating, Child insists that "any person who *apologized* for slavery must be deficient in moral sense" and more specifically charges that Sedgwick, while wishing "well to the Negroes . . . could not bear to *contend* for them, or for anything else. . . . She was very deficient in moral *courage*" (emphasis in original). See Lydia Maria Child, *Selected Letters, 1817–1880*, ed. Milton Meltzer and Patricia G. Holland (Amherst: Univ. of Massachusetts Press, 1982), 506.

8. For a range of debate on this subject, see: Sabina Matter-Seibel, "Native Ameri-

cans, Women and the Culture of Nationalism in Lydia Maria Child and Catharine Maria Sedgwick," in *Early America Re-Explored: New Readings in Colonial, Early National, and Antebellum Culture*, ed. Klaus Schmict and Fritz Fleischman (New York: Peter Lang, 2000); Susanne Opfermann, "Lydia Maria Child, James Fenimore Cooper, and Catharine Maria Sedgwick: A Dialogue on Race, Culture and Gender," in *Soft Canons: American Women Writers and Masculine Tradition* (Iowa City: Univ. of Iowa Press, 1999); Gustavus Stadler, "Magawisca's Body of Knowledge: Nation-Building in *Hope Leslie*," *Yale Journal of Criticism* 12.1 (spring 1999): 41–56; Ezra Tawill, "Domestic Frontier Romance; or, How the Sentimental Heroine Became White," *Novel* 32.1 (fall 1998): 99–124; and Maria Karafilis, "Catharine Maria Sedgwick's *Hope Leslie:* The Crisis between Ethical Political Action and U.S. Literary Nationalism in the New Republic," *American Transcendental Quarterly* 12.4 (December 1998): 327–44.

9. Lora Romero, *Home Fronts: Domesticity and Its Critics in the Antebellum United States* (Durham, N.C.: Duke Univ. Press, 1997), 4.

10. *Ibid.*, 5.

11. *Ibid.*, 110.

12. See, for example, introductions to two of Koppelman's short story anthologies: Susan Koppelman, ed., *The Other Woman: Stories of Two Women and a Man* (Old Westbury, N.Y.: Feminist Press, 1984); *Old Maids: Short Stories by Nineteenth-Century U.S. Women Writers* (Boston: Pandora Press, 1984).

Chronological Bibliography
of the Works of Catharine Maria Sedgwick

LUCINDA L. DAMON-BACH

assisted by ALLISON J. ROEPSCH *and* MELISSA J. HOMESTEAD

This two-part bibliography has been built by consulting the Bibliography of American Literature (BAL) and the bibliographies compiled by Sister Mary Michael Welsh ("Catharine Maria Sedgwick: Her Position in the Literature and Thought of Her Time up to 1860," Ph.D. diss., Catholic University of America, 1937) and Richard Banus Gidez ("A Study of the Works of Catharine Maria Sedgwick," Ph.D. diss., Ohio State University, 1958); library cataloging records; and the personal records of Lucinda Damon-Bach and Melissa J. Homestead. In most cases, entries have been confirmed through books, periodicals, photocopies, or microfilm received through interlibrary loan. We were not able to track down every possible edition (or printing) of each work; foreign editions were especially difficult to acquire. The aim of these two lists is to provide the most comprehensive bibliography to date. We welcome additions and corrections for future editions of this volume.

I. Works Bound Separately
Individually published works bound separately are listed by year, with translations and reprints of each edition gathered under the initial publication of the work, separated by a slash (/). Items are listed in the order in which they appeared within a given year; reprints when known are included to give a sense of the volume's popularity. Page numbers are included for the initial entry only, to give a sense of the book's scope. When known, the byline for each book and in some cases relevant information that appeared on title pages is included. If the title was later changed, the new title is noted; if not, the entry begins with the byline. If the byline is unchanged or unknown, subsequent editions include only publication information. Previously published works revised by Sedgwick for new editions are listed in the year they appeared.

1822
A New-England Tale; or, Sketches of New-England Character and Manners. [Anonymous.] New York: E. Bliss & E. White, 1822. 277 pp.
 A New-England Tale. 2d ed. Revised and corrected by the author. New York: E. Bliss & E. White, 1822. [New preface added.] / Based on 2d American ed. London: John Miller, 1822. ["Miss Sedgwick" on spine.] / *Die-Neu-Englander; oder, Skizzen*

von Charakteren und Sitten in Neu England. Bremen [Germany]: C. Schunemann, 1827. / By Catharine Maria Sedgwick. With a foreword by Cathy N. Davidson. Edited with an Introduction by Victoria Clements. New York: Oxford UP, 1995. / See also 1852.

Mary Hollis. An Original Tale. [Anonymous.] New York: New York Unitarian Book Society, 1822. Printed by Van Pelt and Spear. 22 pp.

2d ed. New York: E. Bliss & E. White, 1822. / By Miss Sedgwick. Concord, N.H.: Union Ministerial Association, 1834.

1824

Redwood; A Tale. [Anonymous.] 2 vols. New York: E. Bliss and E. White, 1824. 565 pp. By the author of "A New England Tale." London: John Miller, and Edinburgh: William Blackwood, 1824. / *Redwood, Roman Americain.* Par M. Cooper Paris: Boulland, 1824. / *Redwood: Ein Amerikanischer Roman.* Von Cooper. Wien, Germany: Kaulfuss und Krammer, 1825. / *Redwood: Nordamerikansk Roman.* Af Cooper. Stockholm, Sweden: G. Scheutz, 1826. / *Redwood: Romanzo Americano.* 2d Italian ed. Di Cooper. Livorno, Italy: Tipografia Vignozzi, 1830. [French, German, Swedish, and Italian versions falsely attributed to James Fenimore Cooper.] / New York: George P. Putnam & Co., 1856. / By Catharine Maria Sedgwick. With a foreword by Edward Halsey Foster. New York: Garrett Press, 1969. / New York: MSS Information Corp., 1972. / See also 1850.

1825

The Travellers. A Tale. Designed for Young People. By the author of "Redwood." New York: E. Bliss and E. White, 1825. 171 pp.

London: Miller, 1825. / Reprinted as "Canadian Travellers." In *Tales For Young People Above Ten Years.* 3 vols. Edited by Mary Russell Mitford. London: Whittaker & Co., 1835.

1826

The Deformed Boy. By the author of "Redwood," &c. Brookfield: E. and G. Merriam, Printers, 1826. 36 pp.

By the author of "Redwood." Springfield: Merriam, Little & Co., 1831. / Collected in *Stories For Young Persons,* 1840, 9–38.

1827

Hope Leslie; or, Early Times in the Massachusetts. By the author of "Redwood." 2 vols. New York: White, Gallaher, and White, 1827. 575 pp.

By the author of "Redwood." London: John Miller, 1828. / *La Jeune Sauvage, ou Les Premières Années de la Province de Massachusetts.* Roman Américain de Miss Sedgwick. Paris: Mame et Delaunay-Vallée, 1828. / By the author of "Redwood." London: H. Colburn and R. Bently, 1830. / *Hope Leslie, oder, Sonstige Zeiten in Massachusetts.* Von Miss Sedgwick. Leipzig: Franz Koehler, 1836. / *Hope Veslie: ou, Vorige*

Tyden in Massachusetts. Deventer [Netherlands]: 1838. / By the author of "The Linwoods," "Poor Rich Man," "Live and Let Live," "Redwood," &c. New York: Harper & Brothers, 1842, 1855, 1862, 1872. / *Hope Leslie.* By Miss Sedgwick. London: G. Routledge, 1850. / By Catharine Maria Sedgwick. Reprint of 1827 ed. With a foreword by Edward Halsey Foster. New York: Garrett Press, 1969. / New York: MSS Information Corp., 1972. / By Catharine Maria Sedgwick. Edited with an Introduction and Notes by Mary Kelley. New Brunswick: Rutgers UP, 1987. / By Catharine Maria Sedgwick. Edited with an Introduction and Notes by Carolyn Karcher. New York: Penguin Classics, 1998.

1828

A Short Essay to Do Good. By the author of "Redwood." Republished from the *Christian Teacher's Manual.* Stockbridge: Webster and Stanley, 1828. 24 pp.

[Includes "Christian Charity," "A Vision," and "Saturday Night."] [Note: Originals not found in *Christian Teacher's Manual.* Vol. 1 [no. 1] ([April] 1828) through no. 6 (September 1828) or vol. 2, no. 1 (November 1828) through no. 2 (December 1828). Boston: Bowles and Dearborn, 1828; Boston: Leonard C. Bowles, 1829. "A Vision" and "Saturday Night" collected in *Stories for Young Persons,* 1840, 142–45 and 146–152. —LDB]

The Sagacity of Dogs. Boston: Marsh & Capen, 1828.

[Note: Originally published as "Dogs" in the *Juvenile Miscellany,* 1828.] Collected in *Stories for Young Persons,* 1840, 153–63.

1830

Clarence; or, A Tale of Our Own Times. By the author of "Hope Leslie." 2 vols. Philadelphia: Carey & Lea, 1830. 588 pp.

London: Henry Colburn and Richard Bentley, 1830. / Collected in *The Novelist: A Collection of the Standard Novels.* London: Foster and Hextall, 1839. / By Miss Sedgwick, Author of "Hope Leslie," &c. Belfast: Simms and M'Intyre, and London: W.S. Orr, 1846. / See also 1849.

1835

Home. By the author of "Redwood," "Hope Leslie," &c. Boston: James Munroe and Company, 1835. 158 pp.

James Munroe and Company reprinted *Home* at least three times in 1835, and in 1837, 1839, 1840 (15th ed.), 1841 ([also labelled] 15th ed.), 1846, 1848 (20th ed.), 1850, 1852, 1854. / New ed. By Miss Sedgwick. New York: T. R. Knox, 1835. / London: Simpkin Marshal, 1836. / By the author of "Redwood," "Hope Leslie," "The Linwoods," &c. Boston: J. Munroe, and New York: G. Dearborn, 1837. / London: Moxon, 1840, and London: Ingram, Cooke, & Co., 1853; both 39 pp. [possibly excerpt]. / *Le Foyer Domestique, ou le Chez-soi.* Guers, [France?]: Mes ve Beroud & Sus, 1842. / Bound with "The H— Family" by Frederika Bremer. London: J. S.

Pratt, 1844. / In Sedgwick's *Select Tales* [includes *Home*, "Wilton Harvey," and miscellaneous tales]. London: James Blackwood, 185–? [1850–59]. / London: William Tegg and Co., and Glasgow: R. Griffen and Co., 18–? / New ed. By Miss Sedgwick. Philadelphia: Davis, Porter & Co., 1865. / New ed. Cambridge, Mass.: J. Wilson & Son, 1875. / New ed. By Miss Sedgwick. New York: J. Miller, 1877. / *Home: A Story of New England Life*. New ed. By Miss Sedgwick. New York: Worthington Co., 1890.

The Linwoods; or, "Sixty Years Since" in America. By the author of "Hope Leslie," "Redwood," &c. 2 vols. New York: Harper & Brothers, 1835. 575 pp.

Reprinted 1836, 1861, 1863, 1873. / By the author of "Hope Leslie," "Redwood," &c. London: Edward Churton, 1835. / *La Famille Américaine; ou, L'Amérique il y a soixante ans*. Par Miss Sedgwick. 2 vols. Paris: A. Pougin, 1837. / By Miss Sedgwick. London: John Cunningham, 1841. [Includes, also attributed to Sedgwick, "The Marriage Blunder. An American Story."] / By Miss Sedgwick. London: Bruce and Wyld, 1844. [Includes "The Marriage Blunder," and "The Jew," by Karl Spindler.] / By Miss Sedgwick. London: J. S. Pratt, 1844.

Tales and Sketches. By Miss Sedgwick, Author of "The Linwoods," "Hope Leslie," &c. &c. Philadelphia: Carey, Lea, and Blanchard, 1835. 285 pp.

[Includes "A Reminiscence of Federalism," "The Catholic Iroquois," "The Country Cousin," "Old Maids," "The Chivalric Sailor," "Mary Dyre," "Cacoethes Scribendi," "The Eldest Sister," "St. Catharine's Eve," "Romance in Real Life," and "The Canary Family"; all had appeared previously in print.]

1836

The Poor Rich Man, and the Rich Poor Man. By the author of "Hope Leslie," "The Linwoods," &c. New York: Harper & Brothers, 1836. 186 pp.

Reprinted 1837, 1838, 1839, 1840, 1841, 1842, 1843, 1847, 1856, 1864, 1872, 1876. / 4th ed. By Miss Sedgwick. London: T. Tegg, 1839; 5th ed. 1842. / *De rige fattige og de fattige rige: en fortaelling for børn*. Bearbeidet efter Miss Sedgwick. Kjobenhavn [Denmark]: C. A. Reitzel, 1841. / By Miss Sedgwick. London: J. S. Pratt, 1845.

1837

Live and Let Live; or, Domestic Service Illustrated. By the author of "Hope Leslie," "The Linwoods," "The Poor Rich Man and the Rich Poor Man," &c. New York: Harper & Brothers, 1837. 216 pp.

Reprinted 1838, 1839, 1840, 1841, 1842, 1844, 1854, 1861, 1876.

A Love Token for Children. Designed for Sunday-School Libraries. By the author of "The Linwoods," "Live and Let Live," "Poor Rich Man," &c. &c. &c. New York: Harper & Brothers, 1837. 142 pp.

[Includes "The Widow Ellis and Her Son Willie," "The Magic Lamp," "Our Robins," "Old Rover," "The Chain of Love," "Mill-Hill," and "The Bantem" [*sic*].] Reprinted 1838, 1839, 1844, 1848, 1860, 1871. / 3d ed. By Miss Sedgwick. London: T. Tegg, 1838; 4th ed., 1839. / By Miss C. M. Sedgwick. London and Edinburgh: T.

Nelson and Sons, 1853, 1883. / [Note: "The Widow Ellis and Her Son Willie" also reprinted separately; see 1845.]

1839

Means and Ends, or Self-Training. By the author of "Redwood," "Hope Leslie," "Home," "Poor Rich Man," &c. Boston: Marsh, Capen, Lyon, & Webb, 1839. 278 pp.
2d and 3d ed. 1839; 4th ed. 1840. / 2d ed. By the author of "Redwood," "Hope Leslie," "Home," "Poor Rich Man," &c. New York: Harpers, 1839, 1842, 1843, 1844, 1845, 1846, 1854, 1860, 1870 [all labeled 2d ed.]. / London: Charles Tilt, 1839.

1840

Stories for Young Persons. By the author of "The Linwoods," "Poor Rich Man," "Love Token," "Live and Let Live," &c. New York: Harper & Brothers, 1840. 185 pp.
[Includes "The Deformed Boy," "Eighteen Hundred Thirty-Eight's Farewell," "Marietza," "Fanny and Her Dog Neptune," "Skepticism," "Ella," "Small Losses," "Spring in the City," "A Vision," "Saturday Night," "Dogs," and "Jacot; An Adventure on Board the St. George."]
Reprinted 1841, 1842, 1846, 1852, 1855, 1860. / By the author of "The Linwoods," "Poor Rich Man," "Love Token," "Live and Let Live," &c. London: W. Smith, [184–?].

1841

Letters from Abroad to Kindred at Home. By Miss Sedgwick. 2 vols. London: E. Moxon, 1841. 572 pp.
By the author of "Hope Leslie," "Poor Rich Man and the Rich Poor Man," "Live and Let Live," &c. New York: Harper & Brothers, 1841, 1855, 1871.

1844

Tales and Sketches, Second Series. Binder's title: *Wilton Harvey and Other Tales.* By the Author of "Hope Leslie," "Home", "Letters from Abroad," &c. New York: Harper & Brothers, 1844. 396 pp.
[Includes "Wilton Harvey," "Cousin Frank," "A Day in a Railroad Car," "The Irish Girl," "Daniel Prime," "A Huguenot Family," "The Post Office," "A Vision," "Second Thoughts Best," and "Our Burial Place"; all had appeared previously in print. Note: "A Vision" is different from the story by the same name collected in *A Short Essay to Do Good* and *Stories for Young Persons*.]
Reprinted 1855, 1858. / See also 1850.

1845

The Widow Ellis and Her Son Willie. The Christian Tract Society, London: J. Chapman, 1845. [Reprint; see 1838.]

1846

The Morals of Manners; or, Hints for Our Young People. By Miss Sedgwick, author of
"Home;" "Poor Rich Man;" &c. New York: Wiley and Putnam, 1846. 63 pp.
Reprinted in 1847. / New ed., revised. By Miss Sedgwick. New York: G. P. Putnam & Co., 1854, 1857. [New preface added: "To Parents and Teachers."] / Revised
ed. New York: James Miller, 1864.

1847

The Boy of Mt. Rhigi. By the author of "Redwood," "Poor Rich Man," "Home," &c.
Boston: Crosby and H. P. Nichols, 1847. 252 pp.
Reprinted 1849, 1850, 1851, 1854, 1857, 1862. / By the author of "Redwood," "Poor
Rich Man," "Home," &c. Boston: Charles H. Peirce, 1848.

1848

Facts and Fancies for School-day Reading, a Sequel to "Morals of Manners." By Miss
Sedgwick. New York, London: Wiley & Putnam, 1848. 216 pp.
[Includes "Reverence the Temple of God," "Respect Your Elders," "Personal Clean-
liness," "Disagreeable Habits," "Small Faults," "Gentle Voices," "Order," "A Filthy
Habit," "Borrowing," "Mine and Thine," "Public Squares," "Reading Aloud,"
"Honor all Men," "Self Education," "Winning Souls," and "Self-Teaching."]
New York: G. P. Putnam's Sons, 1856, 1873. / 2d ed. London: George P. Putnam,
1849. / *Facts and Fancies and Other Stories.* By Miss Sedgwick. New York: James
Miller, 1856, 1864. Bound with *Morals of Manners; or, Hints for Our Young People.*

1849

Clarence; or, A Tale of Our Own Times. Author's Revised Edition. By C. M. Sedgwick.
New York: George P. Putnam, and London: David Bogue, 1849. 515 pp.
["C. M. Sedgwick's Works" on spine; new preface added.] Philadelphia: Carey &
Lea, 1849, 1852. / Boston: Phillips, Sampson, & Co., and New York: J. C. Derby,
1854. / New York: G. P. Putnam, 1856.

1850

Redwood: A Tale. By the author of "Hope Leslie," &c. Author's Revised Edition. New
York: George P. Putnam, 1850. 457 pp.
["C. M. Sedgwick's Works" on spine; new preface added; no other changes.
—LDB]
Tales of City Life. By Catharine M. Sedgwick. Philadelphia: Hazard and Mitchell, 1850.
91 pp.
[Includes "The City Clerk" and "Life is Sweet"; both previously published.]
The City Clerk and His Sister; and Other Stories. Philadelphia: Willis P. Hazard, 1851,
1853. / *Charlie Hathaway; or, The City Clerk and His Sister; and Other Stories.* New
York: [unknown], 1869.
The Irish Girl, and Other Tales. By Miss Sedgwick, Author of "Hope Leslie," "Home,"

"Wilton Harvey," etc., etc. London: Kent & Richards, and Edinburgh: J. Menzies, 1850. 138 pp.

[Includes "The Irish Girl," "A Day in a Railroad Car," "A Huguenot Family," "Daniel Prime," and "A Vision"; all previously published.]

London: Slater, 1850. / London: Thomas Allman, 1853.

1852

A New-England Tale and Miscellanies. By Catherine M. Sedgwick [*sic*], Author of "Hope Leslie," "Redwood," "Clarence," Etc., Etc. Revised ed. New York: George P. Putnam & Company, 1852. 388 pp.

[Includes "A Berkshire Tradition," "The White Scarf," and "Fanny McDermot." Reprints prefaces to first and second editions, followed by a new preface.] Reprinted 1853, 1856. / New York: J. C. Derby, 1854.

1853

Pleasant Words: Being Pretty Little Stories . . . London: George Routledge and Co., 1853.
[Not seen; BAL #17411 states that this is a reprint. —LDB]

1857

Married or Single? Author's edition. By Miss Sedgwick. London: Knight and Son, 1857. 440 pp.

By the author of "Hope Leslie," "Redwood," "Home," &c. 2 vols. New York: Harper & Brothers, 1857, 1858. [545 pp. London typeface smaller. —LDB]

1858

Memoir of Joseph Curtis, A Model Man. By the author of "Means and Ends." New York: Harper & Brothers, 1858. 200 pp.

Reprinted 1871.

1867

Mary Dyre. [No publisher, no date; not before 1867. Reprinted from *The Token*, 1831. Collected in *Tales and Sketches*, 1835. See BAL #17426. Gidez notes reprinted in "hard covers" 1890; no publication information provided. —LDB]

1871

Life and Letters of Catharine M. Sedgwick. Edited by Mary E. Dewey. New York: Harper & Brothers, 1871. 446 pp.

1993

The Power of Her Sympathy: The Autobiography and Journal of Catharine Maria Sedgwick. Edited and with an Introduction by Mary Kelley. Boston: Massachusetts Historical Society, 1993. 165 pp.

II. Works Originally Published in Periodicals and Anthologies

Stories, sketches, and other works originally published in periodicals, gift books, annuals, or other edited volumes are listed according to the first known date of publication. This list does not include works originally published in Sedgwick's own collections; see part I for additional works. Reprints and collections are listed under the initial publication, separated by a slash (/). When known, the byline provided for the original appearance of an item is included. The name of the editor for the magazine or annual in which the work was first published is also provided when known, to give a sense of Sedgwick's publishing network. (We rarely include the names of editors of volumes in which reprints appeared, as it is less likely that Sedgwick negotiated such publications.)

1825

"The Catholic Iroquois." By the Author of "Redwood." In *The Atlantic Souvenir*, 72–103. Philadelphia: H. C. Carey & I. Lea, 1826 [pub. 1825].

> Collected in *Stories of American Life*, vol. 3, edited by Mary Russell Mitford, 1–32. London: Henry Colburn and Richard Bentley, 1830. / Collected in *Tales and Sketches*, 45–66, 1835.

1826

"Modern Chivalry." By the author of Redwood. In *The Atlantic Souvenir*, 5–47. Philadelphia: H. C. Carey & I. Lea, 1827 [pub. 1826].

> Reprinted in *New-York Mirror* [edited by Horace Greeley] (25 November 1826): 137–39. / Collected in *Lights and Shadows of American Life*, vol. 3, edited by Mary Russell Mitford, 226–73. London: H. Colburn and R. Bentley, 1832. / Collected as "The Chivalric Sailor" in *Tales and Sketches*, 117–149, 1835.

1827

"Saturday Night." By Stockbridge S. *Juvenile Miscellany* [edited by Lydia M. Child] (January 1827): 31–39.

> Collected in *A Short Essay to Do Good*, 18–24, 1828. Collected in *Stories For Young Persons*, 146–52, 1840.

"A New England Sabbath." By Miss Sedgwick. *The Casket* (1827): 412–13.

> [This is an excerpt from the opening of *Hope Leslie*, vol. 1, ch. 12.] Collected as "The Sabbath in New England" in *Female Prose Writers*, edited by John S. Hart, 24–25. Philadelphia: E. H. Butler & Co., 1864, 1866.

"Romance in Real Life." By the Author of "Redwood." In *The Legendary*, edited by N[athaniel] P[arker] Willis, 118–61. Boston: Samuel G. Goodrich, 1828 [pub. 1827]. Reprinted in *The Garland*, 198–264. Boston: 1839. / Reprinted in *The Diadem*, 236. New York: 1850. / Collected in *Tales and Sketches*, 237–78, 1835.

1828

"Dogs." By Stockbridge S. *Juvenile Miscellany* [edited by Lydia M. Child] (March 1828): 31–43.

Reprinted as *The Sagacity of Dogs*. Boston: Marsh & Capen, 1828. Collected in *Stories For Young Persons*, 153–63, 1840.

"Some Passages in the Life of an Old Maid." [Anonymous.] In *The Token* [edited by Samuel G. Goodrich], 259–78. Boston: S. G. Goodrich, 1828 [pub. 1827].
[The BAL attributes this anonymous piece to CMS based on a penciled annotation on a copy at the Boston Atheneum. —MJH. Stylistically, seems unlikely; very different from the 1833 story "Old Maids." —LDB]

1829

"The Good Son." By Stockbridge S. *Juvenile Miscellany* [edited by Lydia M. Child] (January 1829): 217–29.

"Mary Smith." By Stockbridge S. *Juvenile Miscellany* [edited by Lydia M. Child] (May 1829): 110–34.

"Scene at Niagara." *Youth's Instructor and Sabbath School and Bible Class* (June 1829): 39.

"Cacoethes Scribendi." By the author of "Hope Leslie." In *The Atlantic Souvenir*, 17–38. Philadelphia: Carey, Lea, & Lea, 1830 [pub. 1829].
Collected in *Stories of American Life*, vol. 3, edited by Mary Russell Mitford, 162–86. London: H. Colburn and R. Bentley, 1830. / Collected in *Tales and Sketches*, 165–81, 1835. / Collected in *Provisions: A Reader from 19th-Century American Women,* edited with an Introduction and Critical Commentary by Judith Fetterley, 49–59. Bloomington: Indiana UP, 1985. / Collected in *The Norton Anthology of American Literature*, vol. 1, edited by Nina Baym, 1007–17. New York: W. W. Norton & Co., 1998.

"The Country Cousin." By the author of "Hope Leslie." In *The Token*, edited by S[amuel] G. Goodrich, 153–93. Boston: Carter & Hendee, 1830 [pub. 1829].
Collected in *Stories of American Life*, vol. 1, edited by Mary Russell Mitford, 97–140. London: H. Colburn and R. Bentley, 1830. / Collected in *Tales and Sketches*, 67–96, 1835.

"The Elder Sister." By the author of "Hope Leslie." In *The Youth's Keepsake*, 99–126. Boston: Carter and Hendee, 1830 [pub. 1829].
Collected as "The Eldest Sister" in *Tales and Sketches*, 183–203, 1835.

1830

"The Canary Family." By the author of "Hope Leslie." In *The Youth's Keepsake*, 118–27. Boston: Carter and Hendee, 1831 [pub. 1830].
Collected in *Tales and Sketches*, 279–85. Philadelphia: Carey, Lea, and Blanchard, 1835.

"Mary Dyre." By Miss Sedgwick. In *The Token*, edited by S[amuel] G. Goodrich, 294–312. Boston: Gray and Bowen, 1831 [pub. 1830].
Collected in *Tales and Sketches*, 151–64, 1835. [Note: According to BAL #17426, also reprinted separately "not before 1867"; according to Gidez, also reprinted "in hard covers, 1890." —LDB]

"A Story of Shay's War." By the author of "Hope Leslie." In *The Atlantic Souvenir*, 281–313. Philadelphia: Carey and Lea, 1831 [pub. 1830].

Reprinted in *Boston Pearl and Literary Gazette* (1835): 301–4.

1831

"Berkeley Jail." By the author of "Hope Leslie." In *The Atlantic Souvenir*, 13–53. Philadelphia: Carey and Lea, 1832 [pub. 1831].

"A Sketch of a Blue Stocking." By Miss Sedgwick. In *The Token*, edited by S[amuel] G. Goodrich, 334–46. Boston: Gray & Bowen, 1832 [pub. 1831].

1832

"Spring in the City." By Miss Sedgwick. *Juvenile Miscellany* [edited by Lydia M. Child] (May and June 1832): 111–34. Collected in *Stories for Young Persons*, 125–41, 1840.

"The Bridal Ring." By Miss Sedgwick. In *The Token and Atlantic Souvenir*, edited by S[amuel] G. Goodrich, 223–46. Boston: Gray and Bowen, 1833 [pub. 1832].

"Le Bossu." In *Tales of Glauber-Spa*, by Several American Authors [J. K. Paulding, William Cullen Bryant, R. C. Sands, William Leggett, and Sedgwick all appear anonymously], vol. 1, [edited by William Cullen Bryant], 25–108. New York: J. & J. Harper, 1832.

Book reprinted 1844, 1856. / Book reprinted (1832 edition) New York: Garrett Press, 1969. / Book reprinted as *Childe Roeliff's Pilgrimage and Other Tales*, by Several American Authors. London: A. K. Newman, 1834.

1833

"Country Pleasures." By Miss Sedgwick. *Juvenile Miscellany* [edited by Lydia M. Child] (March and April 1833): 73–97.

"West Point." By Miss Sedgwick. *Juvenile Miscellany* [edited by Lydia M. Child] (November and December 1833): 237–45.

"Old Maids." By Miss Sedgwick. In *The Offering*, 17–46. Philadelphia: Thomas T. Ash, 1834 [pub. 1833].

Annual reissued as *The Wreath of Friendship*. Philadelphia: 1837. / Story reprinted in *The Casket* (March 1834): 137–39. / Collected in *Tales and Sketches*, 97–116, 1835. / Collected in *Old Maids: Short Stories by Nineteenth-Century U.S. Women Writers*, edited by Susan Koppelman, 11–26. Boston: Pandora Press, 1984.

"A Reminiscence of Federalism." By Miss Sedgwick. In *The Token*, edited by S[amuel] G. Goodrich, 102–43. Boston: Charles Bowen, 1834 [pub. 1833].

Collected in *Tales and Sketches*, 9–43, 1835. / Collected in *The Norton Anthology of American Literature*, vol. 1, edited by Nina Baym, 1017–38. New York: W. W. Norton & Co., 1998. / See also http://www.salemstate.edu/imc/sedgwick/federalism.html

1834

"Ella." By Miss Sedgwick. *Juvenile Miscellany* [edited by Lydia M. Child] (March and April 1834): 11–35.

Collected in *Stories for Young Persons*, 95–112, 1840.

"St. Catharine's Eve." By Miss Sedgwick. In *The Token and Atlantic Souvenir*, edited by
S[amuel] G. Goodrich, 7–36. Boston: Charles Bowen, 1835 [pub. 1834].
Collected in *Tales and Sketches*, 205–35, 1835.

1835

"Our Burial Place." By the author of "Redwood," "Hope Leslie," "The Linwoods," etc.
Knickerbocker [edited by Lewis Gaylord Clark] (November 1835): 388–92.
Collected in *Tales and Sketches*, Second Series, 385–96, 1844. / See also http:
//www.salemstate.edu/imc/sedgwick/burial.html

"Amy Cranstoun." By the author of "Redwood" and "Hope Leslie." In *The Magnolia*,
edited by Henry W. Herbert, 145–76. New York, 1836 [pub. 1835].
Volume reissued as *The Snow Flake*, 145–76. New York, 1853.

"New Year's Day." By Miss Sedgwick. In *The Token and Atlantic Souvenir*, edited by
S[amuel] G. Goodrich, 11–31. Boston: Charles Bowen, 1836 [pub. 1835].

"The Unpresuming Mr. Hudson." By Miss Sedgwick. In *The Gift*, edited by [Eliza]
Leslie, 17–38. Philadelphia: E. L. Carey & A. Hart, 1836 [pub. 1835].

1836

"Daniel Prime." By the author of "Redwood," "Hope Leslie," "The Linwoods," &c. In
The Magnolia, edited by Henry William Herbert, 281–311. New York: Bancroft &
Holley, 1837 [pub. 1836].
Collected in *Tales and Sketches*, Second Series, 215–48, 1844. / Collected in *The Irish
Girl and Other Tales*, 95–128, 1850.

"An Unsolved Riddle." By the author of "Redwood," "Hope Leslie," "The Linwoods," &c. In *The Magnolia*, edited by Henry William Herbert, 131–44. New
York: Bancroft & Holley, 1837 [pub. 1836].

"Full Thirty." By Miss Sedgewick [*sic*]. In *The Token and Atlantic Souvenir*, edited by
S[amuel] G. Goodrich, 212–46. Boston: Charles Bowen, 1837 [pub. 1836].

"Uncle David." By Miss Sedgwick. In *The Pearl; or, Affection's Gift*, 17–37. Philadelphia:
Thomas T. Ash & Henry F. Anners, 1837 [pub. 1836].

My Prisons, Memoirs of Silvio Pellico of Saluzzo. 2 vols. Edited by Andrews Norton.
Cambridge: Charles Folsom, 1836. The following pieces were translated by Sedgwick: "Notices of Italian History . . . ," vol. 2, 131–44; "The Conciliatore . . . ," vol.
2, 145–218; "Fate of Individuals Connected with the Conciliatore . . . ," vol. 2,
219–29. [See BAL 17370.]

1837

"Who, and What, Has Not Failed." By Miss C. M. Sedgwick. *New-Yorker* (17 June
1837): 199. [This piece takes the form of a letter, "To the Editors of the Metropolitan," dated "May 1837, New York"; the original of this reprinted item has not been
located. —MJH, LDB]

"Our Village Post Office." By Miss Sedgwick. In *The Token and Atlantic Souvenir*, edited by S[amuel] G. Goodrich, 164–84. Boston: American Stationers' Company, 1838 [pub. 1837].

> Reprinted as "The Village Post Office" in *New-Yorker* (4 November 1837): 514–16.

"A Memoir of Lucretia Maria Davidson." By the Author of "Redwood," "Hope Leslie," &c. &c. In *Lives of Sir William Phips, Israel Putnam, Lucretia Maria Davidson, and David Rittenhouse*, 219–94. Boston: Hilliard, Gray, and Co., and London: Richard James Kennett, 1837. Vol. 7 of *Library of American Biography*, edited by Jared Sparks.

> Reprinted by Harper & Brothers, 1848, 1856, 1902. / Revised as "Biography of Lucretia Maria Davidson," by Miss Sedgwick. In *Poetical Remains of the Late Lucretia Maria Davidson, Collected and Arranged by Her Mother*, 33–91. Philadelphia: Lea and Blanchard, 1841. / Corrected and revised edition of book published by Lea and Blanchard in 1843; reprinted in 1845, 1846, 1847, 1849. / London: Tilt, 1843. / New York: Clark, Austin, 1850, 1851, 1852, 1854. / Boston: Phillips, Samson, 1854, 1855, 1857. / Boston: Crosby, Nichols, Lee, 1860, 1864. / By Miss Sedgwick. In Lucretia Maria Davidson, *Poems*, 223–68. New York: Hurd and Houghton, 1871. / *Leben der Lucretia Maria Davidson*. Aus dem Englischen der Catherine Mary Sedgwick [*sic*]. Leipzig: Brockhaus, 1848.

1838

"Leisure Hours at Saratoga." By the author of "Hope Leslie" &c. *United States Magazine and Democratic Review* [edited by John L. O'Sullivan] (January 1838): 199–203.

"Our Robins." By Miss Sedgwick. *Southern Literary Messenger* [edited by T. H. White] (May 1838): 318–21.

> [Reprinted from *A Love Token for Children*. New York: Harper & Brothers, 1838.—LDB]

"Passages from a Journal at Rockaway." By Miss C. M. Sedgwick. *Southern Literary Messenger* [edited by T. H. White] (September 1838): 573–75.

> Reprinted in *New-Yorker* (8 September 1838): 386–87.

"Country Life." By Miss C. M. Sedgwick. In *The Religious Souvenir*, edited by L[ydia] H[oward] Sigourney, 26–48. New York: Scofield & Voorhies, 1839 [pub. 1838].

> Annual reprinted as *The Religious Souvenir* and *The Religious Keepsake*. Hartford, Conn.: S. Andrus and Son, 1845 and 1846.

"The White Scarf." By Miss Sedgwick. In *The Token*, edited by S[amuel] G. Goodrich, 1–62. Boston: Otis, Broaders and Company, 1839 [pub. 1838].

> Collected in *A New England Tale and Miscellanies*, 295–334, 1852.

1839

"The Falls of Bash-Pish, or The Eagle's Nest." *Southern Literary Messenger* [edited by T. H. White] (January 1839): 34–39. / By Miss C. M. Sedgwick. *New-Yorker* (26 January 1839): 290–93.

> [Note: The *New-Yorker*'s attribution may be incorrect. The piece was published

anonymously in the *Southern Literary Messenger*, prefaced with a letter from someone claiming to be a resident of the Berkshires. —MJH]

"Matty Gore." By Miss C. E. Sedgwick [*sic*]. *The Religious Souvenir*, edited by L[ydia] H[oward] Sigourney, 50–90. New York: Scofield & Voorhies, 1840 [pub. 1839]. Annual reissued as *The Religious Souvenir*. Hartford, Conn.: S. Andrus and Son, 1846.

"Second Thoughts Best." By Miss Sedgwick. In *The Token*, edited by S[amuel] G. Goodrich, 201–58. Boston: Otis, Broaders, & Company, 1840 [pub. 1839]. Volume reissued as *The Moss Rose*. New York: 1846; and as *The Honeysuckle*. New York: 1848. / Story reprinted in *New-Yorker* (31 August and 14 September 1839): 386–88 and 406–8.

1840

"The Beauty of Soninberg. A Letter from Wiesbaden." By Miss Catharine M. Sedgwick, Author of "Hope Leslie" &c. *The Evergreen* (May 1840): 234–37. [This is a pre-publication excerpt from *Letters from Abroad* (1841). —MJH]

"Lucy Wendal." By Miss Sedgwick. *Pittsfield Sun* [Pittsfield, Mass.] (16 September 1840): 1. Reprinted as "A Tale of Real Life" in *The Talisman, an Offering of Friendship* 67–75. Philadelphia: Hogan & Thompson, 1852 [pub. 1851]. [The appearance of this story in the *Pittsfield Sun* during CMS's trip to Europe is almost certainly not the first appearance of this story, but the original appearance has not been located. —MJH]

1841

"English Literary Men." By Miss Sedgwick. *New-Yorker* (10 July 1841): 259–60. [This is an excerpt from *Letters From Abroad* (1841).]

"The Ballet: An American Lady's Opinion of the Opera." By Miss Sedgwick. *New-Yorker* (14 August 1841): 341. [This is an excerpt from *Letters from Abroad* (1841).]

"A Voyage Across The Atlantic." By the author of "Hope Leslie" &c. *United States Magazine and Democratic Review* [edited by John L. O'Sullivan] (September 1841): 236–49. By Miss Sedgwick. In *New-Yorker* (14 September 1841): 391–92. [This is a letter from CMS's European voyage that was not included in *Letters from Abroad* (1841).—LDB]

"Wilton Harvey." By Miss C. M. Sedgwick. *Godey's Lady's Book* [edited by Sarah Josepha Hale] (January to June 1842): 12–18, 76–83, 122–26, 215–19, 242–46, 326–31. Collected in *Tales and Sketches*, Second Series, 9–162, 1844.

"Miss Burdett Coutts." *New-York Mirror* [edited by Horace Greeley] (February 1842): 70. Reprinted in *Brother Jonathan* (3 June 1843): 143. [This is an excerpt from *Letters From Abroad* (1841).]

"The Irish Girl." By the Author of "Hope Leslie," &c. *United States Magazine and Democratic Review* [edited by John L. O'Sullivan] (February 1842): 129–40.

By Miss Sedgwick, the author of "Hope Leslie." In *The Dollar Magazine* (March 1842): 85–87. / Collected in *Tales and Sketches*, Second Series, 191–244, 1844. / Collected in *The Irish Girl and Other Tales*, 9–32, 1850.

"A Day in a Railroad Car." By Miss C. M. Sedgwick. *Godey's Lady's Book* [edited by Sarah Josepha Hale] (July 1842): 51–55.

Collected in *Tales and Sketches*, Second Series, 169–89, 1844. / Collected in *The Irish Girl and Other Tales*, 33–94, 1850.

"A Vision." By Miss C. M. Sedgwick. *Godey's Lady's Book* [edited by Sarah Josepha Hale] (August 1842): 97–99.

Collected in *Tales and Sketches*, Second Series, 321–30, 1844. / Collected in *The Irish Girl and Other Tales*, 129–38, 1850. [Note: This is not the same story that appeared (with the same name) in *A Short Essay to Do Good* (1828), or *Stories for Young Persons* (1840).—LDB]

"A Huguenot Family." By Miss C. M. Sedgwick. *Godey's Lady's Book* [edited by Sarah Josepha Hale] (September and October 1842): 144–48 and 189–93.

Collected in *Tales and Sketches*, Second Series, 249–89. New York: Harper & Bros., 1844. / Collected in *The Irish Girl and Other Tales*, 54–94, 1850.

1843

"A Sketch." By Miss C. M. Sedgwick. *Godey's Lady's Book* [edited by Sarah Josepha Hale] (January 1843): 19–21.

"Scenes from Life in Town." By Miss C. M. Sedgwick. *Godey's Lady's Book* [edited by Sarah Josepha Hale] (April 1843): 159–63.

"Cousin Frank." By Miss Sedgwick. *United States Magazine and Democratic Review* [edited by John L. O'Sullivan] (May 1843): 512–13.

Reprinted in *New World* (6 May 1843): 537–38. / Collected in *Tales and Sketches*, Second Series, 163–68, 1844.

"Society." By Miss C. M. Sedgwick. *Ladies' Companion* [edited by William W. Snowden] (June 1843): 93–94.

Reprinted in *Brother Jonathan* (3 June 1843): 145.

"The Post Office." By Miss Sedgwick. *Graham's Magazine* [edited by George R. Graham and Rufus Griswold] (August 1843): 61–67.

[Listed in the table of contents and index with the subtitle "An Irish Story."] Reprinted in *Tales and Sketches*, Second Series, 291–319. New York: Harper & Brothers, 1844. [This story is distinct from "Our Village Post Office," first published in 1837. —MJH, LDB]

"Dedicatory Letter." By Catharine Maria Sedgwick. In *Memorials Written on Several Occasions During the Illness and After the Decease of the Three Little Boys. By Those Who Loved Them*, 41. New York: Eleazar Parmly, 1843.

"Preface." By Catharine M. Sedgwick. In *Selections from the Writings of Mrs. Margaret M. Davidson*, xi. Philadelphia: Lea & Blanchard, 1843.

1844

"A Contrast." By Miss Sedgwick. *Graham's Magazine* [edited by George R. Graham] (January 1844): 15–18.

"New York Fountains and Astor Baths." By Miss Catharine M. Sedgwick. *Graham's Magazine* [edited by George R. Graham] (March 1844): 123–25.

"Berkshire." By Catharine M. Sedgwick, Author of "Hope Leslie" &c. *Graham's Magazine* [edited by George R. Graham] (July 1844): 6–9.
[This sketch is distinct from the one collected in *A New England Tale and Miscellanies* as "A Berkshire Tradition." —MJH]

"The College Boy." By Miss C. M. Sedgwick. *Godey's Lady's Book* [edited by Sarah Josepha Hale] (July and August 1844): 27–31 and 115–19.

"The Magic Lamp." In *The Jewel*, edited by Emma F. Alston, 35–41. New York, 1844. Reprinted from *A Love Token for Children*, 34–39, 1837. [Note: Not seen. This may be a wholesale reprint of an 1837 annual, which means that the annual publication could have preceded the story's publication in *Love Token*. —MJH]

"Suzie's Cow." By Miss C. M. Sedgwick. In *Boys & Girls Library*, edited by Mrs. Colman, 1–6. Boston: T. H. Carter & Co., and Cincinnati: U. P. James [BAL #17391 dates this c. 1844]. Also in *The Boys' and Girls' Annual*. Boston: T. H. Carter and Company, n.d.

1845

"Fanny McDermot." By Miss C. M. Sedgwick. *Godey's Lady's Book* [edited by Sarah Josepha Hale] (January and February 1845): 13–20 and 75–83.
Collected in *A New England Tale and Miscellanies*, 355–88. New York: George P. Putnam & Co., 1852. / Collected in *Rediscoveries: American Short Stories by Women, 1832–1916*, edited by Barbara H. Solomon, 113–54. New York: Mentor, 1994.

"An Incident at Rome." By Miss C. M. Sedgwick. *Graham's Magazine* [edited by George R. Graham] (March 1845): 104–8.

"The Last Chapter of the Chronicles of the Berkshire Jubilee." By Catharine M. Sedgwick. In *The Berkshire Jubilee, Celebrated at Pittsfield, Mass. August 22 and 23, 1844*, 225–30. Albany [N.Y.]: Weare C. Little [copyright E. P. Little, Pittsfield [Mass.], 1845.

1846

"Look Before You Leap." By Miss Catharine M. Sedgwick. *Columbian Lady's and Gentleman's Magazine* [edited by John Inman and Robert A. West] (January 1846): 13–17.
Collected in *The Irving Offering*, 168–86. New York: Leavitt & Company, 1851 [pub. 1850].

"New-Year's Day." By Miss Catharine M. Sedgwick. *Columbian Lady's and Gentleman's Magazine* [edited by John Inman and Robert A. West] (February 1846): 83–89.
[This sketch is distinct from the one published in 1835 under the same title.—LDB]
Collected in *The Gem of the Season for 1849*, 11–35. New York: Leavitt, Trow & Co., 1849 [pub. 1848]. / Annual [*Gem*] reprinted as *The Gallery of Mezzotints . . . for 1850*. New York, 1850.

"The Patch Work Quilt." By Miss C. M. Sedgwick. *Columbian Lady's and Gentleman's Magazine* [edited by John Inman and Robert A. West] (March 1846): 123–26.

"The Little Mendicants." By Miss C. M. Sedgwick. *Columbian Lady's and Gentleman's Magazine* [edited by John Inman and Robert A. West] (April 1846): 181–84.

"Imelda of Bologna." By Miss Catharine M. Sedgwick. *Columbian Lady's and Gentleman's Magazine* [edited by John Inman and Robert A. West] (May 1846): 253–61.

"Varieties of Social Life in New York." By Miss Catharine M. Sedgwick. *Columbian Lady's and Gentleman's Magazine* [edited by John Inman and Robert A. West] (July 1846): 13–16.

> Collected in *The Gem of the Season for 1849*, 105–18. New York: Leavitt, Trow & Co., 1849 [pub. 1848]. / Annual [*Gem*] reprinted as *The Gallery of Mezzotints . . . for 1850*. New York, 1850.

"An Auction Sale." By Miss Catharine M. Sedgwick. *Columbian Lady's and Gentleman's Magazine* [edited by John Inman and Robert A. West] (September 1846): 126–28.

"Was it Providence?" By Miss Sedgwick. In *The Mayflower*, [edited by Elizabeth Oakes Smith], 278–80. Boston: Saxton & Kelt, 1847 [pub. 1846].

1847

"The City Clerk." By Miss Catharine M. Sedgwick. *Sartain's Union Magazine* [edited by Caroline M. Kirkland] (July 1847): 35–44.

> Collected in *Tales of City Life*. Philadelphia: Hazard & Mitchell, 1850. / Collected in *The City Clerk and His Sister: and Other Stories*. Philadelphia: W. P. Hazard, 1851. / Collected in *Charlie Hathaway; or, The City Clerk and His Sister*, as part of "Uncle John's Library." New York: Allen Brothers, 1869.

"An Excursion to Manchester." By Miss Catharine M. Sedgwick. *Sartain's Union Magazine* [edited by Caroline M. Kirkland] (September 1847): 111–13.

"Crescent Beach." By Miss Catharine M. Sedgwick. *Sartain's Union Magazine* [edited by Caroline M. Kirkland] (November 1847): 212–19.

"An Apologue." By Miss Catharine M. Sedgwick. *Sartain's Union Magazine* [edited by Caroline M. Kirkland] (December 1847): 247–48.

"Widowhood." By Miss Sedgwick. In *The Mirror of Life*, edited by L[ouisa] C. Tuthill, 165–74. Philadelphia: Lindsay and Blakiston, [1847].

1848

"Straggling Extracts from a Journal Kept in Switzerland." By Miss Catharine M. Sedgwick. *Sartain's Union Magazine* [edited by Caroline M. Kirkland] (March 1848): 115–21.

"Life is Sweet." By Miss Catharine M. Sedgwick. *Sartain's Union Magazine* [edited by Caroline M. Kirkland] (August 1848): 94–95.

> Collected in *Tales of City Life*. Philadelphia: Hazard & Mitchell, 1850. / Collected in *The Gem of the Season*, edited by N[athaniel] P[arker] Willis, 219–22. New York, 1850 [pub. 1849]. / Collected in *The Thought Blossom*, edited by N[athaniel] P[arker]

Willis, 208–11. New York: Leavitt and Allen, 1855. / Collected in *Charlie Hathaway; or, The City Clerk and His Sister; and Other Stories.* New York, 1869.

"A Tale with a Moral." *Pittsfield Sun* [Pittsfield, Mass.] (9 November 1848): 1. [Attribution per Gidez.]

1849

"Rural Life." By Miss C. M. Sedgwick. *American Metropolitan Magazine* (January 1849): 12–16.

"The First Love." By Miss C. M. Sedgwick. *Sartain's Union Magazine* [edited by Caroline M. Kirkland] (February 1849): 81–84.

Collected as "First Love" in *The Dewdrop*, 43–54. Philadelphia: Lippincott, Grambo & Co., 1852.

"Magnetism Among the Shakers." By Miss C. M. Sedgwick. *Sartain's Union Magazine* [edited by Caroline M. Kirkland] (May 1849): 337–38.

Collected in *The Literary Gem*, 69–70. Philadelphia: Van Court, 1854. / Reprinted in *Female Prose Writers of America* [edited by John S. Hart], 19–23. Philadelphia, E. H. Butler & Co., 1864, 1866.

1850

"Might Versus Right." By Miss C. M. Sedgwick. *Sartain's Union Magazine* [edited by Caroline M. Kirkland] (January 1850): 75–80.

"The Mother and Her Family." By Miss Sedgwick. *Rural Repository* (2 February 1850): 70–71.

Collected as "The Whole Family," by Mrs. Sedgwick [*sic*] in *Sweet Home; or, Friendship's Golden Altar*, edited by Frances R. Percival, 132–34. Boston: L. P. Crown & Co., 1856 [pub. 1855].

"Owasonook." By Miss C. M. Sedgwick. *Sartain's Union Magazine* [edited by Caroline M. Kirkland] (June 1850): 399–407.

"The English Colonel and His Wife." By Miss Catharine M. Sedgwick. In *The Gem of the Season: a Souvenir for 1851*, 58–80. New York: Leavitt and Company, 1851 [pub. 1850].

1851

"Love and Health." By Miss C. M. Sedgwick. *Youth's Companion* [edited by Nathaniel Willis] (29 May 1851): 17–18.

Reprinted in *Youth's Companion* [collected selections from the magazine from 1827 to 1927. —LDB]. Edited by Lovell Thompson with three former companion editors, M. A. DeWolfe Howe, Arthur Stanwood Pier, and Harford Powel, 866–72. Boston: Houghton Mifflin Co., and Cambridge: Riverside Press, 1954.

1853

"Mary L. Ware." [Anonymous.] *Putnam's Monthly* [edited by Charles Briggs and associate editors George William Curtis, Charles A. Dana, Parke Godwin, and Frederick Law Olmsted] (April 1853): 370–82.

[Attribution per Gidez.]

"The Slave and Slave-Owner." C. M. Sedgwick. In *Autographs for Freedom* [edited by Julia Griffiths], 24–27. Boston: John P. Jewett & Company; also Cleveland, Ohio, and London, 1853.

"Slavery in New England." By Miss Sedgewick [*sic*]. *Bentley's Miscellany* 34 (1853): 417–24. See also http://www.salemstate.edu/imc/sedgwick/slavery.html

1854

"The Great Excursion to the Falls of St. Anthony." By C.M.S., Lenox. *Putnam's Monthly* (September 1854): 320–25.

1855

"Preface." By Catharine Maria Sedgwick. In *The Mysterious Story-Book; or, The Good Stepmother. By Whom?* vi–vii. New York: Appleton and Company, 1856 [pub. 1855]. [Preface dated 30th May, 1855. See BAL #17415.]

1856

"The White Hills in October." [Anonymous.] *Harper's New Monthly Magazine* [edited by Alfred H. Guernsey] (December 1856): 44–56.
   Reprinted in *The Continental Monthly* (October 1862): 423–44. [Attribution per Gidez.]

1857

"A Reminiscence of a Foreign Celebrity's Morning Reception." [Anonymous.] *Harper's New Monthly Magazine* [edited by Alfred H. Guernsey] (April 1857): 655–58. [Attribution per Gidez.]

"Letter regarding Stephen West." From Miss Catharine M. Sedgwick. Lenox, 27 July 1848. In *Annals of the American Pulpit*, by William Sprague, 551–52. Vol. 1. New York: Robert Carter and Brothers, 1857.

1858

"Bianca Milesi Mojon, A Biographical Notice by Emile Souvestre." [Anonymous.] *Harper's New Monthly Magazine* [edited by Alfred H. Guernsey] (April 1858): 641–53. [Review of Souvestre's biography of Mojon; attribution per Gidez.—LDB]

"Ladies of the Sacred Heart." [Anonymous.] *Harper's New Monthly Magazine* [edited by Alfred H. Guernsey] (July 1858): 205–6. [Attribution per Gidez.]

1859

"Introduction." By Catharine M. Sedgwick. In *Women and Work*, by Barbara Leigh Smith Bodichon, 3–11. New York: C. S. Francis, 1859.
   [According to the BAL, CMS's introduction is not included in the first edition of London, 1857.]

1861

"Our Old 'Meeting-House.'" By Miss C. M. Sedgwick. In *Tales of the Time*, 57–61. New York: H. Dexter & Co., [1861].
    Reprinted in *Knickerbocker* (February 1861): 157–61.

1862

"A Sketch from Life." By C. M. Sedgwick. In *Only Once. Original Papers, by Various Contributors*, 7. Published for the Benefit of the New York Infirmary for Women and Children. New York: J. F. Trow, Printer, 1862.

1864

"The Homestead." Catherine M. Sedgwick [*sic*]. In *Autograph Leaves of Our Country's Authors*, edited by John P. Kennedy and Alexander Bliss, 145. Baltimore: Cushings & Bailey, 1864.

1875

"A Very Short Story." In *The Echo. A Journal of the Fair . . . New York . . . April 10, 1875 to April 24, 1875*, no. 1, p. 5. [Not seen—seems unlikely, post mortem. See BAL #17429.]

Contributors

JOHN AUSTIN received his Ph.D. in English and comparative literature from Columbia University in 2001. He is presently completing a book, titled *American Authorship in the Age of the Annuals.*

CHARLENE AVALLONE is currently writing as an independent scholar based in Hawai'i, having served on the faculties of the Universities of Hawaii and Notre Dame. She has published on antebellum literary studies, most recently in *PMLA* on the gendered limitations of the American "renaissance" critical traditions, and is on the editorial board of *Leviathan: A Journal of Melville Studies.* Her essay is part of a larger work in progress that studies American women's conversation from the 1770s to 1870 as literary discourse.

BRIGITTE BAILEY is an associate professor of English and American studies and coordinator of the American studies program at the University of New Hampshire. Her research and teaching interests focus on nineteenth-century United States literature and visual culture. She has published articles on the travel writings of Irving, Cooper, Kirkland, Fuller, Hawthorne, James, and Wharton in essay collections and journals such as *ESQ, American Literature,* and *American Literary History.* She serves on the board of the University Press of New England series Becoming Modern: New Nineteenth-Century Studies.

JENIFER BANKS is a professor in the English department at Michigan State University, East Lansing. She is coeditor of *The Letters of Washington Irving* and has published on Caroline Kirkland. She is currently studying Sedgwick's correspondence.

VICTORIA CLEMENTS is a professor of English at the College of Southern Maryland, where she teaches courses in American literature, writing, and communications. She edited the Oxford edition of *A New-England Tale* (1995), served as codirector for the 1997 and 2000 Sedgwick Symposia, and is a founding member of the Catharine Maria Sedgwick Society executive board.

ROBERT DALY, Distinguished Teaching Professor of English and Comparative Literature at the University at Buffalo, State University of New York, has published widely on American and English literature and culture; has held Leverhulme and Guggenheim fellowships in England and visiting appointments at Cornell, Cambridge, Essex, and Chapman; and has directed five summer seminars for the National Endowment for the Humanities.

LUCINDA DAMON-BACH initiated and codirected the first two Sedgwick Symposia (1997 and 2000), founded the Catharine Maria Sedgwick Society, and launched the Sedgwick Society Web site at http://www.salemstate.edu/imc/sedgwick. She is an assistant professor of English at Salem State College in Salem, Massachusetts, where she teaches courses in American literature, world literature, secondary education, and writing. She is currently researching Sedgwick's life for a literary biography.

JUDITH FETTERLEY is Distinguished Teaching Professor of English and Women's Studies and Associate Dean of Undergraduate Studies at the University at Albany, State University of New York. She is the author of *The Resisting Reader: A Feminist Approach to American Fiction* (1978) and *Provisions: A Reader from 19th-Century American Women* (1985), and coeditor with Marjorie Pryse of *American Women Regionalists, 1850–1910* (1992). With Joanne Dobson and Elaine Showalter, she founded the Rutgers University Press American Women Writers series. She is the fiction editor of *13th Moon*, a feminist literary journal, and has served on the editorial boards of *American Literature* and *Legacy*. Most recently she has completed, with Marjorie Pryse, *Locating Regionalism*, a critical study of nineteenth-century American women regionalist writers, forthcoming from the University of Illinois Press.

SONDRA SMITH GATES is an assistant professor of English at the University of Wisconsin, Fond du Lac. She received her Ph.D. in American literature from the University of Michigan in 2000. Her research interests include representations of poverty in nineteenth-century American fiction, women's religious writings, and computer-assisted instruction.

DEBORAH GUSSMAN is an assistant professor of English at the Richard Stockton College of New Jersey where she teaches courses in American literature, Native American literature, women's studies, and writing. She has published articles in *College Literature*, *Studies in American Puritan Spirituality*, and *Feminist Teacher*, and review essays in *National Women's Studies Association Journal* and *Studies in American Indian Literature*. She is currently working on a series of articles dealing with the rhetorics of reform in early-nineteenth-century literature.

SUSAN K. HARRIS is Hall Distinguished Professor of American Literature and Culture at University of Kansas, Lawrence. She is the author of *The Courtship of Olivia Langdon and Mark Twain* (1996), *19th-Century American Women's Novels:*

Interpretive Strategies (1990), and *Mark Twain's Escape from Time: A Study of Patterns and Images* (1982). She is coeditor of *Legacy: A Journal of American Women Writers* and has edited *Mark Twain: Historical Romances* (1994), *The Minister's Wooing* (1999), and *Adventures of Huckleberry Finn* (2000). Her forthcoming work includes *Annie Adams Fields, Mary Gladstone Drew, and the Work of the Late 19th-Century Hostess* (2002), "Mark Twain and Gender" (2002), and a new edition of *A New-England Tale* (2003).

MELISSA J. HOMESTEAD is an assistant professor of English at the University of Oklahoma. Her book in progress, *Imperfect Title: Nineteenth-Century American Women Authors and Literary Property*, includes a chapter on Catharine Sedgwick's place in the antebellum international copyright debates. Portions of this book have appeared in *New-England Quarterly* (on Fanny Fern) and *Prospects* (on Harriet Beecher Stowe). Her essay in this volume is a small seed from which she expects to grow a book-length study on Catharine Sedgwick and her relationship to antebellum American print culture.

PATRICIA LARSON KALAYJIAN teaches in the humanities program at California State University, Dominguez Hills. She has published on Catharine Sedgwick and is currently editing an academic anthology of western American fiction that reflects the racial, ethnic, and gender makeup of the West more accurately than do traditional anthologies.

CAROLYN L. KARCHER is a professor of English, American studies, and women's studies at Temple University. She is the author of *Shadow over the Promised Land: Slavery, Race, and Violence in Melville's America* and *The First Woman in the Republic: A Cultural Biography of Lydia Maria Child*. In addition, she has published *A Lydia Maria Child Reader*, and scholarly editions of Child's *Hobomok and Other Writings on Indians* and *Appeal in Favor of That Class of Americans Called Africans*, and Sedgwick's *Hope Leslie*. She is currently collecting material for an anthology cum critical study of nineteenth-century American women's journalism.

MARY KELLEY is Collegiate Professor of History, American Culture, and Women's Studies at the University of Michigan; formerly she was the Mary Brinsmead Wheelock Professor of History of Dartmouth College. She has served on the editorial boards of *Journal of American History, American Quarterly, William and Mary Quarterly, Journal of the Early Republic*, and *New England Quarterly*. She is the author of *Private Woman, Public Stage: Literary Domesticity in Nineteenth-Century America*, the coauthor of *The Limits of Sisterhood*, the editor of *The Power of Her Sympathy: The Autobiography and Journal of Catharine Maria Sedgwick*, and the author of many articles. She also edited the *Portable Margaret Fuller*. Kelley is now completing *"Empire of Reason": The Making of Learned Women in Nineteenth-Century America*, a book on educational opportunity and engagement with public life.

DANA NELSON is a professor of English and social theory at the University of Kentucky. She is the author of *The Word in Black and White* (1992) and *National Manhood* (1998). Her most recent work includes a coedited (with Houston Baker) special issue of *American Literature* on "Violence, the Body and 'The South'" (June 2001) and a coedited (with Russ Castronovo) collection of essays titled *Materializing Democracy* (forthcoming in 2002).

ALLISON J. ROEPSCH is currently a candidate for the Master's Degree in English at Salem State College, with interests in American literature, American colonial history, and gender studies.

KAREN WOODS WEIERMAN is an assistant professor of English at Worcester State College. She conducted her research on Sedgwick's antislavery manuscript as an Andrew W. Mellon Fellow at the Massachusetts Historical Society. Her current book project is "One Nation, One Blood: Interracial Marriage in American Fiction, Scandal, and Law, 1820–70."

Index